The Women's War in the South

Recollections and Reflections of the American Civil War

Edited by Charles G. Waugh & Martin H. Greenberg

CUMBERLAND HOUSE
NASHVILLE, TENNESSEE

Cover design by Bateman Design, Nashville, Tennessee.

Library of Congress Cataloging-in-Publication Data

The women's war in the South : recollections and reflections of the American
  Civil War / edited by Charles G. Waugh and Martin H. Greenberg.
    p.   cm.
  Includes bibliographical references and index.
  ISBN 1-58182-021-6 (alk. paper)
    1. United States—History—Civil War, 1861–1865—Women. 2. United
  States—History—Civil War, 1861–1865—Personal narratives, Confederate.
  3. United States—History—Civil War, 1861–1865—Social aspects. 4.
  Women—Southern States—Biography. 5. Confederate States of America—
  History—Sources. 6. Women—Confederate States of America—History—
  Sources. I. Waugh, Charles. II. Greenberg, Martin Harry.
  E628.W93   1999
  973.7'082—dc21   98-56396
                                                                         CIP

Printed in the United States of America

2 3 4 5 6 7 8 9—04 03 02 01

To Frank D. McSherry Jr.

Contents

REFLECTIONS

Preface

*P*RIOR TO the Civil War, society dictated that women were to stay at home, prepare the meals for their household, bear children, and be seen and not heard. This ideal was called the "cult of domesticity," which maintained that women's natural abilities were limited to the home and that they certainly lacked an aptitude for political issues. The war, however, changed that by forcing women into several roles vacated by the men who had taken up arms. The manner in which women met this challenge was the first step toward equality. The letters, books, diaries, and postwar writings these women left behind reveal this other side of the war—the women's war—excerpts from which make up most of this volume, including first-person accounts taken from late-eighteenth- and early twentieth-century sources.

The greatest contribution of the women in the South, however, was probably the most difficult to see: They kept things going at home. They did what their husbands had done before the war. As the war progressed, women ran the family farms and those with slaves worked with their overseers to keep the crops growing. When their livestock was confiscated, women hitched themselves to the plows. They bought and sold goods. Hands that had known only cooking and needlework became blistered and calloused. Many women in the cities came to be employed by the government and the factories trying to keep the armies supplied in the field.

As the war intensified and casualties mounted, women found themselves entering the nursing profession. In 1862 Confederate nurse Kate Cumming noted: "The foul air from this mass of human beings at first made me giddy and sick. We have to walk in blood and water, but we think nothing of it." Another nurse described finding maggots in the wounds of the soldiers under her care. In one instance she claimed to have pulled a pint of them from a single wound.

Some of the more adventuresome served as spies because the prejudices of the times placed them above suspicion; men did not expect women to take up this dangerous work. Among the most notable and successful Southern spies was Rose Greenhow, a Washington socialite who coaxed incredible information from the politicians and officers who enjoyed her company and conveyed it to Richmond. Details of her story appear in the pages that follow.

A few hundred women surreptitiously joined the ranks of the armies and endured combat. Malinda Blalock from Grandfather Mountain, North Carolina, followed her husband, Keith, into uniform. She cut her hair and enlisted in the Twenty-sixth North Carolina as his sixteen-year-old brother, Sam. When her husband was discharged from the army for disease, Malinda revealed herself and was discharged at the same time. A more sweeping epic concerned Loreta Janeta Velazquez, whose "adventures" span the whole war according to the memoirs excerpted in this book and whose truthfulness has been doubted often.

Southern women had strong feelings about this war and often confronted invading Yankees face-to-face without weapons. Their frustrations were furiously recorded in their diaries, such as Sarah Morgan wrote in 1864: "If I was a man. Oh, if I was only a man! For two years, that has been my only cry. Blood, fire, desolation—rather than submit we should light our own funeral pyre as a memorial to our sorrow and suffering."

The war was something that Southern women supported patriotically, but the war meant shortages and sacrifice. The women of the Confederacy quickly focused on survival, notwithstanding the legend of their willingness to do anything for the cause. When William Tecumseh Sherman's soldiers marched across Georgia, the desperate situation took a turn for the worse as a quarter of a million Southern women became refugees and fled from the invading Yankee army.

As Sherman's army foraged liberally across the countryside from Atlanta to Savannah, it laid waste to the land itself, burning barns, killing livestock, and destroying crops. The only opposition was the Southern women intent on maintaining their property as their husbands had left it. For these women, the war was on their doorstep.

In addition to the hundreds of thousands of men who died in the war, untold numbers of women lost their lives to disease, starvation, and battle. For the survivors, the grieving would not end quickly, but amid their sorrow emerged a legacy of independence and freedom. Women emerged from the wreckage and carnage of the war into a new society, where a woman's place was not always confined to the home.

Women were engulfed by the war, and they were eyewitnesses to the events of 1861–65, recording those memories in letters and diaries. During the decades after the war and into the next century, many recounted these recollections in popular magazines like *Harper's* and *Century.* Many of the articles reproduced in this book come from these sources, recalling their experiences for a new audience.

Acknowledgments

THE SOURCES for the selections in this volume are listed below. The original spelling and punctuation have been followed throughout with only minor typographical variations for the sake of consistency. Reference notes have been combined in a separate section following the text.

Beymer, William G. "Mrs. Greenhow, Confederate Spy." *Harper's* 124 (March 1912): 563–76.

Bleser, Carol K., and Frederick M. Heath. "The Impact of the Civil War on a Southern Marriage: Clement and Virginia Tunstall Clay of Alabama." *Civil War History* 30 (1984): 197–220.

Cabell, William Preston. "Woman Saved Richmond City." *Southern Historical Papers* 38 (1910): 350–58.

Chambers, Jenny. "What a School-Girl Saw of John Brown's Raid." *Harper's* 104 (January 1902): 311–18.

Chancellor, Sue M. "Personal Recollections of the Battle of Chancellorsville." *Register of the Kentucky Historical Society* 66 (1968): 137–46.

Clinton, Catherine. "Southern Women and the Civil War." *Journal of Women's History* 8 (1996): 163–68.

Clune, Michael. "The Siren of Bull Run." *Harper's Weekly* 54, July 23, 1910, p. 20.

Davis, Varina. "Stonewall's Widow." *Southern Historical Papers* (1893): 340–43.

Fischer, Leroy H., ed. "A Civil War Experience of Some Arkansas Women in Indian Territory." *Chronicles of Oklahoma* (Summer 1979): 137–63.

Fordney, Chris, ed. "Letters from the Heart." *Civil War Times Illustrated* 34 (September-October 1995): 28, 73–82.

Gilman, Caroline H. "Letters of a Confederate Mother: Charleston in the Sixties." *Atlantic* 137 (April 1926): 503–15.

Hall, Richard. "'Lieutenant Harry T. Buford,' C.S.A." From *Patriots in Disguise* (New York: Paragon House, 1993), 107–153.

Harrison, Constance Cary. "A Virginia Girl in the First Year of the War." *Century* 30 (1885): 606–14.

Hergesheimer, Joseph. "The Rose of Mississippi." From Hergesheimer, *Swords and Roses* (New York: Knopf, 1919), 67–97.

Holzman, Robert S. "Sally Tompkins, Captain, Confederate Army." *American Mercury* 88 (March 1959): 127–30.

Hunt, John, and Bill McIlwain. "Battling Belles." *American Mercury* 78 (March 1954): 13–15.

Inscoe, John C. "Coping in Confederate Appalachia: A Portrait of a Mountain Woman and Her Community at War." *North Carolina Historical Review* 69 (1992): 388–413.

Jones, Virginia K., ed. "A Contemporary Account of the Inauguration of Jefferson Davis." *Alabama Historical Quarterly* (Fall and Winter 1961): 273–77.

Kimball, William J. "The Bread Riot in Richmond, 1863." *Civil War History* 7 (1961): 149–54.

Lander, Ernest M., Jr., ed. "A Confederate Girl Visits Pennsylvania, July-September 1863." *Western Pennsylvania Historical Magazine* 49 (1966): 111–26; 197–211.

McLean, Mrs. Eugene. "A Northern Woman in the Confederacy." *Harper's* 128 (1914): 440–51.

———. "When the States Seceded." *Harper's* 128 (1914): 282–88.

Mason, Emily V. "Memories of a Hospital Matron." *Atlantic* 90 (September–October 1902): 305–18; 475–85.

Myers, Cynthia. "Queen of the Confederacy." *Civil War Times Illustrated* 35 (December 1996): 72–78.

Owen, Mary Bankhead. "Emma Sansom, Heroine of Immortal Courage." *Southern Historical Papers* 38 (1910): 350–58.

Racine, Philip N. "Emily Lyles Harris: A Piedmont Farmer During the Civil War." *South Atlantic Quarterly* 79 (1980): 386–97.

Reed, Lida Lord. "Woman's Experiences During the Siege of Vicksburg." *Century* 61 (April 1901): 922–28.

Williams, Benjamin B. "The Trial of Mrs. Surratt and the Lincoln Assassination Plot." *Alabama Lawyer* 25 (1964): 22–31.

Wood, Richard Addison, and Joan Fare Wood, eds. "For Better or for Worse." *Civil War Times Illustrated* 31 (May–June 1992): 111–26, 197–211.

Introduction: Southern Women and the Civil War

Catherine Clinton

A WORKSHOP ON southern women's history is always a welcome advent, but especially at this meeting where such an opportunity can create the possibility of even more exciting work. I remember back when books like George Rable's prizewinning *Civil Wars* [1989], LeeAnn Whites's new *The Civil War as a Crisis in Gender* [1995], Drew Faust's forthcoming *Mothers of Invention* [1996], and my own *Tara Revisited: Women, War and the Plantation Legend* [1995] were just gleams in their authors' eyes. In addition to all of this exciting secondary work on women in the Confederacy, primary material is flowing hot off several presses; I call your attention to volumes forthcoming from Carol Bleser's new University of Georgia series, Southern Voices from the Past (and encourage any of you sitting on wonderful letters and diaries to contact Carol about your diamonds in the rough). Civil War specialists should look forward especially to Christine Jacobson's diary of Dolly Lunt Burge [1997], Marli Weiner's volume on Grace Elmore [1997], Elizabeth Baer's project on Lucy Buck [1997], and Lyde Cullen Sizer's anthology of the narratives of women rebel spies. But besides providing bibliography, I wanted to offer comments on southern women and Civil War Studies based on my own rather redheaded perspective. . . . to "locate the emergence of southern women's history within the flowering of American women's history and the broadening of southern history during the 1970s and '80s and on into the 1990s, addressing questions of marginality, and the way in which gender has shifted historical issues dramatically." . . . I will refer you to the introduction for *Half Sisters of History: Southern Women and the American Past* [1994] which covers the historical context [and] my review essay "In Search of Southern Women's History" in the Summer 1992 volume of the *Georgia Historical Quarterly,* plus I know Margaret Wolfe has a new series at Kentucky to go along with her exciting new book *Daughters of Canaan* [1995], and Anne Scott, Mary Jo Buhle, and Jackie Hall have a series at the University of Illinois, where they are publishing Marli Weiner's book on South Carolina plantation mistresses [*Mistresses and Slaves,* 1997]. Also, Nell Painter and Linda Kerber have a series at the University of North Carolina Press, where they are publishing Laura Edwards's book on Reconstruction in North Carolina [*Gendered Strife and Confusion,* 1997]. Indeed, there are now numerous people eager to publish books in this booming field. . . .

My message is not the glories of war nor singing praises of peace, but that struggle can make our work count. We cannot be afraid of war because we call ourselves feminists. We cannot turn our backs on contests we know we can't win, because if we believe "winning isn't everything, it's the only thing," then we've let our enemies seal our fate before we even commence. In this, the closing years of our century, we face dilemmas depressingly similar to those faced by scholars in the 1890s.

During the 1990s, Americans confront intellectual estrangement, divided over questions of sex and race. Isn't our society as embroiled with racial and sexual inequalities at the turn of the twenty-first century as were our forebears as they approached the twentieth? And in our own day, videotaped beatings and race riots, alleged high tech lynchings, and COURT-TV create new and dangerous dynamics. . . .

At the end of the nineteenth century, white women North and South knew the battle they waged for equality would be impeded, if not halted, by their signs of support for African Americans. The rare courageous stands taken during those grim days of political compromise haunt us, reminding us of the decency we might emulate. Today, in academe I think the shoe is wrongly placed on the other foot. . . . We sidestep and softshoe and frankly miss opportunities as we oversensitize ourselves to issues of sex and race. Speaking as an African Americanist who did her undergraduate degree in the field over 20 years ago, who has taught African American history for over 20 years but who is still confronted by such questions as "Can I really teach black history? To black students?," I urge you to be misunderstood rather than to remain silent, to take on the disturbing questions to which predecessors have turned a blind eye. If so, you will produce books rich with contradictions, for which not all critics will take you to task. Messy, original work might distract us from the ticky-tacky, shrink-wrapped studies rolling off university presses even as we speak. . . .

I'd like to see more biographical studies. Working on several encyclopedia projects over the years, I am struck by how impoverished Confederate women are, compared to Confederate men. Work on Confederate women can be incredibly tricky within the wider field of women's history, but even the party lines seem to be criss-crossing in these changing times. Mine sweepers have been working overtime, it's never going to be safe in these waters, but everyone should get into the swim. We need some group biographies like Elizabeth Leonard's *Yankee Women* [1994], and I am particularly eager to read work on such women as Belle Boyd, Pauline Cushman, and Eugenia Phillips. And what about the careers of such Confederate nurses as Ella Newsom King, Phoebe Pember, Kate Cumming, and the indomitable Sallie Tompkins, to whom Jefferson Davis awarded a rank in the Confederate army?

We have seen the emergence of powerful case studies. I am thinking particularly of Joan Cashin's compelling essay in *Divided Houses* [1992]; of Drew Faust's sketch of an abusive mistress in her last essay in *Southern Stories: Slaveholders in Peace and War* [1992]; and John Inscoe's vivid portrait of one woman's climb to slaveholding in the new collection from the University of Georgia, Patricia Morton's *Discovering the Women in Slavery* [1996]. I know there are more women, more dilemmas to be recovered and compiled and added to our expanding mosaic of Civil War experience.

I am fascinated by research on the United Daughters of the Confederacy: its purpose, its role, its mysterious hold. Creative research on the role of memorialization—even on Mammy memorials proposed by this group—is well underway. I have heard wonderful papers and hope to see exciting essays in print soon.

The questions of up-ended gender conventions in the wake of the war have fascinated scholars in the field from Mary Massey down to the present. Suzanne Lebsock, Elizabeth Fox-Genovese, Jacqueline Jones, Victoria Bynum, and others have made compelling and conflicting arguments about black and white women's competing interests during and after the war. Stephanie McCurry's intriguing speculations about class and gender in her new book, *Masters of Small Worlds* [1995], will perhaps lure many into looking at the vast majority of southern women who experienced the Civil War outside the classic dichotomous view of mistress and slave.

I keep hoping a new crop of southern women historians will throw off the shackles of their historical foremothers and sexualize their sights and create new ways of thinking about race and gender which include homosocial as well as heterosexual concerns, which is informed by taboo and desire as well as education and etiquette; some sort of matricidal mania would be a nice finish to the decade.

Much of the new work dealing with race, sexuality, and its southern implications—pioneering research by Adele Logan Alexander, Mary Francis Berry, Peter Bardaglio, Kent Leslie, Karen Leatham, Martha Hodes, Carolyn Powell, to name but a few of these daring scholars exploring rugged terrain—offers me hope. I would also encourage projects on rape (although for the purposes of funding I'd call it nonconsensual sex) and prostitution (again, calling it consensual, commercial sex), and cross-dressing (which I'd call cross-dressing because, what the hell).

I have an essay entitled "Noble Women as Well," forthcoming in Bob Toplin's edited collection on *Ken Burns's The Civil War* [1996], due out from Oxford University Press next year. My title is from a text penned by Susie King Taylor, a forgotten heroine of the war, one of the only black women to publish her wartime memoirs. This former nurse and Sea Island veteran complains in 1902: "There are many people who do not know what some of the colored women did during the war." She goes on to remind us: "There has never been a greater war in the United States than the one of 1861, where so many lives were lost—not men alone but noble women as well."

And you should remember not only Susie Taylor's words, but know when she published her volume in 1902, she feared the corrosive effects of white southern women's Lost Cause zealotry. Their "remembrance of things imagined," their rewriting history attempted to silence the voices of African American women. Taylor, like so many of her fellow freedwomen, had emancipated herself. But in the terrible backlash following Confederate surrender, she lost her husband and her job teaching school and was forced to leave her child behind with relatives while she went into domestic service. Unlike the majority of African American household labor, Taylor broke free from the pattern of perpetual exploitation. She achieved middle-class status, reunited her family, became a Boston clubwoman, and finally wrote her memoir to combat the Age of Amnesia—reminding her readers that black women were a vital part of our national heritage, an important part of Civil War history. She, too, had her comrades, the dynamic of Anna Julia Cooper and Ida B. Wells-Barnett, who would want us, as well, to remember, and to celebrate "Noble Women as Well."

The
Women's
War in
the South

Recollections

1 What a School-Girl Saw of John Brown's Raid

Jennie Chambers

I WAS A mile on my way to the Young Ladies' Seminary in Harpers Ferry, on a Monday morning that I shall never forget, when, coming in sight of town, my heart stopped beating and I dropped my books. As I looked over the edge of the hill, I saw, riding up and down the streets, shouting and brandishing their guns, a crowd of men. It seemed to me they were all yelling; and some of them were firing in the air. There has never been for me a day like that of October 17, 1859, when I saw what I afterwards knew was to go down in history as the John Brown Raid.

My home was a mile back through the woods, in Bolivar Heights, and my heart sank is I thought of the distance to safety. I wanted to cry out, and, even at that distance, to warn those I loved of the horrible, strange peril in the air. Others might have thought it war; I had never seen a soldier. The last war I knew anything about was in 1812.

Just then I thought of a schoolmate who lived near by on the road-side, and that gave me courage.

"It's the Abolitionists," she said, running out as I came up to her doorway; "they're down there arresting all our people." I didn't wait to hear more, but my strength had come back to me, and I ran along through the woods like a deer. I didn't know what minute an Abolition-ist might jump out at me from behind a tree—and eat me. They were cannibals, for all I knew, from some far-off country, like the Hessians, of whom I had been reading in history.

5

The oaks and the chestnuts and the maples arched overhead, in all October's glory, but I thought of nothing as I ran, except to warn my mother. There was a strange silence on the road; I met nobody.

"Oh," said I, when I got breath enough to speak, in our door-yard, "mother, it's the Abolitionists!" Then she told me that a rumor had come of trouble in town, and that father had gone down to the Ferry. Some dreadful thing was happening, but nobody knew what. A team came rattling down the Charlestown Pike, towards the Ferry. "They've got Colonel Washington and John Allstadt," the driver called out as he went by, "and they've got their niggers, and—" He was gone before we could hear the rest of it.

Colonel Lewis Washington and Mr. Allstadt lived back of us up the Pike, four miles from the Ferry. Mother and I felt that if Colonel Washington had been taken, nobody was safe. One of Mr. Allstadt's folks happened along not long after this and told us all their family had been waked up the night before by a noise on the big road. Mr. Allstadt went to the door. Who should he see there but John F. Cook and Charles Plummer Tidd, and other men that we knew, with guns and torches. There was a wagon, and when Mr. Allstadt looked there were Colonel Washington and three of his slaves in it, and two men on the seat with guns in their hands. They didn't make any explanation to Mr. Allstadt, but they made him call out his negroes, and he and two of the slaves were bundled into the wagon, without time for a good-by even, and driven away down the Pike.

All of them must have come right near our house in Bolivar, but none of us heard any of it. "Thank God, they didn't get your father," said my mother.

"Yes," said I, "but he's down there with them, isn't he?" and then I began to cry.

There was something in the air that morning which nobody had ever known of before. Mrs. Sarah Kirby, whose husband worked in the Arsenal, lived at the top of the hill, in sight of the Ferry. She came out on her front porch early, and when she saw men on horses galloping about the streets, she called to a passerby. Misunderstanding his answer, Mrs. Kirby ran into the house and said to her husband:

"Oh, Mr. Kirby, a wild beast has just come over the bridge from Maryland, and all the men are out in the streets with guns."

Now we all knew Mr. Cook, and we liked him; we couldn't think how he got into this. They said Mr. Stevens was with him, and all of us school-girls knew Mr. Stevens. He often called out to us as we went by his boardinghouse in Harpers Ferry, and when his landlady used to treat the girls to pickles, he would tell her not to do it, as it was bad for our health.

By-and-by we remembered that Cook and Stevens and others of these men had been friends of Mr. John Smith, who had been living out at the Kennedy farmhouse on the Antietam road, in Maryland. Smith, as he called himself, lived in that lonely place with his two daughters, quiet, unpretentious people, who had little to say to their neighbors, and that only for their good. We knew Mr. Hoffmaster, their next-door neighbor, and he used to say that Smith, no matter where he came from, was a good neighbor, and a good preacher too. Mr. Smith preached in the little church by the road-side.

The sound of gun-shots came over the top of the hill and echoed through the woods. Now and then we heard a stray word that there was a regular battle going on down at the Ferry, and that Smith was at the head of it.

Somebody on the way back up the Pike said that Mr. Hoffmaster said that he had been to hear Smith preach just last night. And now everybody was saying that instead of being John Smith, this preacher was no other than John Brown, the Abolitionist!

It must have been nearly noon when a crowd of men, most of whom we knew, came up the Pike from the Ferry. At first we were worse scared than ever. When they got close by, I recognized father at the head of them. Then they all came into our yard, and the men called him "Lieutenant Chambers."

"We've organized a company of eighty, Harpers Ferry Guards," said he to my mother, "and I was made captain, but I gave way in favor of John Aris—you know he was in the Mexican War."

"What's it all about?" cried mother, smiling now through her tears.

"It's Brown, Brown of Ossawatomie, the Abolitionist; he's trying to get the Arsenal," said my father; "and all these men he's been gathering here, Cook and Stevens and Tidd, to help him mine copper in Solomon's Gap, were nothing but Abolitionists in disguise. The mining tools they used to get in boxes down at the railroad were muskets and pikes.

"But we couldn't get any guns for ourselves until we found these muskets in one of the government's sheds at the Arsenal. Brown's got his men in there now; and we've got no ammunition.

"We were going to get a butcher-knife apiece and go down at them and be captured—and then cut them to pieces. But just then we found these muskets. Now all you women folks must come and help to mould bullets."

While the lead was melting, there was time for more talk. John Hoff-master, who had been living neighbor to Brown so long, out by Kennedy's farm, had told some of our men that Brown—or Smith, as he knew him—preached a fine sermon not an hour before the raid began. Hoffmaster walked home from church with him, and he said that Brown seemed tired and quiet, like a man who was looking for nothing but bed. Instead of that, Hoffmaster had been waked up an hour or two later by a noise in the big road. When he looked out of his bed-room window there was a crowd with torches and wagons, surrounded by mounted men. They had come down from the Kennedy farm, Brown in the lead. They had pikes, as they called them, in their hands, and the glitter of the torch-light on the steel pike-heads was a strange sight. The men passed on by Hoffmaster's down the Antietam road towards the Ferry.

"The first thing the Raiders did," said one of father's men, "was to seize the railroad bridge." All this time father and the others were putting bullets into their pockets, hot from the moulds. There were just four apiece. "When they got down there they grabbed William Williams, the bridge watchman, and five minutes later Heywood Shepherd, Mayor Fountain Beckham's boy, ran out with a pistol in his hand from the rail-road depot. Shepherd was as fine a slave as there was in this county, and they shot him down like a dog. He was the watchman at the Baltimore and Potomac depot, and when he waked up and ran out, he thought they were robbers. Then they got Dan Whelan; and when Pat Higgins went to relieve Dan, about midnight, the Raiders started for him. Pat knocked one of them down with his fists and started to run. A Raider ran down the railroad track after him, but caught his foot in the frog, and Pat got away.

"There's been plenty of bloodshed already, and there's likely to be more. But we're going to drive them out of the Arsenal, no matter what it costs."

This was the way the Harpers Ferry company started off, as they said, "to bring on the battle." Just how big that battle would be, and whether it would be fought by hundreds or thousands, nobody knew then. The Abolitionists might be pouring down through Maryland!

While we were waiting, we forgot about eating. Presently we heard that Colonel Robert E. Lee would bring Marines from Washington. A company of men were coming from Shepherdstown. And the Jefferson Guards from Charlestown were on the way. Brown and his men had cut the telegraph wires. They had stopped the night train through from the West, when it got to the bridge, but Captain Jack Phelps, the conductor, told them he had mail-cars in his train, and so, after holding it back several hours, the Raiders let it go on through to Washington. That was the way the news reached Washington, and that was what started Colonel Lee. Governor Wise had ordered out the men from Shepherdstown and Charlestown.

A lady who was on the train—I think her name was Mrs. Bedford—said the passengers were scared half to death. A man with a gun ran through the cars shouting, "You're all my prisoners." That was all he said; nobody knew who he was or what it meant. He told the conductor he could run his train over the bridge to the Ferry, but no farther. The women on the train were crying and screaming, and when they got to the bridge, the conductor called out to the bridge-tender and asked him what it all was about. "Harpers Ferry is taken," was the answer, and that was the only explanation.

After it was all over somebody remembered that John Brown had once been in business in Springfield, Massachusetts, where the only other government armory in the United States was situated. Knowing all about armories, he had evidently decided to strike at the one in the South, at Harpers Ferry.

Colonel Washington, Mr. Allstadt, and the rest of the citizens who had been captured in the night were under guard in the government watch-house. By this time there were about thirty of the best men in Harpers Ferry shut up there, knowing less than we did even of what it all meant.

The fighting was going on, the militia were coming in from Shepherdstown and Charlestown, the Marines were arriving from Washington, and the Raiders were retreating to the Arsenal. The women and children back of the hills were waiting in fear of their lives for news of their loved ones; the prisoners in the Arsenal, who would gladly have been fighting, were helpless. Nine of them were taken a little later in the day to the Engine House, that has ever since been known as "John Brown's Fort." It was to force the Arsenal, which the raiders seized first, that the Harpers Ferry Guards marched down the hill. Of course we didn't expect ever to see one of them alive again. What did women and children who had never seen a man in uniform, except the Arsenal guard, and had never heard a gun fired, except a squirrel-rifle, think—what could they think about all this?

The Harpers Ferry Guards divided into four squads; one crossed the Potomac and came down the Maryland side, and seized the bridge. That was where the Abolitionists' re-enforcements were looked for. Another squad took possession of the Shenandoah Rifle Works, and a third guarded the railroad bridge above the Musket Factory. Captain Aris, Lieutenant Chambers, Richard Washington (brother of Colonel Lewis, the captive), William Copeland, John Stahl, Jr., Jacob Bajent, George Coleman, Sr., Ed. McCabe, Mr. Sweeny, Thomas Bird, Mr. Watson, and four others were in the last squad, that headed straight for the Arsenal. There was a scrimmage, and the Harpers Ferry boys ran the Raiders out, killing one of them, Dangerfield Newby, and wounding another, Shields Green. This left Brown only twenty men all told, as it turned out. As we found afterward, his whole army consisted of himself, Captain Oliver Brown, Captain Watson Brown (two of his sons), Lieutenant Owen Brown (another son), John E. Cook, John Henry Kagi, William Thomson, Dauphin Thompson, Albert Hazzlet, William H. Leman, Charles Plummer Tidd, Jeremiah G. Anderson, Edwin Coppie, Aaron C. Stevens, Oliver Anderson, Dangerfield Newby, Shields Green, John Copeland, Barclay Coppie, Stewart Taylor, Lewis Geary. Seven of these were members of the Brown family.

They had started out to upset the nation, with just sixteen white and six colored men. Of these, eleven whites and six negroes met their death.

Now to go back to our Harpers Ferry Guards.

Nobody was hurt, apparently, in the retreat from the Arsenal to the Engine House. Brown had his prisoners with him and prepared to fight it out. As it turned out, he had already released all but Colonel Washington and about eight others of the most prominent citizens. These he took along as much for his own protection, it seemed, as anything else. When they got inside, they took the fire-engine and braced the pole of it up against the Engine House door, and made ready for a siege. The besiegers now numbered Captain Rowen and his Jefferson Guards from Charlestown, the Shepherdstown company, our own Harpers Ferry boys, and the Marines under Colonel Lee.

In the court-room at Charlestown, on his trial, John Brown said that the Harpers Ferriers had whipped him before any help came from abroad. "They had us all penned up in the Engine House," said he, "and it was impossible for us to get out. If it hadn't been for the citizens we held as prisoners, we would have had to surrender at once; the building would have been riddled."

Up back of the hills, the women and children were all day in agony. The sharp crack of the rifles we could hear plainly. We did not know then that our Mayor and five of our citizens had been killed, and ten wounded.

The prisoners in the Engine House were as much at a loss as their families to know what was going on.

The Marines under Colonel Lee were seen approaching the Engine House. The prisoners were set to work to make port-holes in the brick, so the Raiders could fire their muskets through the walls. Phil Luckum, one of Mr. Allstadt's slaves, stuttered badly. Mr. Allstadt told us afterward that Phil kept his head ducking all the time, and was in great distress as he heard the bullets rattling on the roof and the walls of the Engine House. Presently a shot popped right through a port-hole and flattened on the wall close to Phil's head.

"Bub-bub-boss," said Phil, trembling all over, and turning to Captain Brown—"bub-bub-bub-boss, it's a-gittin' tut-tut-too hot for Phil!" and he collapsed.

When the call came from the Marines to surrender, Brown cried out, "No." The men outside brought up a ladder and swung it, end on, as a battering-ram against the door. The door began to shake and to give way; as they looked in they saw Brown, musket in hand, standing close to the door. Coppie, near him, called out, "I surrender." Brown said, "That's one." Thompson was killed. Mr. Resin Cross, one of the prisoners, told us afterward that he saw Stevens lying on his back, and knelt by him and asked him if he was hurt. Stevens said, "Yes; I have four buckshot it in my breast." Mr. Cross had asked Brown to send him out with one of the Raiders to explain to the citizens. Brown let him go, on condition that he would return. It was then that Stevens was shot. Stevens was picked up and carried into one of the houses, and in the intense excitement one of the citizens pointed a gun at Stevens while he was lying on a bed. Stevens gave him such a piercing look of contempt that the man seemed paralyzed, and he dropped his gun to his side and went out of the room. Stevens asked some one to lift him to the floor, saying, "Don't let them shoot me in bed." Miss Christine Fouke threw herself between Stevens and the mob that was rushing in the room, and kept them from shooting him again. While Brown was on trial in Charlestown, he turned to Mr. Cross, who was in court, and said, "Mr. Cross, one word: If things had been different, would you have returned to the Engine House according to your promise to me?" Mr. Cross answered, "Yes, I would." Brown said, "I am satisfied."

Watson and Oliver Brown were shot in the Engine House before the door was battered down. Before death brought relief to them, John Brown seemed perfectly cool, and showed no great sympathy. He charged them to die bravely, without a murmur, for the noble cause in which they were fighting. Our citizens who were shut in there with the Raiders were more moved by the sufferings of the dying men, Mr. Allstadt told us, than any of the

Raiders were. "Die like a man," was what Brown said. Mr. Cross had asked Brown to give him some explanation of what he was trying to do. But Brown bluntly refused. Mr. Cross said that he admired Stevens's bearing all through the fight more than that of any of the other raiders. "Stevens's eyes," said he, "were very dark and bright, and when his gaze was fixed upon you, it was as fierce as a hyena's." Mr. Cross tapped him on the arm playfully, and said, "I would like to fight you." "Why?" said Stevens. "Because," said Cross, "you are the finest built and best-looking man I ever saw." Hazzlet was standing near, and raised his gun as if to shoot Mr. Cross.

All the prisoners agreed afterward that they could not help admiring Brown's iron will and unparalleled bravery. At last Mr. Cross said to him, "Are you not Ossawatomie Brown?" Then he answered, "Yes." This was the first the prisoners knew of it.

Presently the cry "Surrender!" rang out again, over the musket-shots and the shouts. Brown said nothing. The blows of the ladder had loosened the fastenings of the Engine House door to such an extent that the prisoners could see the uniforms of the Marines outside. Brown tried again to fasten the pole of the engine against the door. Then came a tremendous crash and a loud shout. One of the men in uniform, Luke Quinn, sprang into the breach, and instantly was shot down. He was mortally hurt. Another Marine, Rupert, fell before this last volley of the Raiders. Then Lieutenant Green rushed in through the door, before the Raiders could fire a gun, and slashed at Brown with his sword. Others came after him, and Brown was twice wounded. Then it was all over. Brown and the survivors were made prisoners.

But two of Brown's men had escaped from the Arsenal and hid themselves in a cellar near by until night. One of them, Hazzlet, was arrested afterward at Carlisle, Pennsylvania. The other got away entirely. Leman was killed on a small island in the Potomac just above the bridge. He was lying behind a rock, when a man by the name of Scheppert shot him. Leman was unarmed, and it was not considered a brave thing. Mayor Fountain Beckham had been killed on the bridge by a shot fired through a port-hole of the Engine House. George McCabe, one of our citizens, was shot through the shoulder. George Turner and Thomas Boerley, citizens, were killed in the street. Three of Brown's men had been killed at the Rifle Works, one of them being Kagi, who had been designated by Brown, in his scheme of what he called a Provisional Government, as Secretary of War. From Martinsburg, Messrs. Murphy, Richardson, Hammond, Dorsey, Hooper, and Wollett were shot. George Turner, from near Martinsburg, was instantly killed.

Daniel Logan, a well-known citizen from the Cumberland Valley, was the man who captured Captain John E. Cook, and received one thousand dollars reward for it.

The next morning, which was Tuesday, Governor Henry A. Wise said to Brown, "Old man, you had better prepare to meet your God; your thread of life is nearly spun." Brown looked calmly up at him and said, "So had you." Governor Wise then turned to Captain Bayler, a citizen from near Charlestown, and said, "Now is the time to strike." Bayler said, "Strike what?" Wise said, "To break up the Union." Bayler said, "I am not in favor of that."

Some of the poor white men from Loudoun County stole the boots from the feet of the dead Brown men. An old colored man named Charles, a slave of the hotel proprietor, named Fouke, at the Ferry, was living with Mr. Everhart, a farmer who hired him. Charles was so superstitious that he would not let the white men who stole the boots leave them downstairs where he slept.

Tuesday night, after the prisoners were taken to Charlestown jail, a false alarm came from Sandy Hook, Maryland, that thousands of Abolitionists were coming through Pleasant Valley, Washington County, Maryland, killing all the citizens. Our people gathered all their families and put them in the cellars. The church was full of them, mostly women and children. All night long the men of the town waited in terrible suspense, the women and children crying and screaming. Only those who passed through this night of terror could give a correct account of it. It all came about in this way: My father, E. H. Chambers, had been sent out Tuesday afternoon on a scouting party to search for hidden arms. Mr. Jesse Moore, a farmer living in the Valley, hearing our men coming through the mountains, got on his horse and galloped into Sandy Hook, crying, "The Abolitionists are coming down the Valley, killing all the citizens."

While Governor Wise was talking to Brown, Colonel Robert E. Lee stood close by. Brown sat with his head buried in his hands a great part of the time. He answered all questions boldly, said just what he had meant to do, and declared that this was the beginning of the end of slavery.

It certainly was true that a great change came over the slaves immediately after the Raid. Their masters were uneasy, and the slaves were not as reliable as before. Up to that time they had not been allowed to hold meeting, but now they would congregate without the knowledge of their owners. I remember well hearing father come into our farm-house one night and say that he had seen quite a number of negroes on the turnpike above us. Father was himself opposed to slavery. He went up to them and advised them to go to their homes, as they would be surely discovered and arrested. The slaves were dealt with in a more lenient manner than before the Raid.

On the morning of December 2, 1859, John Brown was hanged at Charlestown. Stevens, Cook, Hazzlet, Coppie, Green, and Copeland were hanged with him. About twenty citizens and militia in the attack were killed and wounded.

2 When the States Seceded

Mrs. Eugene McLean

*T*HE WRITER was the daughter of Maj. Gen. E. V. Sumner. In 1849 she married Lt. Eugene McLean, a graduate of the West Point class of 1842. They moved in 1859 from Texas, where he had been stationed, to Washington. McLean was a native of Maryland, and his sympathies were with the South. At the outbreak of the war, he resigned his commission and entered the Confederate army, where he attained high rank in the Staff Corps. His wife's diary was written as a continuous narrative, giving the writer's family a picture of the stirring scenes through which she lived in Washington and later in the South.

Washington, *Nov. 8, 1860.*
Terribly exciting day—State after State going for rail-splitting abolitionism and Lincoln—Black Republicans triumphant—radical Southerners equally so—conservatives thoughtful. "Where will it all end?" I asked Colonel de Russey, who has spent the evening with us. "*Mon Dieu,* who knows? Let us not spoil our digestion and our evening in contemplating it. A game of euchre will give us a better night's rest and fewer wrinkles." And so we played till twelve, when the ringing of bells announced the election *un fait accompli.*

Moved our lodgings to Brown's Hotel, the headquarters of the Disunionists, and already the irrepressibles are pouring in. For the first time I hear the disunion openly avowed, and feel as much shocked as if the

existence of a God were denied; but reflection and history teach me that
there is nothing inherently divine in republics.

It is becoming evident that a broad line will be drawn this winter
between Northerners and Southerners, even in social life. What am I to
do, with so many friends on both sides? Have seriously canvassed the
propriety of getting ill to avoid unpleasant *contretemps,* but with so much
to be seen and heard have not the resolution to shut myself up, and have
decided to act naturally and take the consequences "like a man."

CONGRESS MEETS to-day. The most exciting session ever known pre-
dicted—the question of slavery in the Territories to be decided. Northern men cool, calm, and determined; Southern men vehement,
passionate, and threatening. Sympathize more with the latter; cannot at
all comprehend the cold-blooded policy of the former, some of whom
look as if born to be the natural enemies of mankind. The President's
message satisfies no one—too simple a diet.

WENT TO the Senate to-day with Mrs. Jefferson Davis; more pleased with
her conversation than anything I heard. She is as full of feeling as of wit,
and there are times when both are called into play, though I fear she has
too much of the former to make her a happy woman in a revolution
where she will play so prominent a part as the wife of the acknowledged
Southern leader. Mr. Davis's talents and character alone give him this
unenviable notoriety, as he has said very little so far, and what he has said
has been marked by a temperance and moderation unusual in the Southern man. I believe he would willingly effect a compromise to-morrow
were it in his power.

Mr. Douglas to-day, in a clear, emphatic, and, I fear, prophetic voice,
painted the horrors of a war we are bringing on ourselves, and was
equally severe on the radicals of both sides. There is something very
impressive about him, and I felt as if I were listening to the plain, unvar-
nished truth; but so far as the principal actors are concerned, I believe
they would look just as unmoved if they were to see the hand writing on
the wall or hear a voice from heaven. It seems now as if we were to drift
into a civil war without one helping hand to save us. Mrs. Douglas was in
the gallery of the Senate looking the pride and confidence she felt in her
husband's talents, though there is a modesty in her manner in charming
contrast with her truly magnificent appearance. Every place was crowded
and the ladies generally in full visiting toilette. The diplomatic boxes all
full; observed the G——s in one of them and a celebrated New York

beauty in another—all together a striking *coup d'oeil,* with a certain sort of Spartan heroism in it. We begin to feel we are to be scattered like chaff before the wind, and we go to meet our fate in our best bonnets and with smiling faces. If we must secede, let us do so becomingly. There is very little outside gaiety; not one large party so far, and our evenings are our dull times, so unlike the Washington of other days.

South Carolina has passed her secession ordinance and proclaims herself to be an independent body—rather an unprotected-looking female! It would be an act of charity to lead her—quietly, if possible, forcibly, if necessary—back home again, but the powers that be seem to consider it a matter of not much importance, and our wayward sister is allowed to go in peace, while her representatives are leaving Washington and hastening to her assistance before she gets quite out of sight. I cannot persuade myself it is anything but supremely ridiculous, although I have heard for the last month that if she only leads the way the other cotton States will follow.

SENATE AGAIN to-day. Missed the South-Carolinians, but felt a comfortable conviction that there would be talking enough without them. Toombs, of Georgia, was the lion of the house, pacing up and down in front of his desk exclaiming, "If this be treason, then I am a traitor." A number of the officers of the army from South Carolina have resigned. If worse comes to worst I suppose they will all go, though they say very little about it, and it is an understood thing that so long as they wear the uniform of the United States they are not Secessionists, even in opinion. I have no idea what some of our most intimate friends are going to do, and am amused at the persistence they show in avoiding all discussion of the subject. Such a state of affairs cannot last long. Every one is watching with interest almost too deep for words the action of the Committee of Thirteen, composed of Northern and Southern men, to endeavor to effect a compromise of some sort. God grant they may succeed! Union men say there is little probability of it. Mr. Jefferson Davis announced that the compromise committee could come to no terms, and it was received by that immense audience in a silence like death. His succeeding remarks made a deep impression, and he himself was evidently much affected. He is by far the most interesting speaker in the Senate; his voice alone makes him one of nature's orators—so cold and sarcastic one moment, so winning and persuasive the next, and again rising to tones of command that carry obedience with them. If I did not know him in private life, and did not know his high, honorable, and chivalric nature, I could well understand the influence he exercises; he is one of the few public men I have ever seen who impresses me with his earnestness.

NEW-YEAR'S DAY. A good deal of visiting, but conversation turns on the state of the country, and we cannot help asking ourselves and one another, "Where shall we be next year?" Some one has said anniversaries are the tombstones of time, and I begin to see how they can be made so. The officers of the army, in full uniform, went as usual to pay their respects to the President, and as they passed, with the gallant Scott at their head, a Georgia lady said with a sigh, "How many of them will be our enemies?"

MR. SEWARD drew a crowded house to-day. We went at nine o'clock in order to get seats, and found difficulty in obtaining them even at that early hour. We spend so much time in the Senate that many of the ladies take their sewing or crocheting, and all of us who are not absolutely spiritual provide ourselves with a lunch. The gallery of the Senate is the fashionable place of reunion, and before the Senate meets we indulge in conversation sometimes very spirited, though generally the opposing factions treat each other with great reserve—a very necessary precaution. Mr. Seward spoke for nearly four hours, and I was sorry when he took his seat, yet for the life of me do not know what he said, what he did not say, or what he meant to say; either his speech was above vulgar comprehension or he is the Talleyrand of America, as I find no one knows any more than I do, and yet every one says it was a masterly effort. He chained the attention of a promiscuous audience of all classes and of every shade of opinion for four hours; he offered no compromises; he offered no prejudices; he expressed opinions, but did not commit himself. It was like a skilful fencer who shows great adroitness and dexterity in the use of his weapons, and does not hurt his opponent, only because he has taken the precaution to use blunted foils. It may be a sleight of hand to which politicians are accustomed, but to me it is wonderful and argues great reserved strength. Why does he not exert it to save the country? The North grows more and more unyielding every day; the South more and more defiant. Is there no Curtius to close the gulf?

Went to a levee at the White House last evening. A number of ultra Southerners there and all on the best terms, apparently, with the Administration. Miss Lane, as usual, handsome, well-dressed, and agreeable. Mr. Buchanan politic and polite.

Mississippi secedes, and I suppose the others will follow soon, as it seems to be the policy to "speed the parting guest." The tall, handsome, and belligerent Mississippi woman in ecstasies, and the children making a Fourth of July of it with firecrackers, etc. I am becoming accustomed to it.

ALABAMA GOES out. Another *feu de joie*. A caustic old gentleman remarks that they had better save their gunpowder. It would be an economy if they would all go out together. Johnson, of Tennessee, has consumed two days in his argument against the right of secession. A Southern man and a slaveholder, he is regarded as a renegade. He is a remarkable-looking man, with a piercing eye that might, I should judge, see as far into the millstone as any other that has tried to look. At all events, his arguments seemed to me unanswerable, and I came home convinced that people had a right to be rebels, but no right to be secessionists, which is just what I have felt all the time. The question being settled, it now behooves me (taking future contingencies into consideration) to cultivate rebel proclivities.

Mr. Crittenden spoke to-day in a trembling voice and with tearful eyes, beseeching those who could to save the Union. I could not control my feelings; it was sad to see that old white-haired man, who had devoted his best years to his country, find himself powerless to help it in this its extremity, but, with piteous entreaties to deaf ears and hardened hearts, exhaust himself in the vain effort to bring about a single concession. I shall never forget his appearance, and it will always rise to speak for itself when I hear him reviled by one party as a driveler and by the other as a time-server.

Have seen the wives of some of the United States officers at Fort Sumter. When it was decided to abandon Sullivan's Island and retire into the fort the ladies were sent over to Charleston, but could find no accommodations and were obliged to come North. Not a boardinghouse would receive them, and one woman frankly said that if she did she would lose all her other boarders. I cannot imagine such a state of feeling, and am quite indignant with the Southern chivalry, though they say some few of the gentlemen of Charleston were very polite and offered them rooms in their private houses; but, with the enmity openly avowed toward their husbands, they could not, of course, accept any obligations. They feel very bitter and are ready for the war. In the mean time they are receiving a great deal of attention as the first martyrs.

HAVE MOVED up to Willard's and am in the full odor of Black Republican sanctity. The South "dies daily," and, if I am to believe all I hear, is in just that helpless condition which would justify any generous soul in flying to its assistance. It is a fact, however, that when the Southerners were here they held their own remarkably well, and the accounts daily received of forts surrendered do not seem to argue weakness in anything but the United States army. In the Senate, I am told, some of the radicals out-wigfall Wigfall, but I never hear them or read any of their speeches. Am entirely disheartened, and have lost all the hope and enthusiasm with which I commenced the winter.

States going out and Mr. Lincoln coming in are the only topics of the day; and if the first is beginning to be looked upon as a matter of course, the latter is waited for with impatience by all parties. The Republicans are anxious to carry out their programme; the border States hope to effect some sort of reconciliation, while people generally are beginning to feel as if this state of uncertainty were worse than war, and want the thing decided one way or another. All think the country is not what it was, and if it cannot be reconstructed there are many who will feel at liberty to make a choice between the two sections. I should like to place my plat-form on Mason and Dixon's line, but, not being a "solo" or a prima donna, am not considered entitled to one.

The gathering of the Northern clans has commenced and the House is filled with New-Yorkers, Bostonians, and fresh, bright-looking women from all parts of the North, each one with her own "views"—refreshing, wide-awake people who never go to sleep mentally and never allow any one else to. I find it exhilarating, but a friend from the modern Athens, says, "In the long run it is fatiguing." Any quantity of women with unquiet eyes and eager manners, electioneering for office by denouncing everything Southern and doing the agreeable to everything Northern; some New York belles who have no idea of sacrificing themselves to the public weal by drawing party lines; an unusual number of short-sighted girls flirting through eye-glasses with men in spectacles, and, last, but by no means least, some dignified old ladies with porcupinish principles and propriety exuding from every pore.

ALL WASHINGTON in a ferment about the unexpected arrival of the Presi-dent-elect—Abraham Lincoln. His movements since leaving his home in Springfield, Illinois, have been regularly reported, and by last advices he was in Baltimore to remain for the night, and arrives here to-morrow; but early this morning it was whispered that he was in the house, and by midday all kinds of stories were afloat. Infernal machines with Southern sympathies, plug-uglies, etc., etc.—altogether a state of affairs which, if we may believe Dame Rumor with her hundred tongues, rendered a

Scotch cap and military cloak necessary disguises. Be that as it may, he is here and I have seen him! A tall, thin man with black hair and earnest eyes, not at all a handsome face, but one that inspires confidence and justifies the sobriquet of "Honest Old Abe." The Opposition is delighted with this surreptitious advent, and is not slow in making the most of it in the way of ridicule and sarcasm, while the Republicans themselves look as if it would take a very respectable and well-organized insurrection to satisfy them that it was all right. I have heard a mob was feared in Baltimore, and the advisers of Mr. Lincoln, or those whose advice he took, deemed it wiser to avoid all occasion for trouble before he should be fairly inaugurated. What a fine commentary it all is on "the free choice of the people"! Mrs. Lincoln arrived yesterday—one day after her husband—and again we have rumors of some disgraceful scenes during her stay in Baltimore. It is said she found it difficult to get to the depot, and again it is said she expressed her determination to go there at all hazard. If war on women is inaugurated at this early stage, what is to become of us? One of the large parlors with a suite of rooms adjoining has been appropriated to the use of Mr. Lincoln and family, and already a stream of people meander thither at all hours of the day. About eight in the evening it becomes a rushing torrent carrying everything before it. In other words, Mr. and Mrs. Lincoln receive every evening from eight to ten, and during those hours it is impossible to pass through the main hall; accordingly, the knowing ones take a cup of tea in order to secure good seats, favorable as well for making observations as for hearing those of others. I find most persons see just what they wish to see, and the criticisms passed on the distinguished strangers are as varied as the different shades of politics, or as the hopes of critical office-seekers are sanguine or otherwise. In the meanwhile polite society repeats Mrs. Lincoln's remarks or manufactures them, as the case may be, while the political world busies itself in the selection of a cabinet for Mr. Lincoln. At one moment we hear the conservatives are to be called to his counsel, at another the most radical of the Republicans; all parties, however, seem to consider that Mr. Seward is to be the Secretary of State.

THE FOURTH of March, 1861, has seen Mr. Lincoln successfully installed as President of the United States, despite all predictions to the contrary. For the first time in the history of the United States it has been found necessary to conduct the President-elect to the Capitol surrounded by bayonets, and with loaded cannon at different points on the route, where it was feared his passage might be obstructed—all of which added to the display, if it detracted as much from preconceived ideas of the inauguration of the President of a free Republic. From early in the morning the tramp of the troops could be heard, and dashing aids in showy uniforms seen urging their horses almost to full speed and looking as if the fate, not only of the United States but of the universe, depended on their individual efforts. "Masons" and "Odd Fellows" with marshals of the city and marshals of the day were running against one another at every corner, sublimely unconscious of everything but their destination. By nine the street in front of Willard's Hotel was lined with troops as far as the eye could see, and there they remained under arms until Mr. Lincoln appeared, leaning on the arm of Mr. Buchanan, who had previously driven down the avenue in his own carriage unattended. As soon as Mr. Lincoln stepped into the carriage that was to convey him to the Capitol, the troops presented arms, the band struck up "Dixie," and the sun, which had been under a light cloud all the morning, shone with undiminished splendor, as if nothing should be wanting to give effect to the moment. It was a scene never to be forgotten, and seemed to make an unwonted impression on the spectators, hushing into silence for the instant every dissentient voice. As the carriage, which might be said to contain the destiny of the United States, disappeared the troops filed after it, followed by an immense throng of people of all ages and both sexes eagerly hurrying to the Capitol, where a platform had been erected outside of the building, from which Mr. Lincoln, after taking the oath of office as President of the United States, addressed them. I was not near enough to hear what he said, but on that sea of faces turned toward him I could read every variety of expression from exultation to despair, and felt long before I knew positively that there was no hope for the South. The remainder of the day was a gloomy one for all parties; the excitement of the morning has passed away, leaving reflection, that enemy to all present enjoyment, with dark forebodings to overshadow our future.

The Inauguration Ball. The dullest of all balls—scarcely a familiar face to be seen. The *haut ton* did not come out, because "the Lincolns are not yet the fashion." The strangers who patronized the affair tried to make the most of it, but the room, or tent, was arranged with so little taste and was so badly lighted that it required a brilliant imagination to fancy enjoyment in such a scene. Mr. Douglas opened the ball with Mrs. Lincoln, who looked extremely well in a light-blue "moiré," but did not seem to be in good spirits—it is said she remarked that it had been the most unhappy day of her life.

THE CABINET has been appointed, and the extreme radicals carry the day, which means war, say the prophets. Our prophets look gloomy enough; in the meanwhile we laugh and jest as if Rome were not burning. A medical friend, entertaining us with a detailed account of the elaborate arrangements made for the anticipated "crisis" on the day of the inauguration, says the surgeons were ordered to be in readiness with their instruments and bandages, and that mounted orderlies reported from time to time the progress of the procession to the commander-in-chief, who said nothing until Mr. Lincoln had finished his inaugural, when he thanked Heaven "the country was safe." It is well we can laugh if it is only to save our tears, which are ready to flow, as each hour develops the new policy that would have been hailed by many with delight three months since, but which now comes too late either to prevent or to save.

A Peace Convention, the last hope of the border States, is in session, composed generally of the older and more conservative men, and it is sad to see how, day by day, as hope dies out, they look more and more aged. Mr. Bell, of Tennessee, has grown ten years older in three days, and so have many others. We do not even ask now, "What hope?"

THE UNITED STATES flag has actually been fired on, and the steamer *Star of the West,* carrying provisions to Fort Sumter, forced by rebel batteries to turn back. I thought I had reasoned myself into a conviction that rebellion was justifiable, but I find I was not prepared to see it triumphant and the flag of my country go down at the first fire. It is strange how our sympathies change in a moment. I see men who this morning said—and I believe in all sincerity—that nothing could induce them to fight against the South, ready now to take up arms, while the Southerners in the city are inexpressibly shocked, and many of them speak as if they felt the insult as keenly as their Northern brethren.

The attack on Fort Sumter is the all-engrossing theme. G. T. Beauregard commands the rebels, and Major Anderson the United States forces. So far the latter have been able to hold the fort, but the wise say it is merely a question of time. The Southerners have been erecting batteries for the past month or more, and as they have one of our best engineer officers to direct their works and have not been in the least molested, it is reasonable to suppose they will succeed. In the mean time Northern indignation is at fever-heat. Though I, personally, passed through the crisis when the *Star of the West* was fired on, I feel a deep sympathy for the victims in the fort, and should think it quite natural if they finally emerged secessionists, unless indeed they should feel under obligations to the United States government for "assisting" at their first defeat; nor should I feel surprised if they did take this view, as the theories on that subject are as varied as they are erratic. One man knows no United States out of his own State, and another one knows none in it. One swears fealty to the place of his birth, and another to that of every one's but his own. I have met only one entirely independent man, who was born at sea, and privileged to use the reason God gave him in that natal hour.

Fort Sumter has surrendered after three days' continued firing, and no one killed. War loses its horrors upon a nearer view, and we can read the heroic incidents of the attack and defense with minds at ease as to the fate of our friends on both sides.

Mr. Lincoln calls out seventy-five thousand troops to crush the rebellion, and no one is frightened; but, now that the United States government has condescended to notice the affair, private individuals who did not care about taking the initiative are ranging themselves on either side as principle or feelings dictate, so that we may look for more battles, but I fear none so bloodless as Fort Sumter. Strange, strange, strange how we have accustomed ourselves to the thought, and accept the dissolution of the Union as a natural consequence! Whom have we to blame for bringing us to this state of discipline? Wherever the fault lies, I do not envy them their feelings in this hour, and fear both sections will atone in mourning and ashes for the crime.

It is difficult to realize all this, is it not? And to believe that our native land has been sacrificed on the altar of faction—does it not seem as if the whole country was an insane asylum for the exclusive benefit of the two classes of monomaniacs, abolitionists and secessionists? However, as my lot is cast with the latter, it will be wise in me to follow the stream without asking whence it cometh or whither it goeth.

E. [THE WRITER'S HUSBAND] resigned from the United States army on Monday last, with many regrets, but his feelings are with the South, and, now that the difficulties have passed beyond State limits and assumed a sectional character in which the whole South is arrayed against the whole North, he is determined to act upon their dictates, deeming it dishonorable to remain in a service to which he could not give a cordial support. I believe he sacrifices his interests, but I can entirely sympathize in this sort of self-immolation, and, indeed, after all I have seen and heard this past winter it is refreshing to meet now and then a man capable of a generous sacrifice, and I must do the officers of the army who have resigned this justice. They all believe they are leaving the stronger for the weaker side, and speak of old associations and broken ties with regret and sadness that will never be appreciated by those who forced this issue upon them—and, without having had anything to do with bringing about this state of affairs, it is very evident they will be the first victims.

We left Washington this afternoon, and, though I did not trust myself to bid some of my oldest friends farewell, it has been a most trying day to me, while I have not dared to think of those nearer and dearer ones I am leaving behind. As for the present, imagine me in a small room at the Mansion House, Alexandria, having passed the evening in the parlor and in Mrs. Johnston's room. The General resigned to-day. The parlor was filled with officers of the navy and their families, all in a high state of excitement, evidently put on to cover deeper feelings. One poor little woman with five children could not conceal her apprehensions and anxiety for the future, and was rallied by the others upon a want of proper spirit. I sympathized with her, but was prudent enough to forbear any expression of it, feeling that in strict justice I ought to expend all that sort of sentiment on myself, as I fear my antecedents will not procure me a great deal of consideration in Confederate circles. Mrs. Johnston is sick and in low spirits; she feels the parting from old friends and, I imagine, does not look on the future with a very bright eye, though she is too politic to say so; but we sometimes instinctively feel what others think. At all events, her quiet room was a relief after the noisy parlor, and I remained there until a few minutes since. To-morrow we leave for Richmond.

3 A Contemporary Account of the Inauguration of Jefferson Davis

Edited by Virginia K. Jones

*T*HIS ACCOUNT was written by Mrs. Jefferson Franklin Jackson, formerly Ellen Clark Noyes of Boston, Massachusetts, to a relative. The original letter was deposited in the [Alabama] Department of Archives and History, along with a few other items of her grandparents, by Mrs. Lillian Jackson Coleman in 1940. These gifts were added to the collection of papers of Jefferson Franklin Jackson already on deposit.

Montgomery Tuesday—Feb. 19th 1861

My dear Mary,[1]

Your note and the red garters came this morning in time for Willie[2] to put them on when he dressed and he feels very dressed in them.

Yesterday was the greatest day in the annals of Montgomery. The President with his escort of about 20 gentlemen arrived on Saturday night. Yesterday was bright and pleasant and a very large crowd of people assembled at the Capitol and on the streets to see the procession and attend the inaugural exercises. The newspapers will give you full accounts of it. A Government is formed for the South and no idea of reconstruction is entertained.

I was one of the mass of people in front of the Portico. The balconies and every front window were filled with ladies who went *early*. Emmie had a bad cold and did not go. Annie & Bessie went with me. The crowd about used them up. I fared better.

My share of the interesting occasion was to furnish a most beautiful wreath of Japonicas and hyacinths and small spring magnolias—also a large bunch of flowers for the Vice President. *The wreath for the President:* I did not begin to collect the flowers until 9 o'clock in the morning and went to Mr. Garrett's place[3] with a basket and brought it away full of those crimson and red and variegated Japonicas. The green of the wreath was arbor vitae and box. The front of the wreath was elevated, and was composed of large crimson Japonica, a small one and white hyacinths in the point against a back of arbor vitae. Below the Jap. were purple and white *double hyacinths.* On either side of the centre were half opened pink Jap. and the whole wreath was of dark and light flowers alternating. You have no idea how beautiful it was, at a distance and near too.

As the procession came through the Capitol grounds I handed the flowers to Mr. Watts[4] who was one of the committee and told him the wreath was for the Pres., the bouquet for the Vice Pres. They were laid on the table and after the inauguration Howell Cobb handed him the wreath which he slipped on his arm—and gave Mr. Stephens his flowers. The ladies from above threw down small bunches of flowers which the Pres. gathered and held in his hand.

A levee was held last night in Estelle's Concert Hall. The ladies trimmed Estelle Hall beautifully. Oh the crowd! and such a one. The greatest variety of costume you can imagine. People from town, people from country, young and old. Mr. Watts gave all the introductions. Mrs Fitzpatrick, just from Washington,[5] with black velvet dress, point-lace bertha, and sleeves trimmed with same, and pearl ornaments. A lady next-to-her, perhaps with her, head covered and shawl on. Men in fine clothes and men in home spun. Mr. Watts wore his home spun suit. Most of *our* ladies dressed prettily. Mrs. Thorington came with bonnet and cloak. Emmie could not go. *Bessie wouldn't.* Annie not well. Frank and I went alone. I wore my brown silk with blue flounces which has been entirely made over into a low necked dress with skirt in puffs and ruffles. On my neck I wore my pretty collaret and black lace shawl thrown round my shoulders. My head dress was of blue velvet with black and gold ornaments. My jewelry is blue you know.

When we went up to be presented Mr. Watts said "this is the lady who presented you with the wreath." He [Davis] said it was beautiful and he only wished he had a box which would take it safely to his wife and children. Speaking of the crowd I told him when we built the White House we would give him more room. When Frank was introduced he asked Mr. Davis if he remembered him—he looked at him a moment and said "Sampson Harris! Go on, I can't talk to you now, come and see me and bring your wife." They were together in the sick room of Mr. Harris at Washington.[6]

Every house little and big was illuminated from the Capitol to the Exchange last night. The Theatre was illuminated also. Rockets and bengal lights were thrown from opposite sides of the streets constantly by the Estelle Hall comm. In short yesterday was a *great day* for Montgomery.

I have not yet told you that *Wallace*[7] is at home and sick. He came on Sunday night. He thinks he had a chill while keeping guard and has not been well since. He suffers much pain in the back of his neck at times. His company will be here the last of the week. He lays on the sofa all day. A few days of rest will recruit him I hope.

I suppose our new Government will send on a commissioner with full powers to settle the question about the Forts. Nobody expected the *State Commissions* would accomplish anything though the state went through the form but when the seven seceding states demand through their minister the withdrawal of the troops at the Forts it puts a different face on the matter. Haven't you found out yet that South Carolina can't act any longer independently? Did you know that this Southern Congress has all the war measures in hand now, and Ft. Pickens or Ft. Sumter won't be attacked until they say so?

I am sorry for your reading if you do not get any nearer the truth than in those statements about Mr. Yancy saying the northern counties must be compelled etc. When you see or hear statements that call for your disapproval it would be just as well to stop and consider perhaps— *possibly* it may not be so. as to the Southern Forts why do you object to their being occupied by the people for whose defence they were built? They do not defend Massachusetts or New York and the South *must have them,* because she believes that by delay they will be occupied by large bodies of men who will be placed there to attempt the coercion of the seceding States. Now if you are not willing the Forts should be taken by the South for the purpose of defence—then you are willing to have them reinforced, which from what you read in the papers is the policy of the Republicans about to be in power. If the South *must have them* why not possess them while they can be taken without bloodshed as has been the case—without exception—which if not evacuated must be taken at any cost.

It seems hardly possible that Lincoln will undertake coercion. If he does not he will have to acknowledge the Independence of the South and evacuate the Forts. We will not trouble him to take care of our defences or collect our revenue. You may be sure that nothing will be done until our Congress has sent someone to Washington to treat for the purchase of the Forts and all the other Government property, and arrange a basis of settlement. Buchanan won't want to treat but will try and put it off on Lincoln and no one can say what will be done between now and March 4th.

Emmie & Wallace asked Rosa why she did not go to the Capitol to see the Inauguration, that she would be disappointed if she did not see it. She replied with great dignity that she could not be disappointed in what she knew all about. She had seen *three or four Presidents inaugurated*.

What cold weather you are having? Do keep warm inside and out. Drink something stimulating. I am afraid Mother will suffer from these cold snaps. Keep her very warm. Tell Charles he is very kind to look after your fires these cold mornings. I would go to bed and stay there until it gets warm again. Love to Mother, Charles & Sarah. I will send you papers about our affairs.

Your aff. Ellen

4 Mrs. Greenhow, Confederate Spy

William Gilmore Beymer

To MRS. RICHARD PRICE, Recording Secretary of Cape Fear Chapter Three, United Daughters of the Confederacy, at Wilmington, North Carolina, acknowledgment is made for her courtesy in permitting the use of data relating to Mrs. Greenhow.

Many of the passages in this article have been quoted from Mrs. Greenhow's own narrative.

* * *

These pages record the story of the woman who cast a pebble into the sea of circumstance—a pebble from whose widening ripples there rose a mighty wave, on whose crest the Confederate States of America were borne through four years of civil war.

Rose O'Neal Greenhow gave to General Beauregard information which enabled him to concentrate the widely scattered Confederate forces in time to meet McDowell on the field of Manassas, and there, with General Johnson, to win for the South the all-important battle of Bull Run.

Mrs. Greenhow's cipher despatch—nine words on a scrap of paper—set in motion the reinforcements which arrived at the height of the battle and turned it against the North. But for the part she played in the Confederate victory Rose O'Neal Greenhow paid a heavy price.

During the Buchanan administration Mrs. Greenhow was one of the leaders of Washington society. She was a Southerner by birth, but a resident of Washington from her girlhood; a widow, beautiful, accomplished, wealthy, and noted for her wit and her forceful personality. Her home was the rendezvous of those prominent in official life in Washington—the "court circle," had America been a monarchy. She was personally acquainted with all the leading men of the country, many of whom had partaken of her hospitality. President Buchanan was a close personal friend; a friend, too, was William H. Seward, then Senator from New York; her niece, a granddaughter of Dolly Madison, was the wife of Stephen A. Douglas. It was in such company that she watched with burning interest the war clouds grow and darken over Charleston Harbor, then burst into the four years' storm; she never saw it end.

Among her guests at this time was Colonel Thomas Jordan, who, before leaving Washington to accept the appointment of Adjutant-General of the Confederate army at Manassas, broached to Mrs. Greenhow the subject of a secret military correspondence. What would *she* do to aid the Confederacy? he asked her. Ah, what would she not do! Then he told her how some one in Washington was needed by the South; of the importance of the work which might be done, and her own especial fitness for the task. And that night before he left the house he gave her a cipher code, and arranged that her despatches to him were to be addressed to "Thomas John Rayford."

And so he crossed the river into Virginia and left her, in the Federal capital, armed with the glittering shield, "Justified by military necessity," and the two-edged sword, "All's fair in love and war";—left her, his agent, to gather in her own way information from the enemy, her former friends, where and from whom she would.

It was in April, '61, that she took up her work; in November, Allan Pinkerton, head of the Federal Secret Service, made to the War Department a report in which he said—in the vehement language of a partisanship as intense as Mrs. Greenhow's own:

> It was a fact too notorious to need reciting here, that for months . . . Mrs. Greenhow was actively and to a great extent openly engaged in giving aid and comfort, sympathy and information; . . . her house was the rendezvous for the most violent enemies of the government, . . . where they were furnished with every possible information to be obtained by the untiring energies of this very remarkable woman; . . . that since the commencement of this rebellion this woman, from her long residence at the capital, her superior education, her uncommon social powers, her very extensive acquaintance among, and her active association with, the leading politicians of this nation, has possessed an

almost superhuman power, all of which she has most wickedly used to destroy the government. . . . She has made use of whoever and whatever she could as mediums to carry into effect her unholy purposes. . . . She has not used her powers in vain among the officers of the army, not a few of whom she has robbed of patriotic hearts and transformed them into sympathizers with the enemies of the country. . . . She had her secret and insidious agents in all parts of this city and scattered over a large extent of country. . . . She had alphabets, numbers, ciphers, and various other not mentioned ways of holding intercourse. . . . Statistical facts were thus obtained and forwarded that could have been found nowhere but in the national archives, thus leading me to the conclusion that such evidence must have been obtained from employees and agents in the various departments of the government.

Thus she worked throughout the opening days of the war. Washington lay ringed about with camps of new-formed regiments, drilling feverishly. Already the press and public had raised the cry, "On to Richmond." When would they start? Where would they first strike? It was on those two points that the Confederate plan of campaign hinged. It was Mrs. Greenhow who gave the information. To General Beauregard at Manassas, where he anxiously awaited tidings of the Federal advance, there came about the 10th of July the first message from Mrs. Greenhow. The message told of the intended advance of the enemy across the Potomac and on to Manassas via Fairfax Court-house and Centreville. It was brought into the Confederate lines by a young lady of Washington, Miss Duval, who, disguised as a market-girl, carried the message to a house near Fairfax Court-house, occupied by the wife and daughters (Southern born) of an officer in the Federal army. General Beauregard at once commenced his preparations for receiving the attack, and sent one of his aides to President Davis to communicate the information and to urge the immediate concentration of the scattered Confederate forces.

But still the Federal start was delayed, and the precise date was as indefinite as ever. It was during this period of uncertainty that G. Donellan, who, before joining the Confederates, had been a clerk in the Department of the Interior, volunteered to return to Washington for information. He was armed with the two words "Trust Bearer" in Colonel Jordan's cipher, and was sent across the Potomac with instructions to report to Mrs. Greenhow. He arrived at the very moment that she most needed a messenger. Hastily writing in cipher her all-important dispatch, "Order issued for McDowell to move on Manassas to-night," she gave it to Donellan, who was taken by her agents in a buggy, with relays of horses, down the eastern shore of the Potomac to a ferry near Dumfries, where he was ferried across. Cavalry couriers delivered the despatch into General Beauregard's hands that night, July 16th.

And the source of Mrs. Greenhow's information? She has made the statement that she *"received a copy of the order to McDowell."* Allan Pinkerton was not wrong when he said that she "had not used her powers in vain among the officers of the army."

At midday of the 17th there came Colonel Jordan's reply:

> Yours was received at eight o'clock at night. Let them come; we are ready for them. We rely upon you for precise information. Be particular as to description and destination of forces, quantity of artillery, etc.

She was ready with fresh information, and the messenger was sent back with the news that the Federals intended to cut the Manassas Gap Railroad to prevent Johnson, at Winchester, from reinforcing Beauregard. After that there was nothing to be done but await the result of the inevitable battle. She had done her best. What that best was worth she learned when she received from Colonel Jordan the treasured message:

> Our President and our General direct me to thank you. We rely upon you for further information. The Confederacy owes you a debt.

When the details of the battle became known, and she learned how the last of Johnson's 8,500 men (marched to General Beauregard's aid because of *her* despatches) had arrived at three o'clock on the day of the battle and had turned the wavering Federal army into a mob of panic-stricken fugitives, she felt that the "Confederacy owed her a debt," indeed.

In the days immediately following Bull Run it seemed to the Confederate sympathizers in the city that their victorious army had only to march into Washington to take it. "Everything about the national Capitol betokened the panic of the Administration," Mrs. Greenhow wrote. "Preparations were made for the expected attack, and signals were arranged to give the alarm. . . . I went round with the principal officer in charge of this duty, and took advantage of the situation. . . . Our gallant Beauregard would have found himself right ably seconded by the rebels in Washington had he deemed it expedient to advance on the city. A part of the plan was to have cut the telegraph wires connecting with the various military positions with the War Department, to make prisoners of McClellan and several others, thereby creating still greater confusion in the first moments of panic. Measures had also been taken to spike the guns in Fort Corcoran, Fort Ellsworth, and other important points, accurate drawings of which had been furnished to our commanding officer by me." Doubtless it was these same drawings concerning which the New York *Herald* commented editorially a month later:

> . . . We have in this little matter [Mrs. Greenhow's arrest] a clue to the mystery of those important government maps and plans which the rebels lately left behind them in their hasty flight from Fairfax Courthouse. . . . and we are at liberty to guess how Beauregard was so minutely informed of this advance, and of our plan of attack on his lines, as to be ready to meet it at every salient point with overwhelming numbers.

Poor Mrs. Greenhow—from the very first doomed to disaster. Her maps and plans (if these, indeed, were hers) were allowed to fall into the enemy's hands; despatches were sent to her by an ill-chosen messenger, who, too late, was discovered to be a spy for the Federal War Department; her very cipher code, given her by Colonel Jordan, proved to be an amateurish affair that was readily deciphered by the Federal War Office. She never had a chance to escape detection. Concerning the cipher, Colonel Jordan wrote to Confederate Secretary of War Judah P. Benjamin, October, '61 (the letter was found in the archives of Richmond four years later): "This cipher I arranged last April. Being my first attempt and hastily devised it may be deciphered by any expert, as I found after use of it for a time. . . . That does not matter as of course I used it with but the lady, and with her it has served our purpose. . . ." It had, indeed, served their purpose, but in serving it had brought imprisonment and ruin to the woman.

When the War Department began to shake itself free from the staggering burden placed upon it by the rout at Bull Run, almost its first step was to seek out the source of the steady and swift-flowing stream of information to Richmond. Suspicion at once fell upon Mrs. Greenhow. Many expressed their secession sentiments as openly as did she, but there was none other who possessed her opportunities for obtaining Federal secrets. Federal officers and officials continued their pleasant social relations with her, and she was believed by the War Office to be influencing some of these. Thomas A. Scott, Assistant Secretary of War, sent for Allan Pinkerton and instructed him to place Mrs. Greenhow under surveillance; her house was to be constantly watched, as well as all visitors from the moment they were seen to enter or to leave it, and, should any of these visitors later attempt to go South, they were immediately to be

arrested. The watch on the house continued for some days; many prominent gentlemen called—men whose loyalty was above question. Then on
the night of August 22d, while Pinkerton and several of his men watched
during a hard storm, an officer of the Federal army entered the house.
Pinkerton removed his shoes and stood on the shoulders of one of his
men that he might watch and listen at a crack in the shutters. When the
officer left the house he was followed by Pinkerton (still in his stocking
feet) and one of his detectives. Turning suddenly, the officer discovered
that he was being followed; he broke into a run, and the three of them
raced through the deserted, rain-swept streets straight to the door of a
station of the Provost-Marshal. The pursued had maintained his lead and
reached the station first; he was its commanding officer, and instantly
turned out the guard. Allan Pinkerton and his agent suddenly found that
the quarry had bagged the hunters.

The angry officer refused to send word for them to Secretary Scott,
to General McClellan, to the Provost-Marshal—to any one! He clapped
them into the guard-house—"a most filthy and uncomfortable place"—
and left them there, wet and bedraggled, among the crowd of drunken
soldiers and common prisoners of the streets. In the morning, when the
guard was relieved, one of them, whom Pinkerton had bribed, carried a
message to Secretary Scott, by whom they were at once set free. In his
report Allan Pinkerton says:

> . . . The officer then [immediately after Pinkerton was put under
> arrest] went upstairs while I halted and looked at my watch. Said officer
> returned in twenty minutes with a revolver in his hand, saying that he
> went up-stairs on purpose to get the revolver. The inquiry arises, was it
> for that purpose he stayed thus, or for the more probable one of hiding
> or destroying the evidence of his guilt obtained of Mrs. Greenhow or
> furnished to her? . . . .

This report goes no further into the charge, but that very day, August
23d, within a few hours of his release, Allan Pinkerton placed Mrs.
Greenhow under arrest as a spy.

Of the events of that fateful Friday Mrs. Greenhow has left a graphic
record, complete save that it does not tell why such events need ever have
been, for she had been warned of her proposed arrest—warned in ample
time at least to have attempted an escape. The message which told of the
impending blow had been sent to her, Mrs. Greenhow tells, by a lady in
Georgetown, to whom one of General McClellan's aides had given the
information. The note said also that the Hon. William Preston, Minister

to Spain until the outbreak of the war, was likewise to be arrested. To him Mrs. Greenhow passed on the warning, and he safely reached the Confederate army. But Mrs. Greenhow—why did she stay? Did escape seem so improbable that she dared not run the risk of indubitably convicting herself by an attempted flight? Did she underestimate the gravity of her situation and depend upon "influence" to save her? Or was it, after all, some Casabianca-like folly of remaining at her "post" until the end? Whatever the reason, she stayed.

Day after day she waited for the warning's fulfilment. Though waiting, she worked on. "'Twas very exciting," she told a friend long afterward. "I would be walking down the Avenue with one of the officials, military or state, and as we strolled along there would pass—perhaps a washerwoman carrying home her basket of clean clothes, or, maybe, a gaily attired youth from lower Seventh Avenue; but something in the way the woman held her basket, or in the way the youth twirled his cane, told me that news had been received, or that news was wanted—that I must open up communications in some way. Or as we sat in some city park a sedate old gentleman would pass by; to my unsuspecting escort the passer-by was but commonplace, but to me his manner of polishing his glasses, or the flourish of the handkerchief with which he rubbed his nose, was a message."

Days full of anxious forebodings sped by until the morning of the 23d of August dawned, oppressively sultry after the night of rain which had so bedraggled Allan Pinkerton and his detective. At about eleven o'clock that morning Mrs. Greenhow was returning home from a promenade with a distinguished member of the diplomatic corps, but for whose escort she believed she would have been arrested sooner, for she knew she was being followed. Excusing herself to her escort, she stopped to inquire for the sick child of a neighbor, and there they warned her that her house was being watched. So, then, the time had come! As she paused at her neighbor's door, perhaps for the moment a trifle irresolute, one of her "humble agents" chanced to be coming that way; farther down the street two men were watching her; she knew their mission.

To her passing agent she called, softly: "I think that I am about to be arrested. Watch from Corcoran's corner. I shall raise my handkerchief to my face if they arrest me. Give information of it." Then she slowly crossed the street to her house. She had several important papers with her that morning; one, a tiny note, she put into her mouth and destroyed; the other, a letter in cipher, she was unable to get from her pocket without being observed; for the opportunity to destroy it she must trust to chance. As she mounted the short flight of steps to her door, the two men—Allan Pinkerton and his operative, who had followed her rapidly—reached the foot of the steps. She turned and faced them, waiting for them to speak.

"Is this Mrs. Greenhow?"

"Yes," she replied, coldly. As they still hesitated, she asked, "Who are you, and what do you want?"

"I have come to arrest you," Pinkerton answered, shortly.

"By what authority? Let me see your warrant," she demanded, bravely enough except for what seemed a nervous movement of the fluttering handkerchief. To the detectives, if they noticed it, it was but the tremulous gesture of a woman's fright. To the agent lingering at Corcoran's corner it was the signal.

"I have no power to resist you," she said; "but, had I been inside of my house I would have killed one of you before I had submitted to this illegal process." They followed her into her house and closed the door.

"It seemed but a moment," she tells, "before the house became filled with men, and an indiscriminate search commenced. Men rushed with frantic haste into my chamber, into every sanctuary. Beds, drawers, wardrobes, soiled linen—search was made everywhere! Even scraps of paper—children's unlettered scribblings—were seized and tortured into dangerous correspondence with the enemy."

It was a very hot day. She asked to be allowed to change her dress, and permission was grudgingly given her, but almost immediately a detective followed to her bedroom, calling, "Madam! Madam!" and flung open the door. She barely had had time to destroy the cipher note that was in her pocket. Very shortly afterward a woman detective arrived, and "I was allowed the poor privilege of unfastening my own garments, which one by one were received by this pseudo-woman and carefully examined."

Though wild confusion existed within the house, no sign of it was allowed to show itself from without, for the house was now a trap, baited and set; behind the doors detectives waited to seize all who, ignorant of the fate of its owner, might call. Anxious to save her friends, and fearful, too, lest she be compromised further by papers which might be found on them when searched, Mrs. Greenhow sought means to warn them away. The frightened servants were all under guard, but there was one member of the household whose freedom was not yet taken from her—Mrs. Greenhow's daughter, Rose, a child of eight. It is her letters which have supplied many of the details for this story. Of that day, so full of terror and bewilderment, the memory which stands out most clear to her is that of climbing a tree in the garden and from there calling to all the passersby: "Mother has been arrested! Mother has been arrested!" until the detectives in the house heard her, and angrily dragged her, weeping, from the tree.

But in spite of the efforts of the "humble agent" who had waited at Corcoran's corner for the handkerchief signal, in spite of the sacrifice of little Rose's freedom, the trap that day was sprung many times. Miss Mackall and her sister, close friends of Mrs. Greenhow, were seized as they crossed the threshold, and searched and detained. Their mother, coming to find her daughters, became with them a prisoner. A negro girl—a former servant—and her brother, who were merely passing the house, were induced to enter it, and for hours subjected to an inquisition.

Night came, and the men left in charge grew boisterous; an argument started among them. Mrs. Greenhow tells—with keen enjoyment— of having egged on the disputants, pitting nationality against nationality—English, German, Irish, Yankee—so that in the still night their loud, angry voices might serve as a danger signal to her friends. But the dispute died out at last—too soon to save two gentlemen who called late that evening, a call which cost them months of imprisonment on the never-proved charge of being engaged in "contraband and treasonable correspondence with the Confederates."

Soon after midnight there came the brief relaxing of vigilance for which Mrs. Greenhow had watched expectantly all day. She had taken the resolution to fire the house if she did not succeed in obtaining certain papers in the course of the night, for she had no hope that they would escape a second day's search. But now the time for making the attempt had come, and she stole noiselessly into the dark library. From the topmost shelf she took down a book, between whose leaves lay the coveted despatch; concealing it in the folds of her dress, she swiftly regained her room. A few moments later the guard returned to his post at her open door.

She had been permitted the companionship of Miss Mackall, and now as the two women reclined on the bed they planned how they might get the despatch out of the house. When Mrs. Greenhow had been searched that afternoon her shoes and stockings had not been examined, and so, trusting to the slim chance that Miss Mackall's would likewise escape examination, it was determined that the despatch should be hidden in her stocking; and this—since the room was in darkness save for the faint light from the open door, and the bed stood in deep shadow—

was accomplished in the very presence of the guard. They planned that should Miss Mackall, when about to be released, have reason to believe she was to be searched carefully, she must then be seized with compunction at leaving her friend, and return.

Between three and four o'clock Saturday morning those friends who had been detained were permitted to depart (except the two gentlemen, who, some hours before, had been taken to the Provost-Marshal), and with Miss Mackall went in safety the despatch for whose destruction Mrs. Greenhow would have burned her house.

But though she had destroyed or saved much dangerous correspondence, there fell into the hands of the Federal secret service much more of her correspondence, by which were dragged into the net many of her friends and agents. A letter in cipher addressed to Thomas John Rayford in part read:

> Your three last despatches I never got. Those by Applegate were betrayed by him to the War Department; also the one sent by our other channel was destroyed by Van Camp.

Dr. Aaron Van Camp, charged with being a spy, was arrested, and cast into the Old Capitol Prison. In a stove in the Greenhow house were found, and pieced together, the fragments of a note from Donellan, the messenger who had carried her despatch to Beauregard before Bull Run. The note introduced "Colonel Thompson, the bearer, . . . [who] will be happy to take from your hands any communications and obey your injunctions as to disposition of same with despatch." The arrest of Colonel Thompson, as of Mrs. Greenhow, involved others; it was all like a house of cards—by the arrest of Mrs. Greenhow the whole flimsy structure had been brought crashing down.

Of the days which followed the beginning of Mrs. Greenhow's imprisonment in her own house, few were devoid of excitement of some sort. After a few days Miss Mackall had obtained permission to return and share her friend's captivity. It was she who fortunately found and destroyed a sheet of blotting-paper which bore the perfect imprint of the Bull Run despatch! The detectives remained in charge for seven days; they examined every book in the library leaf by leaf (too late!); boxes containing books, china, and glass that had been packed away for months were likewise minutely examined. Portions of the furniture were taken apart; pictures removed from their frames; beds overturned many times.

"Seemingly I was treated with deference," Mrs. Greenhow tells. "Once only were violent hands put upon my person—the detective, Captain Denis, having rudely seized me to prevent me giving warning to a lady and gentleman on the first evening of my arrest (which I succeeded in doing)." She was permitted to be alone scarcely a moment. "If I wished to lie down, he was seated a few paces from my bed. If I desired to change my dress, it was obliged to be done with open doors. . . . They still presumed to seat themselves at table with me, with unwashed hands and shirtsleeves." Only a few months before this the President of the United States had dined frequently at that very table.

Her jailers sought to be bribed to carry messages for her—in order to betray her; their hands were ever outstretched. One set himself the pleasant task of making love to her maid, Lizzie Fitzgerald, a quick-witted Irish girl, who entered keenly into the sport of sentimental walks and treats at Uncle Sam's expense—and, of course, revealed nothing.

On Friday morning, the 30th of August, Mrs. Greenhow was informed that other prisoners were to be brought in, and that her house was to be converted into a prison. A lieutenant and twenty-one men of the Sturgis Rifles (General McClellan's body-guard) were now placed in charge instead of the detective police. The house began to fill with other prisoners—all women. The once quiet and unpretentious residence at 398 Sixteenth Street became known as "Fort Greenhow," and an object of intense interest to the crowds that came to stare at it—which provoked from the New York *Times* the caustic comment:

> Had Madam Greenhow been sent South immediately after her arrest, as we recommended, we should have heard no more of the heroic deeds of Secesh women, which she has made the fashion.

Had the gaping crowds known what the harassed sentries knew, they would have stared with better cause. They sought to catch a glimpse of Mrs. Greenhow because of what she had done; the guards' chief concern was with the Mrs. Greenhow of the present moment. For during the entire time that she was a prisoner in her own house Mrs. Greenhow was in frequent communication with the South. How she accomplished the seemingly impossible will never be fully known.

She tells of information being conveyed to her by her "little bird"; of preparing "those *peculiar, square* despatches to be forwarded to our great and good President at Richmond"; of "tapestry-work in a vocabulary of colors, which, though not a very prolific language, served my purpose"; and she gives, as an example of many such, "a seemingly innocent letter," which seems innocent, indeed, and must forever remain so, since she does not supply the key whereby its hidden meaning may be understood.

Then there is the story of the ball of pink knitting-yarn, a story which, unlike the yarn ball, was never unwound to lay its innermost secrets bare. Now and then the prisoners passed one another when being marched for their period of exercise in the garden or back into the house again; and it was thus that Mrs. Greenhow one day met Mrs. Philips in the hall. Behind each stalked an armed guard; the ladies might not pause even long enough to bid each other good day. But as she passed on into the house, Mrs. Philips called, "I found your ball of pink yarn in the shrub-bush under your window, and tossed it into your room." Pink yarn! Women-talk!—not worth a soldier's heed, and the sentries gave it none. Out in the garden Mrs. Greenhow restlessly paced up and down; for the first time the brief half-hour seemed too long; for the first time, too, she was glad to be marched back to her room again. Yes! there on the floor in a band of sunlight lay the pink ball—safe. As she dropped it carelessly into her work-basket the guard watched her narrowly, then again languidly seated himself at her door. That is all of the story—except that the ball of pink yarn was wound around a little roll of paper, a cipher message from the South.

By such means she was able to outwit her many guards—though not as invariably as at the time she believed that she had done. Allan Pinkerton reports to the War Department, with a mixture of irritation and complacency:

> She has not ceased to lay plans, to attempt the bribery of officers having her in charge, to make use of signs from the windows of her house to her friends on the streets, to communicate with such friends and through them as she supposed send information to the rebels in ciphers requiring much time to decipher—all of which she supposed she was doing through an officer who had her in charge and whom she supposed she had bribed to that purpose, but who, faithful to his trust, laid her communications before yourself.

But Mrs. Greenhow evidently made use of other channels as well, for the copy of her first letter to Secretary Seward safely reached the hands of those friends to whom it was addressed, and by them it was published in the newspapers, North and South, thereby showing to all the world that a tendril of the grapevine telegraph still reached out from "Fort Green-how." It was not this alone which made officialdom and the public gasp—it was the letter itself. In tone it was calm, almost dispassionate—a masterly letter. The blunt Anglo-Saxon words which set forth in detail the indignities which she suffered from the unceasing watch kept over her came like so many blows. She pointed out that her arrest had been without warrant; that her house and all its contents had been seized, and that she herself had been held a prisoner more than three months without a trial, and that she was yet ignorant of the charge against her. The letter was strong, simple, dignified, but it brought no reply.

The heat of midsummer had passed and autumn had come, and with it many changes. Miss Mackall was one day abruptly taken away and sent to her own home; the two friends were never to meet again. Other prisoners were freed or transferred elsewhere, and yet others came—among them a Miss Poole, who almost immediately sought to curry favor by reporting that little Rose, who for some time had been allowed to play, under guard, on the pavement, had received a communication for her mother; and the child was again confined within the four walls. "This was perhaps my hardest trial—to see my little one pining and fading under my eyes for want of food and air. The health and spirits of my faithful maid also began to fail." The attempt of several of the guard to communicate information was likewise reported by Miss Poole, and the thumb-screws of discipline were tightened by many turns. The kindly officer of the guard, Lieutenant Sheldon, was ordered to hold no personal communication with Mrs. Greenhow; the guard was set as spies upon one another and upon him; they, too, were forbidden under severe penalty to speak to her or to answer her questions. An order was issued prohibiting her from purchasing newspapers, or being informed of their contents. At times it seemed as though her house, and she in it, had been swallowed, and now lay within the four walls of a Chillon or a Château d'If; it was added bitterness to her to look about the familiar room and remember that once it had been home!

Miss Mackall had been making ceaseless efforts to be allowed to visit her friend, but permission was steadily denied. Then the news sifted into "Fort Greenhow," and reached its one-time mistress, that Miss Mackall was ill, desperately ill; for the first time Mrs. Greenhow ceased to demand—she pleaded to see her friend; and failed. Then came the news that Miss Mackall was dead.

Among those friends of the old days who now and then were allowed to call was Edwin M. Stanton, not yet Secretary of War. Mrs. Greenhow endeavored to engage him as counsel to obtain for her a writ of *habeas corpus,* but he declined.

Friends—with dubious tact—smuggled to her newspaper clippings in which the statement was made that "Mrs. Greenhow had lost her mind," and that "it is rumored that the government is about to remove her to a private lunatic asylum." "My blood freezes even now," she wrote, "when I recall my feelings at the reception of this communication, and I wonder that I had not gone mad." When the Judge-Advocate, making a friendly, "unofficial" call, asked, "To what terms would you be willing to subscribe for your release?" she replied, with unbroken courage:

"None, sir! I demand my unconditional release, indemnity for losses, and the restoration of my papers and effects."

The day after Christmas Mrs. Greenhow wrote two letters. The one, in cipher, was found in the archives of the Confederate War Department when Richmond was evacuated; it was deciphered and published in the Official Records:

> December 26th
>
> In a day or two 1,200 cavalry supported by four batteries of artillery will cross the river above to get behind Manassas and cut off railroad and other communications with our army whilst an attack is made in front. For God's sake heed this. It is positive. . . .

The grape-vine telegraph lines were still clear both into and out of "Fort Greenhow."

The other was a second letter to Secretary Seward—a very different sort of letter from the first, being but a tirade on the ethics of the Southern cause, purposeless, save that "Contempt and defiance alone actuated me. I had known Seward intimately, and he had frequently enjoyed the hospitalities of my table." Unlike its worthy predecessor, this letter was to bear fruit.

On the morning of the 5th of January a search was again commenced throughout the house. The police were searching for the copy of the second letter. But, as in the first instance, the copy had gone out simultaneously with the original. When Mrs. Greenhow was allowed to return to her room she found that the window had been nailed up, and every scrap of paper had been taken from her writing-desk and table.

It was this copy of the second letter to Secretary Seward which sent Mrs. Greenhow to the Old Capitol Prison.

It was published as the first had been, thereby clearly showing that Mrs. Greenhow was still able to communicate with the South almost at will in spite of all efforts to prevent her. It was the last straw. The State Department acted swiftly. On January 18th came the order for Mrs. Greenhow to prepare for immediate removal elsewhere; two hours later she parted from her faithful and weeping maid, and she and the little Rose left their home forever. Between the doorstep and the carriage was a double file of soldiers, between whom she passed; at the carriage—still holding little Rose by the hand—she turned on the soldiers indignantly. "May your next duty be a more honorable one than that of guarding helpless women and children," she said.

Dusk had fallen ere the carriage reached the Old Capitol; here, too, a guard was drawn up under arms to prevent any attempt at rescue. The receiving-room of the prison was crowded with officers and civilians, all peering curiously. Half an hour later she and the child were marched into a room very different from that which they had left in the house in Sixteenth Street. The room, 10 x 12, was on the second floor of the back building of the prison; its only window (over which special bars were placed next day) looked out upon the prison-yard. A narrow bed, on which was a straw mattress covered by a pair of unwashed cotton sheets, a small feather pillow, dingy and dirty, a few wooden chairs, a table, and a cracked mirror furnished the room which from that night was to be theirs during months of heart-breaking imprisonment.

An understanding of those bitter days can be given best by extracts from her diary:

"*January 25th.*—I have been one week in my new prison. My letters now all go through the detective police, who subject them to a chemical process to extract the treason. In one of the newspaper accounts I am supposed to use sympathetic ink. I purposely left a preparation very conspicuously placed, in order to divert attention from my real means of communication, and they have swallowed the bait and fancy my friends are at their mercy. *January 28th.*—This day as I stood at my barred window the guard rudely called 'Go 'way from that window!' and leveled his musket at me. I maintained my position without condescending to notice him, whereupon he called the corporal of the guard. I called also for the officer of the guard, . . . who informed me that I must not go to the window. I quietly told him that, at whatever peril, I should avail myself of the largest liberty of the four walls of my prison. He told me that his guard would have orders to fire upon me. I had no idea that such monstrous regulations existed. To-day the dinner for myself and child consists of a bowl of beans swimming in grease, two slices of fat junk, and two slices of bread. . . . I was very often intruded upon by large parties of Yankees, who came with passes from the Provost-Marshal to stare at me. Sometimes I was amused, and generally contrived to find out what was going on. . . . Afterward I requested the superintendent not to allow any more of these parties to have access to me. He told me that numbers daily came to the prison who would gladly give him ten dollars apiece to allowed to pass my open door. *March 3d.*—Since two days we are actually allowed a half-hour's exercise in the prison-yard, where we walk up and down, picking our way as best we can through mud and negroes, followed by soldiers and corporals, bayonets in hand. . . . Last night I put my candle on the window, in order to get something out of my trunk near which it stood, all unconscious of committing any offense against prison discipline, when the guard below called, 'Put out that light!' I gave no heed, but only lighted another, whereupon several voices took up the cry, adding, 'Damn you, I will fire into your room!' Rose was in a state of great delight, and collected all the ends of candles to add to the illumination. By this the clank of arms and patter of feet, in conjunction with the furious rapping at my door, with a demand to open it, announced the advent of corporal and sergeant. My door was now secured inside by a bolt which had been allowed me. I asked their business. Answer, 'You are making signals, and must remove your lights from the window.' I said, 'But it suits my convenience to keep them there.' 'We will break open your door if you don't open it.' 'You will act as you see fit, but it will be at your peril!' They did not dare to carry out this threat, as they knew that I had a very admirable pistol on my mantelpiece, restored to me a short time since, although they did not know that I had no ammunition for it." The candles burned themselves out, and that ended it, save that next day, by order of the Provost-Marshal, the pistol was taken from the prisoner.

But it was not all a merry baiting of the guards—there was hardship connected with this imprisonment. In spite of the folded clothing placed on the hard bed, the child used to cry out in the night, "Oh, mamma, mamma, the bed hurts me so!" The rooms above were filled with negroes. "The tramping and screaming of negro children overhead was most dreadful." Worse than mere sound came from these other prisoners: there came disease. Smallpox broke out among them, also the lesser disease, camp measles, which latter was contracted by the little Rose. She, too, had her memories of the Old Capitol; in a recent letter she wrote:

"I do not remember very much about our imprisonment except that I used to cry myself to sleep from hunger. . . . There was a tiny closet in our room in which mother contrived to loosen a plank that she would lift up, and the prisoners of war underneath would catch hold of my legs and lower me into their room; they were allowed to receive fruit, etc., from the outside, and generously shared with me, also they would give mother news of the outside world." Thus the days passed until Mrs. Greenhow was summoned to appear, March 25th, before the United States Commissioners for the Trial of State Prisoners.

Of this "trial" the only record available is her own—rather too flippant in tone to be wholly convincing as to its entire sincerity. Her account begins soberly enough: the cold, raw day, the slowly falling snow, the mud through which the carriage labored to the office of the Provost-Marshal in what had been the residence of Senator Guin—"one of the most elegant in the city; . . . my mind instinctively reverted to the gay and brilliant scenes in which I had mingled in that house, and the goodly company who had enjoyed its hospitality." There was a long wait in a fireless anteroom; then she was led before the Commissioners for her trial. "My name was announced, and the Commissioners advanced to receive me with ill-concealed embarrassment. I bowed to them, saying: 'Gentlemen, resume your seats. I recognize the embarrassment of your positions; it was a mistake on the part of your government to have selected gentlemen for this mission. You have, however, shown me but scant courtesy in having kept me waiting your pleasure for nearly an hour in the cold.'" The prisoner took her place at the long table, midway between the two Commissioners, one of whom, General Dix, was a former friend; at smaller tables were several secretaries; if there were any spectators other than the newspaper reporters, she makes no mention of them. The trial began.

"One of the reporters now said, 'If you please, speak a little louder, madam.' I rose from my seat, and said to General Dix, 'If it is your object to make a spectacle of me, and furnish reports for the newspapers, I shall have the honor to withdraw from this presence.' Hereupon both Commissioners arose and protested that they had no such intention, but that it was necessary to take notes. . . ." The examination then continued "in a strain in no respect different from that of an ordinary conversation held in a drawing-room, and to which I replied sarcastically, . . . and a careless listener would have imagined that the Commission was endeavoring with plausible arguments to defend the government rather than to incriminate me. . . ." The other Commissioner then said, "'General Dix, you are so much better acquainted with Mrs. Greenhow, suppose you continue the examination?' I laughingly said, 'Commence it, for I hold that it has not begun.'" Mrs. Greenhow's account makes no mention of any witnesses either for or against her; the evidence seems to have consisted solely in the papers found in her house. The whole examination—as she records it—may be summed up in the following questions and answers:

"'You are charged with treason.' 'I deny it!' 'You are charged, madam, with having caused a letter which you wrote to the Secretary of State to be published in Richmond.' 'That can hardly be brought forward as one of the causes of my arrest, for I had been some three months a prisoner when that letter was written.' 'You are charged, madam, with holding communication with the enemy in the South.' 'If this were an established fact, you could not be surprised at it; I am a Southern woman.' . . . 'How is it, madam, that you have managed to communicate, in spite of the vigilance exercised over you?' 'That is my secret!'" And that was practically the end, save that the prisoner said she would refuse to take the oath of allegiance if this opportunity to be freed were offered her.

April 3d the superintendent of the Old Capitol read to her a copy of the decree of the Commission: she had been sentenced to be exiled. But the days passed and nothing came of it. Tantalized beyond endurance, she wrote that she was "ready" to go South. General McClellan, she was then told, had objected to her being sent South at this time. (Federal spies—secret-service men, who, under Allan Pinkerton, had arrested Mrs. Greenhow—were on trial for their lives in Richmond; it was feared that, were she sent South, her testimony would be used against them.) "Day glides into day with nothing to mark the flight of time," the diary continues. "The heat is intense, with the sun beating down upon the house-top and in the windows. . . . My child is looking pale and ill. . . . *Saturday, May 31st.*—At two o'clock today [Prison Superintendent] Wood came in with the announcement that I was to start at three o'clock for Baltimore." The end of imprisonment had come as suddenly as its beginning.

Disquieting rumors had been reaching Mrs. Greenhow for some time in regard to removal to Fort Warren. Was this, after all, a mere Yankee trick to get her there quietly? She was about to enter the carriage that was to bear her from the Old Capitol, when, unable longer to bear the suspense, she turned suddenly to the young lieutenant of the escort: "Sir, ere I advance further, I ask you, not as Lincoln's officer, but as a man of honor and a gentleman, are your orders from Baltimore to conduct me to a Northern prison, or to some point in the Confederacy?" "On my honor, madam," he answered, "to conduct you to Fortress Monroe and thence to the Southern Confederacy." Her imprisonment had, indeed, ended. There was yet the Abolition-soldier guard—on the way to the station, on the cars, in Baltimore, on the steamer; there was yet to be signed at Fortress Monroe the parole in which, in consideration of being set at liberty, she pledged her honor not to return north of the Potomac during the war; but from that moment at the carriage-door she felt herself no longer a prisoner.

To the query of the Provost-Marshal at Fortress Monroe she replied that she wished to be sent "to the capital of the Confederacy, wherever that might be." That was still Richmond, he told her, but it would be in Federal hands before she could reach there. She would take chances on that, was her laughing rejoinder. And so she was set ashore at City Point by a boat from the *Monitor,* and next morning, June 4th, she and little Rose, escorted by Confederate officers, arrived in Richmond. And there, "on the evening of my arrival, our President did me the honor to call on me, and his words of greeting, 'But for you there would have been no battle of Bull Run,' repaid me for all I had endured."

Could the story be told of the succeeding twenty-seven months of Mrs. Greenhow's life, much of the secret history of the Confederacy might be revealed. It is improbable that the story ever will be told. Months of effort to learn details have resulted in but vague glimpses of her, as one sees an ever-receding figure at the turns of a winding road. Her daughter Rose has written: "Whether mother did anything for the Confederacy in Richmond is more than I can tell. I know that we went to Charleston, South Carolina, and that she saw General Beauregard there." Then came weeks of waiting for the sailing of a blockade-runner from Wilmington, North Carolina; quiet, happy weeks they were, perhaps the happiest she had known since the war began. She was taking little Rose to Paris, to place her in the Convent of the Sacred Heart, she told her new-made friends. One morning they found that she and little Rose had gone. A blockade-runner had slipped out during the night and was on its way with them to Bermuda.

Many have definitely asserted that Mrs. Greenhow went to England and France on a secret mission for the Confederacy. No proof of this has ever been found, but the little which has been learned of her sojourn in Europe strongly supports the theory of such a mission there. The ship which bore them to England from Bermuda was an English man-of-war, in which they sailed "at President Davis's especial request." Then there were President Davis's personal letters to Messrs. Mason and Slidell, requesting them that they show to Mrs. Greenhow every attention. In France she was given a private audience with Napoleon III.; in London, presented to England's Queen. A letter written to her by James Spence, financial agent of the Confederates in Liverpool, shows her to have been actively engaged in support of the interests of the South from her arrival in England. But of any secret mission there is not a trace—unless her book, *My Imprisonment, or the First Year of Abolition Rule in Washington,* may thus be considered. The book was brought out in November,

1863, by the well-known English publishing-house of Richard Bentley & Son; immediately it made a profound sensation in London—particularly in the highest society circles, into which Mrs. Greenhow had at once been received. *My Imprisonment* was a brilliant veneer of personal war-time experiences laid alluringly over a solid backing of Confederate States' propaganda. Richmond may or may not have fathered it, but that book in England served the South well. None who knew Mrs. Greenhow ever forgot her charm; she made friends everywhere—such friends as Thomas Carlyle and Lady Franklin, and a score more whose names are nearly as well known to-day. She was betrothed to a prominent peer.

All in all, this is but scant information to cover a period of more than two years. Only one other fact has been obtained regarding her life abroad, but it is most significant in support of the belief that she was a secret agent for the Confederacy. In August, 1864, Mrs. Greenhow left England suddenly and sailed for Wilmington on the ship *Condor*. Though her plans were to return almost at once, marry, and remain in England, the fact that she left in London her affianced husband, and her little Rose in the Convent of the Sacred Heart in Paris, while she herself risked her life to run the blockade, seems strong evidence that her business in the Confederate States of America was important business, indeed. The *Condor* was a three-funneled steamer, newly built, and on her first trip as a blockade-runner—a trade for which she was superbly adapted, being swift as a sea-swallow. She was commanded by a veteran captain of the Crimean War—an English officer on a year's leave, blockade-running for adventure—Captain Augustus Charles Hobart-Hampden, variously known to the blockade-running fleet as Captain Roberts, Hewett, or Gulick.

On the night of September 30th the *Condor* arrived opposite the mouth of the Cape Fear River, the entry for Wilmington, and in the darkness stole swiftly through the blockade. She was almost in the mouth of the river, and not two hundred yards from shore, when suddenly there loomed up in the darkness a vessel dead ahead. To the frightened pilot of the *Condor* it was one of the Federal squadron; he swerved his ship sharply, and she drove hard on New Inlet bar. In reality the ship which had caused the damage was the wreck of the blockade-runner *Nighthawk*, which had been run down the previous night. The *Condor's* pilot sprang overboard and swam ashore. Dawn was near breaking, and in the now growing light the Federal blockaders which had followed the *Condor* were seen to be closing in. Though the *Condor*, lying almost under the very guns of Fort Fisher—which had begun firing at the Federal ships and was holding them off—was for the time being safe, yet Mrs. Greenhow and the two other passengers, Judge Holcombe and Lieutenant Wilson, Confederate agents, demanded that they be set ashore. There was little wind and there had been no storm, but the tide-rip ran high over the bar, and the boat was lowered into heavy surf. Scarcely was it clear of the tackles ere a great wave caught it, and in an instant it was overturned. Mrs. Greenhow, weighted down by her heavy black silk dress and a bag full of gold sovereigns, which she had fastened round her waist, sank at once and did not rise again. The others succeeded in getting ashore.

The body of Mrs. Greenhow was washed up on the beach next day. They buried her in Wilmington—buried her with the honors of war, and a Confederate flag wrapped about her coffin. And every Memorial Day since then there is laid upon her grave a wreath of laurel leaves such as is placed only upon the graves of soldiers. Long ago the Ladies' Memorial Society placed there a simple marble cross, on which is carved: "Mrs. Rose O'Neal Greenhow. A Bearer of Despatches to the Confederate Government."

5 A Virginia Girl in the First Year of the War

Constance Cary Harrison

*T*HE ONLY association I have with my old home in Virginia that is not one of unmixed happiness relates to the time immediately succeeding the execution of John Brown at Harper's Ferry. Our homestead was in Fairfax, at a considerable distance from the theater of that tragic episode; and, belonging as we did to a family among the first in the State to manumit slaves—our grandfather having set free those which came to him by inheritance, and the people who served us being hired from their owners and remaining in our employ through years of kindliest relations—there seemed to be no especial reason for us to share in the apprehension of an uprising by the blacks. But there was the fear—unspoken, or pooh-poohed at by the men who served as mouth-pieces for our community— dark, boding, oppressive, and altogether hateful. I can remember taking it to bed with me at night, and awaking suddenly oftentimes to confront it through a vigil of nervous terror of which it never occurred to me to speak to any one. The notes of the whip-poor-wills in the sweet-gum swamp near the stable, the mutterings of a distant thunder-storm, even the rustle of the night wind in the oaks that shaded my window, filled me with nameless dread. In the day-time it seemed impossible to associate suspicion with those familiar tawny or sable faces that surrounded us. We had seen them for so many years smiling or saddening with the family joys or sorrows; they were so guileless, so patient, so satisfied. What subtle influence was at work that should transform them into tigers

53

thirsting for our blood? The idea was preposterous. But when evening came again, and with it the hour when the colored people (who in summer and autumn weather kept astir half the night) assembled themselves together for dance or prayer-meeting, the ghost that refused to be laid was again at one's elbow. Rusty bolts were drawn and rusty fire-arms loaded. A watch was set where never before had eye or ear been lent to such a service. Peace, in short, had flown from the borders of Virginia.

I cannot remember that, as late as Christmastime of the year 1860, although the newspapers were full of secession talk and the matter was eagerly discussed at our tables, coming events had cast any positive shadow on our homes. The people in our neighborhood, of one opinion with their dear and honored friend, Colonel Robert E. Lee, of Arlington, were slow to accept the startling suggestion of disruption of the Union. At any rate, we enjoyed the usual holiday gathering of kinsfolk in the usual fashion. The old Vaucluse house, known for many years past as the center of cheerful hospitality in the county, threw wide open its doors to receive all the members who could be gathered there of a large family circle. The woods around were despoiled of holly and spruce, pine and cedar, to deck the walls and wreathe the picture-frames. On Christmas Eve we had a grand rally of youths and boys belonging to the "clan," as they loved to call it, to roll in a yule log, which was deposited upon a glowing bed of coals in the big "red parlor" fire-place, and sit around it afterwards, welcoming the Christmas in with goblets of eggnog and apple-toddy.

"Where shall we be a year hence?" some one asked at a pause in the merry chat; and, in the brief silence that followed, arose a sudden spectral thought of war. All felt its presence; no one cared to speak first of the grim possibilities it projected on the canvas of the future.

On Christmas Eve of the following year the old house lay in ruins, a sacrifice to military necessity; the forest giants that kept watch around her walls had been cut down and made to serve as breastworks for a fort erected on the Vaucluse property, but afterwards abandoned. Of the young men and boys who took part in that holiday festivity, all were in active service of the South,—one of them, alas! soon to fall under a rain of shot and shell beside his gun at Fredericksburg; the youngest of the number had left his mother's knee to fight in the battles of Manassas, and found himself, before the year was out, a midshipman aboard the Confederate steamer *Nashville,* on her cruise in distant seas!

My first vivid impression of war-days was during a ramble in the woods around our place one Sunday afternoon in spring, when the young people in a happy band set out in search of wild flowers. Pink honeysuckles, blue lupine, beds of fairy flax, anemones, and ferns in abundance sprung under the canopy of young leaves on the forest boughs, and the air was full of the song of birds and the music of running waters. We knew every mossy path far and near in these woods, every tree had been watched and cherished by those who went before us, and dearer than any other spot on earth was our tranquil, sweet Vaucluse. Suddenly the shrill whistle of a locomotive struck the ear, an unwonted sound on Sunday, "Do you know what that means?" said one of the older cousins who accompanied the party. "It is the special train carrying Alexandria volunteers to Manassas, and to-morrow I shall follow with my company." An awe-struck silence fell upon our little band. A cloud seemed to come between us and the sun. It was the beginning of the end too soon to come.

The story of one broken circle is the story of another at the outset of such a war. Before the week was over, the scattering of our household, which no one then believed to be more than temporary, had begun. Living as we did upon ground likely to be in the track of armies gathering to confront each other, it was deemed advisable to send the children and young girls into a place more remote from chances of danger. Some weeks later the heads of the household, two widowed sisters, whose sons were at Manassas, drove in their carriage at early morning, away from their home, having spent the previous night in company with a half-grown lad digging in the cellar hasty graves for the interment of two boxes of old English silver-ware, heirlooms in the family, for which there was no time to provide otherwise. Although troops were long encamped immediately above it after the house was burnt the following year, this silver was found when the war had ended, lying loose in the earth, the boxes having rotted from around it.

The point at which our family reunited within Confederate lines was Bristoe, the station next beyond Manassas, a cheerless railway inn, a part of the premises was used as a country grocery; and there quarters were secured for us with a view to being near the army, a few miles distant. By this time all our kith and kin of fighting age had joined the volunteers. One cannot picture accommodations more forlorn than these eagerly taken for us and for other families attracted to Bristoe by the same powerful magnet. The summer sun poured its burning rays upon whitewashed walls unshaded by a tree. Our bedrooms were almost uninhabitable by day or night, our fare the plainest. From the windows we beheld only a flat, uncultivated country, crossed by red-clay roads, then knee-deep in dust. We learned to look for all excitement to the glittering lines of railway track, along which continually thundered trains bound to and from the front. It was impossible to allow such a train to pass without running out upon the platform to salute it, for in this way we greeted many an old friend or relative buttoned up in the smart gray uniform, speeding with high hope to the scene of coming conflict. Such shouts as went up from sturdy throats when the locomotive moved on after the last stop before Manassas, while we stood waving hands, hand-kerchiefs, or the rough woolen garments we were at work upon! Then fairly awoke the spirit that made of Southern women the inspiration of Southern men for the war. Most of the young fellows we were cheering onward wore the uniform of privates, and for the right to wear it had left homes of ease and luxury. To such we gave our best homage; and from that time forth, during the four years succeeding, the youth who was lukewarm in the cause or unambitious of military glory fared uncomfort-ably in the presence of the average Confederate maiden.

Thanks to our own carriage, we were able during those rallying days of June to drive frequently to visit our boys in camp, timing the expedi-tions to include battalion drill and dress parade, and taking tea afterwards in the different tents. Then were the gala days of war, and our proud hosts hastened to produce home dainties dispatched from the far-away plantations—tears and blessings interspersed amid the packing, we were sure; though I have seen a pretty girl persist in declining other fare, to make her meal upon raw biscuit and huckleberry pie compounded by the bright-eyed amateur cook of a well-beloved mess. Feminine heroism could no farther go.

And so the days wore on until the 17th of July, when a rumor from the front sent an electric shock through our circle. The enemy were moving forward! On the morning of the 18th those who had been able to sleep at all awoke early to listen for the first guns of the engagement of Blackburn's Ford. Abandoned as the women at Bristoe were by every masculine creature old enough to gather news, there was, for them, no way of knowing the progress of events during the long, long day of wait-ing, of watching, of weeping, of praying, of rushing out upon the railway track to walk as far as they dared in the direction whence came that intol-erable booming of artillery. The cloud of dun smoke arising over Manas-sas became heavier in volume as the day progressed. Still, not a word of tidings, till towards afternoon there came limping up a single, very dirty soldier with his arm in a sling. What a heaven-send he was, if only as an escape-valve for our pent-up sympathies! We seized him, we washed him, we cried over him, we glorified him until the man was fairly bewildered. Our best endeavors could only develop a pin-scratch of a wound on his right hand; but when our hero had laid in a substantial meal of bread and meat, we plied him with trembling questions, each asking news of some staff or regiment or company. It has since occurred to me that this first arrival from the field was a humorist in disguise. His invariable reply, as he looked from one to the other of his satellites, was: "The—Virginia, marm? Why, of coase. They warn't no two ways o' thinkin' 'bout that ar rig'ment. They just *kivered* tharselves with glory!"

A little later two wagon-loads of slightly wounded claimed our care, and with them came authentic news of the day. Most of us received notes on paper torn from a soldier's pocket-book and grimed with gunpowder, containing assurance of the safety of our own. At nightfall a train carrying more wounded to the hospitals at Culpeper made a halt at Bristoe; and, preceded by men holding lanterns, we went in among the stretchers with milk, food, and water to the sufferers. One of the first discoveries I made, bending over in that fitful light, was a young officer I knew to be a special object of solicitude with one of my fair comrades in the search; but he was badly hurt, and neither he nor she knew the other was near until the train had moved on. The next day, and the next, were full of burning excitement over the impending general engagement, which people then said would decide the fate of the young Confederacy. Fresh troops came by with every train, and we lived only to turn from one scene to another of welcome and farewell. On Saturday evening arrived a message from General Beauregard, saying that early on Sunday an engine and car would be put at our disposal, to take us to some point more remote from danger. We looked at one another, and, tacitly agreeing that the gallant general had sent not an order, but a suggestion, declined his kind proposal.

Another unspeakably long day, full of the straining anguish of suspense. Dawning bright and fair, it closed under a sky darkened by cannon-smoke. The roar of guns seemed never to cease. First, a long sullen boom; then a sharper rattling fire, painfully distinct; then stragglers from the field, with varying rumors. At last, the news of victory; and, as before, the wounded to force our numbed faculties into service. One of our group, the mother of an only son barely fifteen years of age, heard that her boy, after being in action all the early part of the day, had through sheer fatigue fallen asleep upon the ground, where his officers had found him, resting peacefully amidst the roar of the guns, and whence they had brought him off, unharmed. A few days later we rode on horseback over the field of the momentous fight. The trampled grass had begun to spring again, and wild flowers were blooming around carelessly made graves. From one of these imperfect mounds of clay I saw a hand extended; and when, years afterwards, I visited the tomb of Rousseau beneath the Panthéon in Paris, where a sculptured hand bearing a torch protrudes from the sarcophagus,

I thought of that mournful spectacle upon the field of Manassas. Fences were everywhere thrown down; the undergrowth of the woods was riddled with shot; here and there we came upon spiked guns, disabled gun-carriages, cannon-balls, blood-stained blankets, and dead horses. We were glad enough to turn away and gallop homeward.

With August heats and lack of water, Bristoe was forsaken for quarters near Culpeper, where my mother went into the soldiers' barracks, sharing soldiers' accommodations, to nurse the wounded. In September quite a party of us, upon invitation, visited the different headquarters. We stopped overnight at Manassas, five ladies, sleeping in a tent guarded by a faithful sentry, upon a couch made of rolls of cartridge-flannel. I remember the comical effect of the five bird-cages (an article without which no self-respecting female of that day would present herself in public) suspended upon a line running across the upper part of our tent, after we had reluctantly removed them in order to adjust ourselves for repose. Our progress during that memorable visit was royal; an ambulance with a picked troop of cavalrymen had been placed at our service, and the convoy was "personally conducted" by a pleasing variety of distinguished officers. It was at this time, after a supper at the headquarters of the "Maryland line" at Fairfax, that the afterwards universal war-song, "My Maryland," was set afloat upon the tide of army favor. We were sitting outside a tent in the warm starlight of an early autumn night, when music was proposed. At once we struck up Randall's verses to the tune of the old college song, "Lauriger Horatius,"—a young lady of the party from Maryland, a cousin of ours, having recently set them to this music before leaving home to share the fortunes of the Confederacy. All joined in the ringing chorus, and when we finished a burst of applause came from some soldiers listening in the darkness behind a belt of trees. Next day the melody was hummed far and near through the camps, and in due time it had gained and held the place of favorite song in the army. No doubt the hand-organs would have gotten hold of it; but, from first to last during the continuance of the Confederacy, those cheerful instruments of torture were missing. (I hesitate to mention this fact, lest it prove an incentive to other nations to go to war.) Other songs sung that evening, which afterwards had a great vogue, were one beginning "By blue Patapsco's billowy dash," arranged by us to an air from "Puritani," and shouted lustily, and "The years glide slowly by Lorena," a ditty having a queer little quavering triplet in the heroine's name that served as a pitfall to the unwary singer. "Stonewall Jackson's Way" came on the scene afterwards, later in the war. Another incident of note, in personal experience during the autumn of '61, was that to two of my cousins and to me was intrusted the making of the first three battle-flags of the Confederacy, directly after Congress had decided upon a design for them. They were jaunty squares of scarlet crossed with dark blue, the cross bearing stars to indicate the number of the seceding States. We set our best stitches upon them, edged them with golden fringes, and when they were finished dispatched one to Johnston, another to Beauregard, and the third to Earl Van Dorn,—the latter afterwards a dashing cavalry leader, but then commanding infantry at Manassas. The banners were received with all the enthusiasm we could have hoped for; were toasted, fêted, cheered abundantly. After two years, when Van Dorn had been killed in Tennessee, mine came back to me, tattered and smoke-stained from long and honorable service in the field. But it was only a little while after it had been bestowed that there arrived one day at our lodgings in Culpeper a huge, bashful Mississippi scout,—one of the most daring in the army,—with the frame of a Hercules and the face of a child. He was bidden to come there by his general, he said, to ask if I would not give him an order to fetch some cherished object from my dear old home—something that would prove to me "how much they thought of the maker of that flag!" After some hesitation I acquiesced, although thinking it a jest. A week later I was the astonished recipient of a lamented bit of finery left "within the lines," a wrap of white and azure, brought to us by Dillon himself, with a beaming face. He had gone through the Union pickets mounted on a load of fire-wood, and while peddling poultry had presented himself at our town house, whence he carried off his prize in triumph, with a letter in its folds telling us how relatives left behind longed to be sharing the joys and sorrows of those at large in the Confederacy.

The first winter of the war was spent by our family in Richmond, where we found lodgings in a dismal rookery familiarly dubbed by its new occupants "The Castle of Otranto." It was the old-time Clifton Hotel, honeycombed by subterranean passages, and crowded to its limits by refugees like ourselves from country homes within or near the enemy's lines—or "'fugees," as we were all called. For want of any common sitting-room, we took possession of what had been a doctor's office, a few steps distant down the hilly street, fitting it up to the best of our ability; and there we received our friends, passing many merry hours. In rainy weather we reached it by an underground passageway from the hotel, an alley through the catacombs; and many a dignitary of camp or state will recall those "Clifton" evenings. Already the pinch of war was felt in the commissariat; and we had recourse occasionally to a contribution supper, or "Dutch treat," when the guests brought brandied peaches, boxes of sardines, French prunes, and bags of biscuit, while the hosts contributed only a roast turkey or a ham, with knives and forks. Democratic feasts those were, where major-generals and "high privates" met on an equal footing. The hospitable old town was crowded with families of officers and members of the Government. One house was made to do the work of several, many of the wealthy citizens generously giving up their superfluous space to receive the new-comers. The only public event of note was the inauguration of Mr. Davis as President of the "Permanent Government" of the Confederate States, which we viewed, by the courtesy of Mr. John R. Thompson, the State Librarian, from one of the windows of the Capitol, where, while waiting for the exercises to begin, we read "Harper's Weekly" and other Northern papers, the latest per underground express. That 22d of February was a day of pouring rain, and the concourse of umbrellas in the square beneath us had the effect of an immense mushroom-bed. As the bishop and the President-elect came upon the stand, there was an almost painful hush in the crowd. All seemed to feel the gravity of the trust our chosen leader was assuming. When he kissed the Book a shout went up; but there was no elation visible as the people slowly dispersed. And it was thought ominous afterwards, when the story was repeated, that, as Mrs. Davis, who had a Virginia negro for coachman, was driven to the inauguration, she observed the carriage went at a snail's pace and was escorted by four negro men in black clothes, wearing white cotton gloves and walking solemnly, two on either side of the equipage; she asked the coachman what such a spectacle could mean, and was answered, "Well, ma'am, you tole me to arrange everything as it should be; and this is the way we do in Richmon' at funerals and sich-like." Mrs. Davis promptly ordered the outwalkers away, and with them departed all the pomp and circumstance the occasion admitted of. In the mind of a negro, everything of dignified ceremonial is always associated with a funeral!

About March 1st martial law was proclaimed in Richmond, and a fresh influx of refugees from Norfolk claimed shelter there. When the spring opened, as the spring does open in Richmond, with a sudden glory of green leaves, magnolia blooms, and flowers among the grass, our spirits rose after the depression of the latter months. If only to shake off the atmosphere of doubts and fears engendered by the long winter of disaster and uncertainty, the coming activity of arms was welcome! Personally speaking, there was vast improvement in our situation, since we had been fortunate enough to find a real home in a pleasant, brown-walled house on Franklin street, divided from the pavement by a garden full of bounteous greenery, where it was easy to forget the discomforts of our previous mode of life. I shall not attempt to describe the rapidity with which thrilling excitements succeeded each other in our experiences in this house. The gathering of many troops around the town filled the streets with a continually moving panorama of war, and we spent our time in greeting, cheering, choking with sudden emotion, and quivering in anticipation of what was yet to follow. We had now finished other battle-flags begun by way of patriotic handiwork, and one of them was bestowed upon the "Washington Artillery" of New Orleans, a body of admirable soldiers who had wakened to enthusiasm the daughters of Virginia in proportion, I dare say, to the woe they had created among the daughters of Louisiana in bidding them goodbye. One morning an orderly arrived to request that the ladies would be out upon the veranda at a given hour; and, punctual to the time fixed, the travel-stained battalion filed past our house. These were no holiday soldiers. Their gold was tarnished and their scarlet faded by sun and wind and gallant service—they were veterans now on their way to the front, where the call of duty never failed to find the flower of Louisiana. As they came in line with us, the officers saluted with their swords, the band struck up "My Maryland," the tired soldiers sitting upon the caissons that dragged heavily through the muddy street set up a rousing cheer. And there in the midst of them, taking the April wind with daring color, was our flag, dipping low until it passed us.

Well! one must grow old and cold indeed before such things are forgotten.

A few days later, on coming out of church—it is a curious fact that most of our exciting news spread over Richmond on Sunday, and just at that hour—we heard of the crushing blow of the fall of New Orleans and the destruction of our ironclads; my brother had just reported aboard one of those splendid ships, as yet unfinished. As the news came directly from our kinsman, General Randolph, the Secretary of War, there was no doubting it; and while the rest of us broke into lamentation, Mr. Jules de St. Martin, the brother-in-law of Mr. Benjamin, merely shrugged his shoulders, with a thoroughly characteristic gesture, making no remark.

"This must affect your interests," some one said to him inquiringly.

"I am ruined, *voilà tout!*" was the rejoinder—a fact too soon confirmed.

This debonair little gentleman was one of the greatest favorites of our war society in Richmond. His cheerfulness, his wit, his exquisite courtesy, made him friends everywhere; and although his nicety of dress, after the pattern of the *boulevardier fini* of Paris, was the subject of much wonderment to the populace when he first appeared upon the streets, it did not prevent him from going promptly to join the volunteers before Richmond when occasion called, and roughing it in the trenches like a veteran. His cheerful endurance of hardship during a freezing winter of camp life became a proverb in the army later in the siege.

For the time nothing was talked of but the capture of New Orleans. Of the midshipman brother we heard that on the day previous to the taking of the forts, after several days' bombardment, by the United States fleet under Flag-Officer Farragut, he had been sent in charge of ordnance and deserters to a Confederate vessel in the river; that Lieutenant R—, a friend of his, on the way to report at Fort Jackson during the hot shelling, had invited the lad to accompany him by way of a pleasure trip; that while they were crossing the moat around Fort Jackson, in a canoe, and under heavy fire, a thirteen-inch mortar-shell had struck the water near, half filling their craft; and that, after watching the fire from this point for an hour, C— had pulled back again alone, against the Mississippi current, under fire for a mile and a half of the way—passing an astonished alligator who had been hit on the head by a piece of shell and was dying under protest. Thus ended a trip alluded to by C— twenty years later as an example of juvenile foolhardiness, soundly deserving punishment.

Aboard the steamship *Star of the West,* next day, he and other midshipmen in charge of millions of gold and silver coin from the mint and banks of New Orleans, and millions more of paper money, over which they were ordered to keep guard with drawn swords, hurried away from the doomed city, where the enemy's arrival was momentarily expected, and where the burning ships and steamers and bales of cotton along the levee made a huge crescent of fire. Keeping just ahead of the enemy's fleet, they reached Vicksburg, and thence went overland to Mobile, where their charge was given up in safety.

And now we come to the 31st of May, 1862, when the eyes of the whole continent turned to Richmond. On that day Johnston assaulted the portion of McClellan's troops which had been advanced to the south side of the Chickahominy, and had there been cut off from the main body of the army by the sudden rise of the river, occasioned by a tremendous thunder-storm. In face of recent reverses, we in Richmond had begun to feel like the prisoner of the Inquisition in Poe's story, cast into a dungeon with slowly contracting walls. With the sound of guns, therefore, in the direction of Seven Pines, every heart leaped as if deliverance were at hand. And yet there was no joy in the wild pulsation, since those to whom we looked for succor were our own flesh and blood, standing shoulder to shoulder to bar the way to a foe of superior numbers, abundantly provided as we were not with all the equipments of modern warfare, and backed by a mighty nation as determined as ourselves to win. Hardly a family in the town whose father, son, or brother was nor part and parcel of the defending army.

When on the afternoon of the 31st it became known that the engagement had begun, the women of Richmond were still going about their daily vocations quietly, giving no sign of the inward anguish of apprehension. There was enough to do now in preparation for the wounded; yet, as events proved, all that was done was not enough by half. Night brought a lull in the cannonading. People lay down dressed upon their beds, but not to sleep, while their weary soldiers slept upon their arms. Early next morning the whole town was on the street. Ambulances, litters, carts, every vehicle that the city could produce, went and came with a ghastly burden; those who could walk limped painfully home, in some cases so black with gunpowder they passed unrecognized. Women with pallid faces flitted bareheaded through the streets, searching for their dead or wounded. The churches were thrown open, many people visiting them for a sad communion-service or brief time of prayer; the lecture-rooms of various places of worship were crowded with ladies volunteering to sew, as fast as fingers and machines could fly, the rough beds called for by the surgeons. Men too old or infirm to fight went on horseback or afoot to meet the returning ambulances, and in some cases served as escort to their own dying sons. By afternoon of the day following the battle, the streets were one vast hospital. To find shelter for the sufferers a number of unused buildings were thrown open. I remember, especially, the St. Charles Hotel, a gloomy place, where two young girls went to look for a member of their family, reported wounded. We had tramped in vain over pavements burning with the intensity of the sun, from one scene of horror to another, until our feet and brains alike seemed about to serve us no further. The cool of those vast dreary rooms of the St. Charles was refreshing; but such a spectacle! Men in every stage of mutilation lying on the bare boards with perhaps a haversack or an army blanket beneath their heads,—some dying, all suffering keenly, while waiting their turn to be attended to. To be there empty-handed and impotent nearly broke our hearts. We passed from one to the other, making such slight additions to their comfort as were possible, while looking in every upturned face in dread to find the object of our search. This sorrow, I may add, was spared, the youth arriving at home later with a slight flesh-wound. The condition of things at this and other improvised hospitals was improved next day by the offerings from many churches of pew-cushions, which, sewn together, served as comfortable beds; and for the remainder of the war their owners thanked God upon bare benches for every "misery missed" that was "mercy gained." To supply food for the hospitals the contents of larders all over town were emptied into baskets; while cellars long sealed and cobwebbed, belonging to the old Virginia gentry who knew good Port and Madeira, were opened by the Ithuriel's spear of universal sympathy. There was not much going to bed that night, either; and I remember spending the greater part of it leaning from my window to seek the cool night air, while wondering as to the fate of those near to me. There was a summons to my mother about midnight. Two soldiers came to tell her of the wounding of one close of kin; but she was already on duty elsewhere, tireless and watchful as ever. Up to that time the younger girls had been regarded as super-fluities in hospital service; but on Monday two of us found a couple of rooms where fifteen wounded men lay upon pallets around the floor, and, on offering our services to the surgeons in charge, were proud to have them accepted and to be installed as responsible nurses, under direction of an older and more experienced woman. The constant activity our work entailed was a relief from the strained excitement of life after the battle of Seven Pines. When the first flurry of distress was over, the residents of those pretty houses standing back in gardens full of roses set their cooks to work, or better still, went themselves into the kitchen, to compound delicious messes for the wounded, after the appetizing old Virginia recipes. Flitting about the streets in the direction of the hospitals were smiling white-jacketed negroes, carrying silver trays with dishes of fine porcelain under napkins of thick white damask, containing soups, creams, jellies, thin biscuit, eggs à acrême, broiled chicken, etc., surmounted by clusters of freshly gathered flowers. A year later, we had cause to pine after these culinary glories, when it came to measuring out, with sinking hearts, the meager portions of milk and food we could afford to give our charges.

As an instance, however, that quality in food was not always appreci-ated by the patients, my mother urged upon one of her sufferers (a gaunt and soft-voiced Carolinian from the "piney-woods district") a delicately served trifle from some neighboring kitchen.

"Jes ez, you say, old miss," was the weary answer, "I ain't a-contra-dictin' you. It mout be good for me, but my stomick's kinder sot agin it. There ain't but one thing I'm sorter yarnin' arter, an' that's a dish o' greens en bacon fat, with a few molarses poured onto it."

From our patients, when they could syllable the tale, we had accounts of the fury of the fight, which were made none the less horrible by such assistance as imagination could give to the facts. I remember that they told us of shot thrown from the enemy's batteries into the advancing ranks of the Confederates, that plowed their way through lines of flesh and blood before exploding in showers of musketballs to do still further havoc. Before these awful missiles, it was said, our men had fallen in swaths, the living closing over them to press forward in the charge.

It was at the end of one of these narrations that a piping voice came from a pallet in the corner; "They fit might smart, them Yanks did, I tell *you!*" and not to laugh was as much of an effort as it had just been not to cry.

From one scene of death and suffering to another we passed during those days of June. Under a withering heat that made the hours preceding dawn the only ones of the twenty-four endurable in point of temperature, and a shower-bath the only form of diversion we had time or thought to indulge in, to go out-of-doors was sometimes worse than remaining in our wards. But one night, after several of us had been walking about town in a state of panting exhaustion, palm-leaf fans in hand, a friend persuaded us to ascend to the small platform on the summit of the Capitol, in search of fresher air. To reach it was like going through a vapor-bath, but an hour amid the cool breezes above the tree-tops of the square was a thing of joy unspeakable.

Day by day we were called to our windows by the wailing dirge of a military band preceding a soldier's funeral. One could not number those sad pageants: the coffin crowned with cap and sword and gloves, the riderless horse following with empty boots fixed in the stirrups of an army saddle; such soldiers as could be spared from the front marching after with arms reversed and crape-enfolded banners; the passers-by standing with bare, bent heads. Funerals less honored outwardly were continually occurring. Then and thereafter the green hillsides of lovely Hollywood were frequently upturned to find resting-places for the heroic dead. So much taxed for time and attendants were the funeral officials, it was not unusual to perform the last rites for the departed at night. A solemn scene was that in the July moonlight, when, with the few who valued him most gathered around the grave, we laid to rest one of my own nearest kinsmen, about whom in the old service of the United States, as in that of the Confederacy, it was said, "He was a spotless knight."

Spite of its melancholy uses, there was no more favorite walk in Richmond than Hollywood, a picturesquely beautiful spot, where high hills sink into velvet undulations, profusely shaded with holly, pine, and cedar, as well as by trees of deciduous foliage. In spring the banks of the stream that runs through the valley were enameled with wild flowers, and the thickets were full of May-blossom and dogwood. Mounting to the summit of the bluff, one may sit under the shade of some ample oak, to view the spires and roofs of the town, with the white colonnade of the distant Capitol. Richmond, thus seen beneath her verdant foliage "upon hills, girdled by hills," confirms what an old writer felt called to exclaim about it, "Verily, this city hath a pleasant seat." On the right, below this point, flows the rushing yellow river, making ceaseless turmoil around islets of rock whose rifts are full of birch and willow, or leaping impetuously over the bowlders of granite that strew its bed. Old-time Richmond folk used to say that the sound of their favorite James (or "Jeems," to be exact) went with them into foreign countries, during no matter how many years of absence, haunting them like a strain of sweetest music; nor would they permit a suggestion of superiority in the flavor of any other fluid to that of a draught of its amber waters. So blent with my own memories of war is the voice of that tireless river, that I seem to hear it yet, over the tramp of rusty battalions, the short imperious stroke of the alarm-bell, the clash of passing bands, the gallop of eager horsemen, the roar of battle or of flames leaping to devour their prey, the moan of hospitals, the stifled note of sorrow!

During all this time President Davis was a familiar and picturesque figure on the streets, walking through the Capitol square from his residence to the executive office in the morning, not to return until late in the afternoon, or riding just before nightfall to visit one or another of the encampments near the city. He was tall, erect, slender, and of a dignified and soldierly bearing, with clear-cut and high-bred features, and of a demeanor of stately courtesy to all. He was clad always in Confederate gray cloth, and wore a soft felt hat with wide brim. Afoot, his step was brisk and firm; in the saddle he rode admirably and with a martial aspect. His early life had been spent in the Military Academy at West Point and upon the then north-western frontier in the Black Hawk War, and he afterwards greatly distinguished himself at Monterey and Buena Vista in Mexico; at the time when we knew him, everything in his appearance and manner was suggestive of such a training. He was reported to feel quite out of place in the office of President, with executive and administrative duties, in the midst of such a war; General Lee always spoke of him as the best of military advisers; his own inclination was to be with the army, and at the first tidings of sound of a gun, anywhere within reach of Richmond, he was in the saddle and off for the spot—to the dismay of his staff-officers, who were expected to act as an escort on such occasions, and who never knew at what hour of the night or of the next day they should get back to a bed or a meal. The stories we were told of his adventures on such excursions were many, and sometimes amusing. For instance, when General Lee had crossed the Chickahominy, to commence the Seven Days' battles, President Davis, with several staff-officers, overtook the column, and, accompanied by the Secretary of War and a few other non-combatants, forded the river just as the battle in the peach orchard at Mechanicsville began. General Lee, surrounded by members of his own staff and other officers, was found a few hundred yards north of the bridge, in the middle of the broad road, mounted and busily engaged in directing the attack then about to be made by a brigade sweeping in line over the fields to the east of the road and towards Ellerson's Mill, where in a few minutes a hot engagement commenced. Shot, from the enemy's guns out of sight, went whizzing overhead in quick succession, striking every moment nearer the group of horsemen in the road, as the gunners improved their range. General Lee observed the President's approach, and was evidently annoyed at what he considered a fool-hardy expedition of needless exposure of the head of the Government, whose duties were elsewhere. He turned his back for a moment, until Col. Chilton had been dispatched at a gallop with the last direction to the commander of the attacking brigade; then, facing the cavalcade and looking like the god of war indignant, he exchanged with the President a salute, with the most frigid reserve of anything like welcome or cordiality. In an instant, and without allowance of opportunity for a word from the President, the general, looking not at him but at the assemblage at large, asked in a tone of irritation:

"Who are all this army of people, and what are they doing here?"

No one moved or spoke, but all eyes were upon the President—everybody perfectly understanding that this was only an order for him to retire to a place of safety; and the roar of the guns, the rattling fire of musketry, and the bustle of a battle in progress, with troops continually arriving across the bridge to go into action, went on. The President twisted in his saddle, quite taken aback at such a greeting—the general regarding him now with glances of growing severity. After a painful pause the President said, with a voice of deprecation:

"It is not my army, general."

"It certainly is not *my* army, Mr. President," was the prompt reply, "and this is no place for it"—in an accent of command unmistakable. Such a rebuff was a stunner to the recipient of it, who soon regained his own serenity, however, and answered:

"Well, general, if I withdraw, perhaps they will follow," and, raising his hat in another cold salute, he turned his horse's head to ride slowly towards the bridge—seeing, as he turned, a man killed immediately before him by a shot from a gun which at that moment got the range of the road. The President's own staff-officers followed him, as did various others; but he presently drew rein in the stream, where the high bank and the bushes concealed him from General Lee's repelling observation, and there remained while the battle raged. The Secretary of War had also made a show of withdrawing, but improved the opportunity afforded by rather a deep ditch on the roadside to attempt to conceal himself and his horse there for a time from General Lee, who at that moment was more to be dreaded than the enemy's guns.

When on the 27th of June the Seven Days' strife began, there was none of the excitement attending the battle of Seven Pines. People had shaken themselves down, as it were, to the grim reality of a fight that must be fought, "Let the war bleed, and let the mighty fall," was the spirit of their cry.

It is not my purpose to deal with the history of those awful Seven Days. Mine only to speak of the rear side of the canvas where heroes of two armies passed and repassed as if upon some huge Homeric frieze, in the manœuvres of a strife that hung our land in mourning. The scars of war are healed, when this is written, and the vast "pity of it" fills the heart that wakes the retrospect.

What I have said of Richmond before these battles will suffice for a picture of the summer's experience. When the tide of battle receded, what wrecked hopes it left to tell the tale of the Battle Summer! Victory was ours, but in how many homes was heard the voice of lamentation to drown the shouts of triumph! Many families, rich and poor alike, were bereaved of their dearest; and for many of the dead there was mourning by all the town. No incident of the war, for instance, made a deeper impression than the fall in battle of Colonel Munford's beautiful and brave young son Ellis, whose body, laid across his own caisson, was carried that summer to his father's house at nightfall, where the family, unconscious of their loss, were sitting in cheerful talk around the portal. Another son of Richmond whose death was keenly felt by everybody received his mortal wound while leading the first charge to break the enemy's line at Gaines's Mill. This was Lieutenant-Colonel Bradfute Warwick, a young hero who had won his spurs in service with Garibaldi. Losses like these are irreparable in any community; and so, with lamentations in nearly every household, while the spirit along the lines continued unabated, it was a chastened "Thank God" that went up from among us when Jackson's victory over Pope had raised the siege of Richmond.

6 Personal Recollections of the Battle of Chancellorsville

Sue M. Chancellor[1]

*C*HANCELLORSVILLE WAS not a village but a large country home. It was built for my grandmother, Ann Lyon Pound Chancellor, by her nephew, Alexander Lorman, of Baltimore.[2] My grandmother was married twice. Her first husband was Richard Pound, whose mother, Fannie Underwood, was the great-granddaughter of William Underwood (a member of the House of Burgesses in 1652 and the husband of a great-granddaughter of Pocahontas). My mother, Fannie Longworth Pound, was the eldest child of Richard Pound, and in her the Indian features were strongly marked.

My grandmother's second husband was George Chancellor, of Chancellorsville. It was after his death that the large Chancellorsville house was built to be used as an inn, for the Plank Road (the main road between Orange, Madison, and all those rich up-country counties and Fredericksburg, the head of navigation) ran through the estate.

My mother married Sanford Chancellor, a younger brother of her stepfather. He served in the war of 1812 as a Major on General Madison's staff. My father's home was at Forest Hall, near United States Ford. He had a bark mill on the canal which ran by the side of the Rappahannock up from Fredericksburg, and I remember the canal boats which used to come up with groceries, dry goods, machinery, and other things, and carry down the bark and farm produce. The engineers who built the canal stayed at our house, and on leaving they gave my mother a silver tea service, which is still in my possession.

After my grandmother's death, which occurred on December 31st, 1860, Chancellorsville was sold and passed out of the family. My father died at the very beginning of the war, February 1860, and my mother bought back Chancellorsville and moved there with her six unmarried daughters and one son. I had one married sister, Mrs. Thomas Charters, and another brother, Dr. Charles William Chancellor, a surgeon who was appointed Medical Director of General Pickett's Division.

My first recollection of the war is of the Confederate pickets. They were stationed near us and came in and got their meals from Mother. We had plenty of servants then, and Mother was a good provider, so they thought themselves in clover. My sisters were very nice to these defenders of our country, and played on the piano and sang for them. They, in turn, taught my sisters to play cards, of which my mother disapproved, but they all seemed to have a good time. They were very nice to me, too. I remember one Sunday a drove of sheep came down the road, and one of the soldiers said, "Sue, wouldn't you like to have a pet?" I, of course, was delighted to think of such a thing, so he went out and bought me a beautiful white lamb. The soldier's name was Thomas Lamar Stark, from Columbia, South Carolina—so I named the lamb "Lamar" and kept it until the house was burned. When the Confederates went away and the Yankees came, I brought the lamb into the house every night to keep it from being killed.

When the enemy made their raids they were different. My sisters were very cold and distant to them. Mother had her whole crop of corn shelled and put under beds in the bedrooms of the house, and all of her stock of meat was hidden under the stone steps at the front door. There were several of these steps and the top one was lifted, the whole stock of hams, shoulders and middling packed in the space underneath, and the top stone replaced. On the whole, however, the Yankees were kind and polite to us, but I can never forget how they used to come in a sweeping gallop up the big road with swords and sabres clashing, and how I would run and hide and pray. I reckon I prayed more and harder than ever in my life, before or since. Once one of them spoke to my sister as "You rebel women," and she said, "Yes, you call us rebels and we glory in the name." We all know better now. Washington and the Continentals might have been rebels, but we stood for our rights, and under the Constitution, the war was a "War Between the States."

After the Battle of Fredericksburg, the two armies went into winter quarters—the Northern troops on the Washington side of the Rappahannock, and our men on the Richmond side. After the emancipation in

1863, our servants ran away to the Yankees, who were not very far away in Stafford County. General Posey and General Mahone had their troops near us, guarding some of the river fords, and they were at our house a great deal. I remember them both well. General Mahone was a little man, but was just as brave and gallant as one could be. It was a pity that he turned Republican after the war. General Posey was also a nice man, with a long beard—I can see him now. General McLaws and General Anderson used to come, and General Stuart, too. We all loved General Stuart; he was so nice and always had a pleasant word for everyone.

We had refugees from Fredericksburg in the house too: old Mr. and Mrs. F—; their married daughter, Mrs. T— Fall Hill; their young lady daughter, Miss Kate and her "Mammy" old Aunt Nancy; and their driver, carriage, and horses.

The main body of our men were down below Fredericksburg. As the spring opened, up there were a great many rumors. It was said that the Yankees were in Fredericksburg and then that they had crossed below Fredericksburg, and then that they had crossed above us and were going around by Gordonsville. Everything was reported. For several days old Mr. F— had been rather anxious to go into town to attend to some business, and Mrs. F— and Mrs. T—, who both had sons in the army, wanted to go too, in order that they might hear from them. On the morning of Wednesday, April 29, Mr. F—'s desires got the better of his apprehensions, and he had the carriage hitched up ready for the trip. They told us all good-bye, gave Miss Kate, with Aunt Nancy, into my mother's care, and left with Miss Kate a covered basket of valuable papers, securities, etc. It was two years before they saw her again.

That evening there was a rendezvous at our house—General Anderson, General Posey, General Stuart, and some of their aides. My sisters, who did everything themselves now that the servants had gone, prepared a good supper and took great pride in waiting on the table and having everything nice. While we were all at the table enjoying the good things, suddenly a courier came with dispatches saying that the enemy was crossing at United States Ford. Immediately all was confusion. Hastily the Generals bade us good-bye, but General Stuart, always so charming took time to say to my sister, "Thank you, Miss Fannie, for your good supper, and as it is always my custom to fee the waitress, take this from me as a little remembrance." With that he gave her a tiny gold dollar. I have it now, and I treasure it as one of my most cherished possessions.

There were in the house by mother, her six daughters and half-grown son, Miss F—, Aunt Nancy, and a little colored girl whose mother had left her when she ran away to the Yankees. Miss Kate put on all the clothes she could, as did we all, and my sisters took spoons and forks and pieces of the silver tea service which the engineers had given my mother and fastened them securely in their hoop skirts. Thus they were preserved, and I have them still. Other valuables were secreted as best they could be. Presently, the Yankees began to come and they said that Chancellorsville was to be General Hooker's headquarters and that we must all go into one room in the back of the house and stay, sleeping on pallets on the floor. They took all of our comfortable rooms for themselves. I often think of all that old mahogany furniture and how glad I would be to have some of it now. General Hooker did not come until the next day. He paid no attention to my mother, but walked in and gave his orders. We never sat down to another meal in that house, but they brought food to us where we were. If we attempted to go out, we were ordered back. We heard cannon fire, but did not know where it was. We were joined by one and another of our neighbors who fled or were brought to the Chancellorsville house for refuge, until there were sixteen women and children in that room. From the windows we could see couriers coming and going, so we knew that the troops were cutting down trees and throwing up breastworks. I know now that they were very well satisfied with their position and seemed to be very confident of victory.

In the meantime, old Mr. and Mrs. T— had run right into what is called the second battle of Fredericksburg. Miss Kate was miserable about them and they were anxious for her, caught in the lines of the enemy without help or protection. Their younger son, Mr. James F—, was killed just at this time and their cup of sorrow was filled and over-flowing.

We got through Thursday and Friday as best we could, but on Saturday, the second day of May, the firing was much nearer, and General Hooker ordered that we be taken to the basement. The house was full of the wounded. They had taken our sitting room as an operating room, and our piano served as an amputating table. One of the surgeons came to my mother and said "There are two wounded rebels here, and if you like you can attend to them," and she did.

There was water in the basement over our shoe tops, so one of the surgeons brought my mother down a bottle of whiskey and told her that she must take some and so must we all. We did, all with the exception of Aunt Nancy. She said, "No sah, I aint gwine to tek it. I spec it's pizened," and she didn't.

There was firing, fighting, and bringing in the wounded all that day. Wonderful today, they did not forget to bring us food. It was late that afternoon when the terrible time came. Oh! Such cannonading on all sides, such shrieks and groans, such commotion of all kinds! We thought that we were frightened before, but this was far beyond everything, and it kept up until long after dark. Upstairs they were bringing in the wounded, and we could hear their screams of pain. This was Jackson's flank movement, but we did not know it then. Again we spent the night, sixteen of us, in that one room. It was the last night in the old home.

Early in the morning they came for us to go to the cellar, and in passing through the upper porch I saw the chairs riddled with bullets and the shattered columns which had fallen and injured General Hooker. Oh, the horror of that day! There were piles of legs and arms outside of the sitting room window and rows and rows of dead bodies covered with canvas. The fighting was awful, and the frightened men crowded into the basement for protection from the deadly fire of the Confederates, but an officer came and ordered them out, commanding them not to intrude upon the terror-stricken women. Presently the same officer came down the steps and bade us come out at once. "For, Madam, the house is on fire, but I will see that you are protected and carried to a place of safety." This was General Joseph Dickinson, but we did not know it at the time.

Cannons were bombing in every direction, and missiles of death were flying as this terrified band of women and children came stumbling out of the cellar. If anybody thinks that a battle is an orderly attack of rows of men, I can tell him differently, for I have been there.

The sight that met our eyes as we came out of the dim light of the basement room beggars description. The woods around the house were a sheet of fire; the air was filled with shot and shell; horses were running, rearing, and screaming; the men were amass with confusion, moaning, cursing, and praying. They were bringing the wounded out of the house, for it was on fire in several places. "Mammy" Nancy had old Mr. F—'s basket of papers and she and the little colored girl were separated from us and told to stay behind. A Yankee snatched the basket from the old "Mammy" and was making off with it, when Aunt Nancy gave a shriek. "Miss Kate for de Lawd's sake, git yeh Pa's basket." An officer turned and sternly reproved the miscreant, and gave the basket into Miss Kate's hands. Slowly we picked our way over the bleeding bodies of the dead and wounded—General Dickinson riding ahead, mother with her hand on his knee, I clinging close to her, and the others following behind. At our last look, our old home was completely enveloped in flames. Mother, a widow with six dependent daughters, and her all was destroyed.

We took the road toward United States Ford, which was held by the enemy, and after a while we got out of sight of the battle. After walking about half a mile, my sister, who had been ill, had a hemorrhage from her lungs. General Dickinson stopped a soldier on horse-back, made him get down, and put my sister on his horse, walking behind her to hold her on. After a while Miss Kate stopped, completely exhausted, and said that she could not go any farther. General Dickinson asked her if she could ride, "for if so, you may take my horse and I will walk at his head." She said that she was much too exhausted to attempt that, but that she could ride pillion fashion behind him. "That is impossible," he sternly said. "I fear I can not provide for you." After a few minutes' pause, we went on. Presently we met an officer, who wheeled on his horse upon recognizing our leader and demanded with an oath, "General Dickinson, why are you not at our post of duty?" I will never forget General Dickinson's reply. He drew himself up proudly and said, "If here is not the post of duty, looking after the safety of these helpless women and children, then I don't know what you call duty."

After walking three miles, we reached the ford where the Yankees had crossed on a pontoon bridge four days before. Here at the old LaRoque house General Dickinson left us in the care of a New Jersey chaplain, and went to see about getting us across the river. We saw here the corpse of an old colored woman, who, they said, had been frightened to death. We all stayed on the porch waiting, not knowing what would happen next. Presently General Dickinson returned, and went with us to the bridge, where he bade us good-bye. A nobler, braver, kindlier gentleman never lived.

The chaplain went with us across the bridge, and I will never forget the "wobbly" sensation as we walked across those boats. When we reached the other side, the chaplain got a horse from somewhere, put my sister on it, and took us to the top of the hill. There sister fainted and was laid on the grass. A little drummer boy named Thacker was so kind to us at this time. He got some ice and a lemon for sister, and took his clean bandanna handkerchief and tied up her head. He said, "If this is 'on to Richmond,' I want none of it. I would not like to see my mother and sister in such a fix."

We stayed there for some time. After a while an ambulance drove up, sent by General Dickinson. My sick sister was put into it, along with Mother, Miss Kate, my little brother, and myself. The others had to walk. We finally came to the house of Mr. John Hunt, at the Eagle Gold Mines in Stafford County. This was in the Federal lines, and here we were kept under guard for ten days. Sister got better; we had good food, and our guards were very kind to us. My other sisters were very cool toward them at first, but after a while they relaxed and relieved the irksomeness of our confinement by talking, playing cards, and music. I even think that there were some flirtations going on.

General Dickinson sent word of our safety to my brother, Dr. Chancellor, and also to Miss Kate's friends. To my mother he sent a return message from my brother. Miss Kate had a brother who was a professor of distinction in the medical college in Philadelphia. She, still with her basket of papers, was sent to Baltimore, where she was met by her brother, and spent the last two years of the war with him at his home. General Dickinson went to see her there, and it was said that he paid her marked attention and even courted her, but I don't know how that was.

When the order came for our release, one of my sisters said to one of the guards, "Well, I reckon you are glad your prisoners are going." "Not at all," he said. "I am glad for you, but sorry for ourselves. I am going to write my mother and tell her what a good time I have had with these rebel ladies." We were put into an ambulance and carried back to United States Ford, where we were met by my sister, Mrs. Charters, who received us as recovered from the very jaws of death. At her home we found "Mammy" Nancy and the little colored girl, and there we learned the particulars of our glorious victory and the sad news of the death of our beloved "Stonewall" Jackson.[3]

The following fall we went to Charlottesville, where I was put in school. Two of my sisters got positions in the valley as teachers, and mother was made matron first of the Midway, afterwards of the Delevan Hospital. There were three hospitals in Charlottesville and my half-uncle there, Dr. J. Edgar Chancellor, was in charge and obtained the position for her. There we stayed until the close of the war. Just about that time a cousin, Mr. Lorman of Baltimore, died and left my mother some money, so we fared pretty well.

I cannot close this paper without commenting on the enduring friendship which sprung up between my mother and General Dickinson. They corresponded, and, as he was deeply interested in verifying the war history of this section, he several times visited the battle-fields, never without coming to see her. He attended her funeral (her death occurred in July, 1892), thus testifying to the respect and affection he felt for her.[4]

And now another incident of interest: In 1876, a party of us boarded the train in Fredericksburg on our way to the Centennial. The name Chancellor caught the ear of a distinguished looking gentleman seated nearby, and presently he came up, asking if we were the Chancellors of Chancellorsville. When he found that we were, he said, "and I am General Hooker." Of course we were surprised, but we invited him to join our party. He shared our bountiful luncheon and we had a very pleasant day, which was a contrast to the three days spent in the same house with him thirteen years before. We never saw him again, but for years we had visits from soldiers, both Northern and Southern, who remembered "the ladies of Chancellorsville."

I married my cousin, Vespasian Chancellor, and have preserved the name. Many on both sides have passed away, and the years have dimmed my memory for incidents and occurrences, yet the horrible impression of those days of agony and conflict is still vivid, and I can close my eyes and see again the blazing woods, the flaming house, the flying shot and shell, and the terror-stricken women and children pushing their way over the dead and wounded, led by that courageous and chivalrous, General Dickinson.

7 Stonewall's Widow

Varina Davis

$\mathcal{N}$O CHARACTER is so difficult to depict as that of a lady; it can be described only by negations, and these do not convey the charm and beauty which positive virtues impress upon us. This thought has been suggested to me by the request for a sketch of Mrs. Stonewall Jackson. Outside the limits of the States in which she has lived little more has been known of her personally than that she was infinitely dear to her heroic husband, and that she bore him a little daughter, who sat on his bed, cooing and smiling, "all unknowing," while he was slowly entering into the rest prepared for him.

Mary Anna Morrison—this was Mrs. Jackson's maiden name—was the daughter of the Rev. Dr. R. H. Morrison, a Presbyterian minister, and the first president of Davidson College, North Carolina, which he founded, and which still remains as his memorial. Dr. Morrison graduated from the University of North Carolina in 1818, with President Polk and many other prominent men. Mrs. Morrison was one of six daughters of Gen. Joseph Graham, of Revolutionary fame, who was successively Governor of North Carolina, United States Senator, and Secretary of the Navy under President Fillmore. Mary Anna was one of ten children born to the couple. Dr. Morrison, on account of his large family, removed to a quiet country home near to several churches, at which he officiated for his neighbors as occasion demanded. The society about their home was of exceptional refinement, and the associations of the family were with the best people.

In due course of time the girls married Southerners, who afterwards became—or then were—men of mark, such as General D. H. Hill, General Rufus Barringer, Judge A. C. Avery, and I. E. Brown. In 1853, Anna, with Eugenie, her youngest sister, made a visit to their eldest sister, Mrs. D. H. Hill, at Lexington, Va., escorted thither by one of her father's friends. General—then Major—Jackson was at that time engaged to Miss Elinor Junkin, to whom he was soon to be married. He was a frequent visitor to General Hill's house, and became so friendly with the cheery little country girls that he rendered them every social attention in his power. Major Jackson left Lexington for rest in the summer vacation, but in August suddenly returned, and spent the evening with his young friends, listening to their songs and parrying their teasing questions. In the morning they learned that he had married and gone on a bridal tour that day, so shy and reticent was the grave young Major, even to his intimates. After the marriage of her sister, Eugenie, to Mr.—afterward General—Rufus Barringer, Anna remained at home for three years.

In the interim Major Jackson lost his young wife, his health failed, and he went abroad to recuperate. After making an extended tour, he returned, and wrote to Anna in such ardent fashion that everyone, but the object of his affection, suspected his state of mind. Soon after he followed, and they were quietly married from her father's home. The young couple set out upon an extended Northern tour, returning only in time for the session of the Military Institute, where the Major's duty lay. Major Jackson soon established himself in his own house, and his young wife, in the privacy of their home, pursued the busy tenor of a Southern woman's way. Before the expiration of a year, a little daughter was born to the young couple, which was not long spared to them. Their lives seem to have flowed on unruffled by domestic dissonance. Her husband's letters call her his "gentle dove" and his "sunshine," and she gives in the life of her husband, which she published some years ago, a pretty picture of her sitting, at his request, and singing "Dixie," so that he could learn the air. After four years had passed, the dread realities of war broke over the young people. Major Jackson was summoned to take the cadets from the Virginia Military Institute to Richmond for occasional service. The first Military duty was followed by his offering himself to the army of Virginia. After a short time he went into the regular Confederate service, and then the young wife was sent to her father, as it was too lonely for her to remain in Lexington.

Here, practically, ended her married life, save for a few happy weeks at Winchester in the earlier part of her husband's service, and an occasional visit to his camp. These, and the loving letters he wrote to her, were all that was left of her domestic joy. She does not seem to have lost heart, however, but looked forward patiently and prayerfully to a happy end of her many trials and deprivations.

When, in 1862, little Julia was born, Mrs. Jackson met alone and uncomplainingly her illness. The baby was five months old before there was a lull in the fierce strife in which General Jackson was so powerful a motor, which allowed the young wife to take the child to its father, and she, with the infant and a nurse, went to find him in the field. After jolting over miles of new-made road, Mrs. Jackson at length found shelter and the comfort of her husband's companionship, but this indulgence lasted only a little over nine days. The dreaded call to arms was issued to confront General Hooker's advancing army, and the non-combatants were ordered on to Richmond. General Jackson hurried, fasting to the field, after a hasty farewell, expressing the hope that he might find time to return to bid his dear ones loving God-speed, but this privilege was not to be granted. Time passed, and the roar of battle shook to its foundation, and Mrs. Jackson was forced to leave the scenes of her happy reunion, while a procession of litters bearing the wounded was being brought into the yard for medical attention. Haunted by the memory of carnage and death, the poor young wife, with a child's faith and a woman's anguish, left her treasure on the battle-field. Then came the death wound, and after a week's detention, Mrs. Jackson reached her husband's death-bed. Spent with the anguish of his wounds, he lay dying, too near the silence of the grave to do more than murmur to his wife: "Speak louder, I want to hear all you say," and feebly to caress his baby with a whispered "My sweet one, my treasure," while the innocent smiled in his dying face. Then was the heartbroken wife and mother given strength to minister both these objects of her love. From her firm lips the dying hero learned that the gates of Heaven were ajar for his entrance. Controlling her bitter grief, she sang for him the sacred songs on which his fainting spirit soared upward to its rest. When all was over and she had followed him to his grave, she again sought her father's roof, and there hid her bowed head among her own people, to live only for her baby. In strict retirement, the young widow husbanded her means until her daughter was grown—a pretty, graceful young woman, and then, to promote her child's happiness, the mother emerged from the privacy in which she had lived since her husband's death, and visited both the Southern and Northern States. In the course of time Julia became engaged to a young Virginian, Mr. Christian, of Richmond, and a few months later was married to him. Shortly after this marriage Mr. and Mrs. Christian removed to California, whither Mrs. Jackson accompanied them. They returned, a short time later, to Charlotte, N.C., where they took a house and lived together. Now, however, the widow's next trial was imminent. Mrs. Christian was attacked by a prostrating fever, and succumbed, after bearing her illness with great fortitude. She died in her twenty-seventh year.

Mrs. Jackson for a time was stunned and inconsolable. Eventually she occupied herself by writing a biography of her husband. When the book was finished she came to New York, and having secured a publisher without difficulty, gave the tragic and tender history of her hero's life to the world.

Then, for the first time, the writer saw her, and was much impressed by her cheerful and simple personality. The most impressive thing about her was her spirit of resignation and contentment—in fact, I left her with the feeling expressed at the outset of this sketch—that the most difficult of all tasks is to depict a lady, but so gently exercised that one does not confess it!

8 A Woman's Experiences During the Siege of Vicksburg

Lida Lord Reed

*I*N THE middle of May, 1863, a dense fog of mystery and conjecture enshrouded the military tactics and immediate future of the Confederate army in the Southwest. Porter thundered at Vicksburg from the river; Grant held Mississippi in the hollow of his hand; Johnston had vanished like a ghost; Pemberton, dignified generalissimo and "pet of Jeff Davis," inspired no confidence; and the government at Richmond gave no sign. But the soldiers and citizens, men, women, and children, penned like sheep in the hot little Southern city, felt from the bottom of their hearts that "some one had blundered"; and the feeling embittered and made less endurable all the subsequent horrors of the siege. Scared from our home by the gunboat shelling, we had passed the entire winter, an unusually severe one for Mississippi, on a lonely plantation in Warren County. The house stood very near the banks of the Big Black River, so near that during the battle of Big Black we could hear the firing and smell the gunpowder, while the atmosphere was dull and leaden with smoke.

On May 16 a neighbor rode over to report the evacuation of Jackson, and we were surprised and dismayed by the news that Pemberton was falling back, closely pressed by Grant, upon Big Black and Bovina. We did not allow ourselves, however, to doubt either the valor or the wisdom of our generals, but felt confident that this ambiguous movement was but a part of a preconcerted plan of Pemberton and Joseph E. Johnston—a plan which would lead up to the speedy surrounding and utter annihilation of Grant's army. We had no foreboding of the fact that Grant's army would in a very short time effectually surround us.

About sunset of the same day a soldier rode into the yard to inquire the road to Bovina.

"What news?" was the eager question, as every one, black as well as white, rushed out upon the front piazza.

But the gaunt gray cavalryman hung his head. "I am ashamed to tell you, madam," was his answer. "We are terribly whipped, and are retiring upon Bovina and Bridgeport Ferry."

All that night we were packing and watching. By daylight the next morning the yard was thronged with tired, hungry soldiers, all with the same words upon their lips: "We are sold by General Pemberton." Our hearts sank like lead. It was a dismal day for Vicksburg if Pemberton was a traitor. But there was little time to spare that day for hopes or fears. From early dawn the cook was busy boiling coffee and baking biscuit, which Minnie, our zealous mulatto maid, handed in buckets and big trays to the scores of dusty, ragged, and foot-sore men who pressed up to the front door. How they enjoyed their breakfast, poor fellows, thanking and blessing the ladies; and how they swore, within bounds, at Pemberton and the Yankees! They did not tarry long, and, strange as it seems now, we were in a tremendous hurry to follow them. I don't believe the people of the North could ever be made to comprehend what an awful bugaboo their armies were to the women and children of the South—unless some few upon the borders still remember their own horror of the "rebels." There were four magnificent bloodhounds upon the plantation, and the quarters were full of muscular and professedly loyal negroes, but no one even suggested making an effort for the protection of our persons or property. The servants and provisions were packed into a wagon and the family into a carriage, the rector followed in a buggy, and the whole train started for town, though we were warned that we ran the risk of meeting the enemy at the cross-roads. The roads, always bad, were simply frightful for the passage of ambulances, artillery, and army wagons, and it was ten o'clock that night when our driver halted upon Prospect Hill, a sharp ridge above Vicksburg, overlooking both river and town. Below to the right and left, before us and behind us in the valleys, were thousands of camp-fires, above us gleamed the stars—all so closely blended in a gloom of haze and smoke that we literally seemed to be within the hollow center of a great star-sprinkled sphere. It was a beautiful, even wonderful sight, but we did not linger to admire it, for behind us on the dark road to Bovina crept closer and closer the awful shadow of—Grant.

From the time that we met our pickets, stationed about half a mile from Vicksburg, the place seemed alive with soldiers. We found rows of them sound asleep upon our own front gallery, and the street full of their wagons and artillery. At midnight the lines were closed, and our little city was in a state of siege. On Monday, except for some picket shooting, all was quiet. On Tuesday morning the musketry began, but our house was entirely out of range. All day the cannonading was terrific and the air was full of conflicting rumors, but toward evening the news was brought that in three tremendous charges the enemy had been repulsed with great slaughter. Then began the moral reconstruction of our army. Men who had been gloomy, depressed, and distrustful now cheerfully and bravely looked the future in the face. After that day's victory but one spirit seemed to animate the whole army, the determination never to give up.

Our own trials began on Thursday, when the gunboats opened fire. The night had been quiet, and we all gathered about the breakfast-table with good appetites and light hearts. The sky was blue, and free from the familiar battle-smoke; the smell of the roses came in through the open windows; on the table were glass and silver and dainty china, delicate rolls and steaming coffee. Our friend the major proved to us conclusively that morning that *we* need have no fear, as our home was out of range from the river, though it was stated as ominous news that the gunboats had advanced as near to the batteries as they dared. Before sunset that evening a bombshell burst in the very center of that pretty dining-room, blowing out the roof and one side, crushing the well-spread tea-table like an egg-shell, and making a great yawning hole in the floor, into which disappeared supper, china, furniture, and the safe containing our entire stock of butter and eggs. We were all in the study, and were just rising to go in to supper, when the roar and crash came. Minnie, after ringing the bell, had gone into the kitchen for the coffee, and so saved her life. At first we were too much stunned to realize what an escape we had made. I think I speak only the literal truth in saying that one minute later we should have been seated about that table, now a mass of charred splinters at the bottom of that smoking gulf.

We very soon decided to seek safety somewhere, and found it temporarily in the cave of a friend. Now, the caves of Vicksburg were not, as many suppose, natural caverns, but hastily dug passages, like the burrows of rabbits, running straight into the hillsides, and many of them in the heart of the city. The streets of Vicksburg form a succession of terraces, very striking and distinct from the river, and it seems miraculous that under the direct fire of the gunboats a single house should have escaped.

Yet, except for broken glass and loosened bricks, many were uninjured. The caves protected the people in them from fragments of shell and cannonballs, but only the mercy of God could have saved them from a bombshell; and the fact may be classed among singular providences that in all that prolonged and heavy bombardment no shell ever struck directly above an occupied cave.

Our refuge consisted of five short passages running parallel into the hill, connected by another crossing them at right angles, all about five feet wide, and high enough for a man to stand upright. In this nest of caves were eight families, with children and servants. Our own was a fair sample as to size. There were eleven of us—three white adults and four children, with our maid Minnie and cook Chloe and Chloe's two little girls. These faithful women served us cheerfully during the siege and stood by us stoutly afterward. In fact, Minnie followed us "into the Confederacy," was an ardent defender of "the cause," and was always called "the secesh darky" by her colored friends.

The people in our cave that night were not counted, but I have heard it stated since that, including three wounded soldiers, there must then have been at least sixty-five human beings under that clay roof; and I can say positively that they were packed in, white and black, like sardines in a box. A big store-box lined with blankets held several babies, and upon a mattress on the damp floor lay a lady accustomed to the extremest luxury, with an infant beside her only eight days old.

All that Thursday night the shelling never ceased. Candles were forbidden, and we could only see one another's faces by the lurid, lightning-like flashes of the bursting bombs. Sometimes a nearer roar, a more startling gleam, would cause us all to huddle closer together and shut our eyes, feeling that our last hour had come. Frightened women sobbed, babies cried, tired and hungry children fretted, and poor soldiers groaned; and a little girl, crushed by a fall of earth from the side of one of the caves, moaned incessantly and piteously. No wonder that the blessed daylight came like heaven.

All that Friday the horrible fight between gunboats and batteries continued. The noise and concussion were deafening, the strain upon nerves and senses unrelaxed for hours. But our greatest misery was the suspense and inaction. The worst sufferers during a battle are the non-combatants. The victors and victims suffer afterward.

In addition to our other woes we were hungry, not having had a morsel to eat for nearly twenty-four hours. But about dusk on Friday, Chloe's husband, a fine fellow, afterward an alderman, came bravely through the heavy firing, bringing us a tray of ham and bread and butter. In the afternoon of the same day a bombshell struck the side of the hill, caving in one of the entrances, and causing a frightful panic. A rush of hot smoke and a strong smell of powder filled the passages. Some one yelled, "Out of these caves!" Some one else cried that the soldiers were killed. Almost immediately a strong voice was raised to quell the confusion. "All right," it cried, "and nobody hurt." But for this timely check there must have been a disastrous crush; for many were rushing for the openings, while others, blinded and terrified, were plunging farther back into the hill. For, truly, though there were horrors enough within, where else could the poor souls go?

We felt, however, that it was quite time for us to move on, and on Saturday morning the major got us a carriage, and we proceeded, during a lull in the storm of shot and shell, to drive out into the suburbs, where, though nearer to the breastworks, we hoped—a last hope—to be out of range of the mortars. The two ladies and four children were in the carriage, the gentlemen on the box, and Minnie, with Chloe and her children, had to follow on foot. After the confinement in the cave the drive in the fresh air was delightful, and we finally found ourselves in a green little valley directly behind the ridge on which the hospital stood. Here, under the protection of the yellow flag, we literally pitched our tent. Sleep was sweet that night, though our bed was a blanket on the grass, and one small canvas roof sheltered the whole party. There was another tent in the valley, occupied by some bright, cheery young ordnance officers, whose chief, General Bowen, had his quarters just around the hill. They were gallant, handsome fellows, whose jokes and genial camaraderie lent a charm even to those dark hours. From that time on they were identified with out daily life, shared our few pleasures and many anxieties, and gave us in return heart and hope, and the benefit of all the thousand incidents and rumors of trench and camp.

These officers worked with the rector and the major, under the hot June sun, to dig us a cave in one of the hills surrounding our valley. When finished it was the coziest cave in all Vicksburg, and the pride of our hearts from that day until the fatal Fourth of July. There was first an open walk, with parapet six feet high cut into the hillside. In one wall of this was a low and narrow opening overhung by creeping vines and shaded by papaw-trees. This was our side door. Here the rector smoked his cocoanut pipe, and the children made mud-pies and played with paper dolls cut from a few picture-papers and magazines that happened somehow to be among our belongings. This cave ran about twenty feet underground, and communicated at right angles with a wing which opened on the front of the hill, giving us a free circulation of air. At the door was an arbor of branches, in which, on a pine table, we dined when the shelling permitted. Near it were a dug-out fireplace and an open-air kitchen, with table, pans, etc. In the wall of the cave were a small closet for provisions, and some niches for candles, books, and flowers. We always kept in tin cups bunches of wild flowers, berries, or bright leaves which the children gathered in their walks. Our cave was strongly boarded at the entrances, and we had procured some mattresses which made comfortable beds. For a time we slept in the tent, and only used the cave for a shelter.

It was curious to see how well trained the little ones were. At night, when the bombs began to fly like pigeons over our heads, they would be waked out of sound sleep, would slip on their shoes, and run, without a word, like rabbits to their burrows. In the daytime they climbed the trees, gathered papaws, and sometimes went blackberrying up the road, but never far, for the first sound of cannonading sent them scampering home.

We took into Vicksburg with us, besides bedding and clothing, a barrel of flour, a barrel of white sugar, some corn-meal, a few sides of bacon, coffee (Rio and ground chicory), tea, butter, and eggs. The fate of the butter and eggs has already been told; of the sugar we made a plateful of taffy to the music of Minie balls and Parrott shells; the rest of the provisions fed the eleven during most of the siege. At the last we would really have suffered for food but for the kindness of a friend who furnished us facilities for buying absolute necessaries from the army stores.

While we had no actual communication with our friends, we heard through the officers and the rector a great deal that was going on in the town. Many of the citizens lived in caves, going to their homes as often as they dared. One young lady, spending a sultry night in her own bedroom, could not sleep, but got up and sat by the window; and while she was there a spent ball went right through her bed, crushing a bonnet-box and bonnet under it. A mother, rushing to save her child from a bursting shell, had her arm taken off by a fragment. Another mother had her baby killed on her breast. My own little brother, stooping to pick up a Minie ball, barely escaped being cut in two before our eyes, a Parrott shell passing over his back so close that it scorched his jacket. There were many other narrow escapes and some frightful casualties; but, taking the siege as a whole, there was among the citizens a surprisingly small loss of life.

The loss in the trenches was heavy. The men suffered terribly. The hot sun burned and blistered them, while the freshly dug earth poisoned them with malaria. They were half starved, shaking with ague, and many of them afflicted with low fevers and dysenteric complaints. There was a "bloody flux" prevalent among them that was both distressing and contagious. Many succumbed and had to be taken to the hospital, where kind ladies tended them as best they could.

If the men suffered, the officers had compensation; they were absolute heroes in the eyes of some of the prettiest girls in the South, who knitted their socks and hemmed their handkerchiefs, put blossoms in their buttonholes when they started for the batteries, and welcomed them back to an evening in the caves, where home-made candies, flowers, songs, flirtations, and whist combined to wring some festivity even out of those gloomy hours. And when the officers could not leave their posts, the girls, fearless as they were fair, made up riding-parties to the forts and trenches, going in the twilight so that they could see and dodge the fuses of the shells.

Speaking of fuses, the rector told us one day a very funny thing he had seen during one of his trips to town. Every day, as long as the siege continued, he crossed that hospital ridge and passed over the most exposed streets on his way to the church, always carrying with him his pocket communion-service, apparently standing an even chance of burying the dead, comforting the dying, or being himself brought home maimed, or cold in death. His leaving was a daily anguish to those who watched him vanish over the brow of the hill. One evening, coming back in the dusk, he saw a burly wagoner slip off his horse and get under it in a hurry. His head appeared, bobbing out first from one side, then from the other. Above him in the air, bobbing too, and with a quick, uneasy motion, was a luminous spark. After a full minute spent in vigorous dodging, the man came out to prospect. The supposed fuse was still there, burning brilliantly. "Darn the thing!" he grunted. "Why don't it bust?" He had been playing hide-and-seek for sixty seconds with a fine specimen of our Southern lightning-bug, or firefly!

Service was held daily in the Episcopal church, and was always well attended by citizens, ladies, and soldiers off duty. No one seemed to be deterred by fear of casualties, though the church was pretty badly riddled by fragments of shell and cannon-balls. However, it was struck only once during prayers, and then there was no excitement or damage. Before the siege ended a great deal of the beautiful ivy that had covered it for years had been torn, scorched, and killed, and every pane of glass was broken; but no drop of blood ever stained its sacred floor. That daily church service was very impressive. The responses were often drowned by the rattle of musketry and the roar of bombs. The gold buttons of the rector, who was also a chaplain, gleamed under his surplice, and many of the women were in deepest black; for Bull Run and Manassas, Fort Donelson and Chickasaw Bayou, had already desolated Mississippi homes.

I need not describe here the daily newspapers printed on wall-paper, for they are historical, and found their way to many a Northern fireside after the siege. I find in one of them a mere mention of the most distressing accident of the whole siege. A family living on the Jackson road were sitting together in their house when a shell came through the roof, and, bursting, killed the mother and one child, not even a fragment of the child being found. I find, also, a little later, the death of Major Hoadley, one of the handsomest officers in the army, and a great favorite with the girls.

In our own cave we lived in constant danger from both rear and river. We were almost eaten up by mosquitos, and were in hourly dread of snakes. The vines and thickets were full of them, and a large rattlesnake was found one morning under a mattress on which some of us had slept all night. We had to buy water by the bucketful and serve it out in rations, so that we realized what thirst meant, and were often hungry, though, when we knew our men were living on mule-meat and bread made of ground beans, we did not grumble at our scanty fare. We tasted a mule-steak once, but did not like it; it was very dry and tough. We heard wonderful tales of the officers experimenting upon rats and mice and cats and puppies, but I believe such stories were canards.

Canards were plenty, and we had rumors enough and to spare. Our ears were always strained to catch the first sound of Johnston's guns; every extra-heavy cannonading was a message of hope, and every courier brought in, it was said, news of most encouraging victories. On Sunday, June 21, our friends, the young ordnance officers, were in jubilant spirits. They had seen an acquaintance, a St. Louis man, one Bob Lowder, who brought despatches to Pemberton, and letters from home for them. They described him as a most daring man, but when cross-questioned admitted some doubts as to his being very reliable. He had passed the gunboats on the Yazoo, dressed as a fisherman, in a skiff full of lines and bait; but at the mouth of the river he saw so many men and boats that he had taken to the woods, and finally had floated down the Mississippi after dark on a plank canoe. He stated that he had been sworn to secrecy, but when eagerly questioned he replied: "Now, boys, *don't!* I can only tell you that in three or four days you will hear the biggest kind of cannonading, and will see the Yanks skedaddling up the Yazoo." He also said that

Johnston's army consisted of the very flower of the South Carolina, Virginia, and Kentucky troops. This was corroborated by a courier, who came in the same day, and reported himself as only three days absent from Johnston's camps. Joseph E. Johnston was our angel of deliverance in those days of siege, but alas! we were never even to touch the hem of his robe.

One memorable day two bombshells burst simultaneously in our small valley. This seems incredible, and still more incredible that none of us were killed. The ground was torn up, and the air was filled with flying splinters, clods, fragments of iron, and branches of trees. The earth seemed fairly to belch out smoke and flame and sulphur, and the roar and shock were indescribable. The tents were in ruins. One of the officers was astride a table, without any idea of how he got there, and one was flat on the ground, with his scalp slightly grazed and bleeding. The mess-cook, a white man, was on his knees, with his hands clasped to his back, frantically clutching his suspenders and howling dismally. He was with much trouble convinced that he had escaped without a scratch.

That evening, in the reaction from our fright, we had quite a merry time. We made taffy, and the "boys" sang us many a rollicking song. One young lieutenant had a beautiful voice, and gave us "Widow Malone" in fine style. Alas! he died of typhoid fever a few days after the siege ended. Another, his bosom friend, was an artist, and carved our profiles in basso-rilievo on the cave walls. A candle was held so as to throw a shadow, and with a penknife the work was very cleverly done. Even the baby in her nightgown was immortalized in clay. So we passed the time trying to be gay, though every face was pale from the recent shock, and every heart heavy with grave anxieties. The entire force, except Cupid, the pony, slept in the cave that night, and before retiring we registered a vow to meet on every anniversary of the raising of the siege, and have a feast and frolic in our stout little underground home.

I mentioned Cupid, and he merits a chronicle of his own. His body was fat and his legs were lean and short, and he was much more like a pug-dog than a pony, but, representing in his own person all the live stock of the united party, he was the idol of every child in the camp. He belonged to the musical lieutenant, and was named Cupid because *her* name was Archer, and Cupid was an archer! Every day his master rode him off to water, and he was always followed down the road by an admiring body-guard of youngsters and darkies. Cupid had something of the look and all of the peculiarities of a mule. He would buck and kick outrageously, and his capers provided fun for the whole camp. In the last days of the siege he disappeared. His fate was a mystery, over which, perhaps, we had better draw a veil, for men were hungry, and Cupid was meat.

There was really no excuse for the city of Vicksburg being so poorly provisioned. The planters of Warren County offered General Pemberton the contents of their well-filled smoke-houses and barns if he would furnish wagons and horses to bring them into town. His answer to the committee which waited on him was, according to common report: "Gentlemen, when General Pemberton desires the advice or the assistance of the planters of Warren County, *he will ask it.*" And so it was that the corn and sugar and bacon of rich plantations fed General Grant's army, while the defenders of Vicksburg starved.

Early in the morning of July 3 came a startling rumor to the effect that General Pemberton, General Bowen, and other officers were to have an interview with Grant. We were at that time sanguine of success and becoming accustomed to hardships, and our soldiers,—and we saw hundreds going and coming on the road through the valley,—though pale and wasted, were enthusiastic and determined. From what quarter came, then, the whisper that that interview foreboded surrender? At all events, there was no firing that night, but in the morning a faint sound of musketry reassured us; for silence meant defeat. Late the night before a statement had been circulated that the flag of truce was sent out to protest against the constant firing on the hospital, and, knowing such a protest was needed, our fears had been lulled to rest. It was therefore a great shock to us all when the rector, pale as death, came into the cave, and said, with almost a sob, "Take the children home. The town is surrendered, and the Union army will march in at ten o'clock." We lost no time in preparations for departure, but, speechless with grief, gathered our few goods together, and, leaving them in charge of our friends, started to walk into town. When we reached the Jackson road we met group after group of soldiers, and stopped to shake hands with all of them. We were crying like babies, while tears rolled down their dusty cheeks, and eyes that had fearlessly looked into the cannon's mouth fell before our heartbroken glances. "Ladies, we would have fought for you forever. Nothing but starvation whipped us," muttered the poor fellows; and one man told us that he had wrapped his torn battle-flag around his body under his clothes.

When we reached our own home we found it almost uninhabitable, but few hearts in Vicksburg that day mourned personal loss. We stood at our shattered windows and watched the wreck of our army pass by. The men were pallid, emaciated, and grimy with dust, panting from the intense heat, and without their colors or arms. But they were our heroes, our brave defenders, and every child knew it was through no fault of theirs that they failed.

But the hardest trial of that bitter Fourth was the triumphant entrance of Grant's army, marching, with banners waving and drums beating, through streets plowed by their cannon-balls and strewn with the ruins of our homes.

The day of the surrender we were in a pitiable plight, having neither food nor candles; but within twenty-four hours we were, with many others, receiving rations as "a family in destitute circumstances"!

Just at first the Federal soldiers gave some trouble, trooping in and out of yards and houses, passing rough jokes with colored women, and bragging not a little. But the officers were uniformly kind and considerate, General McPherson especially exerting himself to make the lot of paroled prisoners and unfortunate people more endurable.

About two hours after the grand entry, we found two men, common soldiers, on our back porch, turning over with their bayonets the contents of a basket of clean clothes. On being reminded that their presence was an intrusion into the privacy of a lady's house, one of them grinned, and said, pointing to gaping walls and starting planks, "Do you call that a lady's house? You ought to keep it in better order." They were promptly ordered off by a man standing near, who wore shoulder-straps and seemed to have authority. After that day every family had protection papers from the provost marshal, and good order and discipline reigned.

I will finish this my true chronicle with an extract from a letter which gives a graphic history of the rest of our experiences with General Grant and his army, and has the advantage of having been written and posted on the spot:

> George came in to-day, and such a description as he gave of the destruction and desolation in the county! Oakland, where our things were, was completely sacked. I had fitted up two rooms with my own furniture, lace curtains, and mantel and toilet ornaments. I left a pantry stocked with provisions for many months, a cedar chest full of handsome clothing, the rector's fine library packed in boxes, and even my little trunk full of sewing-materials, and my writing-desk and work-table just as they stood. The soldiers cut the carpets into strips with their penknives, and tore the lace curtains from the windows with their bayonets. Valuable books were torn from their covers and thrown to the winds. Our clothing was piled in a heap in the yard, and barrels of flour and molasses poured over it. The men stirred the heap with their

bayonets, and called it a "rebel stew." They tore my bonnets up, and tied the pieces to the bedposts, and even went so far in wanton mischief as to kill a sheep in the parlor and cut it up on the handsome table. I had never believed the stories we heard of such things, looked upon them as newspaper items gotten up for excitement, yet ours was only one of many cases.

But I must tell you about our interview with General Grant. After much discussion it was decided that I had better go to Grant, and ask him to send us out with our soldiers as prisoners of war to New Orleans. We feared the exposure of the children to the heat of the July sun, after their underground life and scant fare and the hardships of travel in wagons. So Jennie and I called upon General Grant, who received us with every courtesy, and gave us papers which would secure us transportation through his lines. He behaved throughout our interview like a brave soldier and kindly gentleman. He expressed himself as being anxious to aid the people all he could, admired the heroism and self-sacrifice of our army as much as I could ask, and "as for the women of the South," he said, "they cannot be conquered." Those were his very words.

While we were there Admiral Porter entered, and we were introduced to the man who for eighteen months had been bothering us with bombs. On our way home, we passed a wagonful of Confederate soldiers, who, when we bowed, as we always do when we meet them, filled the air with their cheers. Our whole army is devoted, every man of it, to the ladies who shared with them the trials and dangers of the siege.

9 A Confederate Girl Visits Pennsylvania, July–September 1863

Edited by Ernest M. Lander Jr.

*F*LORIDE CLEMSON was born December 29, 1842, at "Fort Hill," the home of her grandfather, John C. Calhoun, near Pendleton, South Carolina. Floride's father, Thomas G. Clemson, a transplanted Pennsylvania scientist, farmer, and sometime diplomat, had married Anna Maria Calhoun, the favorite daughter of the distinguished South Carolina senator. Clemson's business affairs and governmental work carried him to Europe, New York and Washington; hence, Floride grew up in a cosmopolitan atmosphere and mingled with the best of society. She visited in the White House and formed a lasting friendship with Harriet Lane, President Buchanan's niece and White House hostess.

When the Civil War began, the Clemsons lived at "The Home," a modest dwelling on the outskirts of Bladensburg, Maryland. Thomas G. Clemson and his son, John Calhoun Clemson, returned South to aid the Confederate cause. The elder Clemson served in a civilian capacity in the Nitre and Mining Bureau. The son received a commission as a lieutenant but saw little action before his capture in Mississippi in September 1863. He spent the remainder of the war in prison at Johnson's Island, Sandusky, Ohio.

Meanwhile Anna Maria Calhoun Clemson and Floride remained at The Home until June 1864, when they moved to Beltsville, Maryland. During these years many of their local friends were openly sympathetic to the Confederacy and seemingly came and went with little or no government interference. In December 1864, after much difficulty and delay, the mother and daughter secured passes to return South. They reached Pendleton on December 31, in time to witness the death throes of the Confederacy.

From January 1, 1863, to October 1866 Floride kept a diary,[1] which briefly covers her Pennsylvania visit, July–September 1863, but her private correspondence with her mother reveals much more. There are Floride's descriptions of the countryside, the cities and mountains, her characterizations of her Pennsylvania relatives, and her hidden hopes and anxieties. The letters of both mother and daughter indicate family feuds, and above all, reveal their deep sentimental attachment to the Confederate cause and fear of impending defeat. I have included Floride's letters in their entirety, with spelling and punctuation unchanged. On the other hand, as Mrs. Clemson's letters contain much household trivia and local gossip of little relevance to Floride's narrative, I have quite liberally edited hers.

Altona. July 29th
Wednesday

My Darling Mother,

Every one has gone to take a nap, so I seize this moment of rest, to tell you of my safe arrival here, I was received with great cordiality by cousin Anna, & aunt Hetty,[2] & am very much pleased with them. Cousin Anna is not handsome, but very lady like, & pleasant, so is auntie. This house is one of the hansomest, & most elegant I ever saw, the position & grounds beautiful. Cousin Sarah, & Luly, are both here. The former is a brisk, smart little homely woman, & the latter, who is about 11 years old, seems a sweet, bright, pretty little thing. I am sure I shall have a splendid time. Cousin Sylvester I dont much like, he is quiet, & not more than good looking. I saw Carrie McClelland[3] this morning. She is nearly as tall as I am & really beautiful. She was delighted to see me.

Now I will begin my journal. I felt pretty badly at first, at the idea of leaving you, but soon the excitement of travelling woke me from my dumps, & I began to enjoy myself. At Annapolis Junction, I looked out, & who should I see, but Mrs. Rankin, standing on the platform, looking as much like a nut craker, or the nut cracked, as ever. We had to wait an hour & a half in Balt. & started for Philla. at ten. Uncle [Elias] drew my attention from time to time to the crops, which looked splended but spent his trip mostly in the arms of Morpheus. It began to rain after we crossed the Susquehanna (which you do in the cars, without getting out, they are run on the boat) but it was not very hot. We were perfectly covered with cinders, & uncle used one corner of my veil, greatly to his satisfaction. By half past three we reach the city, of brotherly—not love, in the rain, & nearly starved. I went right to aunt North's[4] & found no one but Walter (who has grown to be a tall thin ugly boy of 17 [?]) all the rest being in Atlantic city except Willy & Clem, who had enlisted to drive Lee from the state. They however returned that same evening, after a six weeks experience of a soldier's life. They are both very handsome. Clem has wiskers, & is extremely good looking. They were very kind, & made me most welcome. After eating something I got Walter to go down street with me, & bought nearly everything I wanted. I enclose a list, which is pretty exact, I believe, & only left off shopping when the stores closed. The next morning I finished my list, but had no time to get shoes, the night before my feet were too swolen to try them on. I went into almost every millenary store in the city but found only one bonnet that *would do* for 7$ as the season is so bad for such things, & that is a white crape, with red moss roses, which though pretty of the kind, is neither becomeing or suitable they tell me here. The dress is grey alpaca 50 cts. a yard, & very pretty. Everything is much cheaper than with us. I went to the depot then, put my things in the trunk, found uncle, & started at 11½ o'clock.

The cars ran very fast, we soon passed by Kate Barton's[5] station, then through the beautiful Chester valley, which looks like a garden spot, it is so luxuriant, & rich,—neat to excess. Uncle pointed out the crops, (which were very heavy) furnaces, & places, and when we came to the mountains, said "yes very pretty," & nodded! Oh mother I never dreampt of such scenery! From Harrisburg, on the beautiful Susquehanna, we wound around through, & by mountains, & followed the banks of the Juniata from its mouth to this place. Oh I nearly went wild, it was so beautiful. Not the lofty, cloud peircing, barren peaks, I thought of, but bold, rocky, & wooded ridges, some wonderfully regular, some tossing wildly like a stormy sea. The woods, and feilds *so* fresh, and the little green islands in the lovely Juniata spotted with Orrange love weed. It was a splended day to travel, little sun, little rain, few cinders, no dust, & just cool enough. I looked till my eyes were blinded by smoke, then rubbed them, & regretted the time it took to do so. I would not have missed it for the world, and uncle nodded! Harrisburg is beautifully situated among the mountains, & by the river, but is in itself indefferent. I love the magnificent mountains, uncle admires the fine barns, & was very kind. We reached Alton which is quite a nice place before nine, & found auntie waiting for us. This appears to be a large neighborhood, & quite gay. Annie was at a party last night, so I did not see her till this morning. I think I shall like her very much. Indeed I have taken a great fancy to all. I have not heard politics broached, & I think they do not bother their heads about such matters. They all think my trunk preposterous, as I thought they would. Tell Mr. Onderdonk[6] if he never was along this road, it is more than worth his while to do so, & get a seat on the right hand side. Tell Mr. Lee[7] uncle says the Hudson is too far out of the way, oh dear! & is not an inspiering companion; *though kind,* he is lame [?]

I hope you all miss me. If not I wont have anything to do with you when I get home. If you were here, I should be perfectly content, but I feel very badly at leaving you alone. Be sure to write twice a week, & tell me how you are & everything. I am quite well. All our relations are well. Uncle William[8] and aunt Sue are at Claymont [Del.]. Mattie[9] they say still has plenty of beaux. There seems to be a great deal of wealth here. This place, & house are really superb. I am tired now, & will go rest for a little while.—I heard a young lady sing with splended voice to day. Cousin Anna plays. Uncle is very affectionate. Now do take care of yourself, & do not show my letters, I write in such a hurry so that I may rest. They keep very early hours here, in the morning & for meals.

Love to Mrs. D. F, Mrs. Calvert[10] & all.

Your devoted daughter
Floride Clemson

This is frightfully scratched, but I am tired & can not stop to think.

Before receiving Floride's first letter from Altoona, Anna Maria Calhoun Clemson on July 30 wrote her daughter a lengthy and rambling letter telling her the news of the neighborhood and The Home. Henry McCeney[11] was working all day and "sitting up all night to guard their garden &c, which are nightly pillaged in spite of all their efforts." Henry had said that his cousin Eliza's family had lost nearly all their servants. Mrs. Calvert had a letter from Ella[12] & talked of visiting her [in Pendleton, S. C.] "& the means of accomplishing it." Mr. Lee "still continues *charming,* & evinces no intention of returning to his *duties,* in W." Mrs. Clemson reported that the body of a Negro man, dead of foul play about two weeks earlier, had washed down on their back property. Mr. Onderdonk was to leave the next day with his sister for New York. "I have not heard from your grandmother [Mrs. John C. Calhoun] since you left, & am getting anxious." She advised her daughter that "I shall expect quite a journal of all your doings," and added: "enjoy yourself & *be quiet.*"

Altona. Aug. 2nd 1863

I have not heard from you yet dearest mother, but I suppose I must wait a little longer in patience, as the mails do not do as they should, & bring the letter in one day. I wrote you a hurried, scratchy letter the day after I got here, and told you in an unsatisfactory, & hasty manner, pretty much all that had happened till then. Now, though I have little of interest to write, I know you want to hear from me, so I will give you the journal of my last four days.

There has been a great deal of visiting to this house, indeed coming nearly all the time, which is pleasant and very filling up, to one's time. There seems to be a great superabundance of young ladies, & very few gentlemen in this country. I have scarcely laid my eyes on one of the other sex, under forty years old. Carrie McClelland lives but a short distance from the enclosure, & comes up every day. Another of my school mates is staying with her now; Lizzie McIlvain. She is a sweet pleasant girl, but not striking.

I have taken the greatest possible fancy to all this family. They are very lovely among themselves. Cousin Annie would please you wonderfully, she is most lady like, and quiet, and seems very affectionate, and simple. Every one loves her. She is twenty seven, but seems, & looks much younger. I should take her to be twenty two. She is not pretty. Aunt Hetty is very sweet. Although she is sixty she would never be guessed over forty five & is very good looking, & not at all fat. I think my dresses might fit her in size. She is also very refined. Lulu is the smartest, & sweetest child I ever saw. She is a little wonder. She sends her love to you; "as she knows me," she says. Her mother is quite intelligent, and very tender hearted, & pure. She is very brisk, and has occasionally a little something Yankee about her, but not much. Dear mother, do you believe it, they have never mentioned politics, & are much more considerate than I ever dreampt of. After all I rather like cousin Sylvester. He is a little cranky but I think he is very honorable, & kind hearted. He seems highly thought of, and is exceedingly quiet.

Uncle has gone East gone, & after his return, means to visit Kentucky, where he has invited cousin Anna, & me, to accompany him; of course I do not think of that, or wish to go. I fear much lest our Niagara scheme may fall through, somehow. Oh mother was it not dreadful about Morgan![13] I felt so badly. I could not bear to read the particulars. I have not seen a paper since I came, so dont forget the *summaries*, or I shall be as badly off as Rip Van Winckle, & ask where the country is, on my return home. They keep but two servants here, although they live in such nice style, & are very industrious. I have sent for my shoes to Phila. by the shoemaker here who took my measure. I had to bye a hat (see the above diagram) for $E. It is black, trimmed with velvet, & becomeing. I had nothing to walk in. I went to the Presbyterian church to day, and heard a very dull sermon.

Cousin Sylvester took me up to the ore bank in his buggy yesterday. It is about five miles off & one of the very largest holes I ever saw. The scenery about here is magnificent, & though this house is not more elevated than Mrs. Calvert's, in proportion to the surrounding country, they have a beautiful view of the mountains, & some intervening rolling ground. There are trees at the back of the house, a lovely garden at one side, nice grounds on the other, & terraces & the view in front. The house is one of the finest I ever saw, & very refined. *Our* furniture[14] looks beautiful in their parlor, & they only want pictures to complete it. The family is badly off for horses just now, & there is little chance for rides until the deficiency is supplied. There is talk of several excursions, to the mountians &c. next week I will try to get my new dress done.

They have put out my wash, but will not hear of my paying for it. I received a letter from Kate yesterday. She heard I had passed, & was hurt at my not telling her. I wrote to day, & explained. She is very affecate. Remember me to Mr. Lee & ask if he misses me—or—!!! To Mr. O. also. I hope to see them both. Love to Henry. Take good care of yourself, & write often to your devoted daughter

Floride Clemson.

Have you heard from father? I am pretty well. It was too cool at first, but is very warm today. All join in love to you. Cousin Sarah hopes to meet you, some day, she says. She is very kind to me. I enclose a likeness of cousin Anna taken some time ago, & is not very good. She has an immense head of hair. Love to Lizzie R:[15] Mrs. Daub &c. Mrs. Calvert & all.

Upon receiving Floride's first letter August 1, Mrs. Clemson answered the next day, giving her daughter the local news, noting the comings and goings of Messers. Lee and Onderdonk, and expressing delight in Floride's pleasant visit. She happily informed her daughter that she had earlier sent news "summaries" and a letter from Ella Clavert Campbell giving news of Mr. Clemson and John Calhoun Clemson. "It is quite a relief to find they are both well, after so long a silence, but I am anxious to hear of your grandmother as Mrs. C[alvert]. has had two letters from Ella, since she enclosed one from her [Mrs. Calhoun]. I do hope she is not sick."

Mrs. Clemson also reprimanded Floride about the newly-purchased bonnet: "I charged you, if you did not find one to suit, to have one made, & not *to pick up anything.*" She strongly urged her to write Mrs. Calvert, and lectured her about her conduct: "Dont get excited. This is all the caution I have to give you. If you can only remain *calm,* I have perfect confidence in your behaving just as I would have you, & making a favorable impression. *Do keep hold on yourself.*"

On August 6 Mrs. Clemson again wrote Floride and complained of having received only one letter from the daughter. Word from Mr. Onderdonk in Baltimore was that news by way of steamer from Charleston was suppressed. The heat and stench in Washington was unbearable. Two days earlier, the mother reported, a trip into the city had made her so ill that she had had to go to bed upon returning home. And the evening before, the foul odor from burning animal carcasses had forced them to retreat indoors and close all windows.

Mrs. Clemson had little news "except the excitement of the draft," and some neighboring visitors. As for Mr. Lee, she wrote that "the gallant defencer, tho possessed with a silent devil, is still quite pleasant, & makes himself generally useful, & manages me as usual." She reminded Floride that August 21 had been appointed in the South as "a day of fasting & prayer."

(Sunday)
Altoona. Aug. 9th. 1863
My Darling Mother,

I received your letter written on Thursday, yesterday, & was delighted that you were getting on so well. I wrote to Mrs. Calvert in the middle of the week, & I must own here little, or nothing of importance to record since, but you must have your letter, whether it merely consists of a few words. You complain of heat; well I must do the same. Although the day only is hot, still I feel it very much, & often wonder if in our own cool home, I could not find a breath of air. This morning I nearly roasted in church & wished myself in some comfortable, free & easy chair, where I should not have to play lady, until I got so fidgetty, & stiff.

I am glad you send me the "Summaries." I can not resist the temptation of reading the papers here sometimes, & they make me feel very gloomy. I have had a fit of the dumps all day, on account of one of these indulgeances this morning. I still have the same forbearence, & kindness to record, for which I am really grateful. My watch is being mended, & I have ordered some shoes from Hipman, through the shoemaker in Altoona. Cousin S. got me a beautiful pair of riding gantlets in Philla., where he spent a day last week.

I wrote to aunt North, Mary C.[16] and Kate Barton. I forgot to tell you that the latter said aunt B. "would be delighted, & would love to see me, with her love!" Strange! Tell Mr. Lee I take regular exercise, & I thank him for taking care of you. I am much obliged for the fencing of my flower beds also. Remember me &c. Govvy[17] seems a fixture. Is he cleaner? I am so glad of such recent, & good news from *abroad* [South Carolina], but hope grandma is well. It seems strange she does not write, does it not? Again I must tell you how kind every one is. They think me wonderfully straight, & say I carry my hight well. They can not understand my weight, (166 lbs.)

My face is a little broken out, but I eat, & sleep *a merveil.* The hours are dreadful, breakfast at seven or a little after, (I am always one of the first down!) dinner at one, or before; a nap soon after, then dress for the evening, supper at six, & to bed after ten. Auntie is an active, neat, clean housekeeper, but the eating is not Mrs. Daub's. I can not get used to so much sweet. Even salad is made sickening with sugar, & ham comes very often. Everything is good of its kind however.

I recorded in the letter to Mrs. C. my two evenings of dissipation. I had to drive the girls in a one horse carriage, & the man had to ride on my old pony. We got along quite nicely, for I trusted to the horse's instinct, & the good road, as I found my eyes useless. The road that passes by here, from Hollidaysburg to Altoona, is made of cinder, & plank, & is excellant, but I find that can be said of no other in this country. It all behooves me to complain, & I doubt whether they are worse than ours, but of a different style,—very stony, & precipitous, & exceedingly ill made, but not as washed, & boggy as ours. They are so beautiful, & pass over such a romantic country however, that in climbing a bad hill, you only think of the view which will entrance you at the top, & the delight lasts until you reach the bottom. Cousin Sylvester, who I like better every day for his kindness, took me a buggy ride of some fifteen miles, which I enjoyed exceedingly. We just missed a shower which we saw near us, though so very partial, as to look like a grey viel, & so did not feel troubled by the sun. He also took me another, & shorter ride, which was perhaps more beautiful, as he did not confine himself to road, but took me to the top of some mountain-like hills, where the views, were most fine. I am quite prepared to answer questions on ore digging, washing, & burning.

There is a derth of horses, which will not be filled until uncle returns from Kentucky, & which keeps us a good deal at home, but the weather has been so warm that I think buggy riding is perhaps as well. I find it quite pleasant, & a novelty. Pet, as cousin Anna calls the pony, has grown quite round, & fat,—too much so for its slight frame, & is still the tricky little imp, it always was. I have tried riding but once since I came & unless I can get a better horse, & a saddle of more respectable dimensions, & shape, I am quite resigned to staying at home. There are still some trips to the most celibrated spots, in contemplation, which may come off any day. However, my imagination can picture nothing more beautiful than I have already seen. Anna's cousin Sadie Sterrit, a tall, thin girl of twenty two, is staying here now. I am happy to say she only intends remaining a week or so, for I have taken a dislike to her. She is just a little too sweet, & cat like, & too fond of kissing, &c. Very polite to me however.

You need not think I am not taken care of. I have coughed a little since I came, for you know I had a cold when I left (which soon got well however), & the sound thereof, being not even as hard as usual, did not meet with the approbation of my kind relatives. So here I am, with enough care taken of me, to keep a gross of tender hot-houseplants, through an Arctic winter. In vain I plead that it does not amount to any thing (& it really does not,) the minute I give a hack, there is a general closing of windows, & getting of sugar & water, shawls &c. It is really amusing. Uncle set them on, retailing yours, & Mr. Lee's accounts of my delicacy. Joking apart, they make more fuss than you; & almost roast me with care.

Poor Carrie McClelland, whose mother died of consumption you know, is quite delicate. She spit (or *spat*) some blood last week, but does not cough. Lizzie McIlvain is still with her, & as interesting as ever.

Uncle got back the day before yesterday. He got the papers he says from you. He will go to Kentucky next week, but we have no intention of accompanying him. His movements are too uncertain. He & cousin S. do not sit horses at all. They have not quarell, to my knowledge; but do not get along. Anna is lovely, & quiet, but not very interesting, auntie ditto. Cousin Sarah is by far the most intelligent, & is the only one of the whole set, who has any enthusiasm. I really love her. She seems to have taken a fancy to me, & is very kind. She is very religiious, & pure, really one of the best women I ever saw. She is an Episcopalian.

The Clemson's are expected, indeffinately any time. I shall be glad to see Sallie[18] & Mary, who I think are the two that are coming. The sentiments of the family with regard to "Mrs. Marton," & others suits me exactly. I really pitty you for that miserable smell, but hope it will soon pass away. Now I have written you a long letter about nothing, & expect a speedy & punctual answer. My love to Leo,[19] & the rest of the family, with oceans to yourself from

> Your devoted daughter,
> Floride Clemson

Keep well all [and?] tell me everything. The family would send love but are napping & at Sunday school. I shall remember the 21st rest assured. I have been doing no work at all.

On August 9, the same day as Floride's latest letter, Mrs. Clemosn wrote of the usual household items: the doings of Mr. Lee and "Govvy" Morris, the heat, anxiety over absence of news from Mrs. Calhoun, the continuing stench from Washington, and the visits of neighbors. She added a bit of gossip picked up in the city from Mrs. Robert Stone[20] to the effect that Lizzie Giles had jilted Washington Baker, a Clemson cousin, for a General Quarles in Mobile. She wrote: "If it is true, she & her mother have both behaved shamefully, & I think your cousin well rid of her . . . . To think of her driving out with him, as his fiancée, while the mother bought her wedding things to marry another man!!!!!"

Mrs. Clemson expressed joy over Floride's pleasant visit and the absence of political discussions, but she warned her to remember "the interest of Northerners cannot be so *vital* as ours in this contest, & that family especially, having no near relative engaged in it, & your uncle's iron being *enormously increased* in value, by it, have no cause for bitterness, indeed the wonder is, that being, as you say, & as I believe, sincere & earnest christians, they or any other good person at the north, could be in favour of a war of invasion, for the avowed purpose of abolition, & subjugation, against their brethren, & can stand calmly by, & see so much innocent blood shed, to *put down the very principles our common forefathers fought for."*

On August 13 Mrs. Clemson wrote again, still complaining about the heat and the "bad smells" of Washington almost making her ill. Mr. Lee was still at The Home, she reported, and "like[ly] to be. He talks no more of being ordered off [by whom? to where?], & is not so pleasant as he has been. What a queer man he is, to be sure! I gave him your messages, & he expressed himself *gratified & sent his respects."* She complimented her daughter on her interesting letters and her punctuality at the Bakers. "I hope you make yourself agreeable, & that they like you as much as you do them." After a little lecture to Floride about proper spelling and word usage ("You speak of a 'buggy *ride.*' You *ride* on horseback—You *drive* a carriage of *any kind*"), she ended with the following note: "The news is not bad & I heard the other day all [Confederates] were in good spirits in spite of the late reverses."

On August 16, Mrs. Clemson, increasingly disappointed at not hearing from Floride, wrote that the weather was still hot; some new neighbors had moved in; she had not been to Washington recently; Mrs. Calvert was quite sick and distressed over no news from Ella; Mrs. Clemson likewise was "anxious at not hearing from your grandmother." She enclosed summaries of the war news and a Carlyle article—"the best satire on the war yet." She added: "Does not Charleston hold out valiantly? God bless the old state."

"There is quite (an almost mightly nuisance,) in the shape of an execrable band from Ft. Lincoln, which comes to make night hideous, for several hours, at Yost's & Barney's.[21] No two instruments accord, & they neither play in time or tune, nor any tune worth hearing, so the only effect they produce is setting one's teeth on edge."

Concerning "Govvy," she wrote: "Mr. L. tells me he persuaded 'Govvy' to join his regiment, & as he has not come out today, I suppose he took the advice. I am not sorry, for tho personally I rather liked him & he had become cleaner, I don't wish that kind of cattle too much about the house." Regarding Mr. Lee, she said: "On the whole he makes himself rather agreeable, but 'too much of a *good thing* is worse than none at all.' He gets no letters that I see. Mysterious is it not? *Govvy* told me he [Mr. Lee] wanted to go to Texas, if there was an expedition sent there. I suppose that is what he is waiting for orders."

She closed the letter with a final but serious warning: "Don't be led into going to make visits to *any of the family*. Get off civilly. You have been away so long must go straight home &c &c. I prefer things to remain as they are."

Altoona. Aug 16th 1863

My dearest Mother,

I have so much to say, that I scarce know where to begin. Last week, we were so constantly on the go; & when at home, so tired, that I had not the time to write to you, but Mr. Onderdonk said he would see you tomorrow, tell you all about me, so you will not miss my letter.

First then, Monday was very quiet; Tuesday we had determined to go up to Cresson, a place about fifteen miles from here, up the Aleghany range, but could not, as the rest of the party were not prepared. So cousin Sylvester took me up to Holidaysburg, in the buggy, & we had a very pleasant drive. It is not so large a place as Altoona, nor so nice a one, but seems to be thriving. Wednesday, we *all*, with several other persons from the neighborhood, made an early start for Cresson. Cousin S. & one or two other gentlemen, constituted the masculine element; the feminine amounting to some sixteen, or more. Cousin S. with his usual kindness to me, determined to get me a stand on the back platform, so that I might enjoy the view to the greatest extent. We had a couple of engines, & a short train, still the grade was so heavy, that we went slowly. I think I never saw anything grander, or more wild, than the scenery was. We mounted in a most circuitous manner skirting ravines, & making the sharpest possible turns. The idea of being nearly on the top of a high mountain on a railway train! It seemed wonderful. I did enjoy it so. Just before we reached our destination we passed through a tunnel, 200 ft. under ground & well on to a mile long. I did not like that.

Cresson is a summer resort, with no natural attraction, except the mountain air, that I could see. Though so elevated, there is no view, & no fine scenery in the immediate neighborhood, but it is surrounded by deep massive hemlock woods, which are not only magnificent looking, but exceedingly productive of ferns & musketoes. There are some strong *un*medicinal springs, a fine large hotel, some nice cottages, & a promiscuous set of people, besides a ten pin alley, two billiard tables, & a bar room. Also many plank walks. Well after waiting till we were tired for a room to lay off our things in, we were shown one very small one which we sixteen ladies, besides some children, occupied in common with a gentleman & baby, besides other congruous elements I suppose. The gentleman (who was probably tall, as his pants were very long) kept us out of the room while he dressed for dinner, but was not otherwise inconvenient.

We spent the morning most pleasantly rolling ten pins, & walking; besides wondering at the different kinds of people it takes to make a world. At the first amusement, I came out third, after two long games with eight others, most of whom had rolled before. Cousin Sylvester gained the first, & Lizzie McIlvain the last game. I liked it exceedingly at the time, but found my muscles did not, next day. We had right good eating, & a pleasant day. About eight we expect[ed] to start home, but the train was half an hour late. When it came, it was so crowded, that we could not all get seats. I managed to get squeezed next to a woman, whose child occupied the whole of the opposite seat, as a bed. I tried to induce her to pick it up, but she said she was too tired to hold it any longer, so after inquiering if it had no infectuous disease, & seeing that it was clean, I picked it up, & provided two more of the party with seats. The child was very heavy! I left two of my hoops at the plank walk, for incredible as it may seem, my new set [?] is too long. That night we slept without rocking. Next day we rested.

Mr. Onderdonk arrived in the morning, & stayed all day, & evening. We invited him to join a party which had arranged for the next day (Friday) to visit the Wopsenonock mountain, one of the highest about her, & the finest view. Six of us went on hoseback, & six in a springless wagon. I was one of the three ladies who rode, Carry, & Anna the others. On account of the scarcity of horses, cousin S. most kindly gave up his (which was lame, & worthless) to Mr. O., & did penance in the conveyance, which cousin Henry McClelland drove. I was on the latter's horse, a huge white beast, which showed much docility of temper in not paying the slightest attention to my whip, & other attempts at urging out of a very hard, & slow walk. My saddle would probably have fitted me at the age of say eight—but I have grown since.

We started about ten o'clock in the hot sun, & thick dust, & I must say I suspected little pleasure from the ride, however after over three hours we reached the crown of the mountains, & as the weather had become a little hazy, & less hot, the road being beautiful, & the company pleasant, I managed to get along passably pleasantly. We had to wait sometime for the waggon, as the roads were well calculated to retard anything like progress, being nothing more nor less than frightful, & nothing but rocks, & holes. After unpacking the lunch, & feeling to see whether there were any bones broken, we seated ourselves in a shady grove right by the Wopsenonock house, a neat tavern, & had a merry, & most refreshing meal. About two o'clock we saddled up, & rode half a mile to the *brink* of the mountain. The brow has been denuded of trees, & you look down near a thousand feet of so abrupt a decent, that a stone can be thrown to the bottom, & a man could roll down, were it not for the bushes. What could be finer than that I can not imagine. It was just dumbfoundering. Though the day was somewhat smoky, we could see over three ranges of mountains, & I believe some 80 miles in one direction. The country looked like a beautiful map. What I had though[t] mountains before, looked like mole hills from there, & Altoona, which was scarce six or seven miles off, seemed just a little place. I do wish you had seen it. It did me good. Most reluctantly, & with many a "longing, lingering look behind," we left it, & after rather a brisker jog back, by an other road, reached home more battered than tired, & with fine food for thought before dark. My horse, who added stumbling, & shying to his phlegmatic temparament, fell with me twice, though he exhibited no symtoms of enough life for the first agrément. However owing to his inertia & my sticking qualities, he recovered without throwing me. Cosuin Anna had a sick headache unfortunatley, & had to take Lizzie McIlvain's place in the wagon coming home. Mr. O. will probably tell you all about this trip himself.

Yesterday Cousin S. took me all over the machine shops in Altoona, which I enjoyed excessively, as he, & Mr. Brasto [?] (the superintendent) explained everything to me. The works are very extensive, & are for the manufacture of the engines, & other rollingstock of the road. I saw all possible kinds of working in iron, especially. It was a great treat; & very dirty, & noisy. I would like to go again. I saw them casting in the evening, at uncle's furnace, the liquid iron in [is] beautiful; but rather warm. Uncle started for Kentucky Wednesday, & will probably be back in a week or so, when he will take us to Niagara he says. Cousin S. has to go tomorrow to the East as far as Bauting [?] to sell iron, & will probably be gone a week. I shall miss him much, he has been so good, & kind to me, taking me about, & showing me sights. I really like him now. The Clemson's, uncle, Mary, & Mattie, are coming early this week. I am so disappointed Sallie is not to be one of them. I send you aunt B's letter without comment, what must I say? I know what to *do*. "This world & 'tother country" deciets & starange things! She tells uncle he must "call by for Kate."

The furniture has arrived, & is splended, especially the looking glass, & etagere. I took my dress body & sack to be made yesterday. I have made the skirt myself. I find I will have to send for more. I got my watch fixed for $1.50. Carrie McC. is very delicate, she spit blood last week.—Mrs. Latrobe & Mary[22] wrote me nice letters from Bethlehem inviting me to join them, which I would do were it not for the Clemson's. I don't know when I shall get home. I want to see you much, *very much*. I received yours, & Mrs. Calvert's letters last week. Glad you are getting on so well. Remember me to Mr. Lee, & tell him to be in readiness to go with us to Niagara if he can. I cant help getting excited I fear, & being noisy, but they seem to like me, & are certainly *very* kind, & considerate, & affectionate to me. Remember me to Mr. O., Mrs. Calvert, Lizzie, Mrs. D., & F. & all, all, all.

I am your devoted daughter
Floride Clemson

*   *   *

Wednesday
Altoona. Aug. 19th 1863.

Darling Mother,

I have just received your letter of the 16th inst., & Monday one from Mrs. Calvert, & an other one from you. It is such a delight to get your letters, & I look so anxiously for them. Though there is not such an immense variety of news in them, you need not feel that you have nothing to say, for every little trifle sounds like a great deal, when one is away from home. I am really sorry you are suffering so much from the heat. We have had some hot weather, to be sure, but the nights were so cool, that we did not mind it. Though rain is wanted, still there is no appearance of drougth yet.

I hope you received my last letter. It was exceedingly *long*, & *interesting* (I always *was* modest, you know.). Today I have not so much to say. Yesterday afternoon we drove to Hollidaysburg, to spend the evening, & night, at Dr. Lander's. There are three pleasant young ladies in the family. There was a *kind of* a party (wing [?]) and we had a merry dance. One of the daughters of the house sings splendedly. We walked over that extensive city, this morning, in search of birth day presents for Luly. I got her the "Arabian Nights." We reached home by one o'clock. Carry went with us, or rather *took* us, as we are scarce of horses yet. The evening before last, we returned some visits, & spent the evening out. On our return we found visitors; among others Mr. Collin, a Sweede who told me much about his country.

Our Niagara trip still holds good. Cousin Sarah, Luly, cousin Anna, Sady Sterritt (her cousin who is still here) & myself, are all going under the shaddow of uncle's wing. My only fear is that his *wing* will not be large enough to cover us all, & I *do* wish we had an other gentleman or two with us. Do tell Mr. Lee to join us, he will be such a pleasant addition & I do not think we will see a thing with uncle, he is so decrepid, & always wants to gallop through night, & day. Then I think a trip will do Mr. Lee *good* &c &c. We will probably go by Pittsburgh, & Cleveland, & get left at our respective homes East, on our way back. Cousin A. is to make a stay in Philla. to attend the wedding of a friend. So Mr. Lee could take me home, without taking uncle so far. Then the party dont want to come down but by the side of the Hudson, or sail on the lake, nor nothing else. I suppose Mr. O. could not go with us, as we will not probably start before ten days, or two weeks. Urge Mr. L., & tell him I wont bother him, *or say a word to him,* if he goes. Wont that do? It will be so agravating, disappointing, vexatious, & stupid to make the trip, & see nothing, but gallop round. Uncle & cousin S. are both away, but will probably return toward the end of this, or the beginning of next week.

I am getting very fat, & well, & have still the same reports to make of kindness & considirateness. I am so happy Charleston still holds out so well. We have not heard from the Clemson's again, but expect them daily. Sallie is not to be one of them, I am sorry to say.—Thank you for correcting my letters & your good opinion of them.

What a fist Emily Wood[23] does write! It dont pay. I some how dont do much of anything but enjoy "dolche for minte." I am sorry Mr. Merrick[24] has left the city. We will have no one we know there soon. Are my gladiolis in bloom, they are nearly over her. They have had no tomatoes yet, is that not late? Remember me to Mr. O, Mrs. C. & all enquiering friends. I will write to Laura[25] I think. Aint aunt B "one of 'em"? All send love to you. I dont because you have all mine.

Yours devotedly,
Floride Clemson

I will write to Mrs. C. soon again.

Private

Now my darling mother, I want to tell you something I have been thinking for some time, very seriously on religious subjects; for, as I have often told you, I could not be satisfied with what *seems* quite sufficient for you, and many others. Still as you say, one's religion must fit as one's cloths, & every one must have religion and I think I need something more tangible. Since Mary Latrobe was at our house, I have had many conversations with Mr. O.[26] on this subject. Without my knowledge, she spoke to him about me, & as the ice was broken, I saught the topic. He very kindly made many points clear to me, but I was still undecided, when I came here. Cousin Sarah has been kind enough to help me, & I feel now as if I should really like, & feel it my duty, to be, baptized.

I do not pretend to say I am a bit better than I was before, or that I have very *strong* faith, yet I want to believe, & have been convinced of the truth of most of the important points for some time, the rest will come I hope, & pray. I have always felt I needed something of this kind, *perhaps* because I am weak, though this weakness may prove strength, but still it *can* do no harm. Do not think that I have been converted, as they say, "all of a sudden," but ask Mr. Lee & Mr. O. if I have not thought about it for some time. I did not think of making up my mind so soon when I left home, for I was uncertain which I liked best the Episcopal, or Presbyterian church, however on investigation, I find the latter does not suit me, & I had rather join the former. Their faiths are the same nearly.

I wont take any step till I get home if you say so, though I think if Mr. Hall comes here, while I still remain, it can be done quieter. I feel very badly about it, & hope you wont object. I dont expect to get any better right off, but perhaps it may help me to become so. However I have long felt as if I should like to do it, & ought to, & I can not rest satisfied without it. Shall I take both, or only one name?[27] Perhaps better both. Now mind, if you had rather, I will wait, but I see no use, for cousin Sarah, who is the only one here to whom I have spoken about it, has used no influence, but just told me what I wanted to know. I do not pretend, to understand many things, but I feel as if it were in the main right & true, & I want to believe.

I spoke to Mr. O. about this matter, which I really feel all important, & whatever I have left unsaid, he may be able to tell you. Write as soon as you get this, & tell me whether it would be better to get uncle Baker to baptize me. Perhaps it would. I do hope & trust I shall be in time, all the better daughter to you for this, & more of a comfort to you, but I know I am weak naturally, & this strength may not make as much change as it should, but it is such a help & comfort to those who earnestly believe & trust. I will say no more, but will wait anxiously for your reply. Indeed mother I do love you so I wish you would think as I do.

Yours devoted daughter
Floride Clemson

(Dont show this)

In her letter of August 20 Mrs. Clemson again expressed pleasure that Floride was enjoying her vacation and that her relatives were so kind. She hoped to be able to welcome them agreeably in The Home.

"As to your aunt's letter [Mrs. Barton], it is simply an impertinence. I see the idea. She would like again to get a foothold, for herself & daughter, in the comfortable quarters she lost by her conduct. *Dont write her.* Answer thro K., that you thank her for her kind invitation, which you 'cannot possibly accept,' &c.&c. Not much—only enough for politeness. Dont go either to your uncle B[aker].'s. When you return home you 'have been so long absent you cannot possibly stop on the road' &c . . . . Be cautious what you say before them. You *don't know where your father is.* Your uncle is very *black.* Old Mr. Latrobe is a nuisance with his letters. When you write Mary put in a kind message for him. Your time can always be too occupied to write such a letter as you would like to send him, &c&c."

As to events around The Home, Mrs. Clemson told of neighborhood visitors, the weather, the flowers, the canary, and that Mr. Lee, "a curious compound," sent his regards but could not join the Niagara excursion. "Dont break your heart!" she significantly added. As usual she had no news from Mrs. Calhoun.

Lastly, Mrs. Clemson discussed at length Floride's queries about baptism. As she believed her daughter needed "a deep & abiding faith," she advised her to be certain that her judgment agreed with her actions. The mother gave her approval of the Episcopal Church, of Mr. Hall to perform the ceremony, and of the use of only the name "Floride." She saw no need for delay.

On August 23 Mrs. Clemson repeated her advice regarding Floride's religion and again warned the daughter not to visit certain relatives. As was her custom she spoke briefly of Mr. Lee, how quiet and uncommunicative he was though still pleasant, and of the other neighbors and doings around The Home. She asked Floride to buy her $5 worth of woolen yarn.

There was not even a rumor from Washington, to which she had not recently been. Pouring out her true Confederate sentiments, she wrote: "Even Charleston affords 'nothing new.' Thank God! That is the best of tidings for *us.* I strictly kept day before yesterday hoping the earnest faith of a whole nation might speak for us. If truth, & justice, can avail, our cause must succeed, but the ordeal is a dreadful one, & my heart aches for my people. I am very anxious about your grandmother. Mrs. C. had a letter from Ella, two days ago, & none from her enclosed—this makes the third, since I have heard, showing she does not write. Something must be wrong, & I imagine everything possible. Perhaps it may be only accidental—I try to hope so. No letters from 'the travellers' [Thomas G. and Calhoun Clemson] either. I cannot but feel this constant suspense."

Allegany Furnace. Aug. 24th. 1863

Darling Mother,

Uncle Baker, Mattie, and Mary, arrived her Friday evening. I was very glad to see them, & they seemed to take equal pleasure in meeting me again. I can see no kind of difference in Mary, except that she is a little stouter, & more womanly, she is still quiet, firm, "little Mary," & has just as little to say. She is *not* pretty, but has such a good, sweet face, that she sometimes looks almost so. Mattie looks older, and thiner. She is not at all strong, and has a more *vague,* weak, undecided look, than ever. She *seems* rather more steady than she was, & Mary says she is much more so. I dont think she *takes* here, though every one likes Mary. Uncle Baker is very pleasant, & takes particular pains to be kind to me, almost affection-ate. He wears a very long beard (none of the thickest) & does not shave at all, which gives him rather a rabinical appearance in the pulpit.

Mattie in her off hand, foolish, way, is the only one that mentions pol-itics, & even she says nothing unkind, so I must say I think every one won-derfully considirate. I myself have not mentioned politics, & to *their* own kind feelings, & this, I suppose I owe the wonderful considirateness I have met with. Indeed mother, from what I see in my hasty glances in the papers, & hear, I feel very uneasy about our noble city [Charleston]. Would it not be frightful if it fell? I can not bear to think about it. The times are indeed dark. It seems to me as if I should give a good deal to hear, & have a good *Southern talk.* Kate B. from what I hear, seems still to retain her moderate feelings, & they say she will in no way work for the soldiers, according to her promise. Every one speaks so highly of her, & the improvement, & change she has undergone. I thought she was earnest. I really feel a deep respect for one who has struggled so hard to do right, with such temptations as she has had, by nature.

Uncle Elias has not yet returned, but we expect him home to day, or tomorrow. Cousin Sylvester we also expect daily. The Clemsons have gone up to spend to day at Cresson, as they got an excursion ticket, for half price, for that place, & they must get it signed there. It only lasts ten days, so they will have to return on Thursday. Friday morning I went to meet Mr. Latrobe, according to his letter, but was happy not to find him, so I wrote to Mary, & told her of my doing; but made no appology for not writing. I also had my traveling dress tried on, by an Altoona dress maker. It will be done tomorrow. I had the body made plain, with long sleeves, &

a point in front, & behing; I had to get cousin S. to send me a couple more yards from Philla. to finish the French sack. It is all trimed with rows of brai[ds] so wide *[diagram]* half an inch.

I will write to Kate B. today, & make all due excuses. As the Clemson's seem so freindly, I may stop there on my way home, for a day or two, as they press me earnestly to do, & get Kate to meet me there, which will straighten all that matter. I think the breech may as well be healed. Uncle says you are "one of the very finest women he ever knew!" Uncle Will, & aunt Sue are away. The former sent me most affectionate messages by Mary, who says he is devoted to me! "The ways of this world are passed finding out," I think. Cousin Anna B. is not at all well. She has constant, & dreadful sick-headaches, which last longer than mine. *I* still continue fat, & well. Kate Russel, a second cousin of mine, is now staying with Carry. She is a small dark girl, about nineteen, with a fine (not handsome) face, full of character, & energy. Remember me to Mr. Lee, & Mr. Onderdonk. It seems much more than a month since I left. We will probably leave for Niagara next Monday. We will wear hats, which is customary all over the North. Break up the canarie's nest. She will kill herself setting to no good. Take away the eggs. Love to Lizzie R. Mrs. D. & F. With oceans to yourself I am, (All send love)

Your devoted daughter
Floride

P. S. We will have to hurry through with our trip as cousin Anna will have to be in Philla, at a friend's wedding by the 20th of next month.

Altoona
August 24th.

(Private)

As Mrs. Calvert wrote me that Dr. Hall had given up coming to Altoona, my dear mother, & Mr. Onderdonk wrote me a short note to the same effect, in accordance to my request that he should; I thought one Northener was as good as an other, and as you said nothing to the contrary, I got uncle Baker to baptize me yesterday. I do not know that I would have spoken to him about it, but he seemed so kind when cousin Sarah did, & so heartily glad of my determination, that I thought it would be better than an entire stranger, as I had to be questioned first. Then Mr. Buck can not feel offended at my not applying to him. Altogether I thought it was better.

When the time came, I must confess I felt very badly, but I thought it was my duty, so I did it. I wanted the cerimony to take place in the evening, but uncle said it was not customary, so I had to go up right after the second lesson in the morning service. It nearly made me sick, & I cried like a baby. The church (St. Luke's) is a very small one, & the congregation still smaller, & as few knew me, I did not mind it so much. Cousin Sarah, & Mary, stood as witnesses. Uncle, & indeed all, were very kind, & I got through pretty well, though I had to go to bed with a headache as soon as I got home. None of the family were there, as there was communion in their church. Auntie advised me to become an Episcopalian, as my family were, & there was no great difference; and then I found I liked that church best after all. I am very glad it is over, & am equally glad to have done it, for it has worried me for a long time. I took but one name, as you said. I was so much obliged to you for your kind letter, & cousin S., & uncle, thought it *beautiful*. Please tell Mr Onderdonk, as he has been so kind to me, also Mr. Lee, Lizzie, & Mr. Buck. Indeed I dont care who knows it.

Tell Jennie King[28] that Mr. Oliver, the minister, here enquiered after her, & sent his love, or something.

I have not taken this step rashly, for I have been thinking about it ever so long, & you know I was always inclined that way. I trust I shall improve more now. I hope you do not mind that Uncle B. performed the cerimony. I think it was more suitable, & I believe he is a good man, though prejudiced. He really gave an excellant sermon in the evening. Do write to me soon again, & tell me how you feel about it. I should be sorry to do anything you would not like. I do not know why it is, but I had rather do anything than make up my own mind. I trust you will find me a better daughter for this.

I do wish we could hear from grandma.—My love to all friends, I am as ever your devoted daughter

Floride Clemson.

P. S. I believe that adult baptism is equal to confirmation. See Prayer book.

Mrs. Clemson's next letter, August 27, complained about the horde of visitors that day, including the tax collector "to whom I paid the sum of $15 very unwillingly." Among her visitors were Mr. Onderdonk and the McCeney family. The latter had recently lost sixteen hands but seemed "to think they must not complain, as others have lost many more." Mr. Lee "is pleasant enough *for him,* & I believe wants to be agreeable." She reported that she had been into Washington to see a number of friends, but the clouds of dust had almost made her sick. "By the way, the bath house has been again broken open, & robbed of the soap, & soap dish, & two towels."

Turning to the war, Mrs. Clemson dismally confided: "I feel, with you, that times are dark with us, but not, I trust, desperate. As to Charleston, I fear more than I hope. Not that I think that the destruction of Ft. Sumter ensures, or *begins even,* the taking of the city, but the position is so without natural defences, such as Vicksburg had, that I fear, *in time,* it must fall. It remains to be seen whether the vandals are willing to pay the price for it. I hope they will get nothing but ashes. I also worry much about your grandmother, father, & brother, but in these dreadful times we must all bear, with patience, the share of suffering which falls our lot."

Finally, she added: "Dont go to your uncles or any where else. *I dont wish it.*"

Thursday 1863
Altoona. Aug. 27th.

Darling Mother,

I received your Sunday letter, the day before yesterday, & was glad to see you were still passing your time quietly. I have had the dumps ever since, on account of Charleston, which seems to me, to be in a bad way, by the *headings* in the papers, for I never trust myself to read more. Yesterday I took a good crying spell over the news. They are so kind, & considerate here, that for the last day, or two, they have kept the papers out of my way, & merely say: "nothing official," when I ask for the news, which I suppose protends *nothing good*. I am *so uneasy.*

I received a nice letter from Laura to day, in reply to one I wrote her last week. She never received my last letters, & seems much hurt about Mr. Lee, but I will send you the letter. I also wrote to Kate, merely thanking aunt B. for the invitation, & saying how much I should like to see Kate, and in no way commiting myself.

We have put off starting on our trip, until next Wesnesday, as Miss Cameron,[29] & some other friends of cousin Anna's, are to come on Monday to stay a day, & night. Uncle got home Tuesday. Cousin Sylvester also returned the same day. Uncle Baker left before either got back, which was fortunate, as he is no favorite with cousin S. at *least*. Mattie, & Mary, were to have gone to day, but the former was quite sick yesterday, so they will start tomorrow. They are both much improved. The one by getting quieter, & the other less so. A favorable exchange.

We have had a terribly cold spell for the last two days & the much-wished-for rain. I found my "gall body," by no means too warm, & had to put on my flanel. I wish I had a skirt with me. To day I am shivering in my traveling dress, which has just come home, & looks quite nicely. I payed $2 for making. I am too unfortunate about my shoes! The ones I had made here, are too broad, & those I sent for to Hipman, an inch too short, so I will have to send them back, & indeed I am put to it for any to wear. It is *too* bad to have such a foot!

Uncle brought *plenty* of horses from Kentucky, & nice ones too, I believe. I have been playing chess a good deal lately, & manage to come out pretty even with my opponents. Mattie [?] & I, have also revived some of our old duetts, to *our* great satisfaction. Yesterday we had quite a house full of company, to spend the day.

Cousin S. told me how sorry aunt North seemed not to see me. I must really stop there on my way back, if I can.—Mrs. Siles' son George, is dead I hear. They say he was engaged to Lizzie W. Mattie heard from cousin Annie[30] last week. All were well. Her youngest child is to be called Louisa, & uncle B. is going to baptize it this fall. They have had a very hard time.—Aunt Hetty is not very well.—We have such a joke on uncle. He was scearched, on suspicioin of picking some one's pocket in the cars! We teaze him terribly. I am as well & fat as possible.

I too am most anxious about grandmother. I wish we would hear how she is at least. I hope [?] she is not sick. I hope you got some of the late rain. I want to get cousin S. to take me to a coal mine, if I can. Remember me to Mssrs. Lee & Onderdonk; Lizzie, & Mrs. Calvert. Tell the latter I have not had time to write lately, but will try to do so soon. All continue as kindly, & *[illegible]* to me as possible, & send love, in which I most sincerely join.

Your devoted daughter,
Floride.

Mrs. Clemson's letter of August 30 gave a rather full account of the activities of their friends and acquaintances. Mrs. Stone was going to Baltimore for a day or two (Mrs. Clemson declined to accompany her); both Mrs. King and Jennie had suffered serious falls; Mrs. Calvert was ill; the Robinsons had paid a nice visit; Mrs. Perdicaris had left for Italy; Mrs. Dodge[31] and Mrs. Fone looked better; but the Gallant Defender was "poorly." She had discharged Moses, who wanted a pay raise, and had secured a substitute hand.

Mrs. Stone had reported that a cousin of Lizzie Giles "got a letter from Mrs. Ould (wife of the commissioner on our side, for the exchange of prisoners,) who says, 'you will be surprised to hear Lizzie Giles has discarded the General she came down to marry'!!! What can we believe, for a friend of Mrs. Stones, also, saw the marriage of Miss Giles, & Gen. Quarles announced in a Southern paper. Mrs. Stone still believes she is married."

Continuing, Mrs. Clemson wrote: "Yesterday I went into the city, & saw the usual set, who were all rejoicing over the taking of two gunboats in the Rappahanock & the capturing, by Moseby[32] of forty waggons, & 'from 700 to 1700' soldiers. The Confederates, 800 strong, were over the river day before yesterday, above Georgetown.—From Charleston there is no news at all. I suppose Ft. Sumter is a mass of ruins, but that has been expected for some time. I send you a *Federal* account of the difficulties yet to be over come, before the city is taken. If only our big iron clads,[33] which have, I hope, started from England, can arrive *in time,* it may yet be saved—If not, I hope they will only get ruins, & even those ruins they cannot occupy, before frost, without certain death. Unfortunately, the islands are healthy. I wish, *for their sakes,* they were dismal swamps." Again: "Dont stop at your uncles or cousin Toms's,[34] *I entreat you.*"

Sunday
Altoona. Aug. 30th./63

I take a small sheet again, dear mother, for I have very few events to record since Thursday, when I last wrote. I received your letter, written on that day, this morning, & am *so* glad to think you are well, & getting along comfortably. Must I add all of my selfishness? Well I am not sorry you miss me, for it would not be pleasant to think that I wanted to see you so much, & that you did not care to have me home again.

Dear mother, it is so hard these heavy days of trial to our country, to be away from any one who can sympathize with you, & feel as you feel. Although I meet with real sympathy, & kindness, for my anxiety, yet it is very different when one thinks that, how ever kind they are, still they are overjoyed at what makes us miserable. I suppose Charleston is doomed sooner or later to fall, & I feel miserable enough about it, & also about grandma. Oh dear!

The Clemsons left Friday, & I was quite sorry to part from them. I will do as you say, & not go to see them, as I can easily get off. Friday afternoon, I drove Sadie Sterrit to Hollidaysburg, in the buggy, as we had a visit to return & some shopping to do. We started right after dinner, & got home before dark. Our horse was a fat, well kept animal, that the weight of a score of years had made swaybacked & siff, so the whipping, & driving, being too much for one, Sadie did the former, & had the hardest work, by far. We have taken a couple of rides in the new carriage, with uncle's fine horses. Both are most excellent. It is wonderful what good taste the old gentleman has in everything. I had to get some flanel, & make myself a skirt, I was so cold. We had to make a fire today.

We have settled to start Wednesday if nothing happens to prevent. We will go, as I wrote you, & expect to spend near two weeks on the trip, as we mean to take it by easy stages, & slowly; as cousins Anna, & Sarah are not strong. Auntie is still in bed, but as it is only one of her accustomed billious attacks we do not count upon her detaining the party, as she is much better. We will be much crowded for time, as cousin Anna will have to be in Philla before the 17, which is not pleasant.

I saw some of these steel collars & cuffs for ladies, & were they not so expensive (2.50) I would get a set to travel in, they are so nice, & pretty.—We took a pleasant, walk yesterday of about a mile & came home just in time to receive three gentlemen who spent the evening here. One of them played, & sang very well.—I have had such a pleasant visit here, that I shall regret leaving, though I expect to enjoy my trip, & want to see you ever so much.—I went, with cousin Sarah, up to the Sunday school today, where there are 100 scholars all ages, & seizes. Afterwards I took a long walk with cousin Sylvester, to a hill, where there is a glorious view of the surrounding country. On our way we stopped at the family burying ground where cousin Woods[35] lies.

Indeed I do not know where to tell you to direct. We expect to spend next Sunday at Niagara but I do not know at what house. Have a letter waiting at the Leupps [in New York City] anyhow. I shall feel very uneasy at not being able to hear from you. All send love. Give my love to all & respects to Messers. Lee & O. I will try to write as often as possible but dont get uneasy if you dont hear.

I am as ever your devoted daughter,

Floride Clemson

Wednesday,
Altoona. Sep. 2nd/63

You see by the date of this letter my dear mother, that we are still here. Auntie did not get well as soon as we expected, so we put off starting one day, though that is decidedly inconvenient, as we will be still more pushed for time. However it could not be helped, and we confidently expect to get off tomorrow morning at eight o'clock. There is good in all evil for this morning I have been sick with one of my headaches, & though it was not a very bad one, still had I been traveling it might have been worse. Auntie is up and about today but cousins Sarah & Anna, have both very bad sore throats I am sorry to say. I hope there will be no more getting sick once we are started, for we have no time to spare on the road. You must not be surprised at the size of this sheet, as all my larger note paper is done, much to my sorrow. Your Sunday letter came to hand this morning, & as usual was most eagerly read, & reread.

Monday afternoon uncle took us (Sadie, Luly, & I) out a lond 25 mile drive in the new turn out [?]. We started about three o'clock, & did not get back till past eight. We passed through eight different towns & villages, & had one of the loveliest drives, I ever took. At one place there was a canal reservoir, which had all the appearance of a lake as it covered some 400 acres of land. It was surround by mountains, & fine bold scenery & had on its banks a place called Cat Fish, at which we got some sugar crackers, candy & apples. Some of the mountains about here look as if they had the *mange,* as the otherwise thick woods is intersperced with bare patches of slate. The effect is very curious. We we got back, we found Miss Jennie Cameron, Miss Mary Willson, & Mr. Blanchard here & they only left this morning. Miss C. is a fine looking, free & easy girl of 25 or so, who put me a little in mind of Miss Laine[36] in figure & style, though not half so lady like & elegant.

By the way, I really have not had time to write to Miss L. I received a sweet letter from Mary C. yesterday. It was by far the pleasantest I ever saw from her. Now mind do not expect my letters *too* hard, for I may not have time to write often. If you get this epistle without a poscript to the contrary, you may know we have started, as I will put it in the post office on our way to the depot.

We went to Hollidaysburg last evening, & in the morning took a walk to the mill where I weight 168 lbs. I am very well & fat you see. I am sorry about the Kings. Miss Cameron sings splendedly & we had some fine duetts to gether. Last evening we had a good deal of company to bid us good bye. I really have not time to write any more so must stop with much love to all & hopes that I shall see you soon, & as well as I am. Auntie & all send much love. Remember me to Messrs Lee & O. Love to Mrs. D. & all. I have no time to write to Mrs. C.

Your devoted daughter
Floride Clemson

* * *

Pittsburgh
Sep. 3rd. 1863

Here we are my darling mother after a pleasant days travel. We started from Altoona at nine o'clock this morning, & reached this place at a little before two. I am now sitting by the open window which commands a view of the Monogahela River, the suspension bridge, the entrances to several coal mines on the other side, & various manufactories of iron, glass &c. The river is very low, & exposes a bank which is paved with cobble stones in an inclined plane on which the waggons go *into* the stream to the boats which lie as near as they can.

Although we have been here so short a time, we have already *done* the principal of the sights. We have driven through the city, & visited a rolling [?] mill for iron, a glass blowing manufactory, & an iron clad ocean steamer, called the [*illegible*], which is 250 feet long. It has only the iron shell completed. The glass blowing was most interesting. We saw them making salt sellars, lamp glasses, & pressed tumblers & dishes. The rolling mill was also very interesting. In coming down here we saw the entrances to many coal & iron mines, which seemed to be very extensive. At a small place called Jackson, we saw a good many of both kinds in the side of the mountain, lying in different strata. They manufacture there considerably.

This place is by far the dirtiest I ever saw. Every thing you touch leaves a black spot on your fingers. The mud is black, the houses are black the atmosphere is dark (It has been raining & drizzleing all day) and the smoke hangs in still heavier clouds than the natural ones. There is nothing but dirt, & chimney stacks. However it is very interesting, & I would not have missed it for the world. The ride down here was beautiful, & the scenery, though not as bold as on the other side of the mountains, was fine. The Conamaugh is not near as large or as lovely as the Juniata, but still very beautiful.

We are a nice party of five, & determined to see, & enjoy all we can. Anna is still weak. We are staying at the Monongahela house, & as I started to tell when I said where we were sitting. We have aching feet (Sadie & I) immersed in a tub of cold water & as we did not have our trunks brought to the hotel, but put all strict nesscissaries in our bags, we are comfortably taking our ease in our night gowns, *en guise de robes de chambres*. We will probably stay at the Clifton house on the Canada side of the falls, which I much prefer, for I long to be out of these United States. I am almost afraid to ask for the news, I am so uneasy. Those ironclads (I saw two) made me feel vicious. Tomorrow we start at one, & will reach Cleveland in the evening. On account of our lost day we will not be able to make any stay there but will spend part of Saturday at Buffalo.

Auntie was much better when we left. I was almost sorry to go, I had enjoyed myself *so* much. I hope you will be able to read this. In hopes [*several illegible words*] be as glad to see me as I will you, I am

Yours devotedly
Floride

10 Emma Sansom, Heroine of Immortal Courage

Mary Bankhead Owen

ORIGINAL EDITOR'S NOTE.—Emma Sansom was born at Social Circle, Walton County, Ga., in 1847. Her father removed his family to the farm near Gadsden, Ala., in 1852. In 1864 she married C. B. Johnson, a Confederate soldier of the 10th Alabama Regiment. She died in Calloway, Texas, in 1900, leaving five sons and two daughters.

On JULY 4, 1907, there was unveiled in Gadsden, Ala., near the site of her immortal deed of courage, a monument to Emma Sansom, the Confederate heroine.

No such signal of honor has been bestowed upon any other woman participant in the daring deeds of those epic years in our history embraced in the early sixties of the nineteenth century.

It is true that a memorial tomb has been placed above the grave of Winnie Davis, in Hollywood Cemetery, Richmond, because she was tenderly cherished as the "Daughter of the Confederacy," having been born to the family of the new republic's President during the existence of that historic government; but the conditions are not comparable.

The United Sons of Confederate Veterans have in operation plans by which they propose erecting in every Confederate State one splendid monument of uniform type to the "Women of the Confederacy." The citizens of Macon and of Sandersville, Ga., respectively, have laid cornerstones of proposed monuments; and Captain E. White has reared a shaft to them in Confederate Park, Fort Mill, South Carolina, but so far, to the girl heroine of Alabama the distinction belongs of having reared in her honor an individual monument, which bears upon its pedestal her figure in Italian marble, and in relief upon the base, scenes from the incidents which gave her fame, together with epigramimatic inscriptions that perpetuate that fame for all time in history.

It was to Emma Sansom's memory also that Dr. John A. Wyeth dedicated his Monumental Life of General Nathan Bedford Forrest. Among the dedicatory lines is found this encomium: "She was a woman worthy of being remembered by her countrymen as long as courage is deemed a virtue," and in the text of the book he says further: "As long as the fame of Nathan Bedford Forrest shall last among men—and it must endure forever—coupled with it in artless womanhood and heroic pose will be the name of Emma Sansom."

Soon after the incident occurred which brought this mountain country girl into public view, and placed her immemorially in the hearts of all who have a true soul and brave, the State of Alabama in General Assembly adopted a series of joint resolutions donating her a section of land and a gold medal "in consideration of public services rendered by her."

To the uninformed as to her specific act, is given a gist of the facts in the eulogistic clauses of the preamble to those resolutions, in which it is told that "'she exalted herself above the fears of her nature and the timidity of her sex,' with a maiden's modesty and more than a woman's courage, tendered her services as a guide, and, in the face of an enemy's fire, and amid the cannon's roar, safely conducted our gallant forces by a circuitous route to an easy and safe crossing, and left them in eager pursuit of a fleeing foe, which resulted in a complete and brilliant victory to our arms within the confines of our own State. By her courage, her patriotism, her devotion to our cause, and by the great public service she has rendered, she has secured to herself the admiration, esteem and gratitude of our people, and a place in history as the heroine of Alabama."

Several times since this act, efforts have also been made to have the State seal changed from its present form to a scene representing Emma Sansom riding behind General Forrest, and directing him to the now immortal "lost ford."

There transpired no more heroic or picturesque occurrence during the War Between the United States and the Confederate States than the adventure in which this incident figured, an adventure reflecting glory upon all participants, Federal and Confederate alike, for it was one calling for high courage, dauntless daring, and the best mettle of true soldiership.

After the battle of Murfreesborough, Major-General W. S. Rosecrans, of the Federal army, determined, if possible, to manoeuvre Major-General Braxton Bragg, commanding the Confederate Army of Tennessee, south of the Tennessee River, in order that the Confederates might not get possession of the natural stronghold of Chattanooga. One step towards this end was to destroy the two railroads leading from that mountain city, one to Atlanta, the other to Knoxville, by which sustenance for the Confederates could be supplied. The undertaking was entrusted to a body of raiders under the leadership of Colonel Abel D. Streight, of India. The plans of "this great enterprise, fraught with great consequences," for it was thus that the order ran, were carefully laid by Rosecrans and his chief of staff, Brigadier-General James A. Garfield, with the aid and advice of the intrepid Hoosier who was to be its leader.

The commands selected to Colonel Streight were the Fifty-first and the Seventy-third Indiana, the Third Ohio, the Eighteenth Illinois, and two companies of Alabama Union cavalry, about 2,000 officers and men in all.

With impatience and high hopes the Streight raiders set out from Nashville on April 10, 1863, under orders to repair "to the interior of Alabama and Georgia, for the purpose of destroying the railroads in that country."

Upon the entrance of the raiders into North Mississippi, they were joined by a considerable force under General Grenville M. Dodge, whose orders were to facilitate the advance of Streight upon his important mission. It was the intent of the Federals to so divert the Confederates under Colonel P. D. Roddey by minor skirmishes in which they engaged them as to cause them to lose sight of the movements of Streight.

On the 26th of April, 1863, just past midnight, through almost impenetrable darkness and steady downpour of rain, Streight's "lightning brigade" rode out of Tuscumbia, Ala., over broken and boggy roads, headed for Mount Hope, thirty-six miles distant, where they were to make their encampment. At sunset, hungry and weary, having made only one halt for food, they reached their destination, with the cheering news, however, from General Dodge that he had Forrest, the "Wizard of the Saddle," whose pursuit was Streight's greatest fear, upon the run in another direction. Early morning found the raiders pushing forward with all possible progress through rain, mud and across swollen streams, buoyed, however, by the hope of success. Again at nightfall they rested, but on the morning of the 29th, scarcely beyond midnight, they once more rode off in the darkness and the rain.

Forrest and his band of 1,000 men had cut loose from in front of Dodge, and they, too, were riding through the night with its ceaseless downpour, in hot pursuit of the confident raiders, and only sixteen miles behind them.

On through these early hours the two bodies of soldiers rode, Streight bound for Rome, Ga., and Forrest bent on capturing Streight. Both forces moved along at a steady gait, and by night of the 29th, the Federals, after having swept the country clean for a swath of several miles on each side of the road, of all the mules and horses, firearms and forage, rode into Day's Gap, the gorge that leads to the summit of Sand Mountain. Here the raiders rested for the night, as quiet and supposedly secure as the Sidonians of old.

Forrest's men rode on in dogged pursuit, mile after mile, with only one hour's rest for man and beast. By midnight they were only four miles behind their quarry. Knowing that his men must have food and rest, Forrest ordered a halt, and soon his band, all except the famous "Forty Scouts," were deep in sleep upon the ground, a thousand inanimate bundles in blankets and oilcloths.

At daylight Streight moved forward, but before he had proceeded two miles his rear guard was attacked by Forrest.

The following three days' contest across Sand Mountain, as these contending foes struggled to outwit, outfight and overmaster each the other, affords a dramatic spectacle rarely equaled in military annals. The setting was most auspicious for the tragic action—a rugged country with precipitous cliffs and deep ravines, cut across here and there with leaping streams; the combatants, two bands of men who were soldiers all, patriots all, venturing for their consciences' sake that for which it is said a man will forswear all things else, his life; the roar of cannon, the rattle of musketry, the clank of crossed swords, the silences of ambush, the cries of victory, the groans of death! And over all, now April-showers had ceased, clear spring skies of the silver rays of the southern moon.

The Alabama soldiers, with the Federals, were familiar with the passes, and this fact was of service to Streight, for with his dreaded foe at his heels, and detachments circling around the mountain sides endeavoring to form a juncture to meet his advance, he seemed to be caught in a trap. As he ascended the western crest of the mountain, which is the southwestern termination of the great Appalachian range, and looked below to the valley which surrounded him, the bold Indianian saw that he was in a capital position to make a stand. He laid an ambush which was measurably effective. Counter-strategem and some vigorous fighting followed, in which Forrest's only two cannon were captured and a number of men and horses killed on both sides.

The "Wizard of the Saddle" told his band that their guns must be retaken if every man died in the attempt, and that they must dismount, hitch their horses to saplings and begin their task, assuring them that if they did not succeed they would never need their horses again. The "fiery, turbulent spirits" under him loved to execute just such desperate orders as their beloved chief was giving them, for they had charged with him at Shiloh, escaped with him from Fort Donaldson, made glory with him at Murfreesboro, at Thompson's Station, at Brentwood, and they knew the inflexible dauntlessness of the man.

From this moment there was a running fight across Sand Mountain, with death to mark the trail. Streight advanced as rapidly as possible, and when finding his rear too hard pressed would take his stand and fight or ambuscade his adversary. Forrest harried him constantly, attempting to circle around him, and steadily shooting at "everything blue" to "keep up the scare." Seeing the difficulty of his movement, because of the natural barriers of gorges, precipitous mountain sides and broken paths, the Confederate chief ordered a portion of his command to advance in "a general direction parallel with the route upon which Streight was moving," to prevent his escape by way of the crossroads, while he himself led the remaining troops in pursuit of the swift marching raiders. Streight still had Forrest's two big guns! The Confederates had been compelled to unhitch their horses from the saplings.

That night the fight was renewed, Forrest, as always, leading the assault in person. The encounter became so spirited and so desperate that the participants grappled hand to hand. When he could no longer withstand the attack, Streight ordered retreat, leaving Forrest his covered guns, which, however, had prudently been spiked. At once, with renewed eagerness, the Confederates were upon the heels of their fleeing foe. Late in the night, under the light of a full moon, there was fighting, following an ambuscade, and again more fighting following another ambuscade.

Assured of thwarting Streight's plans, Forrest allowed his men a brief respite for rest, and while they slept the raiders descended the eastern slope of the mountain, and on May-day entered the little town of Bluntsville, took a little rest, a goodly number of mules and horses, and then their departure.

By afternoon Forrest rode in and fell upon the Federal rear guard with vigor. Ten miles further away, on the banks of the Black Warrior,

Streight was again forced to take his stand and fight in order to secure a crossing over this swift and dangerous stream.

The following morning the raiders reached Black Creek, "a crooked, deep and sluggish stream, with precipitous clay banks and mud bottoms," which has its source on Lookout Mountain, "the southern limit of which range is less than one mile to the north."

Before reaching the bridge which crossed Black Creek there was an unpretentious country home owned and occupied by the widow Sansom and her two daughters. This home was entered by the dreaded "Yankees," and thoroughly searched for firearms and saddles. The only son and protector of the home was far away in a Confederate command fighting for the Stars and Bars. The indignity of this invasion was keenly resented by the three lone women, and to appease their fears the raiders' chief placed a guard around the house "for their protection." Emma, the young sixteen-year-old daughter, true to the traditional "high spirits" of mortals possessing red hair, was still in high dudgeon over the occurrence when General Forrest, a little after the "Yankees" had taken their departure, rode up to the gate. He found an eager little Confederate volunteer.

"They have burned the bridge! They have burned the bridge!" she cried, "but I know the way through the lost ford. No one else can show you. No one else knows!"

"It will take me three hours to reach the bridge above this ruined one," Forrest said, meditatively. "I cannot lose three hours. Come, show me the way."

Streight's rear guard was still posted across the river, and cannon balls and rifle shots were flying through the air.

"There is great danger to you. Maybe you had better go back," the General said to the young girl, whom he had taken up behind him on his horse in his haste to discover the crossing.

"I am not afraid," she declared, stoutly.

"Are you sure about the ford?" Forrest asked, anxiously.

"I have seen our cows pick their way over in low water. I am sure!"

As they neared the place which she indicated they dismounted and crept through the underbrush towards the ford. When they came into view of the raider sharpshooters across the river their lives were in grave peril; but the girl's courage was of the quality of the fearless Confederate leader, and she stood her ground. On they went to the very spot where a reasonably safe footing was to be secured for the daring riders in gray, winding their way down the mountain road. When his young guide had pointed out to him the zigzag course across the swift stream she returned to the little home, which from that hour sprang into existence as among the historic sites in American history, the home of Emma Sansom, the Confederate heroine of Alabama.

When Streight, who had halted in the town of Gadsden, four miles distant, to destroy some commissary stores there, discovered that Forrest was again after him, he felt that indeed he was a veritable wizard, and one, too, that was in covenant with hell and leagued with the devil.

Again the raiders went forward with determination and all possible speed towards their objective, encouraged by the hope of burning the bridge at Rome after they had passed over.

"On to Rome!" they cried. "On to Rome!"

"After them, men!" shouted Forrest, as he dashed forward, in the lead as ever, his flashing sword an oriflamme to his tired men, who, thus ordered, put spurs to their flagging mounts and with a "rebel yell" and but one will, their chieftain's will, answered: "After them!"

The Federals had to their advantage, by virtue of their advanced position, the first choice of fresh horses, which they seized without formality as they passed through the country, not only to procure fresh mounts for themselves, but to thwart their pursuers of them, and also the tremendous advantage of the deadly ambuscade.

The Confederates, but half the Federals in number, had but Forrest for their leader.

Streight sent 200 picked men ahead of his column to seize and hold the bridge until his arrival. Anticipating this move, Forrest dispatched a courier, who rode with the speed of the Persian angari to give warning to the Romans.

When Streight's detachment arrived they found the bridge barricaded and amply protected by the home guard. In the meantime, the main body, their way lighted by the moon and the stars, reached the banks of the intervening river, the Chattanooga.

The ferryboat had mysteriously vanished. Nothing daunted, Colonel Streight led his men for some miles through the dense woods, a wilderness, along the riverside, in quest of a bridge. Many of his band were so exhausted from the ride of 150 miles over the mountain and rough country roads, from hunger, constant fighting and from weary vigils, that they were sound asleep in their saddles. Finally the site of the Chattanooga bridge was reached.

It was but charred ruins, the bridge had been burned!

Still wandering through the wilderness in search of a crossing, the rising sun found the raiders worn and sleep-ridden. At 9 o'clock a halt was called for rest and breakfast. The faithful band, too exhausted to crave food, fell off their horses to the ground and slept. The tireless raider chief was the only wide-awake, unspent soldier of the troop.

A courier presently arrived, bringing the tidings of Rome's defended bridge. Rumors also floated into camp that Confederate troops were advancing to the defense of the city and the railroads. But the paramount evil announced itself—Forrest was again upon his track. Burnt bridges nor sequestered ferryboats had not stayed him. While the raiders wandered through bog and river bottoms in search of a bridge he had rested his followers. Now the pack was in full cry and the quarry in reach! It was to be a fight to the death!

Streight aroused his sleeping band with difficulty from their heavy slumbers to take up arms in defense of their lives.

A desperate, though losing fight, ensued. Seeing his victory, General Forrest sent a number of his staff to Colonel Streight under a flag of truce to demand a surrender. To accede to this demand was the only course left to the brave raider, and honorable terms were agreed upon.

To the three hours which Emma Sansom saved him at Black Creek, Forrest ever attributed this victory of his arms. Not alone was Rome saved, but one of the great Confederate lines of transportation and supply was also saved, and an historian has said that had "the Congress of the Confederate States or the President, in the light of this brilliant achievement, with the recollection of Fort Donelson, Shiloh, Murfreesborough, Thompson's Station and Brentwood, fresh in mind, appreciated the great military genius they were hampering with such a small force and had placed him then in command of all the cavalry of the Army of Tennessee, they would have brightened the prospects of an independent Confederacy, and have won the appreciation and confidence of the Southern people."

11 Woman Saved Richmond City

William Preston Cabell

ORIGINAL EDITOR'S NOTE: The following from the *Memphis Commercial-Appeal*, written by William Preston Cabell, deals with a thrilling story of the war, familiar in most of its aspects to Richmond and Virginia people but of unfailing interest, especially because of the local references:

*H*ISTORY HAS not recorded the fact that Richmond and the lives of Jeff Davis and his cabinet were saved by the art of woman. Ever since the semi-mythical legend of the rescue of Captain John Smith by Pocahontas, all the world reads with romantic interest of the saving of men by the hand of woman.

The daring exploits of Ulric Dahlgren, the one-legged boy-soldier who was only 21 when he rode at the head of his regiment, eclipsed the wildest legends of adventure of the olden time, and they are interwoven with a thrilling episode of unwritten history which reads like romance and fiction.

Early one morning in March, 1864, we were startled by the heavy pounding on the oaken doors of Sabot Hill, the charming home of James A. Seddon, secretary of war of the Confederacy, and situated on the James river, twenty miles above Richmond.

Mr. Seddon was a lawyer by profession, had been a congressman, and was a man of great refinement, experience in public affairs, and wealthy. His wife was the beautiful and brilliant Sallie Bruce, one of the large family of that name in Halifax and Charlotte counties. Her sister, Ellen, another famous belle of the Old Dominion in the palmy days, was married to James M. Morson, and lived on the adjoining plantation, Dover, one of the most aristocratic homesteads in

Virginia. Many of Richmond's inner circle enjoyed the famous social gatherings here, where the society was as delightful as that which adorned the literary circles of the British metropolis in the golden age of Scott, Coleridge, Moore, and Leigh Hunt.

Mr. Morson and his brother-in-law, Mr. Seddon, each owned several sugar plantations in Louisiana, besides cotton lands in Mississippi. Just half a mile distant was another typical old Virginia residence. Eastwood, owned by Mr. Plumer Hobson, whose wife was the accomplished daughter of Governor Henry A. Wise. Eastwood was one of the most delightful homes imaginable and the abode of refinement and hospitality. Mr. Hobson paid $2,500 for Tom, one of the most courtly and graceful butlers, or "dining-room servants," as they were in those days called. There were nine children of the Seddon home—one of the happiest in all America.

On the night before the heavy pounding on the Sabot Hill door, governor, then Brigadier-General Henry A. Wise, had arrived at Eastwood, accompanied by his daughter, Ellen, now Mrs. W. C. Mayo, a remarkably clever woman, with rare intellectual gifts and literary attainments. The governor had come home on furlough from Charleston, S.C., and was joined by his wife, who had preceded him, and with his family reunion, anticipated a brief recreation amid the charms of one of the most attractive communities in the State. He had traveled from Richmond, on the old James River and Kanawha canal, on a very slow and primitive boat, called the Packet, built very much on the plan of Noah's ark. The mode of travel on this ancient canal was something astonishing. A ditch, filled with slimy water, snakes and bullfrogs, and fringed along its banks with lily pads and weeping willows, furnished the waterway for the Packet. A piece of rope, three damaged mules driven tandem, a tin horn and a negro were the accessories, any one of which failing, caused the trip on the Packet to be suspended or delayed until these necessary paraphernalia were provided. The boat was a curiosity, and the toilet facilities for the entire ship's company were a comb and brush, fastened by chains to keep them from falling overboard, and a tin basin similarly guarded—all attached to the side of the boat on a little gangway between the kitchen and the cabin.

General Wise and Mrs. Mayo entered the Eastwood carriage which was awaiting them at the wharf less than a mile from the Hobson homestead, and as Uncle Ephriam, a famous driver, wheeled them along at an exhilarating gait, the candles twinkled in the windows, and the lights from the country store glinted on the vehicle, harness and trappings. It was noticed in the starlight that the northern sky was aglow with what was supposed to be the aurora borealis. Merry, happy greetings and joyous faces met the father and daughter as they entered the Eastwood threshold. Within, the warmth of great wood fires and the good cheer of a delicious supper banished from the good old general every thought of war, as he looked over the rich viands and array of luxuries before him, and contrasted them with the mess pork, "hard tack," "cush," sweet potato coffee, slapjacks, hoppin'-john and hoppin'-jinny and all the horrible makeshifts of food he had endured for months in camp at the front. What a feast it was! Genuine coffee from Mrs. Seddon's, sugar from Mrs. Morson's and sorghum from Mrs. Stanard's. For the first time in many months the general laid his head on snowy pillows and tucked himself away, at midnight, in a Christian bed, with linen, lavender-scented sheets, and warm, soft blankets, to dream of days gone by, when, at his own home by the sea, in time of peace, with oysters, terrapin and canvasback ducks for the feast, judges, statesmen and even presidents had been his guests. He sank to rest, in fancy hearing the sound of salt waves at his tidewater home, and the sighing of the winds through the seaside pines. A soldier of the general's command had come up with him on furlough. His home was some miles beyond Eastwood, in the back country.

At daybreak the following morning, he had sped rapidly back to East-wood to tell the household that he had heard "boots and saddles" sounded, and to warn his dear old general of the danger. The mystery of the aurora borealis was solved; for right around his home he had come upon the bivouac of Dahlgren's troopers. When he was arousing the family, the enemy was coming on the same road, and not more than three or four miles behind him. The news chilled every heart with the sense of imminent peril, the dream of peace and rest was over, and the ashes on the hearth, where last night's revel was held, lay dead. There was hurrying for the stables. In an incredibly short time Tom and Ephraim had brought to the door Pulaski, the blind warhorse of the general's dead son, Captain O. Jennings Wise, of the famous Richmond Light Infantry Blues, who had been killed at Roanoke Island, and Lucy Washington, Mr. Hobson's thoroughbred riding mare. They were not a moment too soon. The general and his son-in-law, Mr. Hobson, galloped off with whip and spur to Richmond to notify the authorities of the enemy's proximity, and the militia, home guard and private citizens were hurried to the trenches.

Dahlgren's original purpose was to cross the James River at either Jude's ferry, on the Morson place, or at Manakin ferry, three miles below, and to approach Richmond by the south bank of the James. Reaching Belle Isle, he proposed to liberate the 12,000 Federal prisoners encamped thereon, who, reinforced with his regiment, could easily sack the Confederate capital, as Richmond was then in an almost defenseless condition, the reserves having been sent to Lee at the front. There was found upon Dahlgren's body a memorandum, in which the young man had made a wager that he would hang Jeff Davis and his cabinet on that raid. But the fates were against him, as he was repulsed that evening in a desperate charge on the fortifications and later killed.

He was ignorant of the depth of water at the ferry crossings, and therefore paid a burly, black negro man from the Stanard place, who professed safe knowledge of the ferry, $10 to pilot the troop of cavalry safely across to the south bank. They had not proceeded half way across the stream when the advance horsemen were over their heads, and one of the number drowned. A retreat was promptly ordered, the negro was hanged after a "drum-head" court martial, and his body left swinging from a limb over the roadside. The neighbors allowed this coal-black corpse to hang there for a week as an object lesson to impress the slaves of the vicinage with a new idea of Northern feeling towards the blacks. I shall never forget when a seven-year-old boy, and passing along the road one evening at twilight, how the cold chills ran over me when this gruesome spectacle met my horrified vision—the neck of the darky thrice its ordinary length and his immense pedal extremities suspended scarcely three feet above the ground. When Dahlgren and his staff dashed up to the Hobson home at dawn with drawn revolvers, one of the men inquired, "Where is the man that hanged John Brown?" Mrs. Mayo, who had come out on the porch, replied, "If you mean my father, General Wise, he is not in this house." At this very moment, Mrs. Mayo could see her father and Mr. Hobson entering the woodland in a sweeping gallop about 400 yards distant on the road to Richmond. The negroes had advised Colonel Dahlgren that General Wise was visiting Eastwood, and a hasty search was made for the man who was Governor of Virginia when John Brown and his confederates were captured at Harper's Ferry and hanged at Charlestown.

A handsome stone barn on the Morson place, which cost $65,000, and three fine stables with the horses in them, were burned that morning, and there was great consternation at these three homes—all in plain view of each other. At this time Mr. Morson was on a visit to his Southern plantations, and his elder children, who were left with their aunt at Sabot Hill, could hear the groans of their father's horses in the burning stables and see the flames wipe out the magnificent buildings at Dover, while the residence was saved by the faithful slaves. Dahlgren had been told that Dover was Mr. Seddon's home, and his object was to destroy the property of the Secretary of War. At Dover, a number of the troops, half drunk, found Mrs. Morson's handsome wardrobe, replete with a variety of elegant toilettes, donned her wedding gown and other costly feminine costumes, formed a cotillion, and danced all over the yard in this ridiculous "fancy dress" apparel. At Sabot Hill, the old black "mammy," Aunt Lou, rushed into the nursery that morning, crying out, "Lawdy, chillun, git up and dress as quick as yer kin, de whole hillside is blue wid Yankees." Uncle Charles, the dining-room servant, begged the bluejackets not to burn and destroy the property of his master and mistress, and was as true and loyal as "Aunt Lou," who hurried the children to a safe hiding place. When Dahlgren knocked at the doors of Sabot Hill, Mrs. Seddon came forward with that high, womanly spirit which characterized so many patriotic Southern women when all the men were absent at the front and their homes were in danger of the enemy's torch..

The intrepid young officer, standing upon a wooden leg, and leaning upon a crutch (his leg had been amputated by reason of a wound in the ankle, received at Hagerstown, Md., in July, 1863), introduced himself as Colonel Dahlgren. Mrs. Seddon asked him if he was related to Admiral John A. Dahlgren. When the response came that he was a son of the admiral, the wife of the Confederate Secretary of War replied, "Your father was an old beau of mine in my girlhood days when I was a schoolmate of your mother's in Philadelphia." This seemed to touch a tender chord, and the Colonel at once doffed his hat and promised Mrs. Seddon protection and immunity from harm for herself and property. Whereupon she invited the gallant officer and his staff to walk into the elegant parlors of this old Virginia mansion with twenty-six rooms, and built at a cost of $64,000. Mrs. Seddon ordered Uncle Charles to bring from the cellar some blackberry wine of the vintage of 1844, and quickly a hostile invader was converted into an amiable guest, whose brain was soon exhilarated with the sparkling wine, and his manly soul captivated by the gracious diplomacy and finesse of his father's quondam sweetheart. It was by this device and strategy that Mrs. Seddon detained Colonel Dahlgren about the length of time required by General Wise and Mr. Hobson to speed to Richmond and notify her husband of the great peril to the young nation's capital, for she was advised of their flight to Richmond. Thus, it was late that evening when young Dahlgren reached the beleagured forts around Richmond.

12 Letters of a Confederate Mother: Charleston in the Sixties

Caroline H. Gilman

*T*HE SOUTHERN animus of Mrs. Gilman's letters derives a special piquancy from the facts that she 'first saw the light where the Mariners' Church now stands, in the North Square,' in Boston, 1794, and that her father, Samuel Howard, a shipwright, was one of the sixty protestants who attended the Boston Tea Party. Caroline Howard married, in 1819, the Samuel Gilman who was later to distinguish himself by writing 'Fair Harvard.' Immediately upon their marriage, the two young New Englanders settled in Charleston, South Carolina, where Mr. Gilman was ordained pastor of the Unitarian church. The greater part of Mrs. Gilman's long life, until her death in 1888, was lived in the South. She was the editor of one of the earliest periodicals for children, *The Rosebud*, and the author of *Mrs. Gilman's Gift Book* and a number of other volumes. From a voluminous correspondence extending over a period of seventy years, 1810–1880, these vivid reminiscences of the Civil War have been chosen.—ORIGINAL EDITORS' NOTE

Charleston, S. C. *(No date)*

Dear Mr. Dodge:—

Answers to your eight questions.

1. It is wonderful, considering the inexperience of the men and the crowded state of the Forts, that so few mishaps have occurred. It is also strange that, though it poured rain half of last month and the sentinels

133

have been drenched, while the men on the night boats are standing half the time in water, or in the marshes, guarding the creeks and inlets, there has not been a death from disease.

2. Of course business is in a very different state from what it would be in the palmy time of peace, but as the revolution was not sudden, people prepared themselves. Our banks were particularly provident and cautious. If it is hard to collect money, people are very patient & hopeful, which balances the difficulty.

3. With regard to young men being drafted & forced—the trouble is that they are too eager to volunteer, and become restless as clerks and apprentices. The Gov. has refused hundreds.

4. The men are building fortifications at every available point, but from what I hear from Washington and Willie, they are all willing and cheerful. I heard of one youth who refused to *sweep* under orders, but no other mutiny or discontent.

5. The idea of parties of soldiers entering houses & demanding money is the merest fiction.

6. The only family I have heard of as removing, was old Mr. Gibbon with his wife, two children, and two nurses. They all came back last week and are at their home in New Street.

7. The wealthy *are* called upon and willingly contributing to furnish uniforms, clothing to the military volunteers. Mr. Mordecai has given ten thousand dollars to the State. Plowden Weston, a member of the legislature, whose income is 75 thousand per year, has kept twenty-five thousand for himself, and given the remainder to the use of the State. It has not been published. He also entirely furnished a Georgetown company. Planters are sending rice, potatoes, etc. gratuitously. Washington says that a farmer up the road sent two loads of cabbages to Morris Island. One of the exquisites of our city, wanting some milk for his coffee, took a cabbage in one hand, and his tin cup in the other, and coaxed a stray cow to stand still while he milked her. A few of the donations are mentioned in the papers, but not one third. The merchants continue the salaries of their clerks, while at the Forts. Frank pays six, and does not employ more than two, at the Counting House. Mr. Atkinson, Frank's friend in England, wrote to him to draw on him for $100 for the city's wants.

Circles of ladies all over the city are at work for the soldiers.

That there must be pecuniary pressure by and by, I suppose no one can doubt. If Fort Sumter is attacked, which I pray God to avert, Charleston must be a city of mourners and the widows and orphans destitute.

8. You ask if Mr. Petigru and Mr. Bryan are the only Unionists. I doubt not that there may be others. So many were proud of our beautiful mother, but they are hidden by the mass who think themselves aggrieved.

I have been led to speculate on the subject of war, now that it has been brought so near. Next to the fact that all animals prey on other animals, this seems the most difficult to reconcile to the idea of a God of Love. But I must bow in humble faith, trusting that He 'doeth all things well.'

Farewell all. Whatever betide, let us keep a kindly and loving spirit, and so 'fulfil the law of Christ.'

Your affectionate Mother

Charleston, S. C., *Dec. 16th, '60*

My dear Children:—

The Arsenal in Cannonsboro belongs to the U.S. A Federal officer is in command, with a few soldiers.

The state of things seems to be this, as far as I can learn, though I have seen nothing official. When our citizens (for it was common movement) decided on a revolution or Secession, there was danger that they would seize the Arsenal, in some moment of excitement; there was danger, on the other hand, that the Federal Gov. would send more troops.

Either of these movements might have led to civil war, which was foreign to the original plan.

The Governor of our state, as I understand, guaranteed the safety of the Arsenal to the Pres. and ordered the Washington Light Infantry to keep guard. The State soldiers and the Federal officer are on amicable terms. It is a peculiar state of things, but if kept in good faith on both sides, may save bloodshed.

I had a conversation recently with James. I told him that I wished him to understand the cause of the difficulty between the North and South. I said, 'You know the old thirteen states made laws together, called a constitution, and promised to keep them. One of the laws was that runaway slaves should be returned to their owners. The North has broken the law, encourages the slaves to run away, and sends them to Canada. They do not take them home and make ladies and gentlemen of them, but put them in a freezing climate, to labor for their own living, good and bad together.

'Another trouble is about the territories. Can you tell me, James, who owned Louisiana before the U.S. bought it?'

'The French, ma'am,' said he, without hesitation.

'Well, that state, and the other territories were bought by all the States, North and South. The South paid as much money as the North and had the same right to them. After a while some of the Northern States began to say the Southerners should not carry their slaves into new territories. Of course they could not live without their slaves, who are their support, and this made another difficulty. Now the South wants to separate from the North and have nothing more to do with them. James, do you understand all this?'

'Yes, ma'am. Thank you, ma'am.'

'Now James, I hope and trust there will be no fighting, but if there is, you must take good care of me, and I will take care of you.'

'Yes, ma'am.'

To show you how tranquil I am, dear children, I tell you that I sleep alone, on this floor, without fastening my door. Can the Northern ladies say the same?

In all events your

Loving Mother

East Battery, Charleston, Aug. 7th

Dear, dear Daughter:—

I have a few moments to write you by a private opportunity to tell you of our health and welfare. *We do* see all the worst threats of the North in our papers and so are prepared, but *you* cannot see the calm indomitable spirit that prevails here. Every old man and boy is prepared all over the South. You need not be told what the military are after the experience at Bull Run; and as for the blockade, it is almost a farce. One would think that Pres. Lincoln and his Cabinet had never studied geography. They have overlooked the numberless creeks and inlets on our shores, that must, from their peculiar navigation, be the outlet for privateers, while dangerous to outsiders.

As yet we are unstinted in our wishes for the good things of this life— our markets full—dividends good, and everybody willing to bear a reverse if it should come. I write you thus, that your fears for us may be removed.

Mother

Charleston, S. C., March 12, 1861

Dear Children:—

The dearth of public amusement here is made up by the excitement of slipping the blockade. In the last month *thirteen vessels* have run out, and three steamers have come in, the Ella Warley, the Catawba, and one large steamer, now lying in full sight from my window, whose name I have not yet learned. How these vessels pass over and through Lincoln's hulks and by the fleet is wonderful. In the history of the war the daring of Southern sailors will form a conspicuous part of the picture. . . .

Frank is with us until the 20th and Willie also. They are preparing for their destination *for the war;* Washington has gone. We do not know when we shall see any of them again. If Charleston is in real danger we shall go to Greenville, where we have a house engaged.

I have said nothing about the Naval victory at James's river, for even that will be a nine days' wonder over, when this reaches you. Well may Lincoln be in tears. He with his Cabinet has made two nations weep.

I know nothing of my Island House, which is open for the soldiers. So farewell, dear ones all.

Mother

Charleston, S. C., *March 31, 1861*

My dear Children:—

I was able to give the Wilkies great pleasure, by taking them with my permit to Sullivan's Island on Friday. The wharf presents a very animated appearance from the number of soldiers and the different uniforms—the Zouaves I think the most picturesque. Lieut. W. met us at the Cove, after we had passed the guard. In a short time Willie and Washington joined us. Lieut. W. borrowed the State wagon, and putting some of our chairs for extra seats, the party were made very comfortable for a drive to Fort Washington, the quarters of the Washington Light Infantry. Washington drove me in a buggy. The first battery on the way, now finished and mounted, is the next lot to mine, the terrible cannon pointing Sumter-wise. We stopped to see the recruits (regulars) drill. The second battery is on Mrs. McDowell's lot; the third is Fort Moultrie, where the fearful machinery of war is so artistically arranged; the fourth and fifth are near the Curlew grounds, and the Myrtles. After our drive of three miles, so different from our Summer associations, we turned at East End, and saw the battery now named Fort Washington, which our boys have been blistering their hands in building. Lieut. Wilkie ordered the guns to be fired that we might see the force of their action. The first regiment of rifles, including the Washington Light Infantry, are all in tents, at the East End, and form quite a picturesque village. We went first to the Officers' tent, where Lieut. Wilkie unrolled a new flag beautifully wrought with a Palmetto symbol and recently presented by Mrs. Beauman of Charleston. Knowing where to touch the heart of a W.

L. I. man, I asked to see the old Eutaw Standard. He unrolled it reverently. It is of red damask and in tatters.

From the Officers' tent we went to Willie's. Willie was full of fun as waiter, with his tin drinking cups, and Washington was over-running with sentiment about Carrie, who was absent, and for whom he made a charming bouquet, with an appropriate kiss sentiment hidden in the centre. After about an hour of chat and inspection we drove home, with Fort Sumter in view, the calm waters and glittering beach in all their old beauty. Fort Sumter looks like a noble stag at bay, with Morris Ft. where the largest force is stationed, and James Fort bristling with cannon in the rear, Sullivan's in front; and the floating battery ready for the first note of reinforcement, for Beauregard says all is ready. When will it be surrendered? The men, ours, have finished their work, and are growing impatient of delay. It requires all the wisdom of their superiors to keep them cool. Think of so many thousand men leaving plantations, mercantile life, shops, colleges, and every department of labor, since December, and working like journeymen. The dragoons, who have been waited on all their lives, curry their own horses.

Such is my faith in peace, that I carried down a gardener to arrange my flower beds.

Mother

Charleston, S. C., April 16, 1861

My dear Children:—

On Thursday the 11th we heard that the attack on Sumter was to commence at 7 o'clock P.M. We went with beating hearts to Lou, but all was still. At ten Caroline and the children went home, and as Frank was with his company at Morris Is., I decided to remain with Lou until his return. I had an agitated night, but fell asleep towards morning. At half past four I was awoke by the signal gun, which I thought was to be the forerunner of death in its most horrid form. Then followed the action, with which by this time you are familiar. The wind was in a direction to blow the sound towards us, and from that time, until seven in the evening, we heard every gun. Instantly, after every firing on the Islands and at Fort Sumter a cloud of white smoke rose before the explosion, and thus, the sight of every discharge was as distinct as the sound. We could hear the whiz of the balls, and feel the house shake at each concussion. A strange fascination drew us to the windows, to gaze and tremble. Many friends came in and out through the day, and the most part of them were immediately employed in making cartridge bags. A group of ladies, from time to time, cutting them out in the dining-room. They are made of strong red baize, and sewed with worsted, as cotton thread ignites more readily. For the largest guns, they are about ½ a yard long and a quarter wide. Little was said, except when rumours were brought in by the few gentlemen who could call and then we clustered around them, as if life and death hung on their words. At seven, the guns of Fort Sumter stopped for the night, but all through the next ten hours, the relentless shells rose from the batteries like stars, careered in light prismatic shades over Fort Sumter, and then dropped their fearful burdens within the walls, or sent up a shower of spray outside. All the long night this went on, and amid a thunder storm I still saw them and saw too the flag we once loved so well, waving unhurt.

In the morning, a glorious morning in nature, Anderson, the brave soul, resumed fire, but about eight our hearts stood still, for a shout came from the spectators—Fort Sumter was in flames. Still the flag waved, as if only a summer breeze stirred its folds. We forgot our people, we forgot everything, for a few moments, but the gallant band within the burning crater. You know the rest. You will read of the courtesy and even tenderness of our military commanders, to a man whom they cannot but honor in defeat.

Your loving Mother

Charleston, S. C., *Oct. 20, 1861*

Dear Annie:—

Are your ladies as busy as ours are for the soldiers? The amount of work done, and the zeal which characterizes it, is wonderful all over the Confederacy.

At the Island, recently, Capt. Wagner of Fort Moultrie gave out that he wanted several thousand cartridge bags in twenty-four hours, for the Coast. Some ladies sat up all night, and we rose at daylight. Of course the order was completed. You see everywhere ladies knitting stockings for the soldiers.

Lou and I were driving, and little Lou took a small basket with pieces of carpet about an inch square, and began to ravel in the carriage. I asked her what it was for, and she said 'for the sick soldiers' pillows.' Wool is very scarce. Madame Girard has a society of little children, for the purpose, in her school. . . .

I referred a little while since to the state of our country. Let me beg you to distrust all extracts you may see from the *Mercury* against our Authorities—the editor belongs to a little clique, who have no influence of importance. Pres. Davis is almost idolized by the mass of the people, and the military commanders are still more popular.

What a curious picture the South presents, storing piles of their staple every hour; in a few weeks they will open the ground for new planting. The sea-coast only will be disturbed, and plans are laid for the negroes to fall back, after the fortifications are completed, to safe residences. The utter impossibility of simultaneous attacks on our immense coast, and the greater impossibility of the Lincolnites leaving an army of occupation behind them, renders the margin of retreat for the negroes very wide. I suppose it is pretty well understood that the Southerners do not mean to retreat.

Whatever I am besides,

Your loving Mother

Charleston, S. C., Nov. 3rd, 1861

My dear Daughters:—

The history of the Gordon seems like a romance. Three weeks ago, dismantled of her guns, dressed with flowers, and christened Theodora (God's blessing) she left this port and passed the blockading vessels with our Commissioners Slidell and Mason with four ladies and their female attendants. Frank, who is agent for the Theodora, says the young girls were as gay and lighthearted on that momentous night at 12 o'clock, as if they were going to a party, and in raptures with the beautiful roses with which Lou had decorated the cabin. Now she lies at one of our wharves, having discharged a splendid return cargo. In view of the expected attack at Bay Point, near Beaufort, by the Lincoln Fleet, she was engaged immediately on her arrival yesterday as a transport. Frank and Willie went down to her wharf last night, at 9 o'clock, and returned this morning at six, having employed twenty laborers and four drays all night.

I had the pleasure of seeing Mr. Slidell, who does not look the 'wily politician' he is said to be.

This is one of the most agitating periods of the war, as the Great Fleet is momentarily expected. A telegraph just announces that two of the Lincoln transports are aground off Georgetown, but they can afford to lose a few.

The buoyancy of our people is wonderful, and so calm too.

Mrs. Harleston was at church this morning, pale but cheerful. No one here thinks that her son and the other privateers will be sentenced. If they are, God be with the prisoners here, for man will hardly help them. The retaliation will be fearful.

Jan. 25th, '62

After writing the above, Mason and Slidell were captured, and I had no spirit to continue.

Mother

Charleston, S. C., *Feb. 1st, '62*

My dear Children:—

I think all your letters must have reached me safely; mine, giving most substantial evidence of the inefficacy of the blockade, you have acknowledged, five in all.

The second instalment of the Stone blockade was deposited one week ago, seen by observers from Sullivans Is., with good glasses. Last night six vessels went out over our bar, from our wharves, two of them probably carrying letters from me. I hoped to have sent P. D. a map of the burnt district drawn by a friend, but have not rec. it in season. . . .

My Orange Street house was struck by a shell, through the pantry, which entered the cellar without exploding.

It is no child's play here.

Your loving Mother

Greenville, S. C., *March 27, '63*

My dear Children:—

The incident of the past month has been a call from one of the surgeons on the Coast, for our Ladies Aid Society, for flags and rosettes for his department, the flags to be nailed to fences and trees from a battle field to a hospital, to designate the road, and the rosettes to be attached to the arms of those who are to carry the wounded. I volunteered at the Directors meeting to have twenty flags made, and Lou gave the material. All that were required were completed and sent seaward in thirty-six hours, but the expected attack at the last 'spring tide' has not taken place. We are now awaiting the third of April when it (the tide) serves again in our harbor.

The Confederate authorities also called on us to have a hundred sheets made for a receiving hospital in Greenville for convalescent soldiers from other hospitals in case nearer ones should be wanted after a fight. In a week the ladies had everything ready. Beauregard is a splendid officer for precaution; minute details are not below his large military vision.

One year since we came to Greenville and not subjugated!

Your loving Mother,
C. G.

Greenville, S. C., *Aug. 21, '63*

Dear Children:—

Situation public

Charleston besieged. Men fighting on the Islands, women nursing in the City—singularly few casualties. Many private families not removing. Mrs. Crafts and Mrs. Miles, for instance, are still on the battery. Supplies and men coming in. All willing to meet the emergency. Frank says we should not know Sullivans Is. The houses on Front Beach from my lot, where Battery Bee is, to Fort Moultrie pulled down and batteries in place. To-day is Jefferson Davis's Presidential Fast.

Situation private

And now, dear children, farewell. No matter if you *wish* or *fear* that Charleston may fall. Vicksburg and Hudson have gone, but look at the rallying along the Mississippi, where the abolition commerce trembles under its treble guards; so will it be in South Carolina; let Charleston be annihilated (for it never will be taken) and resistance will spring up in every new form that valor and ingenuity can devise.

In Greenville, among the negroes, you would still not think of war. Like other refugees, they are mending up their old clothes, but they are not yet losing fathers and brothers like the whites. The same merry laugh is heard, the same willing labor seen.

Your loving Mother

(no date)

My dear Annie:—

We have a constant succession of Frank's relatives and friends here. He is so hospitable that he will share his last with others. Not a week passes but we have an improvised bed, what the soldiers call a 'shake-down' in the parlor.

Willie is a paroled prisoner and came home on a walk of two hundred miles from Johnston's army. Notwithstanding *the times* he and Nina went to a surprise party last night and stayed until the small hours.

We are living in a strange way now. Isolated by the cutting off the R. R.s we have only accidental communication with the outer world, no stores for two years open; without currency; no post-office, that is, no paid P. M., and a future dependent on the strangest combination of human affairs. It requires more than Adriadne's thread to carry us through this labyrinth.

Love to the children,

Your loving Mother

Christmas Day, 1864

My dear Eliza:—

Savannah has gone; Charleston is in danger, and though they are not *the* Confederacy, and there is a strong recuperative power after every blow, yet the suffering must be immense. By the way, Atlanta has started a newspaper again, and the road is open to Macon.

The children rose at daylight to examine their stockings, for we sympathize with them. By a singular accident my gifts were quite belligerent, *fighting cocks,* made of pumpkin seeds, and worsted *balls.* To give you an idea of prices, Lou gave twenty dollars for an india rubber round comb for Louly, and $1.50 for a set of wire knitting needles. I paid $10 for the *making* of a pr. of leather shoes for little Phillis, and Lou found the material. Men's coarse shoes are $90. You should see Frank's bill for his yard family, eleven in number.

Lou had a grand present from her friend Jennie Wardlaw yesterday— sausages, chines, hogs-cheese, butter and eggs. By the way, eggs were offered at the door yesterday at five dollars per doz! And yet strange to say, we hear of no real want in Greenville.

I suppose Sherman will not turn the women and children out and burn Savannah as he did Atlanta, but keep it as a base of operations.

How that march through those feminine foes in Georgia will read in History! The cry of those ruined households will sound along the ages, when he might, like our General Lee, have made it so glorious by lenity.

Whatever happens, however, do not think the South gives up for the burning of her cities. The field is too wide for that. It will still be a give-and-take game, while our internal resources are so varied.

By the way, I just heard Frank say, 'Albert, gather me a quantity of poison berries (Pride of India) to make some blacking.' Three cheers for Confederate blacking!

Your loving Mother

Greenville, S. C., *August 5th, 1865*

If you have rec. all my letters, you will have learned, my dear daughter, that Frank after covering his wagon, and making a whip, borrowed two hundred dollars and went to Charleston to buy goods. You and Annie who have been purchasing about that amount lately, can fancy the quantity. On his return, he hired *by the week,* an empty store, and he and Willie placed their stock of Eng. goods in a bow window, and glass case, in one corner, with a bag of coffee, some boxes of herring etc. near the door of entrance. It is a large store, well arranged, and it was amusing as well as sad to see the empty shelves beyond. Every evening Willie comes home and hands over his little purse to Frank, and they have as long a talk as when they bought thousands of dollars worth of cotton. One very funny incident occurred in the store, luckily to Frank, and not to Willie. Two girls came in dressed in homespun, with sunbonnets. They fell into great admiration at the straw hats trimmed with red feathers, which Frank had brought from Charleston, and immediately selecting two, put them on. On asking the price, Frank told them five dollars a piece.

'Wait a bit' said one, and stooping a little, she raised her dress, turned down her stocking and handed out the amount in greenbacks. This is worthy of Sterne's *Sentimental Journey*.

We had no greenbacks in circulation, the garrison having arrived only two days previous, so the greenbacks told their own story.

Frank and Lou and I were driving in Main Street, when the garrison, arriving from the cars, took possession of their quarters. There was no demonstration of feeling of any kind. A gaze of curiosity in the negro population; a grave stolidity in the conquered rebels. They have been here three weeks, and our people walk opposite. By the way, I was saddened by your allusion to Peace celebration, the contrast was so strong. All here was so still, so Poland-like in its cold, stern acquiescence. I hear, however, that 'in fifty years the South will be proud of the Union.'

Did you know that all the old residences on Ashley River were burned by the Northerners, except Drayton Hall, which was used by them for a small post?

Your loving Mother

1865

I destroyed *my will* yesterday, 'circumstances having altered cases' as the copy book says. Caroline calls it *my won't*. It was with a very peculiar feeling that I ran over the items donated to all of you children and grand-children, now either in possession of a Northern soldier, or destined to be sold for my temporary support. The silver and your father's college table I shall retain.

I asked Lucas R. in a recent letter, to write you my account of the recovery of her family portraits. We have them here, and Louisa says she is becoming attached to them, as they look at us, some of them sadly mutilated, in our parlor. Gov. Ed. Rutledge we cannot recover. It is probably in some hovel. When the raiders, who came during the armistice, found nothing valuable to them in a box, they threw out the contents to the negroes and women of ill fame who surrounded them. I cannot divine the motive for their cutting the figure of the full-length by Romney from the back-ground, for it required some time to do it. We have it here. The features can all be recognized and the form is entire, but the coloring is almost lost. It has been trodden under foot, in a negro yard, I suppose in mere recklessness or carelessness.

Frank has just returned from his country trip, and there is the usual amount of bustle. I dare not dwell on the idea that we shall never be a united or loving family again. Time is a healer, but the scars are *so* deep! Poland! Poland! Will Frank ever be Annie's Frank in this world? How he did love her next to his own children!

Frank exchanged his coffee for corn, to a family of maiden ladies and decrepit old woman in an old fashioned house, and fairly set them dancing with delight. He says it is one of the drollest sights he ever saw, to see the old ladies fly around when they heard the word coffee. He says the corn crops are splendid; no starvation but—no cotton.

Now I have shown you all in these few phrases, can you fancy us as we are? With love to the dear children, your 'owny, downy'

Mother

June 2nd, '65

My dear Eliza:—

I think you will be interested in an account of the Raid in Greenville, which, occurring as it did after the announcement of the armistice, may not be published.

On the 2nd day of May, Louisa, Caroline, the children and myself, seated ourselves at the dinner table, with some pleasant jests on the subject of a roast pig, which Lou had provided, as a great treat, after a long series of bacon. A sense of calm, if not happiness, was shed over us by the thought that our friends were not in mortal combat, and we had full confidence that the flag of truce would be respected. What was our horror, then, to hear a cry from the servants. 'The Yankees are coming.' We sprang from the table, and rushing to the piazza, saw Albert throwing up his arms in a phrenzied manner, calling out 'Lord Jesus, the Yankees are coming! The Yankees are coming!' Presently a negro man, in a cart, whipping his horse to a full gallop, came tearing along to escape, but in vain; a dozen of the enemy's cavalry came after him and fired. In an instant, almost, his horse was unharnessed and taken possession of.

Not having any immediate object to pursue, the riders, who were a portion of Stoneman's Brigade, under Major Lawson, turned back and

Caroline and I went to the front gate, where she hailed them with 'Have you an officer here?' One of them rode in advance, the rest followed. 'Yes,' was the reply. 'I am Lieut. West.' 'Will you give us a guard?' 'That is not at all necessary. Our men have strict orders to respect private property.' 'But,' I urged, 'there may be stragglers, or your men may become intoxicated. Pray let us have a guard.' 'I assure you, madam, your houses are perfectly safe.'

Caroline ran up the piazza steps, and taking her baby from the nurse's arms, stood by the Lieut. who was on horseback. 'I have heard' she said, 'that some of Sherman's men tore the clothing of infants to strips. Do give me a guard for this one.' The *gallant* Lieut. stooped from his horse, took Clare in his arms, and caressed her under the boughs of the apple tree which reached his head. Our servants, twenty in number, were peeping from every accessible opening. The Lieut. glanced at his followers, and then called to a stolid looking man, and said, 'Shertz, guard this house strictly, and watch the streets. Let none of our men disturb these ladies.' Then giving Clare back to her mother, he added, 'Madam, I have been four years in the war, and I can say I have never injured a woman or child.'

'But,' said I, before he rode away, 'How is it that you come to a place like this, where there are only non-combatants, during the Armistice?' 'Oh, madam,' was the reply, 'The Armistice did not hold after Lincoln's death.' He rode off, promising to look after us. . . .

Shertz took his stand on the piazza. Clusters of horsemen passed, looked, and rode on without a question, while in other houses they were searching for arms and horses. One man came on foot, while I was leaning over the rails, and demanded coffee. I said I had been without coffee two months. 'I hear you have coffee,' said he, 'and if I find it is so, I'll be damned if I don't burn your house down.' Shertz pointed his musket towards him and he went away.

The Raiders, about two hundred in number, went to Main Street and opened the Commissary Stores, robbed the Bank, pillaged every article from the rooms of the Ladies' Association, and then proceeded to private houses and property. The Refugees from the Coast had put their property in various closed chambers in empty stores three years ago, all over the town. Everything was rifled; books, costly plate, wines, pictures and bed linen thrown into the streets to be picked up by any passer-by. All the afternoon we saw white and black, laden with goods, passing by the house.

At twilight I was on the piazza, when Lieut. W. made his appearance with a stand of U.S. colors. 'I hope you will excuse me, madam,' he said, 'for bringing my flag, which I have captured in the foundry. I hope I don't hurt your feelings,' walking into the parlor and unrolling it. 'I should be very sorry to do so. You will allow me to place it here,' extending the flag staff along the high, old fashioned mantel, and letting the colors spread out at full, against the wall.

'We are in your power, and of course you must do as you choose,' I replied.

He sat down to supper, we remaining near, but not joining. Louisa waited on him, but did not sit. After some remarks he said, 'Will you tell me, ladies, why we engaged in the war?' After a pause Lou said, 'to subjugate us and free our slaves.'

'You never were more mistaken,' said he. 'We do not want to subjugate you, nor do we want to touch a negro or your institution. The U.S. only wants her own territory, and she will have it.' 'Ah,' said he, looking up to a youth about seventeen, who entered the door, 'Here is one of my boys, Mr. Simpson. I hope you will give him some supper. He is a perfect gentleman.'

The 'perfect gentleman' had just thrown off a broadcloth cloak which we afterwards heard he had stolen from the Rev. Dr. Boyce, at the same time taking his watch. He wore a new velvet waistcoat which he had taken from a locked trunk of Mr. Burckmeyer's, that was under Dr. B's care. Immediately, on being seated, the 'perfect gentleman' said, 'Well, Lieut., how many Rebs have you bagged to-day?' 'None,' was the answer, 'but I captured a splendid number of guns, and a stand of colors at the foundry.' . . .

Starting up, the Lieut. said they were 'under orders to be off in an hour. But Gen. Brown,' he added, 'will be here with five thousand men at twelve o'clock to-night.' So they departed, taking our friend Shertz with them.

We none of us undressed for several nights, but Gen. Brown did not appear.

Two young ladies here, pretty girls, had no matron to protect them, so one of them, only fifteen years old, but quite an adept in masquerade, dressed herself like an old woman. Fifteen privates went to their house and demanded supper. She waved her hand with great dignity and said to a servant 'Give them men their supper in the kitchen.' They obeyed her orders. When they enquired for fire-arms she told a servant to bring the poker and shovel, and ordered about her elder sister with a severe manner of authority.

The Lamb family had eight hundred dollars in gold and all their jewelry, diamonds included, taken from a wagon on the road where they were sending them for security.

The Raiders pointed a pistol at Mrs. Forsyth's little son, eight years old, and called him a little Rebel. The child, who has a nervous temperament, fell insensible, and has never recovered from the shock.

I did not mention that almost every lady in Greenville had on two suits of clothes to save them. I put Mr. Jervey's new silk over an alpaca. Fortunately the weather was cool.

So ends the history of the Greenville Raid, which occurred, as I wrote before, *during an Armistice.*

Your loving Mother

Thirty thousand dollars in gold was taken from the Bank—'private property.'

Greenville, S. C., *Sept. 17*

My dear Eliza:—

Fearing that my letter of 15th may not have reached you, I write again to express my sympathy with your happiness, and approval of your choice. May the anxiety of the past settle into gentle domestic calm. My wedding day was 14th.

Frank has returned from another of his terrible journeys for goods. Willie has an assistant behind the counter in Huger Smith, Eliza Mason Smith's third son, who is to receive a dollar per day. I saw his brother Robert volunteer to bring heavy boxes into the store with the drayman. He hauls wood for the use of his family.

Mrs. Williman has not a servant left, and Mrs. Pyot, one of the wealthiest women in Charleston, with an infant, does her own cooking. These are specimens.

The negroes appear to think that even if they receive wages, besides their old privileges, the are not free as long as they are with their old masters, and you see them leaving their comfortable homes and living in miserable shanties, often seeking a day's work for food.

On the other hand, there was a Saturday picnic yesterday, where they gathered, in their Sunday clothes, and they have a school with a colored teacher.

Since the announcement of their freedom in our yard, we have not heard Albert's old Methodist hymns at his work, and Handy, who said he would 'like to be sworn at,' because it made him more 'perticular,' has been surly and disrespectful, although his wife has just given birth to a little freeman. The policy among them will be to get to the Coast, and Frank's idea, is that it is best, as it seems to be theirs, ultimately to part.

I mentioned rice fields. . . . Does it seem possible to you that in this State we should not have had any rice on our table for five months? It will probably be imported for some time to come, from the old world.

Your own Mother

Charleston, S. C., *Dec. 12, '65*

My dear Eliza:—

I closed my last Greenville letter just a month ago. On the morning of the 14th, Frank, Lou, and all the children rose at four o'clock and sat down to the last breakfast to be prepared for us by the family servants. And a nice breakfast it was, and bountifully did Lou supply our meals for the journey. Kissing the whites and shaking hands with the blacks, we departed at six.

One of the saddest spectacles on our way was the gangs of negroes, with weird, tired, hungry faces, going coast-wise to take 'possession of the lands.' Many of them, most of them, leaving comfortable homes and kind masters. But what of that?

It occupied us seven hours to reach Columbia. How gladly I would have escaped what may now be called Sherman's Desolation. Scarcely a farm house, not an elegant and hospitable plantation residence on the way, all ruin, ruin; and in Columbia the last rays of twilight were on the ruins. We were glad to leave early in the morning and start on the car for home, *Home!*

In 1858 I journeyed with a coffin, where was laid my love and earthly hope, and came *home*. In 1865 I journeyed with the dead South, and came *home*.

I found by G. Howard's kindness a furnished bedroom and parlor and Laura Geddings had superintended Caroline's room, by her request, which looks fresh and bridal. It was interesting to see the remnants of the past. Your father's Bust unharmed during four years of destruction, looking so calm, that it filled me with a sense of sacred repose. The Apollo and Diana, in their classical beauty, gave me welcome.

One great event took place. James unearthed the box he had buried in 1861, which contained the beautiful tea set Frank gave me, the glass finger bowls and various toilette keepsakes from friends. Mr. Dodge's pretty inlaid vase was ruined, also window transparencies and everything of woodwork, but strange to say, amid mould and destruction, at the bottom of the box, the framework fallen to pieces, and seemingly exposed to every possible injury, Annie Loring's face looked up with its young loveliness, unharmed.

My books, private papers, and pictures are all stolen. The pillagers must have had some object beside robbery in their selection. Everything valuable as an autograph is gone.

You remember the eight little white books your father inscribed for me and seemed so fond of; they are gone.

James came a fortnight ahead of us, laid the carpets and prepared the bedding, and we had every reason, when placing our heads on our pillows, to thank God for a home.

Soon after my arrival Mr. Stebbens called and sympathized with me in my plans for restoring the Cemetery. I was fortunate in securing a gardener, who was engaged to clear the four years débris and overgrowth for eighty dollars. I have pledged fifty of Louisa Loring's, and Mr. Stebbens promises thirty. Other persons will doubtless help on the good work. I could not help thinking yesterday, as I saw the flowers look up and smile when the superincumbent weight and decay and ruin were removed, that they set us a good example politically. But then, flowers have no memory.

And now a new era in my life has begun. My prayer for usefulness has thus far been granted. Perhaps my heaviest trial may come when that ceases.

One of my favorite poems has it,—

> At sixty-two life is begun,
>   At *seventy-two* begin once more;
> Fly swifter as you near the sun,
>   And brighter shine at eighty-four;
> For life well spent is ever new,
>   And years anointed younger grow.

In life or in death, dear child,

                                        Your own Mother

13 A Northern Woman in the Confederacy

Mrs. Eugene McLean

I BEGIN AT last to appreciate the fact of the Southern Confederacy, and that I am in and of it—though, as I look around upon this beautiful city, I hope it may escape its share of the consequences. Already, however, there is some talk of making it the capital, and a large party is in favor of it, while the residents of the city make strong objections, some fearing one thing, some another, dreading the influx of "people no one knows," while outside barbarians hint that a little piquant demoralization is the one thing needed to make Richmond society perfect. Just now, adorned with the "pomp, pride, and circumstance" of war, without its honors, it is one of the most attractive places I have ever seen.

Col. Robert E. Lee is here in command of the state forces, looking calm and cool, but much more grave than I have ever seen him, and has already impressed himself upon people as a leader.

Gen. Joseph E. Johnston is also here, another of Virginia's distinguished sons from whom much is expected; with the dashing Colonel Magruder, who accepts the war as philosophically as he does everything else, and will undoubtedly win renown. Already he is at work with his accustomed energy and will speak in loud tones when next heard from.

I see a great deal of Mrs. Johnston, our conversations ranging from grave to gay, from lively to severe, in the most impartial manner. She is altogether the most agreeable woman I have ever met.

To-day a Marylander and an old friend of my husband's came to see me, and, in the most delicate manner, begged that I would call upon him for any pecuniary assistance I might need before the return of E. [the writer's husband]. This relieves me much, as, owing to the United States Government refusing to give E. the pay that was due him, I arrived here with only ten dollars. Since that was an inadequate sum to commence life on, I had resolved in a committee of ways and means to invest in lemonades and sherry-cobblers for the benefit of myself and friends.

The Northern papers received to-day are filled with details of warlike preparations, broken roads, and burned bridges, all of which makes me feel quite uneasy about E., nor do I at all fancy the possible contingency of being launched on the revolutionary stream in my own frail bark, without rudder, without anchor, and without convoy.

Richmond.

I have passed the last three days in walking, driving, visiting. Troops are hurrying in from all directions, and as rapidly hurrying away again, though it is not proper to ask why or wherefore, and I suppose none but spies and officers in command have any accurate information. Conversation turns on "strategic points," "bases of operations." "lines of defense," and glorious plans for the capture of Washington City, while men of all ages and sizes are "deploying" about the hotels and "skirmishing" up and down the streets. The street immediately in front of this hotel is the drill-ground for a South Carolina company, and it is one of my occupations to see how naturally these polka-dancing young men take to the "double-quick." This company represents the flower of South Carolina chivalry, and numbers in its ranks Prestons, Hamptons, Mannings, Rublidges, Middletons, etc., certainly a very handsome body of men, though my old associations will forever prevent my comprehending or appreciating the status of these high privates. Last evening a Sergeant Somebody was introduced, and I received him with that sort of mental "gulp" with which I receive everything nowadays; but I soon discovered that he wanted only ten minutes' start to prove himself a most charming man, with a fund of conversation that never once trenched on war or politics. It seems a great waste of material to put such men in the ranks, but it's encouraging to know that they are willing to go; and indeed there is no sacrifice—whether of life, money, tastes, habits, or associations—that these men are not ready to make.

E. returned yesterday after encountering annoyances of all kinds, but feels himself quite fortunate in running the gantlet without serious detention. He describes the same scenes that we are surrounded by, and says the Northern people are in earnest, but feel quite secure behind their seventy-five thousand volunteers and the Seventh New York regiment. The wise ones here predict that Mr. Lincoln will have to treble and quadruple his call before long, and we hear that General Scott is of the same opinion, and is consequently looked upon as an old fogy by the "Veni, vidi, vici" kind. E. has decided to offer his services to the Confederacy, though many of his friends advise him to take an appointment under the "Sic semper tyrannis." If one must be in a revolution, I think, myself, that the center is more desirable than the circumference. I shall write you from our new capital, if I'm not completely demoralized in passing through the Cotton States. Till then, good-by.

Montgomery, Ala.

After a most fatiguing journey from Richmond, enlivened only by military manœuvers of awkward squads and patriotic speeches in every town, large and small, we arrived here about dark, and without warning were ushered into the crowded parlor of the Exchange Hotel. There sat all the world and his wife, in full evening toilette, and before I could make my escape I was recognized through the *incog.* of a thin brown veil and several layers of dust. We afterward ascertained that the house was so full that every available spot was covered with cots, and nothing of the reception-room left but the name over the door. Accordingly, E. left me so seek accommodations, and my observations led me to the conclusion that, though the scene was changed, the actors were not.

I had not more than time to take a general survey of the small fry before E. came in with Major B., to say that he had secured a room at the Washington Hall, of which we took immediate possession, and in which I am now writing as well as the extreme heat of the weather and the mosquitoes will permit.

Yesterday I drove over the town with Mrs. Jefferson Davis, and was delighted with out new capital. There are some beautiful residences, with flower-gardens attached, while the State Capitol, in which the Confederate Congress holds its sessions, is a most imposing-looking building, situated on a hill which commands a view of the whole town. The Congress is known as "the Provisional," and is said to be acting with great unanimity, passing laws every day without the excitement of a shadow of opposition.

The uniform of the Confederacy is to be gray, with insignia of rank on the collar and sleeves. The ornaments are well enough, but I fancy a whole army in gray will look lugubrious. The flag is very much like the United States flag—the same colors, with the blue field and white stars; but, instead of the stripes, three bars of red. At the President's I saw a very poetical one made of flowers and sent to Mrs. Davis by the young girls of a neighboring seminary. The bars were red and white roses, the blue field was larkspur, and the stars were jasmine, so ingeniously woven together that it could be handled without falling in pieces. Many persons object to the Confederate flag because it is so like the Union one. I like it for that very reason, though it can never recall as many pleasant associations, whatever it may become in the future. The President occupies a very pretty cottage in about the center of the town, and there Mrs. Davis has her weekly receptions, at one of which I was present yesterday. I saw little to distinguish it from ante-revolutionary gatherings. No homespuns as yet, though the more enthusiastic talk of adopting them, and I suppose they will when everything becoming is exhausted.

The atmosphere of Montgomery is certainly much less warlike than that of Richmond, or any other place I have been in, nor do people seem to be half so much in earnest, while it is said the Government itself is not making the most strenuous exertions to put the country on a war footing. The different states are sending to Europe for arms and ammunition, but an official said the other day that the Government intended to take them from its enemies. Yesterday E. mustered into service a regiment of fine-looking men, said to represent fabulous wealth, as the best and wealthiest men are going into the ranks. It makes me sad to see them, and I cannot help believing—in that little corner of my brain which ought to be paralyzed for the present—that those who are left will find little difficulty in counting their fortunes by the time the war is over.

Mrs. Davis has made herself somewhat unpopular by saying openly that she has no personal feeling against her Northern friends, of whom she likes to talk, and takes great interest in their welfare. It is almost a pity she says so much, as there are always some who are willing to use it to her disadvantage, for already jealousies have crept into our model republic, and some, of old standing, have been imported with congress and other respectable institutions. How long will it last?

Richmond

How shall I describe the events of the last ten days, or give you any idea of the feeling by which I have been agitated? It seems as if ten years had rolled over my head, and that the scenes of suffering I have witnessed had burned themselves into my heart, withering every association of the past and every hope of the future. We have talked of battles, and said that they were fought here and there, or would be, but the 21st of July, 1861, made us realize for the first time what war means.

The day dawned quietly, calmly, beautifully. Although we knew Mr. Davis had gone to Manassas Junction, we never suspected the object, but enjoyed the day as one of rest, few of us even going to church. Nor was there anything to disturb the calm, except the sad duty of attending the funeral of a friend's child at five o'clock in the afternoon. I remarked to Mrs. Davis and Mrs. Johnston, who were in the carriage, that the people in the streets looked excited and I thought there must be some news, but they laughed at my nervous fancies, and I was somewhat reassured by Mrs. D. saying that we would certainly know if there was any news of importance. However, upon our return, I again remarked the same anxious expression on every countenance, and, more to convince me of my error than anything else, Mrs. D. asked a gentleman who was passing if there was any news. "Yes, madam," he replied, "they have been fighting at Manassas since six o'clock this morning." I do not know how we got into the hotel, but when there we were met by the ladies, who had just received the same information, and were perfectly beside themselves with terror and anxiety. There were ten of us whose husbands were known to be on that field, while all the others had sons, brothers, or some near relation, and one poor lady's family was represented by her husband, two sons, a brother, and a brother-in-law. Three hours passed in this suspense before we received a private telegram from Mr. Davis, with a list of officers killed and wounded, which, while it relieved most of us, brought a crowning sorrow to Mrs. Barstow. Fortunately she was not in the room when it was read, and we were enabled to defer until the next day a communication which no one felt willing to convey. So we retired to our rooms with grateful hearts, though death came too near for us to feel any elation at Mr. Davis's other telegrams, which announced to the people victory, in these words: "We have won a glorious, though dearly bought victory. Night closed on the enemy in full flight and closely pursued."

The next day was one of clouds and darkness, with a pouring rain which disturbed the working of the wires. For nearly twenty-four hours we were without another word from Manassas, and no one would have imagined Richmond to be the capital of a victorious people. It seemed as if a pall had fallen on every house, and people spoke low to each other as they waited to learn with what price victory was bought. Every family had its representative with the army, and the women who had talked so freely of their willingness to sacrifice them were bowed down to the dust, fearing they might be called upon. Among ourselves, with that poor stricken woman in the midst of us, there could be nothing like rejoicing, and one of our number, coming out of her room, said, "God help us if this is what we have prayed for!" The day wore on, and it was not until late at night that telegrams began coming in, each one bearing its message of joy or sorrow; but by the morning of Tuesday, which opened brightly, the Richmond people began to look up. There was more of good news than bad for them, and by the time Mr. Davis had returned and had addressed them in one of his stirring speeches they were almost wild with enthusiasm. To me, one of the saddest moments in all that time was when everything appeared the brightest—when Mr. Davis had returned, and the parlors were illuminated, and friends were congratulating one another, and the street in front of the house was crowded with a multitude cheering for "the President," "the Confederacy," "the Generals," and "the Army"; while, like a passage in the minor key in some brilliant piece of music, I heard at a distance the "Dead March," and knew that the bodies of General Barstow and General Bee were being escorted to the State Capitol. I left the parlor feeling that, let war bring what it would, I should always hear the accompaniment of that sad note. The next day the bodies lay in state in the Senate Room, where they were visited by hundreds. Eloquent eulogies were pronounced by their personal friends, and the determination to avenge them recorded on high. The trains also began to bring in the wounded. Richmond threw open the doors of its private houses, and ladies who would have shrunk a few days before from the sight of blood devoted all their time to dressing wounds and caring for the sick.

On the fourth day after the battle Mrs. Johnston and I, hearing of a good opportunity to go to Manassas, procured the necessary permission from the Secretary of War, and, without listening to any remonstrances, took the early morning train.

On the way we met the train containing Union prisoners, but they seemed to enjoy their situation so much, laughing and singing, and were such a horrible-looking set, that we felt it would be going quite out of our way to sympathize with them, tacitly agreeing to look on them as so many curiosities. Upon our arrival at the Junction we were met by General Johnston and several officers of his staff, who conducted us in safety through the scene of confusion that surrounded the depot. There were congregated, the sick, the well, and the wounded, Unionists and Disunionists, conquerors and conquered, people who had just found their friends, and others, alas! who had given up all hope of ever seeing theirs in this world, while surgeons and hospital attendants were either placing those of the wounded who could be moved into the return train, or anxiously looking for the medicines and little comforts that were expected from Richmond. By some strange carelessness or oversight the medical department found itself, after the battle, deficient in the very articles it most needed, and many a poor wretch lay there groaning when a little morphine would have relieved him. We were successfully pushed and piloted into the carriage that stood in waiting, and soon reached the headquarters, a small farm-house with nothing to distinguish it but its temporary occupants. Almost the first things we saw were the captured cannon, and the first thing we heard was an account of the thirty thousand handcuffs that had been taken. This hinted at such an uncomfortable state of subjection that I worked up a very respectable feeling of rebellion, when a well-meaning but stupid man informed me there was nothing in it—that one box of handcuffs was taken, and that it was quite proper an army of that size should have that number. I thought to myself that shackles for the feet would have been more useful under the circumstances.

In a few moments E. came in to say that his "mess" were in readiness to receive and welcome us; so, declining the kind invitation to remain in the house, I walked over to the encampment and found it just what might have been expected. However, in times of excitement creature comforts are a matter of minor importance. After a fatiguing day's journey one can sleep very well on a camp cot, with nothing to separate one from the outer world but a Sibley tent—more especially if one feels, as I did, that everything had been done to render it as comfortable as circumstances would permit. It was not until the next morning, when I discovered that my occupancy of the tent had obliged all the gentlemen to bivouac under trees, that I fully realized what an unjustifiable imposition I was. Tents, it seems, are not among the superfluities of the Confederacy; and indeed, the more I see and hear, the more impressed am I with the belief that we are going to war with very few of its requisites. But what surprised me more than all else was to hear intelligent men express the opinion that the war was over, that this one battle had decided it. They have convinced themselves that the North can never raise another army. If this should prove to be so, I trust that I shall be quietly removed from all participation either in the self-complacency of the South or the pusillanimity of the North. As a people, we are given to boasting. I look forward to the future with great horror, whichever party is victorious, but privately entertain the idea that neither will be till both have suffered enough to teach them a proper respect for each other. I remember hearing some gentlemen in

Washington discussing this very question, and they agreed that the North needed a defeat to unite it—opposite views, I confess, but I give them to you for what they are worth.

Of course I heard many interesting incidents of the battle, each one having an experience of his own to relate. I also heard a great deal of the technical part of it, which I did not understand, and when I was taken over the field I knew less than I did before. If you are so behind the times as to imagine that a battlefield is anything like the pictures you see, disabuse yourself of the idea at once. If you suppose, as I did, that two lines of men are drawn up opposite to each other on a level piece of ground with nothing to do but fight, you confess a lamentable ignorance. This battlefield covered some seven miles in extent. In that territory there may have been some level spots, but I saw nothing but a broken country interspersed with woods, streams, and quite respectable little hills, and when I heard that the enemy advanced in such and such a direction, and perhaps some two miles distant was shown the exact spot where some brilliant manoeuver dislodged or scattered that enemy, you will not wonder that I could not understand, though General Beauregard himself condescended to explain. By the by, he looks like one of Napoleon's marshals, and was evidently meant for a soldier. The only facts I really appreciated were the numbers of new-made graves, and the atmosphere, which in some portions of the field was almost insupportable.

I also fully realized the situation of our old friend Captain Ricketts, who is wounded and a prisoner. He is in a house at about the center of the field, which, because of the convenience of its location, was converted into a temporary hospital. There I found Federals and Secessionists occupying adjoining rooms, all suffering alike and all miserable for the lack of some articles which a little forethought might have provided. Hearing that Captain Ricketts was in a deplorable condition, I ransacked the mess-chest for such things as I thought he might need, and succeeded in raising a bottle of brandy, some rice, and some sugar, which, with the only blanket we had, I was conveying to him, when, in passing the room that adjoined his, I saw a young Middleton of South Carolina lying on a heap of straw in the corner, gasping his life away from exhaustion. His wound had been pronounced mortal from the first, but, having no stimulants to give him, his poor father and brother, who sat beside him, felt that he was dying sooner than he needed to. I shared the brandy I had with them, and, after making some arrow-root, went into the next room, where lay Captain Ricketts and several other Federal officers. Mrs. R. had arrived the previous evening from Washington and was doing all that could be done with their limited means and poor accommodations. The Captain was suffering dreadfully from his wound, but was better off than the Confederate wounded, as he lay on a camp cot instead of on the floor. He never alluded to the battle except once, when he pointed to the place where he lost his guns and where young Ramsay was killed. Mrs. R. described the scene that greeted her as she entered the house, not knowing whether her husband was dead or alive, and fearing to glance at the large table in the lower hall, which, she told me, was an amputation table, on which lay stretched a man who had died under the operation. Then the groans of the wounded and the shrieks of the dying met her ears, and she felt absolute relief when she found her husband no worse than he is, though it is by no means certain he will not lose his leg. I had known and liked Captain R. so well in happier times that I was completely overcome as the contrast between past and present rushed upon my mind. The other officers were slightly wounded, and, I thought, looked on in that cold, critical manner that people sometimes assume when dissatisfied with themselves and everybody else. After leaving them I saw one of the medical directors, and asked him to procure, if possible, some more comfortable place for Captain Ricketts and his wife; but he said they preferred to remain where they were; and indeed Mrs. Ricketts thought it was better for the Captain to remain with his friends, while she was willing to submit to any discomforts for herself.

Just as I had bade the Ricketts a tearful good-by I saw in the room opposite a pair of eyes glittering with such an extraordinary expression that, without asking any questions or looking to the right or left, I walked straight up to them and, laying my hand on the head of the apparition, asked if there was anything I could do. The eyes rolled toward me, and, without any change in that same glittering look, their possessor told me that he was from Brooklyn, had been wounded, had had his leg amputated twice, once by a Federal surgeon, and once by a Confederate, and was waiting for them to come and cut it off a third time, adding, with a resolute air, "But I can stand it as long as they can." His voice never faltered till he spoke of his mother, to whom he asked me to write. While I was taking down the address he caught my hand, saying, "I will write myself," and without the least perceptible tremor he wrote a short note which I have this day mailed, but which was such a curiosity, considering the condition of the writer, that I showed it to several surgeons, who pronounced it as wonderful as the incident told of Marshal Lannes, who smoked a cigar while his leg was being amputated.

I found some few of the constitutional grumblers dissatisfied because our army had not pushed right into Washington, but the majority were content to believe that there never had been such a victory, and never would be, unless the Yankees should have the temerity to fight again. A few, a very few, acknowledged that it had been a hard day's struggle, and considered Kirby Smith's opportune arrival providential, while they seemed to think that it would have been quite impossible to do more, considering the fatigued condition of the men. Some of them went into battle after a half-day's march, and all of General Johnston's men had been marched and counter-marched for the two weeks previous. Besides, there was a great deal of confusion among the independent gentlemen soldiers, who had done all they thought necessary for the time.

Every one agrees that General Johnston is magnificent on the field, but the friends of Beauregard claim for him the entire credit for the plan of the battle, which the others are not willing to yield. Mrs. Davis gives equal credit to both, and one would suppose there was glory enough for all; but military men seem inclined to be monopolists in this respect, and from present appearances I think it not unlikely that the more battles we fight with the enemy, the more "scrimmages" we shall have among ourselves.

E. returned with me, completely broken down from the effects of diphtheria and the exposure and fatigue to which he had necessarily been subjected. The night after the battle he, with General Johnston and all the staff, slept under a tree. He says they were so tired that they were only too glad to find any place to lie down. He is now in the hands of the physicians, who have prescribed entire rest and sulphur baths. We leave to-morrow for the Montgomery White Sulphur Springs. I have been so much occupied in getting ready for this hurried start that I know nothing of the *on-dits* of the city; I hear the battle is the only thing talked about. A Washington paper received to-day almost claims a victory for the Federals, and is minute in its description of the cannon, which have been placed in the square to show that none fell into the hands of the enemy! Private accounts from there, however, represent an immense amount of consternation and confusion. A great many letters were picked up on the field, most of them a disgrace to the language in which they are written, and I cannot imagine what part of the United States could have produced the writers; but I cease to be astonished at any kind of brutality or demoralization that this war may develop since hearing of a New Orleans "tiger"—as he called himself—displaying a toothpick and candlestick made from the bones of a dead Yankee. What a deliverance the war would be if it would only kill off such wretches on both sides!

Memphis (Early Winter).

Will you believe it? I have been in a battle! And, availing myself of the privilege granted to "veterans," will henceforth tell the story on all occasions. Left Memphis about a week ago for a little trip to Columbus, where I had some business, taking passage in a Government boat which did not carry passengers, but had a place fitted up especially for us, so that I was the only woman on board, though there were some half a dozen gentlemen in the forward cabin. The weather was delightful, and we had a charming time, stopping long enough at Fort Pillow to walk over its very extensive but unfinished works. As we approached Columbus we heard rumors of a battle; but such rumors are always afloat, and in this instance gained no credence, though, as we neared one of our batteries on the Missouri side, a shot across our bow led us to suppose that we were to stop for some reason. We were about obeying the mandate when one—two—three—four—five—ten shots were fired at us, not one hitting us, though two went between the boilers, and all came near enough to scare us considerably. As it was evident by this time, the enemy had possession of our guns, and were turning their fire against us. Why we were not struck I cannot imagine, a steamboat being an uncomfortably conspicuous target when one happens to be in it—as was keenly realized by an unfortunate Irishman of the Bob Acres school. For myself, not appreciating the danger, I did not dread it. Indeed, I was engrossed in watching the Irishman, whose first movement was to divest himself of a uniform coat and red sash, in which he had "splurged" most satisfactorily, while in piteous accents he entreated the captain to turn the boat, exclaiming, from time to time, "Thirs shills! Thirs shills!" So I was thinking less of the cannon than of the coward, as the more novel sight of the two. I will also divulge to you, in strict confidence, that it was my intention, if things got much worse, to creep under my berth, having always had an ostrich inclination to hide my head in case of alarm. But not a word of this, for I woke next morning to find myself a heroine, and have not felt called upon to disprove it.

As soon as the boat could be turned and rounded to, at a wooding-place, the gentlemen went on shore to make inquiries, but could learn nothing very satisfactory from the only persons they met—the stragglers and the "lame who started early"; who, to justify themselves, were obliged to represent the Confederates as being cut to pieces, Columbus evacuated, and all in full retreat. This being the only information to be procured, G. gave it as his opinion that the boat had best proceed to Columbus, as, in case of disaster, it would be needed; and accordingly we

prepared to run the gantlet again. But there is a tide in the affairs of battles, as in everything else, and by the time we were opposite the battery
again the Federals were in retreat, making for their gunboats, and closely
pursued by the reinforcements that General Polk led onto the field about
two in the afternoon. The United States troops under General Grant
attacked General Pillow at Belmont (opposite Columbus) in the early
part of the day, with complete success, but were forced to retire later,
losing all they had gained, and leaving their dead and wounded on the
field. All this we learned from an officer who stepped on board the instant
the boat touched the Columbus landing, with an order that it should
proceed at once to the opposite, or Belmont, side.

There was, of course, no time to get my things together and disem-
bark, therefore I stayed on board, not sorry to keep up the excitement,
and without any idea of the ghastly sights I should see. First, some prisoners were brought on, poor, miserable, dejected-looking creatures, with
whom I could not help sympathizing, as they were forced to listen to the
taunts and jeers of the common men on the boat. I was roused to active
demonstrations at hearing them say to a wounded officer: "Let him lie
on that pile of bricks—it is good enough for him"; and I went in search
of Mr. McLean, who saw him as comfortably placed as was possible, and
gave him some brandy, which restored his failing strength, but failed to
impart a gentlemanly politeness. He took all that was offered to him, as a
matter of course, and in response to Mr. McLean's kind inquiry as to
where he was wounded, gruffly replied, "In the back, sir, but not in running away from the enemy." "I should not have insinuated such a thing
under the circumstances, whatever may have been the probabilities," said
Mr. McLean, turning away disgusted, with the remark to me that "the
United States uniform did not inevitably cover gentlemen nowadays." I
thought little more of him, one way or the other, as by this time other
wounded were being brought on board.

While bathing the face of a man in the agonies of death, I chanced to
look round, and there by my side were thirty or forty corpses that had
been brought on board, rolled in the blood-stained blankets in which
they had been carried from the field, and wearing every expression by
which the human face is distorted. I had always heard that persons dying
of gun-shot wounds preserved a happy expression, but on those ghastly
faces was fixed anger, revenge, suffering, and one man, with a demoniac
stare in his eyes, had his right hand raised and clenched, as if to defy death
itself. Of all who lay there I saw but one who seemed to have died in
peace: a young boy of about seventeen, with light hair, beautiful features,

and a heavenly expression, as if he had been translated far from that scene of woe and suffering. As I looked in his large blue eyes that no kind hand had closed, I thought of the distress awaiting those to whom he was dear, and, stooping down to brush his hair aside, could not restrain the tear which fell on his white face, seeming to mar its placid purity so much that I hastily wiped it off, feeling as though he had silently reproached me for my sorrowing. Among the sufferers was a son of General Pillow, who received neither more nor less attention than any one else; all lay crowded together, dead and dying, friends and enemies—civil war in all its hideousness! I wished that the picture could have been daguerreotyped on the brains of those who let us drift into it—it would have been punishment enough, even for them.

When the boat was filled with its pitiable cargo we returned to the Columbus side of the river, where ambulances were in waiting to convey their temporary occupants either to the hospitals or to their graves. We went to General Polk's headquarters, but found it entirely deserted, nor did the General and his staff return until nine o'clock at night. The firing across the river became more and more animated till darkness closed on the scene, while the town of Columbus itself was rendered as unsafe as the battlefield by the irregular and constant firing of the volunteers who were left there, and who expended their excitement by shooting at everything, anything, or nothing. I was more alarmed than I was on board of the boat, and did not at all relish the idea of being accidentally shot. When General Polk and his staff returned, flushed with victory and proud of the day's deeds, reveling in the excitement of danger met and overcome, and recounting to one another their individual experiences, I felt that I could have been a soldier myself; I forgot for the moment the dark side of the picture, and wondered if these men could ever degenerate again into every-day mortals. There is something electrical in glory, and the old General, with his head thrown back and his eyes sparkling with the fire of youth, seemed more like a paladin than a bishop of the Church, and it would be difficult for any one in his presence to condemn his exchange of the miter for the sword, so thoroughly is he persuaded that he is right.

Later in the evening, all the glamour of war faded out of our minds as we saw G. W. Butler, of Louisiana, brought into the house mortally wounded. He was a great-grandson of Martha Washington, and had just returned from Europe, where he had been attached to various legations. His handsome personal appearance and chivalric bearing had attracted attention as he went into the battle which Fate had ordained should be his first and last, and there was something so noticeable about him that after he was wounded and the Federals were in retreat a United States officer, who chanced to see him, dismounted, gave him some water, and threw his own blanket over him, saying, "Poor fellow, I wish I could do more for you!" I shall never forget the scene as I entered the room. The wounded man lay on the trestle which had borne him from the field, his younger brother leaning over him in great distress, while a brutal doctor announced in loud, harsh tones that there was no hope, and therefore no use in doing anything. He refused even to dress the wounds, so that Butler's shattered arm lay just as it had been struck, while his life blood welled from a wound in his breast. I never felt more indignant, and, taking the doctor aside, observed that at least a little morphine would ease the sufferer. "Nothing will do him any good or any harm, and I have no morphine to waste," was the response. During this colloquy, I shuddered to perceive that pain had not so deadened the sufferer's faculties that he was prevented from hearing every word. But he beckoned to me, saying in the gentlest manner, but with all the spirit of his race in his eye, "Never mind, I know I am dying, but I shall have proper attention"; and from that moment he seemed to revive, while I administered stimulants from time to time, determined that if human means could save him he should not die. Alas, all our care and all the surgical skill that had been exhausted on him were in vain, and after deluding us with false hopes for some twenty-four hours he passed quietly away without a struggle. In those few hours, I felt as if I had gained and lost a friend. All the pain and agony that he suffered seemed to reveal in stronger relief his many noble traits of character and his gentlemanly breeding—his firmness, his gentleness, his delicate consideration for others, that never left him till the end; and as I afterward saw him lying in his coffin, with the Confederate flag folded over him, I felt for the first time that those colors were sanctified. If *I* feel so, how dear must they be to those who have sacrificed their all to it! General Polk was with Major Butler when he died, and offered one of the most earnest prayers I have ever heard. Immediately afterward he said to me, with a great deal of feeling, "What a terrible scourge is this war!"

If I could only get up a wholesome, hearty hatred for one side or the other side, it would be so sustaining; but my wishy-washy way of sympathizing with everybody that happens to be hurt is perfectly contemptible, and I am losing all self-respect. By way of encouraging a more healthy frame of mind, however, I have taken to knitting socks, in the hope that I shall become so raveled up that there will be no extrication; besides, an enlightened public opinion demands a certain number of these articles from every woman's patriotism. Accordingly, I have been cramping my fingers and puzzling my brain in "heeling" and "toeing," "rounding off" and "taking up," till I am at times entirely oblivious of the weightier matters of the war, though never of the conversation that usually accompanies this engrossing occupation when we patriots meet, with our respective socks in their various degrees of advance and decline. "Our poor soldiers" is echoed in every possible inflection of the female voice, and, like a game of ball, it is only necessary to keep it up to insure complete success. Occasionally an energetic woman, with a superabundance of vitality, breaks out against the "Goths, Vandals, and infidels of the North," but it is not necessary to notice it if you knit. So, if you wish to picture me to your mind's eye, fancy a coarse, misshapen sock with a subdued appearance at the other end of it, and you will have all that is left of Margaret Sumner McLean.

The telegraph announces this morning a terrible accident at Columbus. It seems that a new gun, which was being tested, exploded, severely injuring General Polk and killing several officers and soldiers. I feel as if every step were on a grave.

To-morrow we leave for Richmond, and, thanks to the "bridge-burners" in East Tennessee, we shall be some six days *en route*. With "foes without and fears within," it needs a St. Paul to possess one's soul in patience.

14 "Lieutenant Harry T. Buford," C.S.A.

Richard Hall

I

To be a Second Joan of Arc [proved to be] a mere girlish fancy, which my very first experiences as a soldier dissipated forever.
— Memoirs of Loreta Janeta Velazquez

O N A HOT summer day in Washington, D.C., July 20, 1861, the Federal hierarchy had decided that it was time to take decisive action. A Confederate force under Brigadier General P. G. T. Beauregard was in position near the vital Manassas railroad junction, a scant twenty-five miles west and south of the city. A Federal army commanded by Brigadier General Irvin McDowell was sent to drive them away, and destroy them if possible. A crowd of picnickers and onlookers, including some government officials, tagged along expecting to see a glorious spectacle.

The battle of First Bull Run (or Manassas) on the next day was the first large-scale clash of armies during the Civil War. For many regiments on both sides, it was their first exposure to all-out combat. Many of them approached it with enthusiasm, under the common self-delusion that they would quickly dispose of the enemy; it would be a short and glorious war. A number of regiments on the field had been enlisted optimistically for only three months' service. For the most part, the green troops were led by ill-trained and inexperienced officers.

On the Confederate side, eager for battle, was a young "independent" lieutenant, Harry T. Buford, not formally attached to a specific unit.

167

Unbeknownst to fellow officers, "Lieutenant Buford" was a woman in male disguise, complete with artificial beard and mustache. Her real name was Loreta Janeta Velazquez. Born in Cuba from a wealthy family, she was raised in New Orleans, Louisiana, by an aunt. She was able to pay for all her own supplies and equipment, and sought combat assignments or commissions from battlefield commanders on an opportunistic basis.

Traveling with Velazquez, and apparently unaware of her female identity, was a black servant, Bob. They had participated in the skirmish at Blackburn's Ford on July 18th and helped to bury the dead. When a company commander was killed, "Lieutenant Buford" had been placed in temporary command. Now "Buford" was eager to distinguish herself by leading the company in battle before being replaced by a more senior officer. All Velazquez wanted was "an opportunity to make a first-rate display of my fighting qualities."

On July 20th, Confederate reinforcements arrived on the field near Manassas Junction, including Barnard E. Bee with the 4th Alabama and 2nd Mississippi Regiments and a few companies of the 11th Mississippi. For part of that day, "Lieutenant Buford" served as a courier for General Barnard Bee, and that night fell into a deep and dreamless sleep. She later recalled:

> I had fancied that sleep would be impossible to me under such circumstances; but a very little experience as a soldier was sufficient for me to be able to fall into a soldier's way of doing things, and I soon learned to take my rest as naturally and composedly upon the bare ground as if on the most downy couch, and not even the excitements and anxieties incident to an impending battle could prevent my tired eyes from closing after a long and fatiguing day passed under a broiling July sun.

Next morning the battle commenced. From the Confederate perspective, clouds of dust rising from tramping boots signalled the approach of the enemy.

Velazquez later reported in her memoirs:

> The morning was a beautiful one, although it gave the promise of a sweltering day; and the scene presented to my eyes, as I surveyed the field, was one of marvelous beauty and grandeur. I cannot pretend to express in words what I felt, as I found myself one among thousands of combatants, who were about to engage in a deadly and desperate struggle.
> The supreme moment of my life had arrived, and all the glorious aspirations of my romantic girlhood were on the point of realization. I

was elated beyond measure, although cool-headed enough. . . . Fear was a word I did not know the meaning of; and as I noted the ashy faces, and the trembling limbs of some of the men about me, I almost wished that I could feel a little fear, if only for the sake of sympathizing with the poor devils. I do not say this for brag, for I despise braggarts as much as I do cowards.

Loreta Janeta Velazquez's childhood fantasy was coming true. As a young girl she had eagerly read books about kings and princes and soldiers. "The story of the siege of Orleans, in particular, I remember, thrilled my young heart, fired my imagination, and sent my blood bounding through my veins with excitement," she would later recall. "Joan of Arc became my heroine, and I longed for all opportunity to become another such as she. I built air-castles without number, and in my day-dreams I was fond of imagining myself as the hero of the most stupendous adventures. I wished that I was a man . . . and could discover new worlds, or explore unknown regions of the earth."

The battle broke on the hilly terrain near the creek called Bull Run; the rolling hills sometimes concealed maneuvering soldiers until they were practically on top of each other. Complicating matters further, at this early stage of the war, some Federal soldiers had gray uniforms and some Confederate soldiers were garbed in blue. The resulting hesitations and doubts in identification of friends and foes often proved fatal. The skirmishers appearing suddenly over a rise, the choking dust and smoke, the close range cannon fire, led to widespread confusion and disorder.

Reverberations of artillery could be heard all the way to Alexandria, and even in Washington, as clouds of smoke rose out of the woods. The dust and heat quickly became stifling. At first the thin Confederate ranks had difficulty holding back the large Federal columns. The left of Beauregard's line was severely pressured, and everything seemed to be going for the Union forces through a series of attacks and counterattacks during the morning. By late morning the Federal commanders thought they had won, but their celebration proved to be premature.

Through late morning and into afternoon, fresh forces continued to arrive on the battlefield, and were hastily rushed into position by the opposing commanders. Beauregard continued to shift reinforcements to the beleaguered left of the line, among them Jubal Early and M. L. Bonham, and gradually the Confederate forces converged on Henry Hill. The battle for Henry Hill began in earnest about 2:00 P.M., continuing for about two hours.

In mid-afternoon, two of Bonham's regiments arrived on the left of the Confederate line to reinforce the 6th North Carolina regiment which had been valiantly defending the exposed left. Sometime between 4:00 and 4:30 P.M. the right of McDowell's Federal battle line began crumbling, and with timely help from Jubal Early's troops, the Confederate left broke through and sent the Federal army fleeing in full retreat.

"Lieutenant Buford," with Bee's command at the focal point of the final crucial battle, had watched as the panorama unfolded:

> Ere the morning was far advanced, the sharp rattling of the musketry, the roar of the artillery, and the yelling of the soldiers, developed into an incessant tumult; while along the entire line, for miles, arose clouds of yellow dust and blue smoke, as the desperateness of the conflict increased, and the men on either side became excited with the work they had in hand.

"Buford" was chagrined when Bee, finding his soldiers surrounded on three sides and the 4th Alabama in danger of being overrun, ordered a retreat.

> I was wrought up to such a pitch of excitement, while the fight was going on, that I had no comprehension whatever of the value of the movements being made by the different commanders. I only saw the enemy before me, and was inspired by an eager desire to conquer him . . . so, when by the general's command, we were compelled to fall back, I was overcome with rage and indignation, and felt all the shame and mortification of a personal defeat.

But the wisdom of Bee's move soon became apparent. "This movement on the part of Bee," Velazquez wrote,

> afforded me an opportunity to cool off a little, and to observe the ebb and flow of the tide of battle more critically. . . . From this point, therefore, the battle became more interesting than ever, and while none the less exciting, simply as a personal adventure—for my spirit rose and sank as victory or defeat seemed likely to rest upon our banners—I was more under the dominion of my reason, and less of my passions, than I had been when the fight commenced.

As the battle reached a peak, she said, it was a spectacle that "was grand beyond description," bringing to mind scenes of the Sahara Desert, with a broiling sun and roiling clouds of dust mingled with smoke, and dry, choking air. The smoke rose in huge columns, marking the most hotly contested points on the field. "It was a sight never to be forgotten," wrote Velazquez. "One of those magnificent spectacles that cannot be imagined, and that no description, no matter how eloquent, can do justice to . . . a sublime, living drama."

(The following spring, as McClellan's army retreated at the conclusion of the Virginia Peninsula Campaign, having failed to take Richmond, the final battle at Malvern Hill, with its panoramic artillery barrage and hail of musketry, light flashes and smoke clouds, would similarly cause Sarah Emma Edmonds to wax rapturous about the grand spectacle she observed.)

"The fiercer the conflict grew the more my courage rose," said Velazquez. "The example of my commanders, the desire to avenge my slaughtered comrades, the salvation of the cause which I had espoused, all inspired me to do my utmost; and no man on the field that day fought with more energy or determination than the woman who figured as Lieutenant Harry T. Buford."

At midday a courier rode up with a message for General Joseph Johnston that a heavy force of Federals had arrived on the field. "Fortunately, however, the advancing troops were those of [Confederate] Kirby Smith," she reported, "and consisted of about two thousand infantry and Beekman's artillery. The arrival of this force decided the fate of the battle, and the Federals fled, defeated, from the field." (Actually, though Smith's arrival close to noon was very beneficial, it was Jubal Early's timely appearance in late afternoon that helped carry the day.)

By the end of the day Velazquez was satisfied that her performance under fire deserved recognition:

> After the battle, I appealed to General [Thomas "Stonewall"] Jackson for the promotion which I considered that I had fully earned, and he gave me a recommendation to General Bragg for a recruiting commission. This I did not care about, for I thought that I did not need his permission or his aid to do recruiting duty, and determined to wait and see if something better would not offer.

The Confederate victory at 1st Bull Run elated the South and shocked the North. The battle "only quickened my ardor to participate in another affair of a similar kind . . . there is a positive enjoyment in the deadly perils of the occasion that nothing can equal" she concluded.

For several months the opposing armies jockeyed for position in northern Virginia, the Confederate forces lurking just across the Potomac River menacing Washington, D.C. Finally, one of those accidental battles developed that have happened throughout history, when elements of opposing armies stumble onto each other and fate takes over. What started out as a "demonstration" by a brigade commanded by Colonel Edward D. Baker, across the Potomac toward Leesburg, Virginia, where Brigadier General Nathan G. Evans had a small Confederate force, quickly evolved into a sharp, bitter fight on October 21, 1861.

On October 10th, "Lieutenant Buford" had gone to General Evans's headquarters seeking an assignment, but there were no vacancies. On October 21st, she tagged along with the 8th Virginia Infantry into battle.

The Union force had climbed a narrow pathway up Balls Bluff, a 70-foot precipice on the Virginia side of the Potomac, about twenty-five miles up the river northwest of Washington. However, not expecting anything more than a scouting mission, they committed a fundamental mistake by failing to arrange for vessels to recross the river or for an alternate escape route in case they needed to retreat. This proved to be a fatal error.

The scene that greeted "Lieutenant Buford" atop the bluff was:

> a tolerably open piece of ground, cut up somewhat by ridges and hollows, and surrounded by a thick growth of woods. This timber for a while concealed the combatants from each other, and it was impossible for us to tell what force we were contending with. The woods seemed to be alive with combatants, and it was thought that the enemy was strongly fortified. . . . The enemy certainly fought exceedingly well, especially considering the precariousness of their position, although, of course, we did not know at the time the attack was made that our foes were in such a desperate predicament.

Shortly after the Confederate attack began, "Lieutenant Buford" took charge of a company that had lost all of its officers and endeavored to "set them an example." After the battle, the 1st lieutenant of the company reappeared and relieved her, claiming that he had been taken prisoner but had managed to escape. She had serious doubts about his story, and assumed that he had run for cover when the firing started.

As dusk approached, the Union forces found themselves hemmed in on three sides and finally broke, scrambling and tumbling back down the bluff, discarding their equipment as they fled. Struggling soldiers quickly swamped the one or two boats on hand and, floundering in the swift current, dozens were drowned. The Confederate soldiers, shrieking and yelling, stood atop the bluff raining lead down into the frantic Yankees, like shooting fish in a barrel. It was bloody murder, and for the first time Velazquez had doubts about the "glory" or "nobility" of war:

This horrible spectacle made me shudder. . . . I was willing to fight them to death's door in the open field, and to ask no favors, taking the same chances for life as they had; but I had no heart for their ruthless slaughter. All the woman in me revolted at the fiendish delight which some of our soldiers displayed at the sight of the terrible agony endured by those who had, but a short time before, been contesting the field with them so valiantly.

Her impulse was to try to stop the carnage, even at the expense of betraying her secret, but she restrained herself. "Such scenes as these," she noted, "are inseparable from warfare, and they must be endured by those who adopt a soldier's career." But the experience soured her on war. "[It] had the effect of satisfying my appetite for fighting for a time; and after it was over, I was by no means as anxious for another battle, as I had been after the victory at Bull Run."

The sight of the enemy stampeding like buffalo into the river, and hundreds being shot down, had made her "sick with horror."

As the cold shivers ran through me, and my heart stood still in my bosom, I shut my eyes for a moment, wishing that it was all over, but only to open them again to gaze on a spectacle that had a terrible fascination for me, in spite of its horrors.

Still, she fired her revolver at a Union officer as he was jumping in the river, and saw him spring into the air and fall. "[I] then turned my head away, shuddering at what I had done, although I believed that it was only my duty." As she watched the boats overloaded with the wounded and dying sink into the river, she "turned away, sick at heart, unable to endure the sight of it."

In the aftermath, Velazquez reassessed her career and decided it was time to make a change. Disillusioned, and bored with the routine of camp life, she began to think of other ways to contribute to the Confederate cause. Battles were exhilarating, but they were few and far between, and sometimes disturbing in their inhumanity.

"To be a second Joan of Arc," she decided,

was a mere girlish fancy, which my very first experiences as a soldier dissipated forever . . . convincing me that a woman like myself, who had a talent for assuming disguises . . . was possessed of courage, resolution, and energy, backed up by a ready wit, a plausible address, and attractive manners, had it in her power to perform many services of the most vital importance, which it would be impossible for a man to even attempt.

Thus began her career as a spy. Leaving Bob with others, she resumed female garb, lying to a Negro woman to obtain some women's clothes from her:

> I really felt sorry at deceiving her, but quieted my conscience with the thought that lying was as necessary as fighting in warfare, and that the prospects were that I would be compelled to do much more fibbing than this before the errand upon which I was about starting would be achieved.

Her free-lance experimentation with spying proved to be short-lived. Crossing into Maryland, she made her way into Washington, D.C. There she mingled in society and claimed to have met Lincoln and other Federal officials. She found it disconcertingly easy to pry information from Union officers and officials, and yearned for an official appointment in the Confederate detective corps to show what she could do.

After about two weeks of trying out her wings, Velazquez concluded that she had the abilities to be a good spy and detective who could obtain valuable information for the cause. Satisfied with this, she made her way back to Leesburg and retrieved her uniform from the Negro woman who had concealed it for her. She would look for a detective commission down the road, but for now she was drawn back into uniform.

Resuming male disguise, Velazquez rejoined Bob and set out for Columbus, Tennessee, determined to seek an assignment from General Leonidas Polk. Sadder and wiser, and more realistic about the true nature of war, she now understood that it would be a long and difficult affair:

> It became apparent . . . that a single battle was not going to finish the war, and that if the South was to achieve its independence, it must go through a long and bloody conflict. My visit to Washington more than confirmed the opinion I had formed, that the Federals were in command of enormous resources in comparison with ours, and that they were settling down to a deadly determination to bring all their resources to bear for the purposes of fighting the thing out to the bitter end.

General Polk assigned her to the detective corps, as a military conductor on railroad cars on the Nashville Railroad. Armed with powers of arrest, her duties included examination of passes and furlough papers. "Lieutenant Buford" found the female passengers all too eager to flirt with the jaunty young officer:

> I was a personage of considerable importance, not only to the officers and soldiers who were going back and forth, but to the ladies, who

courted me with remarkable assiduity, with a view of inducing me to grant them favors. The women folk tormented me a good deal more than the men did, for the average masculine [*sic*] had a wholesome dread of the rigors of military discipline, and was consequently manageable, while my own sex relied on accomplishing, by means of their fascinations, what was impossible to the men.

The women, she said, would make all kinds of excuses and tell all kinds of improbable stories to persuade "Lieutenant Buford" to pass them:

> Occasionally some of my would-be charmers, finding it impossible to make any impression on me, would abuse me roundly for refusing to grant their request. This, of course, did not have any other effect than to afford me much amusement; but it enabled me to understand why my predecessor seemed so well pleased at being relieved, although I have doubts as to whether he was as strict in enforcing the regulations as myself.

On one occasion a would-be passenger who "Buford" would not let travel without the proper papers trumped up a false charge against the lieutenant in retaliation. To check on the situation, General Polk himself boarded the train and tried to persuade "Lieutenant Buford" to let him travel without proper travel papers. "Buford" stood "his" ground, until Polk—laughing—produced legitimate leave papers. He later apologized, but "Buford" was upset by his lack of trust and his surveillance of her: "I told him very plainly . . . that I did not like that sort of thing, and that I proposed to tender my resignation shortly."

Her stint as a military conductor had lasted barely three weeks. After an interlude of partying, during which she played up to the ladies to enhance her masculine image, she returned to the field and was involved in the battle of Fort Donelson, Tennessee, during February 13–16, 1862.

Velazquez had arrived at Fort Donelson the day before the battle and sized up the situation. She was struck by the contrast with 1st Bull Run, which had been fought in open country during hot summer weather, and she had a premonition of defeat:

> It was a very different thing, from defending a series of earthworks from a combined attack, by land and by water, in the dead of winter. . . . The whole proceeding seemed unseasonable, and this peculiar feeling, combined with a singular sense of discomfort and constraint at being shut in fortifications from which there was next to no escape, except by driving off the enemy, or surrendering to him, had a powerful effect in dampening my ardor.

She and Bob pitched in to work on the entrenchments, hoping for the best. Velazquez noted in her memoirs that Bob proved to be a "much better man than I was" when it came to shoveling dirt:

> There are some things which men can do better than women, and digging intrenchments [sic] in the frozen ground is one of them . . . nature had evidently intended me for a warrior rattler than for a dirt-digger.

Volunteering for picket duty, "Lieutenant Buford" had problems adjusting to the wintry climate. When the weather abruptly turned intensely cold, she began to doubt her qualifications for this kind of service: "I confess that, as the sleet stung my face, and the biting winds cut me to the bones, I wished myself well out of it, and longed for the siege to be over in some shape, even if relief came only through defeat."

Her only consolation was that there were "thousands of brave men around, who were suffering from these wintry blasts as much as I."

Fort Donelson, on the Cumberland River, blocked Federal forces from controlling Kentucky and western Tennessee. An up-and-coming general named U. S. Grant advanced his army of about 15,000 into position to attack the fort. The initial assaults by several Illinois regiments were repulsed, with heavy casualties. In charge of defending the fort were Brigadier General John B. Floyd, Major General Gideon L. Pillow, and Brigadier General Simon B. Buckner.

The Illinois troops dug in within rifle range of the fort, without tents or other supplies. "'At dark," according to an early history of the war,

> a cold, heavy rain began to fall, which soon turned into sleet and snow, accompanied by fierce gusts of wintry wind. It was a night of great hardship and suffering. . . . For twelve long hours the men lay in the cold, pelting storm.

The plan was for the army to besiege the fort, while Flag Officer Andrew H. Foote's gunboats poured shells into it from the river and forced the garrison to surrender. Foote's flotilla steamed upriver on February 14th, but were met by deadly fire from the high ground above the river. Two of the gunboats were disabled, and Foote was wounded in the foot and forced to withdraw. It became evident that if the fort were to be taken, it would have to be by the ground forces.

Meanwhile, the Confederate commanders deliberated and decided that their only chance was to fight their way out by breaking through the Union lines upriver and escaping to open country toward Nashville. A force under General Pillow succeeded in breaking through the Union lines, not only leaving an open road for the garrison to make its escape, but also threatening to sweep the entire field. But Grant, who had been absent consulting with Admiral Foote, arrived on the field and ordered an all-out assault on the fort, which was captured by nightfall.

After several days of battle, the only course available to the Confederate defenders who had fought their way out was to escape with as many troops and resources as possible to fight again another day. The defeat at Fort Donelson was rather overwhelming to Loreta Velazquez:

> Immediately after the defeat at Fort Donelson, especially, I was greatly depressed in spirit, and it was long before I could shake off the disposition to shudder, and the feeling of intense Melancholy, that overcame me to such an extent, that I almost resolved to give up the whole business, and to never allow myself to be put in the way of witnessing anything of the kind again.

She was sick, physically from exposure and fatigue, and mentally from the horrors of battle; it would take awhile to restore her health and spirits. Bob also had been taken sick during the battle. They made their way to Nashville to rest and recuperate.

II

My experimental trip to Washington satisfied me that it was as a detective rather than as a soldier, that my best successes were to be won.
                              —Memoirs of Loreta Janeta Velazquez

AFTER THE fall of Fort Donelson, the atmosphere in Nashville was electric with excitement. The southern cause had received a serious setback, and it was time for an agonizing reappraisal of military strategy. Velazquez found herself caught up in the turmoil and felt compelled to return to service sooner than she had planned. She felt she was needed now more than ever before to help prevent further Federal victories. Sending Bob away in charge of a friend, Velazquez reported to General Albert Sidney Johnston and asked for an assignment. She was again assigned to the detective corps.

Not long afterwards, however, she was wounded in the foot during a skirmish, and fearing detection by a surgeon slipped away to join Bob and to rest for a while. For that purpose she made her way to New Orleans and took up quarters at the Brooks House. The city was in turmoil, apprehensive of an attack, and authorities were alert to possible spies in their midst. Thinking she was among friends, Velazquez let her guard down:

> During the eight or nine months I had been wearing male attire, I had . . . seen a great deal of very hard service. My clothing was well worn, and my apparatus for disguising my form was badly out of order; and the result was, that I scarcely presented as creditable a manly appearance as I did upon the occasion of my last visit to New Orleans. . . . [I] had grown careless about a number of little matters that, when attended to properly, aided materially in maintaining my incognito.

Velazquez was thunderstruck when she was arrested on suspicion of being a spy and was taken before the provost marshal. She was outraged by the charge, but feared that if her identity were exposed at this point, her career would be over. Accordingly, she decided to put up a bold front. She would challenge them to prove anything against her:

> I entered a vigorous protest against the whole proceeding to the officer who made the arrest, and I could see, from his hesitating and indecisive manner, that he was in possession of no definite charge against me, and was inclined to be dubious about the propriety or legality of his action. . . . My protest, however, was of no avail.

The provost marshal quickly decided that there were no grounds for holding "Lieutenant Buford" and released him from custody. But the very next evening, Velazquez was again arrested, this time on suspicion of being a woman: "Now what I had so long dreaded was come to pass, and there was nothing to do but to get out of the difficulties which environed me the best way I could."

Taken before Mayor Monroe, she was interrogated and, assuming that she was a woman, he ordered her to change into female apparel. Velazquez demanded that he prove she was a woman. This disconcerted him, she says, but he put her in jail until the matter could be settled. While in jail a reporter interviewed her for a story, indicating that her circumstances had become generally known. She insisted to the reporter that a great mistake had been made.

Her next visitor was a Dr. Root of Charity Hospital, whom she felt knew she was a woman. Giving up the pretense, she confessed to Mayor Monroe, hoping he would release her immediately. To her surprise and disgust, he fined her and sentenced her to ten days in jail instead. (A contemporary news story reports that she was imprisoned for three months; see chapter notes.)

Eventually Velazquez was released: "At length, after long and impatient waiting, I was free once more; and now the problem was to get out of New Orleans as quickly as possible, before I was recognized by too many people." She hit on a plan that would get her quickly back into the army, though on a risky basis. Proceeding to the recruiting office, she enlisted in Captain B. Moses's company, of the 21st Louisiana Regiment. The company started for Fort Pillow next day to join the rest of the regiment.

As a formally enlisted soldier, instead of an independent officer, her freedom of motion and independence would be severely restricted, so she did not intend to continue in this role for long:

> In this manner I contrived to get clear of New Orleans, but, as I had no fancy for going on duty as a private soldier any longer than was absolutely necessary . . . my next thought was to resume my independent footing at the earliest moment.

Going privately to Brigadier General John B. Villepigue, commanding Fort Pillow, she showed him her commission as an officer, making up some story to account for her enlistment. Since there were no vacancies, Villepigue could not assign her the duties of an officer. Therefore she applied for a transfer to the Army of East Tennessee, which was "very cheerfully granted." Thus did she extricate herself from enlisted soldier life and regain her independent status.

After some dalliances at Memphis, "Lieutenant Buford" and friends were ordered to Corinth where a major battle was impending. Reporting to General William J. Hardee, she participated in the initial attack at Pittsburg Landing (Shiloh) on April 6th that overran the Federal camp. Afterwards, seeing her old company recruited from Arkansas, she received permission from Hardee to join it and reported to the captain, Thomas C. DeCaulp. They had known each other in Pensacola during training, and DeCaulp was delighted to see his old friend "Lieutenant Buford."

Another deeper relationship also existed between the two. DeCaulp had also known Loreta as the wife of a friend, and when he had been killed in a training accident, DeCaulp had courted the widow. They had kept in touch mostly by mail and considered themselves engaged to be married. What DeCaulp did not know was that "Lieutenant Buford" and Loreta were one and the same person.

As plans for resuming the battle commenced, Velazquez looked around and saw a lot of familiar faces, and down the line saw the 11th Louisiana Regiment commanded by a friend, Colonel Sam Marks. She looked forward eagerly to going into battle alongside Captain DeCaulp and among other old friends.

When the battle resumed:

> We had not been long engaged before the second lieutenant of the company fell. I immediately stepped into his place, and assumed the command of his men. This action was greeted by a hearty cheer from the entire company, all the veterans of which, of course, knew me, and I took the greeting as an evidence that they were glad to see their original commander with them once more.

At the close of the first day's battle the Confederates were successful at all points, but the advantage was not pressed. Velazquez had hoped for a great victory, but was disillusioned by what she observed of the leadership. That night, she reported, "a heavy rainstorm, in the middle of the night . . . drenched everyone to the skin, and seriously disturbed the slumbers of the wearied soldiers."

When the tide turned next day and what had seemed to be victory became defeat, she was furious, and considered giving up altogether. To make matters worse, she had been separated from DeCaulp and Bob had wandered off on the wrong road into Federal camp and disappeared.

> I remained in the woods all night, the roads being perfectly blocked up with the retreating army, trying to shield myself as best I could from the furious storm of rain and hail that came on, as if to add to the miseries which the wretched soldiers of the Confederacy were compelled to endure on their weary march back to Corinth. . . . I managed, however, after the worst of the storm was over, to find a tolerably dry place, where, completely used up by the fatigues I had undergone, I fell into a sound sleep.

Reflecting on events the next day as she headed back to Corinth, Velazquez feared for the cause. She had experienced defeat for the second straight time, and began to think that plunging into battle might not be the best contribution she could make in the future. Perhaps she should stick to her previous decision and go into secret service instead.

Along the way to Corinth she came across the camp of the 11th Louisiana and stopped to visit. Captain G. Merrick Miller wanted to bury the dead of his company, so she started back toward the battlefield with him to help. While engaged in burying soldiers on the battlefield, Velazquez was knocked down and stunned by a sudden shellburst. Shrapnel severely wounded her in the right arm, which dangled helplessly.

A soldier helped her onto a horse and started back to camp with her, but the pain was excruciating:

> My fortitude began to give way before the terrible physical suffering I was compelled to endure; all my manliness oozed out long before I reached camp, and my woman's nature asserted itself with irresistible force. I could face deadly peril on the battlefield without flinching, but this intolerable pain overcame me completely, and I longed to be where there would be no necessity for continuing my disguise, and where I could obtain shelter, rest, and attention as a woman. My pride, however, and a fear of consequences, prevented me from revealing my sex, and I determined to preserve my secret as long as it was possible to do so, hoping soon to reach some place where I could be myself again with impunity.

By the time they reached camp, her arm and hand were badly swollen, and her companion had to rip the sleeve of her coat in order to treat the wound with cold water. An ambulance was called, and she was taken to the railroad to be evacuated to the South. But the cars stopped at Corinth for two hours, so she sent for a young surgeon whom she knew and asked him to help relieve her suffering:

> He immediately examined my arm, and, as I perceived by the puzzled expression that passed over his face, he was beginning to suspect something, and guessing that further concealment would be useless, I told him who I really was. I never saw a more astonished man in my life.

Her shoulder was found to be dislocated, her arm cut, and a little finger lacerated. The surgeon dressed the wounds and put her arm in a sling. He urged her to stay in Corinth for treatment, but she persuaded him to obtain travel papers for her so she could press on to Grenada:

> Before the information that a woman, disguised as an officer, was among the wounded on the train, we were, to my infinite satisfaction, speeding out of sight, leaving behind me the camp occupied by a defeated army.

At Grenada she rested for two days, "visited by a great many ladies of the place, who presented me with bouquets, delicacies of various kinds, and bandages for my wound, and who otherwise overwhelmed me with attentions, for which I hope I was duly grateful." But restless and uncomfortable from her wounds, Velazquez had a strong desire to get far away from the army "before the fact that Lt. Harry T. Buford was a woman became generally known."

At Jackson she was too ill to go on, feverish, arm and shoulder inflamed. There, a widow and her daughter took her in and nursed her back to some semblance of health. Gradually she continued on to New Orleans. Once there she saw that the city was about to fall into Union hands, and so put away her uniform and resumed female garb. With the city under Federal occupation, she saw an opportunity for conducting secret service missions as a woman:

> I was very well satisfied to abandon, for a while at least, a soldier's life for the purpose of undertaking work more naturally congenial than campaigning, and for which my sex, combined with my soldierly training, peculiarly fitted me. My experimental trip to Washington satisfied me that it was as a detective, rather than as a soldier, that my best successes were to be won.

To establish her cover, Velazquez worked to gain the confidence of Federal officers in New Orleans by expressing Unionist sentiments, deliberately alienating some of her friends. This enhanced her credibility with the provost marshal and other authorities, who gave her passes to travel through the lines:

> I soon became known as one of the few advocates of the Federal Government in New Orleans, and not only secured myself from molestation, but gained the entire confidence of our new rulers. . . . It was better for me to risk the temporary loss of my friends, in the hope and expectation that vindication of my conduct would come with time, than to risk anything by an incautious word, or even look.

General Benjamin F. Butler, military governor, was her prime target. Ruling harshly, he was handing out severe penalties to spies who were apprehended by Union authorities. Starting a career as a blockade runner, Velazquez carried messages through the Federal blockade to Havana, Cuba, and contacted Confederate agents there. On the return trip, she smuggled in badly needed supplies and drugs. While "running the lines," she pretended to be an English widow in reduced circumstances waiting for money from home in order to return there. She had purchased a passport and other identification papers from an English woman who was sympathetic to the Confederate cause.

Eventually a Confederate officer to whom she had given some dispatches was captured, and the documents were traced back to her. Summarily arrested, she was taken before General Butler who tried to browbeat her into a confession. But the charges could not be proved. Taking refuge in her fake British citizenship, she persuaded the British consul to intervene and was released from prison. Fearing recapture and exposure she tried to leave the city, but was refused a pass. Paying a fisherman to carry her across Lake Ponchartrain, she made a hurried escape, carrying a concealed six-shooter in case of betrayal. Fleeing to Jackson, Mississippi, she resumed disguise as "Lieutenant Harry T. Buford" and sought more detective or scouting duties, but nothing materialized and she became restless again. Hearing that Bob had escaped from the Federal camp after Shiloh and was in Grenada, she went there and was reunited with him.

Deciding that she could accomplish more in the East, Velazquez headed for Richmond with thoughts of establishing herself as a spy for the Confederate government. She had not counted on the fact that authorities in the beleaguered city were alerted to suspicious-looking strangers. Accordingly, she was quickly arrested on suspicion of being a woman in disguise; her disguise, she said, was "not in good order."

General John Henry Winder, provost marshal general, had a rigorous martial law in effect, and all strangers entering the city were closely watched. Once under observation, she surmised: "Some lynx-eyed detective was not long in noting certain feminine ways I had, and which even my long practice in figuring as a man had not enabled me to get rid of."

"Lieutenant Buford" was unceremoniously deposited in Castle Thunder, one of the major Richmond prisons during the war. But good luck sometimes comes in odd ways. The superintendent of prisons, G. W. Alexander, and his wife befriended Velazquez and treated her so kindly and considerately that she was induced to tell them her whole story and what her aspirations were in regard to secret service. Although shocked that a woman would take on male disguise, they took a strong interest in her cause, and Alexander interceded with General Winder.

At last, her dream was realized and she received an official assignment in the secret service corps. General Winder immediately put her to a test, sending her off with dispatches for General Earl Van Dorn. However, the "dispatches" were nothing but blank papers and a letter explaining the trick he was putting her through. Then he telegraphed ahead to the provost marshal in Charlotte, North Carolina, to have her arrested when the train stopped there.

Accordingly, at Charlotte a guard took her into custody and demanded to see the papers in her pocket. But Velazquez perceived that the guard was not accustomed to arresting officers, and so refused to acknowledge his authority. The guard showed his orders, which were correct, but she still refused to comply. Instead, she offered to return to Richmond with the papers and report to General Winder. This confused the guard who thought there must be some mistake, and he didn't know quite how to proceed. "Lieutenant Buford" suggested that he send a telegram back to headquarters asking for further instructions. This satisfied the guard that he must be making a mistake, and soon she was released and on her way again; her bluff had worked.

When the package was delivered to General Van Dorn, he read the letter, looked at "Lieutenant Buford," and laughed. "This might be good fun for Van Dorn and Winder," she later wrote, "but I did not particularly admire having been sent all this distance on such a fool's errand, and was very much disposed to resent it." On reflection, she realized that she had carried out her orders and avoided the snares set in her path, and so had reason to be satisfied.

Back at Richmond, Velazquez settled down to carry out assignments for the secret service. All was not well, however. Her arm was still stiff and sore from the wounds, rumors were floating around about her, and she was having trouble with her disguise:

> It seemed to be an impossibility for me now to avoid getting into continual trouble about my disguise. Not only were a number of people fully informed of all the particulars of my career since the outbreak of the war, but it began to be whispered about among the soldiers and citizens that a woman dressed as a man had been discovered, and some highly-exaggerated rumors with regard to my exploits were diligently circulated. My having received a wound . . . appeared to be a particularly attractive episode to the minds of many people; and my performances at that battle were believed, in some quarters, to have been of a most extraordinary nature . . . I was credited with exploits of unparalleled heroism.

Shortly after returning from Van Dorn's headquarters, while on a trip to Lynchburg she was again arrested on charge of being a woman in disguise. Since her notoriety had preceded her, curious crowds gathered to see the Confederate heroine. But Velazquez was not prepared to give up yet:

> My position was a most unpleasant one, and it required very skillful management for me to play the part of a man to advantage. What gave piquancy to the situation was, that, while it was generally believed that I was a woman . . . my visitors were none of them quite sure which sex I belonged to, and all their efforts were directed to solving the mystery.

On one occasion, hearing feminine voices and footsteps approaching up the stairs of the second-floor jail cell, she braced herself for the ordeal:

> During the two years and more I had been wearing male attire, I had not only learned the general carriage of a man, but had picked up a good many little masculine traits, which I had practiced until I was quite perfect in them. . . . When I heard these visitors coming, I stuck my feet up on the window-sill, and, just as they were opening the door, I turned my head, and spat.

This ruse seemed to convince the mother and daughter who had come to lecture her that the prisoner must be a man after all.

Another visitor was a "motherly old lady" who began grilling the prisoner about her gall in pretending to be a man if she were really a woman. When Velazquez offered to reveal her sex to the woman,

> It had an astonishing effect. . . . She got red in the face, her eyes flashed, and, muttering something that I did not hear, she bounced out of the room, leaving me to enjoy a hearty laugh at the comical termination of the adventure.

Finally, with nothing being resolved by local authorities, Velazquez obtained her release from jail in Lynchburg and proceeded to Charlotte, North Carolina. It was now the summer of 1863. Lee was back in Virginia after the battle of Gettysburg, and the impending action was in Tennessee. General William S. Rosecrans was on the march, and General James Longstreet was detached from Lee's army at Richmond to reinforce General Braxton Bragg.

At Charlotte, she met a number of old friends and acquaintances who were awaiting transportation to various points. Velazquez determined to head into Tennessee with Longstreet's forces to join the action and perhaps win some distinction. She managed to talk her way onto Longstreet's train, headed south.

On reaching Atlanta, Velazquez received a number of letters from relatives, for the first time in months. Two were from her father, one from a sister in Latin America, and one from her brother who (she learned for the first time) was serving in the Confederate army in the Trans-Mississippi Department. Her brother was not aware of her male disguise.

At Atlanta she also learned that Captain DeCaulp, whom she had not seen since the battle of Shiloh, was with Van Dorn's army near Spring Hill, Tennessee. Eager to resume the "strange courtship," she even considered telling DeCaulp the truth. She felt a strong impulse to go to him, and if necessary, abandon army life and resume conventional life as a woman. Her obvious indecision about what she wanted to do, whether to be a soldier or a spy, apparently led her to consider a third alternative.

Heading toward Spring Hill to see him, she fell in with Brigadier General John Pegram's cavalry. En route, she saw "the handsome General Frank Armstrong, an officer for whom I entertained an intense admiration." Unable to reach Van Dorn's camp due to the shifting military situation, Velazquez was forced to change her plans, and turned back to Ringgold, Georgia.

Impatient for action, she decided once more on some free-lance secret service work. She would penetrate enemy lines dressed as a woman and gather information about the strength and disposition of the Union forces. Donning female garb from an abandoned farmhouse, she hid her uniform and other gear in an ash barrel, ate a makeshift meal from leftover supplies, and headed toward the Union lines. Unlike a single soldier in battle, she mused, her present activity depended entirely on her own skill and ingenuity, an individual contest of wits with the enemy; this she found exhilarating. Unfortunately, she felt, spies were generally held in low regard:

> According to all military law, he [the spy] is an outlaw, and is liable to be hung if detected. . . . Nothing has been left undone to render the labors of the spy not only perilous in the extreme, but infamous; and yet the spy is nothing more nor less than a detective officer, and there cannot be any good and sufficient reason assigned for the discredit which attaches to the occupation. (Sarah Emma Edmonds expressed very similar views on the ignoble reputation of spying.)

Using the name "Mrs. Williams" and representing herself as a widow trying to escape the Confederacy to join friends in the North, she asked to see General Rosecrans. After questioning her at some length, he gave her a pass to go north. Making her way to Martinsburg, West Virginia, she checked into a hotel. There she made the acquaintance of a Federal quartermaster. Claiming to be from Cincinnati, she enlisted his help in search of a brother, "Dick," whom she said was missing and presumed killed or wounded.

> The little game I was playing with the quartermaster will serve as a very fair specimen of the methods which a secret service agent is compelled to use for the purposes of gaining such information as is desired. A spy, or a detective, must have a quick eye, a sharp ear, a retentive memory, and a talent for taking advantage of small, and apparently unimportant points, as aids for the object in view. . . . Among other things, I had learned the name of a Federal soldier belonging to General [William W.] Averill's command, and I made a mental note of it for future reference . . . my purpose now was to use it as a means of making the Federal officer by my side at the hotel table useful to me.

At her request, the officer went to headquarters and learned that the missing brother had been killed. Feigning tears and acting distraught, she asked where he was buried so that she might visit the grave. He arranged for an ambulance to take them to the gravesite.

> My escort proved to be so exceedingly communicative, that before we returned to the hotel, I was informed of the exact number of troops in the neighborhood, their positions, their commanders, where the enemy were supposed to be located, who they were commanded by, the results of the recent conflicts, and a variety of other matters of more or less importance. The man was as innocent and as unsuspicious as a newborn babe, and I could scarcely keep from laughing sometimes at the eagerness he displayed in telling me all manner of things that, had he been possessed of ordinary common sense, he would never have revealed to anyone, much less to a total stranger, with regard to whose antecedents he knew absolutely nothing.

Realizing that the information in her possession would be valuable to Confederate commanders if conveyed to them quickly, she slipped through the Union lines that night and passed on what she had learned to Colonel John S. Mosby's command. Then, "with the extraordinary good luck which so often attends bold ventures," she succeeded in getting back to the hotel undetected.

After another week, Velazquez learned something that induced her to return south to Chattanooga. There she represented herself as a soldier's wife trying to see her husband, and she was allowed to stay within the Federal lines. Returning to the farmhouse where she had concealed her uniform, she found the buildings in charred ruins! After searching through the debris, she managed to find her uniform still intact within the ash barrel where she had concealed it.

Making her way back inside the Confederate lines by crawling through the underbrush, she resumed the guise of an officer. When she tried to present herself as an escaped prisoner from Morgan's command, the officer who interviewed her scanned her papers skeptically. These consisted of her transportation pass and

> the letter to General Polk, which had been given to me in the early part of the war. . . . I was much afraid lest he should suspect something, for I had no mustache, and having become somewhat bleached, was not by any means so masculine in appearance as I had been at one time. I, however, bore his scrutiny without flinching, and he apparently did not know what to do but to receive me for what I appeared to be.

After being fed, and debriefed on what she had learned about the Federal army, Velazquez slept until noon. In the afternoon she borrowed a horse and rode to Dalton, Georgia, where she learned that Captain DeCaulp was sick at Atlanta. She resolved to go there and see him one way or the other. However, quite by accident she reinjured the foot that had been wounded at Fort Donelson, and was so lame that she was sent to Atlanta for medical treatment.

Checking into a hotel, "Lieutenant Buford" was immediately surrounded by a bunch of officers who wanted to know how things were going at the front. After a while she had a quarrel with one of them, a General F., whose drunken and insulting manner she found offensive, but friends persuaded her to go to her room.

That night her condition worsened; her foot was sore and she became feverish. So she was sent to the Empire Hospital where she was treated first by a Dr. Hammond and then by a Dr. Hay. There she learned that DeCaulp was close by, in Dr. Benton's ward which was adjacent to that of Dr. Hay. Increasingly, she longed to reveal her secret to him and marry him. Meanwhile, she tossed and turned feverishly on her sick bed, taking stock of "the strange life I had been leading."

> I had some understanding now of what the great discoverers, adventurers, and soldiers, who were the idols of my childhood imagination, had been compelled to go through with before they won the undying fame that was theirs, and I comprehended, to some degree, how hard a thing it was to win fame. For myself, I had played my part in the great drama of war with what skill I could command; and, although

I had not played it altogether unsuccessfully, the chances that fame and the applause of future ages would be mine, seemed as remote as ever.

Loreta Janeta Velazquez found herself disappointed, frustrated, and in poor health. "I was following a will-o'-the-wisp in striving to gain for myself a great name by heroic deeds," she mused. "I had had enough of this, and . . . it was time for me to exchange my uniform for the attire of my own sex once more, and in good earnest, with the intention of never resuming it again."

In this reflective mood, she recalled vividly a romantic Spanish tale from her youth in Cuba, because of certain resemblances it had to her own experiences. It was called "The Story of Estela."

"The heroines of these old Spanish romances," Velazquez noted, "seem to have a decided fancy for masquerading in male attire, and it is not unlikely that this propensity on their part had some effect in encouraging in me a desire to assume the dress of the other sex for the purpose of seeking adventures."

The fair Estela was beloved by a handsome, rich, and gallant young man, Don Carlos, and was deeply in love with him. Eventually a young and wealthy grandee also fell in love with Estela, and became a favorite of her parents. Don Carlos was forbidden to see her, but with her maid and his page making arrangements for them, they met secretly.

During their secret courtship, Don Carlos's page took sick and died. Not long afterwards, a handsome youth applied for the position of page, and was soon taken into his confidence. The youth, however, was a woman who had fallen in love with Don Carlos and had taken the extreme measure of pretending to be a boy in order to be near him and to try to win his love.

This new page—the female pretender—was soon employed as a messenger between Don Carlos and Estela. Very quickly she realized that Estela stood in her way in her effort to win over Don Carlos, and that her rival must be removed. So she set out to devise a plan that would accomplish that purpose.

An opportunity arose when Estela alerted Don Carlos that her parents were trying to pressure her into a quick wedding with the grandee. Don Carlos realized that, unless he acted decisively, he would lose her, so he persuaded her to elope with him.

The young page, of course, was informed of their plans and quickly decided on her own course of action. With the date of elopement set, Estela wrote a letter to her parents explaining her reasons for avoiding their planned match and announcing her intention to elope with Don Carlos. The page was entrusted to deliver Estela to a rendezvous with Don Carlos, but instead betrayed the trust by delivering her to Moorish pirates who carried her off to Algiers to be sold as a slave. As a precaution against treachery, however, the pirates forced the page to go with them. Thus Estela learned that her betrayer was a woman, and the reason for her action.

When Estela's disappearance was discovered, the only clue was her letter to her parents. Don Carlos was accused of spiriting her away, and suspected of having murdered her. The grief-stricken Don Carlos was overwhelmed by the accusations. But as time passed and nothing was heard of her, he began to believe that she had been false to him and had run away with the (presumably male) page. Suspicion of him increased and a murder trial was ordered. Don Carlos fled to Italy and joined the army of the emperor Charles V as a common soldier.

Meanwhile, after many strange adventures, Estela managed to make her escape in male disguise and she, too, joined the army of the emperor. In a skirmish thereafter, she had occasion to save the life of the emperor, who—not suspecting her to be a woman—appointed her to an important position in his entourage. In time, she became the emperor's favorite officer and he showered honors on her. But she longed to return to Spain and seek out Don Carlos.

One day Estela was amazed to encounter a soldier in the ranks who reminded her strongly of Don Carlos. After some conversation, she realized that it really was him. Without revealing her identity to him, she befriended him and gradually drew out his story, including the fact that he doubted Estela's honor. Before telling him who she was, Estela wanted to change his opinion of her. She made Don Carlos her secretary, and in almost daily conversation tried to persuade him that Estela might be guiltless. Although he confessed that he still loved Estela despite her behavior, Don Carlos could not be persuaded that there might be an innocent explanation for her disappearance.

At length, Estela learned that the governor of her native city had died, and she applied to the emperor for the position. Her request was granted, and Don Carlos went with her, feeling that he would be safe as part of the new governor's household, or at least he would receive a fair trial. However, when Don Carlos appeared, Estela's parents pressed charges against him. The governor (Estela) promised that justice would be done, and he remained free in her custody.

In the days leading up to the trial, she redoubled her efforts to make him acknowledge that Estela might be faithful after all. Finally he confessed that, deep down inside, he had faith in her and dreamed some day of being reunited with her.

On the day of the trial, Estela sat as chief magistrate with the other judges to hear the case. Witnesses related the story of Estela's disappearance. Her letter announcing her intention of eloping with Don Carlos was produced. The servants who knew about their secret meetings told what they knew. The accused could only deny his guilt.

The governor and chief magistrate (Estela) sternly announced that the only way his innocence could be proved was by the appearance of Estela, but that if she could not be produced, it would be necessary to condemn the accused in view of the weight of evidence. Don Carlos threw himself at the feet of the governor, reminding "him" of confessing privately to his love for Estela, and asking that true justice be done despite the circumstantial evidence against him.

Moved by his entreaties and unable to restrain herself, Estela proclaimed to the assembly that she knew Don Carlos to be innocent and would order his release. A loud murmur of disapproval arose. The governor, commanding silence, then revealed herself to the astonished audience as the lost Estela. She asked for Don Carlos's forgiveness for the trials she had put him through while testing his faith in and love for her. They were married and, of course, lived happily ever after. Don Carlos was appointed governor in place of Estela, who preferred to resume her female identity.

Velazquez notes that the only reason for including this story in the narrative of her personal adventures

> was because it was so much in my thoughts at the particular period of which I am now writing, and because it inspired me to imitate Estela's example so far as to seek to obtain a confession of love from Captain DeCaulp, before I should reveal myself to him. I was filled with an eager desire to hear what he would say of me to his friend, the supposed Lieutenant Buford.

Loreta Janeta Velazquez yearned for a "happy ending."

III

I have now to tell, not of battles and sieges, but of stratagems and wiles.
—Memoirs of Loreta Janeta Velazquez

CAPTAIN THOMAS C. DECAULP was delighted to see his old friend "Lieutenant Buford," who dropped in for a visit unannounced in Dr. Benton's

ward of the Empire Hospital in Atlanta. They had known each other in
Pensacola, and had fought together at Shiloh. For her part, Velazquez was
primed for a resolution of their strange courtship. She had every intention
of revealing her secret to him, provided she could hear directly from him
an expression of his love for her, in the manner of her fictional childhood
heroine Estela. Ever since her husband's death in a training accident at
Pensacola, she and DeCaulp had stayed in touch, and they considered
themselves engaged to be married. But wartime assignments had kept
them apart.

"Lieutenant Buford" found DeCaulp worn and haggard, but apparently on the way to recovery. During their conversation, he pulled out her
photograph and expressed his love for Miss Velazquez, pointing out that
he had not seen her for three years. Loreta was hard-pressed to choke back
her emotions, but she was hesitant to reveal the truth for fear that he
would react negatively to her masquerade as a male soldier. Should she
reveal the truth to him?

Abruptly, she reached over and took the picture of herself out of his
pocket, and asked him whether he was sure he had not seen somebody like
that within three years. She wondered if he would look at the real thing
standing there and suddenly realize the truth. DeCaulp, puzzled by the
question, silently looked at the picture and then at her, without recognition.

"Well, captain," she finally said, "don't you think the picture of your
lady-love looks the least bit like your friend Harry Buford." DeCaulp,
suddenly taken aback, gasped for air; perspiration broke out on his fore-
head. Grasping her hand, he asked breathlessly, "Can it be possible that
you are she?" Anxiously, Velazquez confirmed her identity and asked the
astonished DeCaulp, "Will you despise her because she was not willing
to stay at home like other women, but undertook to appear on the battlefield in the guise of a man?" To her great relief, DeCaulp replied, "I love
you ten times more than ever for this, Loreta."

Assured of his love, Velazquez went into a long explanation of her
reasons for acting as she had, and outlined her adventures to him. But
realizing that DeCaulp still was very weak and that they both were agitated by the interview, she broke it off, promising to see him again soon.
They had agreed to marry, and she was "supremely happy."

After a brief side trip to Alabama on business, she returned next day
to the hospital and found DeCaulp out of bed and much improved.
Together they went to the Thompson House where she engaged a room
and set about preparing the wedding. To avoid gossip and sensation,
DeCaulp and Velazquez took Drs. Benton and Hammond into their

confidence, telling them the whole story and asking them to witness the ceremony. Loreta obtained a wedding dress, "the main thing being that I should be dressed as a woman when the ceremony took place, for fear of creating too much of a sensation, and, perhaps, of making the clergyman feel unpleasant should I appear before him, hanging on the captain's arm, in my uniform."

Next day they were married in the parlor of the Thompson House by the Rev. Mr. Pinkington, the post chaplain. They looked forward to a pleasant life together after the war. When Velazquez expressed her desire to continue in uniform and accompany her husband into the field (contrary to her previous decision to give it all up), he argued that she had done enough and should now devote herself to their future together. Reluctantly, she assented. After a brief honeymoon, he felt well enough to report for duty, "notwithstanding my entreaties for him to remain until his health was more robust." She felt that he was not as healthy as he should be to face the vigors of army life. But he persisted, and left to report to his command. Before he got there, however, DeCaulp had a relapse, was taken prisoner, and died in a Federal hospital in Chattanooga.

DeCaulp's unexpected death was devastating to Velazquez. She felt that it left her "nothing to do but to launch once more on a life of adventure, and to devote my energies to the advancement of the Confederate cause." Sadder and wiser, she was fed up with her heroic vision and reluctant to go on as "Lieutenant Harry Buford":

> My secret was now known to a great many persons, and its discovery had already caused me such annoyance that I hesitated about assuming my uniform again. . . . I had seen enough of fighting, enough of marching, enough of camp life, enough of prisons and hospitals, and I had passed through enough peril and suffering to satisfy any reasonable human being.

She was weary of war and

> getting out of the notion of subjecting myself to the liability of being locked up by every local magistrate within whose jurisdiction I happened to find myself, simply because I did not elect to dress according to his notions of propriety. . . . On reviewing the whole subject in my mind, I became more than ever convinced that the secret service rather than the army would afford me the best field for the exercise of my talent.

While she had been in the hospital, General Bragg had gained an important victory at Chickamauga (September 19–20, 1863). Lee was successfully defending Richmond. The South was holding on, hoping that antiwar sentiment in the North would turn the tide, or that England or France would intercede on the side of the Confederacy. Though there had been some serious setbacks, the situation was not hopeless.

In the fall of 1863, Velazquez returned to Richmond and called on General Winder and President Davis, seeking a secret service appointment. Neither obliged her, but finally Winder gave her a letter of recommendation to the commanding officer of Confederate forces in the South and West and authorized transportation papers for her. This was not exactly what she had wanted, but at least it opened the door for her to strike a blow for the Confederacy.

At Mobile, Alabama, Velazquez took up residence at the Battle House, where she met a number of officers whom she had known on various battlefields. While there, she received a mysterious note one day asking her to meet the writer on a certain street corner. No reason was given. She hesitated, but decided to go through with it, and was met by a Lieutenant Shorter of Arkansas. He recruited her for an important secret service assignment ("especially," he said, "as you seem to have a talent for disguising yourself") to penetrate enemy lines and deliver a dispatch to a certain party. If interested, she was to meet him next day in Meridian, Mississippi, for final instructions.

At a hotel in Meridian, Shorter informed her that they had captured a spy from Federal General Stephen A. Hurlbut's command who had important papers giving accurate information about the forces and the movements of several Confederate generals. The Confederates proposed to play a counterintelligence game by falsifying the papers to throw the Federal forces off the track. Velazquez was to take the altered papers to Memphis and see that they were delivered to General Cadwallader C. Washburn and convince him that it was accurate intelligence. Also, Shorter had a dispatch for General Nathan Bedford Forrest that she was to deliver to a Confederate agent in Memphis.

Velazquez was given letters of introduction to various Confederates who could assist her along the way, and a password to allow her to communicate with the Memphis agent. At Lieutenant Shorter's suggestion, she impersonated a poor countrywoman whose husband was lost in the war, seeking protection in Federal lines after being badly treated by the rebels. Although her health still was not good, Velazquez found the opportunity appealing and was determined to proceed.

As she approached the Federal lines, Velazquez made contact with the lieutenant in charge of pickets, who would prove to be a valuable—if unwitting—ally. After listening to her story about having papers for General Washburn, the lieutenant personally escorted her on the Memphis and Charleston Railroad to headquarters at Memphis. Since her credibility was greatly enhanced by having a Union escort, she played up to him with flattery, and he seemed attracted to her and looking for a conquest. In answer to questions about her personal life, she told the officer that she was foreign born, had French and Spanish parents, and that her deceased husband had lived in Ohio. Her interest now, she told him, was to return to Europe as soon as possible.

When they arrived at Memphis, the lieutenant engaged a carriage and escorted her to headquarters, where she was ushered in to see the provost marshal. Thanks to the lieutenant's presence, she was not unduly questioned. She told the provost marshal that she was carrying a dispatch and a confidential message from a spy within Confederate lines that she was to deliver personally to General Washburn. However, the general was said to be indisposed and unable to see her. As a last resort she wrote out a note to the general explaining the circumstances and handed over the altered dispatch, expecting the general to contact her later.

Next the lieutenant escorted her to the Hardwick House hotel, where she registered as "Mrs. Fowler." After disposing of the lieutenant by telling him she was tired and needed to rest, asking him to call again in the morning, Velazquez set out to accomplish the other part of her mission. Obtaining some better clothes with the help of hotel personnel, she set out to contact the Confederate agent to deliver the dispatch for General Forrest. Since she had a description of the Memphis agent, Velazquez recognized him on sight and, giving the password, was quickly admitted to his room. She delivered the dispatch, along with verbal instructions from Lieutenant Shorter, and urged the man to get it to General Forrest at once. However, the agent was concerned about imminent movements of Federal troops and asked her to find out what she could at headquarters before he set out on his mission to Forrest's command. To avoid being seen together, they agreed on a means of communicating messages.

While returning to her hotel, Velazquez was startled to see approaching her from the other direction none other than her Federal lieutenant friend, walking along with another officer. "My heart leaped into my mouth when I saw who it was," she said, "but as there was no retreat, I trusted to the darkness and my change of costume, and glided by them as swiftly and quietly as I could, and fortunately was able to gain my room without discovery."

Next morning the smitten lieutenant dutifully called on her and increased his attentions. Since she had pretended to be short of money, he raised some for her, and also helped her obtain better clothes. After a while, other officers and an officer's wife came to call. Velazquez was something of a celebrity, a poor but honest and patriotic woman who had brought important information to headquarters. In casual conversations with her newfound friends, she learned the disposition and numbers of Federal troops and conveyed this information to the waiting Confederate agent, who started at once for Forrest's headquarters. Among other things she had learned that there was a concentration of troops at Colliersville, anticipating an attack in that area, but this left a gap in the Federal line beyond Grand Junction.

A day or two later word was received that Forrest was on a grand raid through western Tennessee. After several weeks, Forrest slipped back past Federal lines into Mississippi, with cattle and other booty. Velazquez felt that her work, in concert with the other Confederate agents, had played an important role in the success of Forrest's raid.

The Federal lieutenant reported back to camp, but returned a day or two later with a 10-day leave and bringing an extra horse for her. While she bided her time, she allowed the lieutenant to escort her around, and went riding with him. They even attended church together. One Sunday at church, she recognized a man in the congregation, in civilian clothes, as a Confederate officer who was in her brother's command. He did not know her as a woman, but had seen her as "Lieutenant Harry Buford." After church she followed the man, with the Federal lieutenant on her arm, hoping to find an opportunity to inquire about her brother. She saw him go to the Hardwick House hotel and, excusing the lieutenant, quickly followed, but the man had vanished.

Later that evening, going to dinner with the lieutenant, she spotted the man in the hotel dining room and maneuvered her escort to a table next to him. Scribbling a note on a card, she directed the lieutenant's attention elsewhere and quickly dropped the note on the floor in plain view of the Confederate officer. He dropped his napkin on top of the card, and stooped to pick it up. The note read: "Meet me at my room, at half past ten o'clock this evening, unobserved. Important." When the man later got up to leave, she turned and gave him a meaningful look to reinforce her message.

That night at the appointed time he showed up at her room, and was perplexed when she promptly identified him as "Lieutenant B. of

Arkansas." But at the mention of her brother's name, his face brightened up and he was visibly relieved. From him she learned that her brother had been captured about four months ago and was a prisoner at Camp Chase, Ohio. As a result of this news, she gave up her plans to return to Mobile and decided to go north to visit her brother, and assist him in any way she could. The news was an additional inducement to practice her secret service skills in the North, something she had thought about for a long time. Lieutenant B. gave her names of various Confederate agents or sympathizers who might be in a position to help her.

Her Federal lieutenant suitor was dismayed to learn that Velazquez was leaving. His attentions had been getting more ardent every day, and he obviously hoped for a conquest. She told him she was going to New York, and promised to write him from there. Although disappointed, the Lieutenant obtained a pass and transportation papers for her from General Washburn, and she was on her way.

In Columbus, Ohio, she took a room at the Neil House, then called on the general in command at Camp Chase. Pretending to be a strong Unionist from New York, she asked to visit her "rebel brother." The request was granted and she was given a permit and directed to Tod Barracks. "I found a one-armed major in command," she wrote. "He told me that he had lost his arm in the Mexican war." Her brother was brought in for an emotional reunion, as they had been separated for a long time. Discreetly, the major let them use his private room to talk. Once they were alone she instructed him to refer to her as his "Union sister from New York." She promised to try to arrange his release.

Later, at her hotel, she discovered that Governor John Brough of Ohio was staying there, and she arranged for an introduction. "He took quite a fancy to me," she wrote, "so much so, that he promised to use his influence to obtain a parole for my brother." Governor Brough kept his word, and her brother was released in her custody, with instructions to report first to General George Cadwallader in Philadelphia and then to General John A. Dix in New York City, where he was supposed to stay with her. Then, leaving her brother in New York City, she proceeded to Washington, D.C., to seek spying opportunities for the Confederate cause.

It was now the winter of 1863–1864. Velazquez took stock of the situation. She could see the relative wealth and prosperity of the North, and realized that the South might lose by sheer force of numbers. But the growing antiwar sentiment in the North and the presidential campaign offered some hope, as did strong sentiments against conscription. Draft riots and secret societies for resisting the draft had spread across the North by 1863. She resolved to use her skills in the enemy homeland in any way that would help the cause, even by encouraging political dissension and supporting the antiwar movement.

During this period of her life, Velazquez expressed sentiments very similar to those of Sarah Emma Edmonds, her Union counterpart:

> It is impossible for me to reflect upon some of the features of my career as a Confederate secret service agent at the North with anything but regret that I should have been forced by circumstances to do what I did, or to associate with the men I did. [She characterizes her account of those activities as a] plain, unadorned statement of the enterprises in which I was engaged during the last eighteen months of the war.

Velazquez set out to establish contacts with the authorities in Richmond, as well as Confederate agents across the North and in Canada. She also worked on building up her social contacts with Federal officials and officers. Finally her efforts paid off when she obtained an introduction to Colonel La Fayette C. Baker, chief of detectives for the War Department. She described him as having a "wiry frame" and eyes that were a "cold gray. I have felt cold creeps all over me as he looked me straight in the eyes and spoke in that cutting tone of voice he was in the habit of using on occasions."

Since Baker was reputed to be very successful at catching Confederate spies, Velazquez felt she should get to know him and study him. Applying for a position in Baker's service, she expressed bitterness toward the South and claimed to have been treated badly by southerners. She expressed her motives as being both monetary (for self-support) and revenge. Since no position was offered right away, she went to visit her brother in New York City.

In New York she found that her brother was on the verge of being paroled to the South, and Confederate agents were after him to carry some documents. But he was being cautious about it. She contacted the agents and revealed herself to them sufficiently to obtain cooperation, and they asked her to do some work for them. Her brother was then exchanged, and delivered a verbal message to Richmond officials on her behalf.

Working with the New York City Confederate agents, Velazquez honed her skills by undertaking various minor missions. Meanwhile, she kept in touch with Colonel Baker, making it a point to give him some information that would be useful in breaking up fraudulent practices by Federal contractors. Gradually, she gained his confidence while operating right under his nose. Eventually Baker used her services and she became a double agent, maintaining the deception for almost eighteen months.

During the summer and fall of 1864, as Confederate fortunes ebbed, the secret service activities increasingly turned toward "back door" operations out of Canada to confuse and harass the Federal forces and undermine support for the war. Various plots were hatched, many bordering on desperation measures. Schemes were afoot to raid northern towns, to liberate Confederate prisoners at Johnson's Island on Lake Erie and elsewhere, to organize escapees into a makeshift army, to engage in guerrilla warfare and create diversions in the North, and the like. There was even a futile attempt in November to torch New York City and occupy it.

Velazquez was to play a role in the attack on Johnson's Island, and had her instructions from Richmond. Approaching Colonel Baker, she claimed to have information that a noted Confederate spy had been captured and imprisoned in the North. She proposed to go to Richmond and pass herself off as a Confederate to learn not only who the spy was and where he was imprisoned, but also what he and his colleagues might be planning. She knew that this would appeal to him, because the rumors of planned raids on northern prisons were widespread and Baker was concerned about them.

Initially reluctant and skeptical that she could pull it off, Baker finally consented to let her try, warning her that if caught, she might hang. Baker arranged passes for her through Union lines, and once clear of them, she had no problem entering Richmond since she was able to identify herself and her real mission to Confederate authorities. Once there, Velazquez immediately delivered various communications from agents in the North and in turn received information about plans for the northern raids to carry to Canada. On her return North, she was so laden with important Confederate documents that she took a wide detour via Parkersburg, West Virginia, just to play it safe. From there she made her way to Baltimore. While staying at the Barnum's Hotel in Baltimore, she found herself short of funds and ill, and was forced to send for a doctor.

Always resourceful, she obtained some funds from a storekeeper whose name had been given to her in case of emergency, and she made the acquaintance of a young Federal captain at the hotel, telling him a story about her bitterness toward the South. The pliant captain introduced her to General E. B. Tyler, who arranged a pass to New York for her. From Baltimore, she conducted some business in Delaware, rendezvousing with a blockade-runner, and then on to Philadelphia where she took a room at the Continental Hotel. There a communication was received that she quotes, indicating that she was using the cover name "Mrs. Sue Battle." Moving on to New York City, she took lodging at Taylor's Hotel.

Once in New York City, Velazquez learned that some Federal detectives were on her trail, and she feared that Colonel Baker had found her out. Running scared, she set out for Canada carrying letters, orders, packages, and a very large sum of money that would be impossible to account for if it were discovered. At the train depot she spotted a detective following her, but thought she had shaken him until the train arrived in Rochester: "To my infinite horror, he entered the car where I was, and took a seat near me," she later wrote. When the conductor came through, the detective said something to him that she couldn't hear and showed him a photograph. The conductor shook his head, and she heard the detective say: "I'll catch her yet."

Sizing up the situation, Velazquez resolved to talk directly to the detective, hoping to confuse and mislead him. She struck up a conversation, trying to learn how much they knew about her. To her dismay, she found out that they knew quite a bit about her, including the fact that she was on the way to Canada carrying important information and a large sum of money. Something critically important that the detective did *not* know about her was exactly what she looked like.

Upon arrival in Canada, the detective gallantly carried her satchel off the train (documents, money, and all), unaware of its contents. "I took the satchel from him, and thanking him for his attention, proceeded to get out of his sight as expeditiously as I could."

Once in Canada, Velazquez met with agents there, delivering dispatches and participating in long conferences about proposed raids on Federal prisons in the Great Lakes area. Her assignment included a visit to Johnson's Island to alert Confederate prisoners to the planned raids and to enlist their aid in plans to "liberate" them in order to open a "second front" or initiate guerrilla activities in the North, the goal being to divert Union forces from southern fronts. In order to accomplish her mission, she needed to exploit her connection with Colonel Baker, so she returned to Washington: "not without many apprehensions."

Velazquez announced herself to Baker as being "just back from Richmond," and was greeted cordially. She told him that she had learned the name of the Confederate spy she had set out to discover on his behalf, some description of him which would help identify him, and also that he was believed to be at Johnson's Island. Playing a dangerous "double agent" game, she fed him a mixture of truth and fiction about what she had learned in Richmond.

It was a very delicate situation. On the one hand, she was working for Baker and his agency as a "trainee" spy, trying to gain his confidence while funneling whatever information she could to him in good conscience, mostly about fraud and corruption by Government contractors. On the other hand, she was trying to exploit her connection with him to gain access into northern prisons while helping to plan the northern raids. "I had much confidence in my own power of reading character and detecting motives," she said. Yet, she never felt sure whether Baker was taken in by her stories, suspected her, or even had definite information about her. It was enough to give her the "creeps."

Next day, Baker approved her proposed trip. She was encouraged to go to Johnson's Island or other northern prisons in order to track down the alleged spy and find out what he was up to, including possible plans for a prison break. It was agreed that she would pass herself off as a Confederate secret service agent intimating that something was afoot as to the rescue or release of Confederate prisoners. Baker was eager to learn whether any escape or rescue plans were in the works.

Baker then confided in her:

> Some of my people are after a spy now who has been traveling between Richmond and Canada, but they don't seem to be able to lay their hands on her. If they don't catch her soon, I have half a mind to let you try what you can do, if you succeed well with your present trip.

"I could not help smiling at the idea of Baker employing me to catch myself," she said.

The presidential elections were now a few weeks away and the Democratic candidate was George B. McClellan, the soldiers' hero. But Velazquez had more hopes for the northern raids than for McClellan's election. She headed west as a secret agent for Baker, via Parkersburg, West Virginia, Cincinnati, Ohio, and finally to Sandusky, Ohio, and the Johnson's Island prison camp. There she spied a young officer who knew "Lieutenant Harry T. Buford." She conferred with him and told him of the liberation plans, but then reported back to Baker that her spy suspect was not at Johnson's Island. This gave her an excuse to press on to another prison camp in Indianapolis, Indiana.

Upon arrival in Indianapolis, she found two men from St. Louis waiting for her, with whom she conferred at length. Her orders were to gain access to the prison and encourage the prisoners to try to escape. She gained entry by accompanying a woman known to the guards who was selling cakes to prisoners. The woman told the guards that Velazquez was her sister. Inside, she spotted a major whom she had met in Richmond "but who had never seen me in female attire." She urged him to help plan a prison break, pointing out that there were few troops to stop them, and told him the general plan of trying to raise a guerrilla army to harass the North and draw troops away from the front.

Then, continuing her double game, Velazquez wrote to Colonel Baker informing him that the man she was looking for (on behalf of the Union) was not in the Indianapolis camp, and she now claimed to have information that he might be at the Alton, Illinois, prison camp. She told Baker that she proposed to go to Alton, and if he was not found there she would give up the search. In reality, she did not plan to go to Alton at all.

Velazquez then called on Governor Oliver P. Morton seeking employment, using the cover story that she was a widow whose husband had been killed in the war. While waiting for further orders for secret service, she hoped to establish contacts in Indianapolis and to find new avenues of information for the Confederate cause. The governor had no jobs to offer, but gave her a letter of introduction for employment at the Federal arsenal where other women were employed manufacturing munitions. There she was given a job packing cartridges. Seeing a golden opportunity, Velazquez plotted to blow up the arsenal, but after about two weeks decided it could not be done without taking many innocent lives.

Since the volume of her correspondence was beginning to attract attention at the post office, she waited anxiously for an assignment, finally receiving money and orders to report to Cairo, Illinois, and then to St. Louis. Following her instructions, she stopped at Planters' House to learn what she could about Federal movements from officers using the hotel as headquarters. Playing the role of a widow in greatly reduced circumstances, Velazquez applied for a job as chambermaid at Planters' House, but to her chagrin there were no openings. Snooping around, she was unable to learn much of value, but did determine the hours during which the officers were least likely to be in their rooms. Lacking any other approach, she determined to surreptitiously enter the rooms in search of information.

Befriending a chambermaid, she managed to steal a passkey and began to pursue her dangerous errand. Slipping into three rooms, she read a number of dispatches of some importance. While leaving the third room, she was almost caught by a bellboy, who turned into the corridor just as she had finished locking the door. Pretending to be lost and confused, she asked the bellboy where the servants' stairway was. He paid little attention to her, and she scurried away in relief.

The information she was able to obtain was forwarded to the proper agent, along with the message that it seemed unlikely she could learn any more at Planters' House. In reply, she was ordered to Hannibal, Missouri, to pick up a package and deliver some dispatches. Here she learned the bad news. The elaborate plan to liberate the Johnson's Island prisoners had failed when the agents were unable to capture the Federal gunboat *Michigan,* a key element of the plot, and the agent who attempted to do so was himself captured. To Velazquez's disgust, the man was carrying papers that revealed the plot, he confessed, and the entire operation came unglued.

> I did not know who was to blame for this failure, but I felt that if all the rest had done their duty as efficiently as I had done mine, success would have crowned our efforts. I, therefore, resolved to return East, and to dissolve all connections with my late co-workers, and with more than half a mind to have nothing more to do with such schemes . . . in the future.

As 1864 drew to a close, Confederate secret service operations took on an air of desperation. With deepening pessimism, the agents in the North still clung to faint hope that they could disrupt the war effort and demoralize the citizens. Velazquez, deciding on a change of pace, took on a new and more lucrative career managing blockade running operations. Ships were loaded with contraband goods from northern cities and Europe, officials were bribed, and cargoes reached southern ports via the Caribbean.

Visiting Cuba once more, she found old acquaintances from 1862 still actively engaged in blockade running. However, she was struck by their "cold-blooded" and "purely pecuniary" attitudes, more concerned that the war might end soon and cut off their source of riches, and seemingly unconcerned about the fate of the Confederacy.

Back in New York City, Velazquez flitted on to other projects, always on the lookout for any opportunity to strike a blow for the cause. She professed to be outraged by the rampant corruption and profiteering in the North, with cynical "war merchants" engaging in all sorts of illegal ventures, but infiltrating these operations made it possible to turn them to the advantage of the South. One of the biggest scandals of all was a ring of thieves and counterfeiters in the Department of Treasury trafficking in bogus Confederate and Federal securities.

Velazquez went to Washington and, after paying a courtesy call to Colonel Baker, contacted a clerk in the treasury who was a known Confederate sympathizer. The man was willing to do anything he could to help, short of risking his personal safety. "He was not the sort of a man I had much liking for," Velazquez noted, "but in the kind of work I was engaged in prosecuting, it did not do to be too fastidious about the characters of one's associates." The clerk gave her an introduction to a very high official who could arrange her entry into the printing bureau; so high up that she was astonished to learn his identity. To him, she proposed a scheme to become involved in the ring and share in the profits, at the same time using the bogus securities to aid the Confederate cause.

Velazquez became the go-between, delivering both real and bogus bonds, currency, and even electrotype plates used to print securities, pilfered from the printing bureau, to brokers in Philadelphia and New York City. The main market for Confederate securities was England. A huge and highly lucrative business was done involving immense sums of money, and she used substantial amounts of her profits to finance continuing Confederate secret service operations.

Finally, when she learned that Colonel Baker was beginning to look into treasury operations, Velazquez quickly severed all connections there, having already accumulated a large sum of money. When Baker tried to expose the treasury ring, he was thwarted by high officials and members of Congress whose attempts to discredit Baker she found "disgraceful." She *knew* Baker's suspects were guilty, she said, because she had been associated with them. She also noted that "during the whole time that the investigation was going on, I was in mortal terror lest Baker should discover that I was implicated."

Velazquez and her associates also took advantage of the widespread, illegal substitute-broker and bounty-jumper operations resulting from the unpopular draft in the latter part of the war. In big cities like New York, immigrants, drifters, and others seized on the Federal offer of bounties to enlist and were paid sizeable sums of money, but then more often than not immediately deserted, only to enlist again elsewhere to make a fast profit. A brokerage ring quickly arose to capitalize on the opportunity for large profits.

Similarly, draft evasion flourished since a man subject to military service could pay a substitute to serve in his place. Fees were determined by supply and demand, and substitute-brokers were in business. The substitutes, too, deserted and repeated the cycle, so that very few actually reached the army. At its worst the system bred totally corrupt brokers who engaged in kidnapping, drugging, forging of papers, and a long list of other crimes in order to produce a marketable "warm body" for delivery to the army.

New York City was a major haven for the brokers. Early in 1865, Colonel Baker went there to investigate the practices, checking in at the Astor House and concealing his presence to prevent his targets from finding out before he was ready to deal with them. According to Velazquez, he requested her to call on him in the evening at the Astor House and asked for her help in cracking the broker rings. Velazquez gave him some suggestions, later alerting her immediate colleagues to his presence and dropping out of the business, too.

To see for himself how the system worked, Baker arranged to be personally "brokered"—hired to serve as a soldier or to substitute for one. With elaborate use of trickery, he manipulated a large group of the brokers into a position where he could (and did) make mass arrests. But when the news of Lincoln's assassination reached him, Baker returned immediately to Washington, where he played a role in the capture of assassin John Wilkes Booth.

Before that, however, Velazquez had been persuaded to undertake one more Confederate secret service assignment out west, another attempt to free prisoners. Though skeptical about the project, her sentiments for the prisoners induced her to try. Maybe she could at least give them some aid and comfort, she thought. So it was back to Dayton, Ohio, this time dressed as a poor girl looking for housework.

Learning the names of some "copperhead" families (southern sympathizers), she obtained work in a copperhead household. There she was quickly befriended and treated as an equal—even a privileged guest—when she let it be known that she formerly was a person of substance, now reduced to scrabbling around for a living. Gradually, she learned of a network of copperheads who were helping escaped prisoners. They would rendezvous in Cleveland to obtain the means to escape south. By now Velazquez had accumulated almost $150,000, a large portion of which she carried as cash. Heading to Cleveland to help, she was intercepted at Columbus by an urgent dispatch directing her to go to Canada at once. Having no time to take other steps on behalf of the soldiers, she contributed $3,000 for their relief before departing for Canada.

Reflecting the frantic times, her activities became a blur. From her unstated mission in Canada, she headed for New York, then to London to see after the sales of bogus Confederate bonds, which were still profitable even at low prices. Then to Paris, where news of Sherman's march gave the impression the war was almost over, and then to Liverpool. Returning by steamer to New York City, she arrived in the harbor just as news of Lee's surrender reached the ship. "[The news] fairly stunned me," she wrote. Immediately she settled her "secret banking and brokerage transactions" accounts, which again must have been substantial.

Apparently "hope springs eternal," for she refused to believe that Lee's surrender necessarily ended the war; there were other armies that could carry on the fight, she thought. While other Confederate agents in New York City were highly pessimistic, Velazquez "was not disposed to give up while a southern soldier remained in the field." The last remaining hope was the scattered armies in the West. Eager to do what she could to help, Velazquez headed there carrying dispatches for guerrilla leader William Quantrill. On the return trip, in Columbus, Ohio, she learned of Lincoln's assassination. Like many thinking southerners, she was deeply concerned about the possible backlash on the South. The unexpected event also disrupted all her plans. She was at a loss as to what to do next.

Returning to Washington, D.C., to confer with her colleagues, Velazquez again met with Colonel La Fayette Baker. To her consternation, he finally enlisted her aid in catching the female Confederate spy who kept slipping through their fingers. Considering the timing of his request, she wondered whether Baker suspected the woman (her) of being in on the assassination plot. The people's mood bothered her; if caught, she could be railroaded as a conspirator. Perhaps, she thought, it would be prudent to leave the country for a while until things calmed down. She had until next morning to decide on his offer.

Next morning before Baker called, Velazquez received a letter from her brother who expected to be in New York City in a few days with his wife and children. He suggested that they all go to Europe together. On the basis of his letter, she decided to accept Baker's assignment as a cover story, but to go to Europe and stay as long as necessary. By now, Joseph E. Johnston's army had surrendered (April 26, 1865) and she was resigned to the fact that the cause was lost, and therefore her mission was at an end. Now she needed to consider her own welfare, and that of her family.

Baker gave her instructions on a general plan for capturing the female agent. "I was astonished to find how much he knew of some of my movements," she wrote. "He and his men must have been on the point of capturing me many times, and they undoubtedly would have done so, had I not had the wit to take the course I did in cultivating his acquaintance."

Velazquez started for New York ostensibly on a search for the female spy, but in reality to wait anxiously for her brother and to get beyond Baker's reach. Before long her brother arrived with his wife, two children, and a nurse in tow, and they had a joyful reunion. One of the children had been named after her. Wasting no time, they left for England on a Cunard Line steamship. From England they went on to Paris where her brother had been educated, visiting the College de France and the medical school where he had studied. Both she and her brother spoke French and appreciated the French culture, so they hired a fancy rig and toured Paris in style, taking in theaters, museums, cathedrals, and monuments.

A side trip to Reims, where Velazquez's childhood idol Joan of Arc had won fame, caused her to observe with some irony:

> [At this time] I was of a more practical turn of mind than I had been a few years before. The romance had been pretty well knocked out of me by the rough experience of real life; and although I was better able to appreciate the performances of Joan of Arc at their true value, somehow they did not interest me to the extent they once did.

The grand tour obviously must have been sponsored by Velazquez's wartime profits, and it continued for some time. They toured Germany, then Poland, and back to Paris, where at the Hotel de Louvre she encountered some Confederate officers who had known "Lieutenant Harry T. Buford." It appears to have been common knowledge shortly after the war ended that "Buford" had been a woman. Without identifying herself to them, Velazquez questioned the officers about "Buford's" career. They praised her valor, but one denounced her for wearing male attire.

The party then toured London, and made a side trip to the factory town of Manchester. By now they were all getting homesick for America, and it was time to decide where they would stay and what they would do. Her sister-in-law wanted to live in Spain, but she and her brother decided to return to the United States. Once they reached New York, however, her sister-in-law persuaded him to move to Mexico. This did not appeal to Velazquez, so they parted company.

The memoirs do not say how much time passed during the European tour. Presumably it was long enough for Velazquez to feel comfortable about dealing with Colonel Baker and traveling openly through the East. The assassination conspirators had been hanged on July 7, 1865, and the country was beginning to emerge from the period of national mourning. The action had shifted away from military conflict to the political arena,

President Andrew Johnson and the Congress struggling over Reconstruction issues.

Her Confederate contacts had sternly warned Velazquez about the
dangers of going to Washington, but she was stubborn. Fully realizing
that Baker must be aware that both she and the female agent under pursuit had vanished, she decided to beard the lion in his den. At the very
least, she would have some tall explaining to do. At most, she might be
thrown in prison and implicated in the assassination conspiracy. Still, she
went to Washington. As it happened, Baker was out of town.

"I do not know to this day," she reported in her 1876 memoirs,
"whether he ever discovered that I was a Confederate secret-service
agent." (Baker died in 1868.)

Velazquez had decided to tour the old Confederate states and take
personal stock of the situation before taking up a new life. As she continued through Richmond, North and South Carolina, and Atlanta, meeting old friends along the way, she found that her reputation had preceded
her. Everyone wanted to meet the woman who had served as a male soldier, and she was pleased by their attention and recognition.

Aside from the personal gratification of being praised for her deeds,
though, Velazquez found nothing but ruin and despair everywhere in
the South. "It is no wonder," she noted, "that at this dismal time, certain
ill-advised emigration schemes found countenance with those who saw
no hope for themselves or their children but either to go out of the country, or [go far away] to start life anew under better auspices than were
then possible [in] the late Confederacy."

New Orleans, her former hometown, she found in a pitiful plight,
the desolation sickening, which she attributed to "ambitious and
unscrupulous politicians" furthering their own ends. "I longed to quit
the scene of so much misery, and fully sympathized with those who
preferred to fly . . . and to seek homes in other lands, rather than to
remain and be victimized." She felt that most of the emigration
schemes, to various Central and South American countries, were
started by swindlers.

The exploitation of the people yearning to start new lives, she said,
"is one of the saddest and dreariest pages in the history of the country." She was among those earnestly looking for a new home, but she
was "street smart"—having observed at close hand all the wartime
scams—and unlikely to be taken in by amateurs. Giving up on emigration schemes, Velazquez put the war behind her and went west looking
for opportunity.

Postscript

MUCH OF her remaining story, as far as it is presently known, shows her pitted against opportunists and swindlers. Yet, she herself did not hesitate to gain profit toward the end of the war and to use it to travel and explore, for her personal advantage, all over Europe and the western United States.

Whatever her motives, clearly she was personally interested in emigration possibilities and she decided to investigate the 1866 plan for colonization of former Confederates in Venezuela. She and her colleagues were skeptical of the pie-in-the-sky claims made for benefits to be provided by the host country, and she resolved to investigate them personally. Just prior to embarking to Venezuela, she married her third husband, a Major Wasson, who unfortunately, caught "black fever" and died shortly afterwards in Caracas.

The villain of the piece apparently is one "Captain Fred A. Johnson" (his real name apparently was Johnson), whom she denounced in letters to friends in New Orleans, strongly advising against emigration to Venezuela. "My experiences in Venezuela," she said, "convinced me that it was no place for poor Americans to go."

From here on, her memoirs increasingly take on the airs of a travelogue. She goes into great detail about the cultural and natural resources of Venezuela, and she is very interested in its mineral wealth. From there, she goes on to visit her childhood home in the Caribbean, stopping at Havana where she was wined and dined and lauded by Spanish officials who knew of her career as a Confederate soldier.

Back in the United States she decided to try her fortunes in the West where everything was up for grabs. Traveling first to Omaha, Nebraska, and then beyond on stagecoach routes, she was exposed to western adventurers and desperados, largely perceived as whiskey-drinking, card-playing, gun-toting fanatics.

In 1868, she married again (her fourth husband), a miner in Nevada. They prospered for a while, but she had a low opinion of her husband's colleagues, and persuaded him to pull up stakes and move to California, where they bought a home in the Sacramento Valley. But her husband had "gold fever," prospecting for a year in Utah, and spending all his money without accomplishing anything. (During this period, her account suggests that they probably were separated for a time.) Then they moved on to Salt Lake City where they stayed for several months, during which she gave birth to a baby boy. She had become disenchanted with the entire milieu of miners and mining, and professed to have learned some lessons, including the fact "that mining speculations are things that people who have consciences should have as little as possible to do with."

From this point on in her memoirs, mentions of her husband became scarcer. She reports seeking fortunes in Colorado, New Mexico, and Texas. While describing a trip down the Rio Grande Valley, she mentions "traveling companions" and a gentleman who is kind to her and her young son, but there is no mention of her husband. In modern terminology, they appear to have been "estranged."

The memoirs of Loreta Janeta Velazquez end abruptly in post–Civil War Texas. After the memoirs were published in 1876, some book reviews and correspondence exist to partially document her career for the decade of the 1870s. Having squandered her fortunes, she wrote the memoirs (rather hastily, judging by internal evidence) to support herself and her young son. General Jubal Early denounced her as a fraud, even refusing to believe that she was a southern woman.

She wrote to Early on May 18, 1878 (using the title "Correspondent Le Buletin Commercial, Rio de Janeiro, Empire Brazil"), protesting his apparent effort "to injure me and my book." In a plea for sympathy, she told him, "I have had trials enough to have driven almost any proud spirited woman to madness, or to commit suicide . . . and with God's protection I have lived above it all, and all I now ask from you is justice to my child. I live for him and him alone."

After about 1880, she literally fades from the pages of history, and no record has been found of her life after that, or of her death. Far from attaining the fame and glory that she originally sought, Velazquez vanished into obscurity.

15 Memories of a Hospital Matron

Emily V. Mason

*W*HEN THE war broke out, we were living in Fairfax County, Virginia. We boasted of fifteen families of "cousins" with whom we were in constant and most affectionate intercourse. This the neighborhood of the Episcopal Theological Seminary of Virginia is renowned for its delightful society. Besides our kinsfolk, we had as neighbors the families of the professors at the seminary, the family of Bishop Johns, the Fairfaxes of Vaucluse, Captain Forrest, U.S.N. and C.S.N., Mrs. Scott of Bush Hill, and others. Through President Pierce our older boy (the son of my widowed sister) received an appointment to West Point. He had been there but two years, and the other boy had just received his warrant for the navy, when the war came to break up our home and drive us forth wanderers for four long years. I heard in Congress the impassioned and sorrowful appeals of Mr. Davis, General Breckinridge, Mr. Pendleton, and others in the interests of peace, and saw the bitterness and anger of our foes. But it was impossible for us who had never seen war to realize what would be the invasion of our country. And who could believe that armed men (Americans like ourselves) could be brought to enter our beloved Virginia with hostile intent,—that "Old Virginia" which all professed to honor?

I was in Washington the night that the troops crossed the Potomac. Never can I forget the dull, heavy tramp of the armed men as they passed under my window. Each foot seemed to fall upon my heart, while tears rained from my eyes. Next day I bade adieu to the city I was not to see again for twenty-five years. Already I found sentries stationed along our roads, and before evening we were prisoners in our own house. My sister had a few hundred dollars in Mr. Corcoran's bank. How to get this money before we were entirely cut off from the North was the question. Already our "West Pointer" had gone to join the Virginia forces, and our neighbors and friends who had sons and husbands were following them South. My sister and her family were anxious to go. Our younger boy, a lad of sixteen, volunteered to find his way on foot through the woods, to cross the Potomac above Georgetown, get to the bank in Washington, and bring safely the money which would be so much needed. This was a fit beginning for his after adventures. Chased by soldiers, fired upon by sentinels, he managed to conceal himself in the woods, and came in after dark, weary and footsore, after twenty-five miles of travel, with the money concealed in his bosom,—the last United States money we saw for four years.

I resolved to remain at home and take care of my property. Having been much associated with the army, I was sure to find old friends among the officers to protect us. We were non-combatants, and in modern warfare it was never known that women had been disturbed in their homes. To our anxious friends I quoted how, in the late Italian and Austrian war, the women stood on the balconies of the Italian villas and looked down upon the battlefields of Magenta and Solferino. But the French and Italians had no "Billy Wilson's men," recruited from the purlieus of New York, no raw levies, ignorant and prejudiced, who thought to do their country service by insulting "Secesh" women. Our houses were entered with pretense to search for arms; in reality to steal thimbles and jewelry, and even to take earrings from the women's ears. Trees were cut down, gardens rifled, storerooms invaded. In vain was complaint made to the commandant in Alexandria. He said he had no power over such men, and advised our retreating (where it was possible) to the security of our own "lines," then about Manassas; but I held out a little longer. Barricading, at night, windows and doors with tables, piano, and bookcases, we were alarmed by thumps upon the doors and threats to break in; and at mealtimes soldiers would enter and devour everything which was set before us. They robbed the henroost and the cellar, burned our fences, and insulted us in every way. My sister resolved to take refuge, with her daughters, at a friend's house just within our lines. She was not allowed to take her own vehicle, but was forced to pay thirty dollars to the military authorities for a carriage to convey the party of four (including the son, who was eager to enter the army) about ten miles. Only one trunk was allowed for all of this family, who were leaving their home never to enter it again! How often, in the after days of the Confederacy, had they reason to regret the warm flannels, furs, and silk gowns left behind! Our house, occupied at first by friends from Alexandria, was not allowed to remain long out of the enemy's hands. General Phil Kearny, command- ing the New Jersey troops, soon took forcible possession of house and furniture. Happily, I was spared the distress of witnessing these things. My niece and adopted daughter, living in New Jersey, and married to an officer of General Scott's staff, became ill, and I was asked to come to her; her husband feeling certain that he had it in his power to send me home when my presence should be no longer needed. Alas, he little knew how impossible would be what he so confidently promised, and I so con- fidingly believed! Advising with the officer in command at Alexandria, I turned my back upon my dear home, and went to the North; not, how- ever, before I had seen how rapidly the work of destruction was going on in our neighborhood. The glass of our greenhouse was wantonly broken by muskets, our roses were trampled down, and the carriage was cut into bits; a neighbor's piano sharing the same fate. In my last walk in the neighborhood, for which I was obliged to get a permit (as well as for the cow to go to pasture, and the man to go to the market), I saw a party of rude soldiers sitting on the porch of one of our clergyman friends, read- ing and tearing up his correspondence! I wonder how they liked mine, which they had soon after?

No sooner did I reach New Jersey than I found myself an object of interest and suspicion. Only those who lived through that terrible time can understand the excited state of the public mind, North and South. I saw myself announced in the papers as a "Secesh spy," sent by General Beauregard to arouse the Catholics of the North, and by Mr. James M. Mason to stir up the Democrats. A full description of my person was given, and my "qualifications" for such a task. These were infinitely flat- tering to my abilities; for it was confidently asserted that I was clever enough to take in every detail of "fortifications," and ingenious enough to establish an underground system of communication with the "Rebels"! My letters were intercepted, and the people were so clamorous to read them at the post office that the mayor of the town was obliged to take them out and bring them to me, which he did with every apology. He behaved in the most gentlemanlike manner. But my position became every day more painful and embarrassing, especially as it involved the peace and security of the family with whom I was staying, who were nat- urally regarded as my "accomplices." They besought me not to go out, or speak to any one. It was not difficult to obey in this last point, for nobody would speak to me. A leper could not have been avoided with surer signs of horror and aversion. Having gone to early church to ease my anxious heart, I read in the paper that I went at that early hour to meet my "confederates," and threats were made that a few days would see me safe in Fort Lafayette!

To give an idea of the extraordinary system of espionage carried on at this time, I must relate the following incident. Being a Catholic, and never having seen Archbishop Hughes, who was famed for his eloquence, I yielded to the suggestion of a friend of mine in New York, a Protestant lady, and a firm "Republican," who offered to introduce me. She came for me and took me to New York, and we went in the street omnibus to the archbishop's door, were most amiably received, and had a pleasant talk, all of us carefully avoiding a subject on which we could not agree,— the war. Both going and coming, I remarked a man who sat near the door of the omnibus and often looked at us, got out where we did, and even accompanied us to the ferry on our return. After this I received a most anxious letter from an officer in Washington, a friend, telling me he had been at a dinner at Mr. Seward's with Archbishop Hughes and others, and Mr. Seward was called out on business of importance. Presently the archbishop was sent for. When he returned he said to this officer: "What a curious thing has happened, showing the state of the public mind! A Catholic lady, Miss Mason, calls upon me, as does every Catholic coming to my diocese. She is followed and watched, and here comes a telegram to Mr. Seward telling him that I have received this 'spy.' He calls me out, and I tell him the lady is no more a spy than I am." Fancy the feelings of my friend! He was ready to fall from his chair with alarm. And no sooner was he at home than he wrote to beseech me not to leave the house again, lest something befall me.

This incident determined me to get away, if possible. I was distracted about my people. Six months had elapsed; I could get no letters, and the newspapers were filled with the most exaggerated accounts of the suffering in the South. I was told that if I attempted to leave the North I would be arrested. But I resolved to risk this rather than suffer, and make my friends suffer, such anxiety. First I wrote to some Sisters of Charity, who were announced to be going South, to ask if I might go with them in any capacity. Then I prayed the bishop, who was full of concern for me, to send me off "some way." In vain. He said that if I were found with these Sisters it would injure their mission; that I could never escape the vigilance of the government; and he advised me to be patient. But *that* I could not be. Some Sisters from New York came to see me soon after, to say that they were sure I would get through "somehow," and to beg me to take some letters with which they were charged, from agonized wives and mothers whose husbands and sons had been taken prisoners at the battle of Manassas, and were now in the military prisons of Richmond. I could not carry the letters, but I promised to learn them by heart, take the names of the men, and, if I ever reached Richmond, find the prisoners, and repeat the news and messages from their families,—which I really did, as much to my own satisfaction as to theirs.

After many plans revolved, and dismissed as impracticable, some friends living at Easton, Pennsylvania, came to spend a week with us, and it was arranged that one of these ladies' trunks should be left behind, at her departure, and mine taken in its stead; and that when an opportunity arrived, I should slip away, go to Easton, take up my luggage, and go to Kentucky via Philadelphia. Once in Kentucky, I was sure I could be concealed for a time, and find a way to get into the Confederacy through Western Virginia, where General Rosecrans was in command of a division of the Union army. Months before I set out I wrote to Newport, Kentucky, to my cousins there, that I should make the attempt to see them "on or about the 2d of November." And this message, couched in most ambiguous terms and without signature, received an equally ambiguous answer,—"Ready to hunt with you at time specified." To have money for this undertaking, I must go to New York, to a bank in which my brother-in-law had some money and North Carolina bonds which I might use. Hardly had I entered the ferry when I saw the same man who had accompanied me on my visit to the archbishop, weeks before. He kept his eye upon me till I entered my friend's house on Second Avenue. To her I told my fears and my errand. She assured me I should dodge my persecutor, and after a time led me through the back yard to the stable, where we entered her carriage, drove out by the alley far away to Bloomingdale, and then, by circuitous streets, to the bank, where my friend's husband brought me my moneys. We concealed them in the puffings of my sleeves, and at the ferry we bade good-by with many tears.

I mingled with the crowd, and thought myself safe, when somebody touched me upon the arm. Looking round, expecting to see my detective, I found the face of one of my childhood friends from Kentucky, who, reading in the papers of my peril, came to see if he could aid me, being a "good Union man." He had not the courage of a Caesar, but he had the heart of a Kentuckian, and he told me how for days he had been watching and waiting for an opportunity to communicate with me. It was agreed that I should make my attempt the next day. He would go on to Philadelphia, and wait for me till the following midnight. Driving out with my invalid niece the next morning, I left her for a moment, ostensibly, but I took the first train for Reading, in fear and trembling, picked up my luggage, and, under the escort of a stout journalist whose paper had been burned the day before for sympathizing with my side, I reached Philadelphia at the appointed hour. I drew a long sigh of relief when once on the railway, bound for the West. Arrived at Newport, I found my young cousins on the ferryboat, armed and equipped as for a "hunt," bade good-by to my old friend, and went to consult as to what should be my next move.

It was resolved that my best chance would be to throw myself upon the charity of the old Archbishop of Cincinnati, an ardent Union man, who had known my family, and whom I had known, in other days. To his door I went, shut in a close carriage, to find him out of town. Turning to go away, his brother appeared in the hall, and said: "Miss Mason! My brother has been expecting you for some days." "Expecting me?" I rejoined. "Impossible! I have just run away from the North, and am concealing myself near here." "Yes," said he, "my brother saw your name at the custom house in a list of a thousand 'suspected,' and opposite your name was, 'Dangerous. To be watched.'" I dropped into a chair, exclaiming: "I wish the earth would open and swallow me! It is plain I shall never get away to my people, with whom I have not communicated in six months." He consoled me with the assurance that if I got into prison his brother would be able to get me out, since he knew I had done nothing against "the government." I explained that I had come to pray him to find means to get me home, and he promised to inform me when his brother should return and be able to see me. Anxious days passed while I lay *perdue,* afraid to go out. Yet among the "initiated" my presence was known, for I had offers of aid from many quarters. A poor little priest and some poorer Sisters offered me their tiny all, to help me on my perilous way. At last came a note from the good bishop, to whom I went with my tale of woe. "God bless my soul!" said he. "I have already thirteen women on my hands, some of them French Sisters, who are trying to get to New Orleans." I prayed him to get me off first, as I had been his old friend. And having eaten of the stale cakes and drunk of the sour wine which he offered me, I was ready to go. He then pulled from his pocket a long, lean purse, from which, after much searching, he drew forth a gold piece, the only one, and pressed it upon me, saying, "You will want it for some poor soul, if not for yourself." God rest his soul, and reward his charity a thousandfold, in that country where there is no North, no South, no Catholic, no Protestant, but all are as the children of God!

In an article published in the Charleston News and Courier, some years ago, I gave an account of my journey through the lines, by Western Virginia, and this appeared afterwards in a book, Our Women of the War. But as this book was little known, and is now quite rare, the story may well be repeated here. Armed with a letter from the bishop, I went to a hotel in Cincinnati where were some gentlemen going on a government steamer to carry forage and provisions to the Federal army in Western Virginia. I had a letter to General Rosecrans, whom I had known in happier days, and was sure he would send me into the Confederate lines by flag of truce, if I could reach him before he received communications from Washington. The gentlemen to whom I was recommended were to set out the next morning, and were most kind in offering to take me with them. So behold me on board, with two well-bred men,—one a volunteer officer, the other his brother-in-law, a physician, and both from Boston. They were too polite to ask my errand, and I was too prudent to disclose it. If they assumed that I was going to the Union army to nurse soldiers, it was not necessary to disclaim it. We discussed everything but politics on that journey of three weeks, and became fast friends. We traveled by day only, as both sides of the river were said to be infested by Rebel scouts, ready to fire upon us at any moment; and I was not allowed to go upon the guards of the boat, lest I should be a mark for their bullets. Longingly I looked for the Rebel cavalry, and prayed they would come and take us, and thus end my difficulties. But they did not come, and one day we ran upon a snag, and to save our steamer we were obliged to give to the waters all our grain and forage. My trunk only was saved from the wreck, and empty-handed we proceeded to our destination. When about ten or twelve miles from "headquarters" my gentlemen left me, to report the disaster, and by them I sent my letter of introduction to the commanding general, with one of my own, reminding him of our former acquaintance, and stating the circumstances which had brought me to his camp; saying that I waited at a respectful distance, not to see what he would wish concealed from my people, and assuring him, if he would let me pass through his hosts and send me to my own lines, I would not in any way make use of any knowledge I might obtain, to his disadvantage. In a few hours came a telegram, saying that a flag of truce would go out at daylight next morning, and that his own servant and ambulance would be sent for me during the night.

While awaiting an answer, I had observed that the steamer was being loaded with great bundles discharged from wagons on the high bluff above us, and that these bundles came sliding down from the banks on a plankway, falling heavily upon the lower deck.

"What are you loading?" I asked one of the boatmen.

"These are sick men come in from camp," he replied.

"An outrage upon humanity!" I exclaimed, and ran down the companion way to examine the live bundles, which were coughing, groaning, and moaning. Here were men in all stages of measles, pneumonia, camp fever, and other disorders incident to camp life, sent in wagons over thirteen miles of mountain road, on a December evening, without nurses, without physician, and with no other covering than the blanket in which each man was enveloped. They assured me they had been sent out in the early morning, without food or medicine, and were expected to remain without any attention till the sailing of the steamer to a hospital twenty miles below. In spite of the remonstrances of the boatmen, who declared the "company" had let the boat to the government to transport horse feed, and not men, I had the poor fellows taken into the cabin and placed in the berths, denuded of mattresses and bed covers, and then proceeded to physic and feed them as best I could. No entreaties could prevail upon the steward of this "loyal" company to give me anything for them to eat. I had tea, however, in my stateroom, and some crackers. The doctor had a box of Seidlitz powders, a great lump of asafœtida, and a jug of whiskey. There were thirty men to be doctored. To the chilly ones I gave hot whiskey and water, the most popular of my remedies; to those who wailed the loudest the pills of asafœtida proved calming; and the Seidlitz powders were given to the fever patients, whose tongues and pulses I examined with great care; and where there was doubt, and fear of doing harm, the tea was safely given. Hardly was the jug emptied and the last pill and powder administered, when the captain and the doctor returned from camp, and announced that the ambulance waited for me. The doctor was not a little indignant at my having appropriated his whole medical supply, but was kind enough to go around the group of patients, examine them, and tell me their real condition; so that I left them in his hands, and departed with their thanks and blessings. And this was the beginning of my ministrations amongst soldiers, which lasted to the end of the war, and which became the life of my life.

It was midnight when I left the steamer, with a thankful adieu to my kind hosts. Once more on my native heath, though seated upon my trunk, with rain and sleet beating in my face, I felt neither cold nor fatigue, for at last I saw home and friends before me. After crossing a mountain, over the worst road imaginable, we reached the camp at daylight, through miles of white tents and formidable-looking outposts. We drove to the general's tent, and his orderly came to say that I must go to a lady whose house was within the camp: and there I should rest, get breakfast, and be ready to set out at eight o'clock. By this time my strength had given out; want of sleep, fatigue, and excitement had made me really ill. I had to be lifted from the ambulance, put to bed, and fortified by sundry cups of strong coffee, to prepare me for an interview with the general and for my departure. I have had the opportunity many times since to thank this lady for her kindness, and to talk over with her the strange fortune which brought us together at this juncture. The camp was upon her plantation, and on the top of the mountain above us was stationed her husband, an artillery officer of the Confederate army, whose guns were pointed toward the camp, but who could not fire without endangering the lives of his wife and children. The kind general came to greet me and give instructions for the journey. He warned me to be careful of my luggage, as he was obliged to employ on escort duty men noted in camp as thieves and freethinkers. But over these men he placed two experienced officers, to see that the men did their duty and treated me with proper respect. How accomplished his thieves must have been may be inferred from the fact that, though I sat upon my trunk and carried my bag in my hand, not only were my combs and brushes stolen, but my prayer book and my Thomas à Kempis, for which they could have no possible use.

The general further reminded me that I should follow in the path of war, that ruin and desolation would be on every side, and that there was but one house which he could count upon where I might find shelter before I reached the Southern lines. In this house, once the finest in the country, I would find a woman as beautiful as Judith, and as fierce. He declared that she had been a thorn in his side for many months. Driven almost to madness by the depredations of his soldiers, her husband and son in the Confederate lines, her cattle and horses stolen or mutilated, she waged war upon her enemies with relentless fury. Leading his men into ambuscades, she would betray them to the Southern scouts, and, while the fighting went on, would sit upon her horse and pick off his men with her pistol. She had been summoned to his camp to answer these charges, but always defied him, bidding him "come and fetch her." In vain had he tried to appease her. As she lived in this fine house at the foot of a great mountain, he counseled me to force myself upon her, if necessary, and demand shelter for a night; if I should be ill, to stop there, and send on the flag of truce for succor.

I parted with tears from this the last friend of "the other side;" and though I invited the general to come to Richmond, and he promised to do so, he never got so far! My friend loaded me with messages for her husband and family, begging them to come and release her from her forced sojourn with the enemy, and at the last moment gave me a package of clothing for a poor woman on the mountain side, whose house had been burned the previous day, and whose loom, her sole means of support, had been destroyed by the soldiers. As we drove off, the general dropped a gold piece into my lap, saying, "That's for the poor woman on the mountain," and before I could thank him the escort "closed up," and we were off to Dixie's Land.

We found the poor woman sitting amidst her ruins, the snow making more hideous the scene of desolation. The road on every side was marked by burned houses and barns, and torn and disordered fences. Now and then a half-starved dog or a ragged negro would peer from some ruins, and then hide from us. Crossing over mountains and fording streams, we reached at last the inhospitable mansion at which the general had recommended me to knock so loudly. In answer to our summons appeared a tall, dark woman, with flashing eyes and jet-black hair, behind whom peeped a fair girl, in contrast to our virago. The latter, without waiting for us to speak, waved us off with a most imperious gesture. "Go on," she said; "this is no place for you. You have done me harm enough. There is nothing more for you to steal."

Leaning from the ambulance, I implored her to take me in for the night. Half dead with cold and fatigue, I could go no farther. I assured her that I was a Southern woman trying to get to my family, of whom I had had no news in six long months.

"You are in very bad company for a Southern woman," she rejoined, "yet as you are a woman I will let you come in; but these men shall not enter my doors."

After explaining that we had a flag of truce, and that if they abandoned me I could never get on, as she had neither horse nor wagon to give me, she consented to admit the two officers, and to allow the men to sleep in an outhouse. By a blazing fire she told me the story of their sufferings, gave me a good supper and bed, and next morning I took my last taste of real coffee for many a long day. But the officers did not find the coffee so good, as the pretty blonde daughter vented her spite upon them by withholding the sugar, and they were too much afraid of her to ask for it.

The next evening brought us to our lines. As we approached these the escort became unwilling to go on, and declared they were afraid of "bushwhackers." It was necessary to use blows and drawn swords to get them on. How my heart bounded when I saw the first "man in gray"! I soon found that, in spite of all reports to the contrary, he was well armed, well dressed, and looked well fed. We fell upon the pickets from a South Carolina regiment, and I was proud to show to my escort that the men were all gentlemen of refinement and elegance. It was impossible for me to get to the Confederate camp that night, and impossible to allow the flag of truce to approach nearer. I was forced to sleep in one of the two log huts belonging to the pickets, while the other was allotted to the Ohio officer who had me in charge and his Confederate host. They had but one bed. What was to be done? I was informed next day by the Ohioan that there was a long struggle between the representatives of the contending armies as to who should occupy the bed. At last it was determined they should sleep together. "I had no objection to sleep with a South Carolinian," said the Northern officer, "but I can imagine what it cost him to sleep with a Yankee!" The flag of truce went back next morning, with a letter of thanks from me to the general. Then came from the Confederate camp a carriage exhumed from some long-disused coach house. It was driven by a little Irishman, who announced that he had heard a "Yankee lady" had come through the lines, and he wanted to see how she looked. So far already had the two countries drifted apart that the people spoke as if the separation had endured years instead of months. Mounting the ladder-like steps of this primitive vehicle, I drove through a camp of thousands without finding one familiar face, though every man came to stare at the unwonted sight of a carriage and a woman. As my courage was about to give way, I was greeted by the familiar voice of a young physician,—"a family connection,—who hurried to my assistance, got into the carriage, and promised to find me shelter and set me on to Richmond. Alas, shelter was not easy to find. Every house near the camp, every barn, every cabin, was filled with sick and wounded soldiers. There was no town within twelve miles, and the stage to Richmond passed only twice a week. I must wait somewhere two days. We drove from house to house. The poor people either had their rooms filled, or they had suffered so much from disease, resulting from their hospitality, that they were afraid to take any one in. I was fainting with fatigue, when, at the door of a neat-looking house, a young girl, who heard her father's refusal, cried: "Father, let the lady come in! I will give her my bed!" Upon the assurance of the doctor that I had no disease, and was ill only from fatigue, they admitted me to a delicious feather bed, from which I emerged the next day for dinner.

At the table I observed the mistress of the house preparing Sunday messes of "bacon and greens" to send to some sick men in one of her outhouses. I followed the servant, to find seven East Tennesseans lying on dirty straw, in every stage of camp fever. The air was stifling; the men were suffering in every way, especially for medicine and for clean beds and clothing. With the aid of the one least ill, we brought in clean straw, had water heated in the big iron pot standing in the chimney corner, while bits of rag served for towels and toothbrushes, and we soon changed the atmosphere and the aspect of things. The water of boiled rice made them a drink, and when the doctor came to see me he prescribed, and agreed to come out from the camp every day and visit them. "Do not be afraid of losing them," he added. "You cannot kill an East Tennessean." I did not feel so sure of this. So before parting we prayed together (they were good Baptists), and begged that God would spare us to meet again. I promised to come back in a week or ten days, armed with power to open a hospital and bring them into it; and here I will add that at the end of a fortnight I had the happiness to see my East Tennesseans drive up to the hospital, waving their caps to me,—not one of the seven missing.

The night before the anxiously expected stage arrival, I saw drive to our door a wagon, which deposited a fine-looking young officer. He walked feebly, and I went to meet him. He was looking for the coach to take him to his family in Richmond. I saw that he was very ill, and found that he had been six weeks in camp with fever. He begged that I would not let the people of the house know it, or they would refuse him a lodging. We took into our confidence the young girl whose kindness had secured me entrance, and soon we helped our patient up the steep ladder stairs, and saw him fall heavily upon the bed. While she went for hot water, I drew off, with difficulty, the heavy spurs and wet boots, rubbed the cold feet and bathed them, washed the fevered mouth, and administered hot tea. When fairly in bed, and after I had promised under no circumstances to leave him behind, he exclaimed, "This is heaven!" And heaven sent him refreshing sleep.

Next morning we left our kind hosts, the sick man resting his weary head on my shoulder; and so we jolted over the rough way till we reached the neighboring town, Lewisburg, and drove to the office of the medical director to ask what should be done with our precious burden, by this time delirious and unable to proceed farther. After some delay (for the town was filled with the sick and dying) we found a good lady who agreed to take him, though every room in the house was full. I saw the poor fellow comfortably disposed in her drawing-room, where he was as carefully tended as by the mother who was soon summoned to his aid.

This was the first campaign of a terrible winter, which proved so fatal to Southern men, called from luxurious homes, where they had never known ice and snow, to die amidst these cruel mountains, with every disease incident to cold and exposure. In this town all the women opened their houses and gave their services. The churches and courthouse were turned into hospitals. I went through one of the former to aid in giving food and medicine. In every pew lay a patient, cheerful sufferer, and into the inclosure round the altar they were constantly carrying the dead, wrapped in a single blanket. Side by side lay master and servant, rich and poor. War, like death, is a great leveler. I saw come in from the camps ambulance after ambulance with their sad loads, the dead and dying in the same vehicle, and tried in vain to stay many a parting breath. How could I leave such scenes, where there was so much to do? Impelled by the hope of coming back with aid and comfort, I hurried away.

There was no way of communicating with my family to tell them of my escape, and arriving in Richmond alone and at night, I did not know how to find any one. At last, as I was passing along one of the main streets, I saw through an open window, seated by a bright fire, my cousin Mrs. Sidney Smith Lee. Entering unannounced, I was informed that they all thought me in a "Yankee prison." It was not long before I found all my dear ones, and I told them of my resolve to leave them again, after a few days' preparation, to return to the mountains, gather up my patients, and go to work. The President said to me at parting: "God bless your work! Remember, if you save the lives of a hundred men, you will have done more for your country than if you had fought a hundred battles." From him and from the surgeon general I had *carte blanche,* free transportation wherever I should go, hospital stores, and nurses *ad libitum,* could I have found any of these willing to encounter the winter's snow on the mountains, where were defeat and disaster, sickness and suffering. With one faithful man servant I set out, so full of enthusiasm as not to feel cold and fatigue, everywhere encountering that sympathy and kindness from our people which never failed me in all my wanderings. We slept at Staunton; and when I asked for my bill, the landlord said that he had none for a woman who went to nurse soldiers: and so it befell me everywhere.

"Jim" was my protector on my journey; and when we opened the hospital at the Greenbrier White Sulphur Springs, he was my cook, nurse, maid, sympathizer, everything, and he did all things well. He slept in the room adjoining mine, and I would often wake in the night and cry out:

"Jim, I am frightened! I cannot sleep! I see the faces of the men who died to-day!" "Go 'long, Miss Embly," he would grumble out, "dead men ain't agwine to hurt you. You was good to them. Go 'long to sleep." My fears thus quieted, I slept.

We had our own little troubles. Looked upon as an interloper, I was also viewed with suspicion as having recently come from "Yankeedom." But my kind chief surgeon, Dr. Hunter, stood by me, and soon stilled the evil spirits. Also the neighbors, the Caldwell family, to whom the springs belonged, were most kind. With the family of Mr. Cowardin of Beauregard—near by—I formed an intimacy, cemented by our mutual trials, which has continued ever since. Thrown together again in Richmond (where Mr. Cowardin was editor of the Despatch), we saw the last act of our great drama; and my association with the younger generation through all changes and chances has never been interrupted. In the summer of 1889 I saw again, for the first time since the war, the scene of my early hospital experiences. With what emotion I found myself upon the spot sacred to such memories! Every room had its own story; and saddest of all was the place where we had laid the dead, unmarked by a single stone! I had difficulty in finding the spot. Oh, my poor fellows! Was it for this you left your Southern homes, the "land of flowers," Florida, Georgia, Alabama, Carolina,—to die amidst these cold mountains, and be forgotten?[1] In the ballroom, in the dining room, where now the gay world assembled, I saw a sight they could not see. I heard a voice they could not hear. Yonder were sixty typhoid cases, there sixty wounded men. Every cottage had its quota of the eighteen hundred men we gathered in. "Carolina Row" held the diphtheria patients, and here, in one room, on a bright, sunshiny winter's day, died four men at the same hour, while I ran in vain from one to the other, trying to tear with my fingers the white, leathery substance which spread over the mouth, and even came out upon the lips. Up to the time of the war I had seldom seen death. A merciful Providence had spared me the sight of it in my own family, in the cases of my parents. And now, in this great family, I saw eighteen die daily, and could not go fast enough from one to the other, to say a last prayer and hear a "last word."

Both the North and the South soon found that it was necessary not only to have love and devotion, to nurse well, but also that successful nursing required knowledge and experience, which few of us had. The Sisters of Mercy of Charleston, South Carolina, were offered by the bishop of that state to go wherever they were needed, and I was the happy person to secure their aid. They arrived at midnight Christmas

Eve, in a blinding snowstorm; but they soon cleared the sky about them. Our labors were systematized, and I learned much from their teachings. The men were shy of them at first, few of them having ever seen a Catholic, much less a "Sister." But very soon my pet patients hesitatingly confessed: "You see, captain" (as I was called), "they are more used to it than you are. They know how to handle a fellow when he's sick, and don't mind a bit how bad a wound smells." It was not that they loved me less, but they loved the Sisters more—and I forgave them.

Here we labored until the spring brought a "Yankee raid" from the west, and we "fell back" to Charlottesville, where we were under the supervision of the famous Dr. Cabell. But soon came the Seven Days' Fight before Richmond, and I was sent to Lynchburg to open the Methodist College building and prepare for the wounded, who already filled Richmond to overflowing, and polluted the air with the odor of blood and wounds. At Lynchburg we had also a camp of Federal prisoners, which I visited with the priest. But there were no wounded, and few sick. Here, as elsewhere, we met with the greatest hospitality and kindness. Mr. McDaniel's carriage met me at the station, and to his house I was taken while we made ready the new hospital, which the McDaniels helped to stock with dainties from their own stores. My sister, Mrs. Rowland, who had been nursing soldiers, since the battle of Manassas, at Warrenton Springs, joined me at Charlottesville, and together we labored to the end. The Sisters of Mercy had been called away to another field of duty. At Lynchburg arrived, day after day, hundreds of mutilated bodies, with unbroken spirits, and many to whom fatigue and exposure brought pneumonia and fever.

I frequently visited the camp of Federal prisoners, who had been captured by Jackson in the Valley of Virginia, carried dainties to their sick, and wrote many letters for them to their homes. Then I became ill, the only time during the war that I lost a day from "duty." The odor of wounds poisoned me, and for a fortnight I gave orders from my bed. It was here that I met Mrs. J. E. B. Stuart. She lost a lovely little girl of ten or twelve years, who vainly asked to see her father, then far away with the army. The skill of our chief surgeon, Dr. Owings, and the pure mountain air brought healing to us all, and we were sorry when the investiture of Richmond obliged us to leave this beautiful region to open the great Camp Winder Hospital, near Richmond, where my sister and I took charge of the Georgia Division, numbering about eight hundred men.

What stories of heroism I might relate, of faith and endurance, amongst men the most illiterate and the most uninteresting in exterior; of sufferings from fevers, of agonies from wounds and amputations; arms and legs with gangrene, the flesh all sloughed off or burned off with caustic, leaving only the bone, the blue veins, and muscle visible! I must put cotton wet with camphor in my nostrils, to stand by these cases. Man after man I have seen carried to the amputating room, singing a Baptist or Methodist hymn as he passed on his stretcher. As I walked beside him, holding his hand, he would say: "Tell my mother I am not afraid to die. God knows I die in a just cause. He will forgive my sins." Standing by the table upon which lay a man to be operated upon for an enormous aneurism, whose chances for life were small (this must have been in Lynchburg), I wrote down his last words to his family, while he coolly surveyed the instruments, the surgeons with bared arms, and the great tub prepared to catch his blood. The doctor held his pulse, and assured me that, with all these preparations in view, it never quickened its march. His courage saved him; but he was so weak, after so great a loss of blood, we could not move him from the table, nor even put a pillow under his head. He was one of the "tar-heels" of North Carolina, who are hard to beat.

It was after the battle of Fredericksburg, or perhaps the Wilderness, that we were ordered to have ready eight hundred beds; for so many our great field hospital accommodated. The convalescents, and the "old soldiers" with rheumatism and chronic disorders who would not get well, were sent to town hospitals, and we made ready for the night when should come in the eight hundred. The Balaklava charge was nothing to it! They came so fast it was impossible to dress and examine them. So upon the floor of the receiving wards (long, low buildings, hastily put up) the men nurses placed in rows on each side their ghastly burdens, covered with blood and dirt, stiff with mud and gravel from the little streams into which they often fell. The women nurses, armed with pails of toddy or milk, passed up and down, giving to each man a reviving drink to prepare him for the examination of the surgeons; others, with water and sponges, wet the stiff bandages. As I passed around, looking to see who was most in need of help and should first be washed and borne to his bed, I was especially attracted to one group. A young officer lay with his head upon the lap of another equally distinguished-looking man, while a negro man servant stood by in great distress. I offered a drink to the wounded man, saying, "You are badly hurt, I fear." "Oh no," he replied. "Do not mind me, but help the poor fellow next me, who is groaning and crying. He is wounded in the wrist. There is nothing so painful as that. Besides, you see, I have my friend, a young physician, with me, and a servant to ask for what I need."

So passing on to the man with the wounded wrist, I stopped to wet it again and again, to loosen the tight bandage, and to say a comforting word; and then on and on, till I lost sight of this interesting group, where there was so much to absorb my attention, and forgot it till in the early morning I saw the same persons. The handsome young officer was being borne on a litter to the amputating room, between his two friends. His going first of all the wounded heroes proved that his was the most urgent case. Rushing to his side, I reproached him for having deceived me with his cheerful face. "Only a leg to be taken off," he said,—"an everyday affair."

I followed to see him laid upon the terrible table which had proved fatal to so many. Not only was his leg to be taken off at the thigh, an operation from which few recovered, but he had two wounds beside. From this moment I rarely lost sight of the doomed man. He was of a Louisiana regiment (the Washington Artillery, I think, for he came from Washington, on the Red River). One could see that he was of a refined and cultivated family; that he was the darling of the parents of whom he constantly spoke. Yet he never complained of his rude straw couch, or seemed to miss the comforts which we would fain have given him; nor did he lament his untimely fate, or utter a murmur over pangs which would have moved the stoutest heart. He could not lie upon his back, for a gaping wound extended from his shoulder far down upon it, nor could he get upon one side, for his arm was crushed. We were forced to swing him from the ceiling. Soon the mutilated leg became covered with the fatal gangrene, and all the burning of this "proud flesh" could not keep death from the door. Even in his burning fevers, in his wild delirium, every word betrayed a pure and noble heart, full of love to God, to country, and to home. He could be quieted only by the sound of music. We took turns, my sister and I, to sit beside him and sing plaintive hymns, when he would be still, and murmur: "Sing. Pray, pray." Thus we sung and prayed for three long weeks, till we saw the end draw near, and lowered him into his bed, that his "dull ear" might hear our words, and his cold hand feel our warm touch. One evening he had been lying so still that we could hardly feel his pulse, and the rough men of the ward had gathered about the bed, still and solemn. Suddenly the pale face lighted with a lovely glow, the dim eyes shone brilliantly, and rising in his bed with outstretched arms, as if to clasp some visible being, his voice, clear and cheerful, rang out, "Come down, beautiful ladies, come!" "He sees a vision of angels!" cried the awestricken men. We all knelt. The young soldier fell back, dead!

In another ward lay upon the floor two young men just taken from an ambulance,—dead, as was supposed. Their heads were enveloped in bloody bandages, and the little clothing they had was glued to their bodies with mud and gravel. Hastily examining them, the surgeon gave the order, "To the deadhouse." I prayed that they might be left till morning, and bent over them, with my ear upon the heart, to try and detect a faint pulsation, but in vain. Yet neither of them had the rigidity of death in his limbs, as I heard the surgeon remark. Turning them over, he pointed to the wounds below the ear, the jaws shattered, and one or both eyes put out, and reminded me that even could they be brought to life, it would be an existence worse than death,—blind, deaf, perhaps unable to eat; and he muttered something about "wasting time on the dead which was needed for the living."

"Life is sweet," I replied, "even to the blind and the deaf and dumb, and these men may be the darlings of some fond hearts who will love them more in their helplessness than in their sunniest hours."

And so I kept my "dead men;" and the more I examined the younger one, the more was my interest excited. His hands, small and well formed, betokened the gentleman. His bare feet were of the same type, though cut by stones and covered with sand and gravel. After searching for a month to these bundles of rags, we forced a small tube between the lips with a drop of milk punch, and had the satisfaction to perceive that it did not ooze out, but disappeared somewhere; and all night long, in making our rounds and passing the "dead men," we pursued the same process. At last, with the morning, the great pressure was over, and we found a surgeon ready to examine and dress again the wounds, and we were permitted to cut away by bits the stiff rags from their bodies, wash and dress them, pick out the gravel from their torn feet, and wrap them in greased linen. With what joy we heard the first faint sigh and felt the first weak pulsation! Hour after hour, day after day, these men lay side by side, and were fed, drop by drop, from a tube, lest we should strangle them. The one least wounded never recovered his mind, which had been shattered with his body, and he afterwards died. The younger one, though he could neither speak nor see, and could hear but imperfectly, showed in a thousand ways, though his mind wandered at times, that he was aware of what went on about him, and he was gentle and grateful to all who served him. As he had come in without cap or knapsack, and there was no clue to his identity, over his bed we wrote, "Name and regiment unknown."

In the meanwhile, by flag of truce from the North, had come newspapers and letters making inquiries for a young man who, in a fervor of enthusiasm, had run away from school in England to fight the battles of the South. His mother having been a South Carolinian, he wrote his father he had gone to fight for his mother's country and for his mother's grave. Traced to Charleston, he was known to have gone to the Army of Northern Virginia, and to have entered the battle of the Wilderness as color bearer to his regiment, in bare feet. As nothing had been heard of him since the battle, he was reported dead; but his distracted friends begged that the hospitals about Richmond might be examined, to learn if any trace of him could be found. We perceived instantly that this runaway boy was our patient. Informed of our convictions, the assistant surgeon general came to see and examine him, being himself a Carolinian and a friend of the mother's family. But the boy either would not or could not understand the questions addressed to him. Many weeks and months passed in the dimly lighted room to which he was consigned, before we could lift the bandage from the one eye, before he could hear with the one ear and eat with the wounded mouth. Fed with soups and milk, he grew strong and cheerful, and was suspected of seeing a little before he confessed it, as I often noticed his head elevated to an angle which enabled him to watch the pretty girls who came from the city to read to him and bring him dainties. These, moved by compassion for his youth and romantic history, came to help us nurse him, and risked daily choking him in their well-meant endeavors to feed him. At last all the bandages were removed, save a ribbon over the lost eye, and our "dead man" came forth, a handsome youth of eighteen or nineteen, graceful and elegant. Now the surgeon general claiming him for his father, with much regret we gave him up to the flag-of-truce boat, and he was lost to us till the end of the war. He had a new eye made in England, and came to see us after the fall of Richmond, bringing me a fine present, his enthusiasm and his gratitude nothing damped by time and change. Even with the two eyes, he saw so imperfectly that he was soon obliged to seek for a life companion to guide his uncertain steps. In Charleston he fell in love with one of his own family connection, and, like the prince and princess in the fairy tale, "they were married, and lived happy ever after."

At the beginning of the war we had no scarcity of provisions, such as they were, and we early became accustomed to rye coffee and sassafras tea. We had always been able to give the "sweet-'tater pudding" to the Georgian, made after his mother's fashion, and the biscuit demanded by the North Carolinian, "dark inside and white outside."

But as the war went on, only peas, dried peas, seemed plentiful, and we made them up in every variety of form of which dried peas are capable. In soup they appeared one day; the second day we had cold peas; then they were fried (when we had the grease); baked peas came on the fourth day; and then we began again with the soup. Toward the last we lived on corn meal and sorghum, a very coarse molasses, with a happy interval when a blockage runner brought us dried vegetables for soup from our sympathetic English friends. A pint of corn meal and a gill of sorghum was the daily ration. Each Saturday I managed to get to the Libby Prison or Belle Isle, and many a hungry Confederate gave me his portion of more delicate fare, when such was to be had, to give to the prisoners who might be sick, and were "not used to corn bread." If beans and corn bread were not always wholesome, they certainly made a cheerful diet; and full of fun were the "tea parties," where we drank an infusion of strawberry and raspberry leaves. I never heard any one complain save those greedy fellows the convalescents, who could each have eaten a whole beef. I could only sympathize when they clamored loudly for a change of diet; for what could we do when we had only peas, corn bread, and sorghum! At last convalescing nature could stand it no longer. I was told that the men had refused to eat peas, and had thrown them over the clean floor, and daubed them on the freshly whitewashed walls of their dining room. The unkindest cut of all was that this little rebellion was headed by a one-armed man who had been long in the hospital, a great sufferer, and in consequence had been pampered with wheaten bread and otherwise "spoiled." Like naughty schoolboys, I found these men throwing my boiled peas at one another, pewter plates and spoons flying about, and the walls and floor covered with the fragments of the offensive viand.

"What does this mean?" I asked. "Do you Southern men complain of food which we women eat without repugnance? Are you not ashamed to be so dainty? I suppose you want pies and cakes."

"They are filled with worms!" a rude voice cried. "I do not believe you eat the same."

"Let me taste them," I replied, taking a plate from before a man and eating with his pewter spoon. "This is from the same pea-pot. Indeed, we have but one pot for us all, and I spent hours this morning picking out the worms, which do not injure the taste and are perfectly harmless. It is good, wholesome food."

"Mighty colicky, anyhow," broke in an old man.

The men laughed, but, taking no notice of a fact which all admitted, I said: "Peas are the best fighting food. The government gives it to us on principle. There were McClellan's men, eating good beef, canned fruits and vegetables, trying for seven days to get to Richmond, and we, on dried peas, kept them back. I shall always believe that had we eaten his beef, and they our peas, the result would have been different."

This was received with roars of laughter. The men, now in good humor, ate the peas which remained, washed the floor and cleaned the walls. Such is the variable temper of the soldier, eager to resent real or imaginary wrongs, yet quick to return to good humor and fun. But the spoiled one-armed man had "General Lee's socks" put on him, and went to his regiment the next day.

This discipline of General Lee's socks was an "institution" peculiar to our hospital. Mrs. Lee, it is well known, spent most of her time in making gloves and socks for the soldiers. She also gave me, at one time, several pairs of General Lee's old socks, so darned that we saw they had been well worn by our hero. We kept these socks to apply to the feet of those laggard "old soldiers" who were suspected of preferring the "luxury" of hospital life to the activity of the field. And such was the effect of the application of these warlike socks that even a threat of it had the result of sending a man to his regiment who had lingered months in inactivity. It came to be a standing joke in the hospital, infinitely enjoyed by the men. If a poor wretch was out of his bed over a week, he would be threatened with General Lee's socks: and through this means some most obstinate cases were cured. Four of the most determined rheumatic patients, who had resisted scarifying of the limbs, and, what was worse, the smallest and thinnest of diets, were sent to their regiments, and did good service afterwards. With these men the socks had to be left on several hours, amidst shouts of laughter from the "assistants;" showing that though men may withstand pain and starvation, they succumb directly to ridicule.

After the "beans riot" came the "bread riot." Every one who has known hospital life, in Confederate times especially, will remember how the steward, the man who holds the provisions, is held responsible for every shortcoming, by both surgeons and matrons as well as by the men. Whether he has money or not, he must give plenty to eat; and there exists between the steward and the convalescents, those hungry fellows long starved in camp, and now recovering from fever or wounds, a deadly antagonism, constantly breaking out into "overt acts." The steward is to them a "cheat,"—the man who withholds from them the rations given out by the government. He must have the meat, though the quartermaster may not furnish it, and it is his fault alone when the bread rations are short. Our steward, a meek little man, was no exception to this rule. Pale with fright, he came one day to say that the convalescents had stormed the bakery, taken out the half-cooked bread and scattered it about the yard, beaten the baker, and threatened to hang the steward. Always eager to save the men from punishment, yet recognizing that discipline must be preserved, I hurried to the scene of war, to throw myself into the breach before the surgeon should arrive with the guard to arrest the offenders. Here I found the new bakery—a "shanty" made of plank, which had been secured at great trouble—leveled to the ground, and two hundred excited men clamoring for the bread which they declared the steward withheld from them from meanness, or stole from them for his own benefit.

"And what do you say of the matron?" I asked, rushing into their midst. "Do you think that she, through whose hands the bread must pass, is a party to the theft? Do you accuse me, who have nursed you through months of illness, making you chicken soup when we had not seen chicken for a year, forcing an old breastbone to do duty for months for those unreasonable fellows who wanted to see the chicken,—me, who gave you a greater variety in peas than was ever known before, and who latterly stewed your rats when the cook refused to touch them? And this is your gratitude! You tear down my bakehouse, beat my baker, and want to hang my steward! Here, guard, take four of these men to the guardhouse. You all know if the head surgeon were here forty of you would go."

To my surprise, the angry men of the moment before laughed and cheered, and there ensued a struggle as to who should go to the guardhouse. A few days after there came to me a "committee" of two sheepish-looking fellows, to ask my acceptance of a ring. Each of the poor men had subscribed something from his pittance, and their old enemy the steward had been sent to town to make the purchase. Accompanying the ring was a bit of dirty paper, on which was written:—

FOR OUR CHIEF MATRON
In honor of her Brave Conduct on the
day of
THE BREAD RIOT

It was the ugliest little ring ever seen, but it was as "pure gold" as were the hearts which sent it, and it shall go down to posterity in my family, in memory of the brave men who led the bread riot, and who suffered themselves to be conquered by a hospital matron.

What generous devotion was seen on all sides! What unanimity of feeling! What noble sacrifice! I have known a little boy of six or eight years walk three miles to bring me one lemon which had come to him through the blockade, or one roll of wheat bread which he knew would be relished by a sick soldier. In passing through town to go to meet exchanged prisoners, my ambulance would be hailed from every door, and the dinners just served for a hungry family brought out to feed the returned men. They would all say, with General Joseph Anderson, when I prayed them to retain a part of their dinner, "We can eat dry bread to-day." As I recall those scenes my heart breaks again. I must leave my pen, and walk about to compose myself and wipe the tears from my eyes. I see the steamer arrive, with its load of dirty, ragged men, half dead with illness and starvation. I hear the feeble shout they raise, as they reply to the assembled crowd in waiting. The faint wail of Dixie's Land comes to my ears. Men weep, and women stretch their arms toward the ship. A line is formed, and the tottering men come down the gangway to be received in the arms of family and friends. Many kiss the ground as they reach it, and some kiss it and die! Food and drink are given; doctors are in attendance; the best carriages in Richmond await these returned heroes; the stretchers receive those who have come home to die. And these soldiers, in this wretched plight, are returned to us from "a land flowing with milk and honey,"—from those who so lately were our brothers,—a land where there are brave men and tender women!

I can never forget a poor fellow from whose feet and legs, covered with scurvy sores, I was three weeks taking out with pincers the bits of stocking which had grown into the flesh during eighteen months' imprisonment. Every day I would try to dispose his heart to forgiveness; every morning ask, "Do you forgive your enemies?"—when he would turn his face to the wall and cry, "But they did me so bad!" Vainly I reminded him, "Our Lord was crucified, yet He forgave his enemies," and that unless he forgave he would not be forgiven. Only the last day of his life did he yield, and with his last breath murmur: "Lord, I forgive them! Lord, forgive me!"

One day, while at Camp Winder, there was brought into the hospital a fine-looking young Irishman, covered with blood, and appearing to be in a dying condition. He was of a Savannah regiment, and the comrades who were detailed to bring him to us stated that in passing Lynchburg they had descended at the station, and hurrying to regain the train, this man had jumped from the ground to the platform. Almost instantly he began to vomit blood. It was plain he had ruptured a blood vessel, and they had feared he would not live to get to a hospital. Tenderly he was lifted from the litter, and every effort made to stanch the bleeding. We were not allowed to wash or dress him, speak, or make the slightest noise to disturb him. As I pressed a handkerchief upon his lips he opened his eyes, and fixed them upon me with an eagerness which showed me he wished to say something. By this time we had become quick to interpret the looks and motions of the poor fellows committed to our hands. Dropping upon my knees, I made the sign of the cross. I saw the answer in his eyes. He was a Catholic, and wanted a priest to prepare him for death. Softly and distinctly I promised to send for a priest, should death be imminent, and reminded him that upon his obedience to the orders to be quiet, and not agitate mind or body, depended his life and his hope of speaking when the priest should appear. With childlike submission he closed his eyes, and lay so still that we had to touch his pulse from time to time to be assured that he lived. With the morning the bleeding ceased, and he was able to swallow medicine and nourishment, and in another day he was allowed to say a few words. Soon he asked for the ragged jacket which, according to rule, had been placed under his pillow, and took from the lining a silver watch, and then a one-hundred-dollar United States bank note greeted our eyes. It must have been worth one thousand dollars in Confederate money, and that a poor soldier should own so much at this crisis of our fate was indeed a marvel.

I took charge of his treasures till he could tell us his history and say what should be done with them when death, which was inevitable, came to him. It was evident that he had fallen into a rapid decline, though relieved from the fear of immediate death. Fever and cough and those terrible night sweats soon reduced this stalwart form to emaciation. Patient and uncomplaining, he had but one anxiety, and this was for the fate of the treasures he had guarded through three long years, in battle and in bivouac, in hunger and thirst and nakedness. He was with his regiment at Bull Run, and after the battle, seeing a wounded Federal leaning against a tree and apparently dying, he went to him, and found he belonged to a New York regiment, and that he was an Irishman. Supporting the dying man and praying beside him, he received his last words, and with them his watch and a one-hundred-dollar bank note which he desired should be given to his sister. Our Irishman readily promised she should have this inheritance when the war ended, and at the earliest opportunity sewed the money in the lining of his jacket and hid away the watch, keeping them safely through every change and amidst every temptation which beset the poor soldier in those trying times. He was sure that he would "some day" get to New York, and be able to restore these things to the rightful owner. Even at this late day he held the same belief, and could not be persuaded that the money was a "fortune of war;" that he had a right to spend it for his own comfort, or to will it to whom he would; that even were the war over, and he in New York, it would be impossible to find the owner with so vague a clue as he possessed.

"And did you go barefoot and ragged and hungry all these three years," asked the surgeon, "with this money in your pocket? Why, you might have sold it and been a rich man, and have done a world of good."

"Sure, doctor, it was not mine to give," was the simple answer of the dying man. "If it please Almighty God, when the war is over, I thought to go to New York and advertise in the papers for Bridget O'Reilly, and give it into her own hand."

"But," I urged, "there must be hundreds of that name in the great city of New York. How would you decide should dishonest ones come to claim this money?"

"Sure I would have it called by the priest out from God's holy altar," he replied, after a moment's thought.

It was hard to destroy in the honest fellow the faith that was in him. With the priest who came to see him he argued after the same fashion, and, as his death approached, we had to get the good bishop to settle this matter of "conscience money." The authority of so high a functionary prevailed, and the dying man was induced to believe he had a right to dispose of this little fortune. The watch he wished to send to an Irishman in Savannah who had been a friend, a brother to him, for he had come with him from the "old country." As for the money, he had heard that the little orphans of Savannah had had no milk for two long years. He would like "all that money to be spent in milk for them." A lady who went to Georgia the day after we buried him took the watch and the money, and promised to see carried out the last will and testament of this honest heart.

But space would fail me to tell of all. There were those noble Israelites of Savannah and of Carolina, who fought so bravely and endured pain so patiently, and were so gentle and grateful when placed with their own people, that generous family of Myers, whose hearts and purses were open to us all. And my poor, ugly smallpox men! How could I fail to mention you, in whose sufferings was no "glory,"—whose malady was so disgusting and so contagious as to shut you out from companionship and sympathy! We had about twenty of these patients in tents a mile away, near Hollywood Cemetery, where they could well meditate amidst the tombs. Often in the night I would wake, thinking I heard their groans. Lantern in hand, and carrying a basket of something nice to eat, and a cooling salve for the blinded eyes and the sore and bleeding faces, I would betake me to the tents, to hear the grateful welcome, "We knew you would come to-night!" "Can I have a drop of milk or wine?" A few encouraging words and a little prayer soon soothed them to sleep.

These were my favorites, except some men with old wounds that never would heal, and our "pet" whom we rescued from the deadhouse.

In war as in life it is not always December; it is sometimes May. Even in hospitals, as I have shown, there are often droll scenes and cheerful laughter. One day a young Carolinian was brought in, wounded in the tongue. A ball had taken it half off, and a bit of the offending member hung most inconveniently out of his mouth, and prevented his eating and speaking, obliging him to be fed through a tube. In vain he made signs to the doctor, and wrote on a slate that they must cut off this piece of tongue. The surgeons refused, fearing the incision of the small blood vessels would be fatal. One day, when he was left alone with the faithful servant who had been with him in every danger, he obliged this man to perform the operation. After doing it, the poor negro was so frightened he ran to us, exclaiming: "I done cut Marse Charlie's tongue off! Come quick!" Fortunately, he had but a very dull pocket knife, and so the blood vessels filled as he cut, and there was little or no harm done. "Marse Charlie" got well, and went to fight again. I forget if he could talk understandingly.

In the intervals of nursing and cooking we wove straw for our bonnets, and dyed it with walnut hulls, and made gloves from brown linen and ratskins. From old pantaloons we got our boot tops, which were laced with twine and soled by some soldier. Woolens and cottons were woven in the country, and we cut the gowns with less regard to form than to economy. After General McClellan's retreat from the peninsula, we had quantities of captured kitchen furniture, which was divided amongst the hospitals. I went to town to get my share. A mirror hung in the shop, high over the door. Glancing up, I saw in it a strange-looking woman, in an ill-hung gown of no particular color, a great cape of the same, and a big blue apron, while her head was surmounted by a shapeless hat of brown straw. "Do I look like that?" I asked, surprised. The much-amused man replied that I certainly did.

As the "lines" drew in closer and closer, the men nurses (convalescents) were taken to the field, and our servants, many of them, ran away. Then came our daughters and the young ladies of the city to assist us. The dainty belles of Richmond, amongst them General Lee's own daughters, would be seen staggering under a tray of eatables for a ward of forty patients, which food they would be enjoined to make go as far as possible. Miss Jeannie Ritchie had a wonderful knack at making a little go a great way, often satisfying her men and having something to spare to the others who had not enough to go round. I have seen three or four of these belles drag from an ambulance a wounded man fresh from the lines at Petersburg, washing and dressing him with their dainty fingers.

It is wonderful how we slept, those last two years in the beleaguered city, with guns booming night as well as day, and the whistle from the railway giving signal continually of a load of wounded from the lines.

Yet these guns seemed less near and less fatal than those at Charleston, where I went during the siege of that city, on my way to Georgia to beg for our hospital. We were in need of everything,—sheets for the beds, shirts for the men. We had not a rag with which to dress wounds, and even paper for spreading poultices and plasters was difficult to obtain. I had transportation with the soldiers, and traveled with them in box cars, sleeping on the floor, covered with a big shawl, with a little carpet bag for a pillow. When we stopped to change cars, I lay down with the men on the platform of the station, and slept as soundly as they did, always meeting with kindness and offers of service. Sometimes my transportation got me a provision train loaded with grain, where I slept comfortably on the bags of corn, and so reached Augusta. The Messrs. Jackson, who had fine cotton mills, generously gave me sheetings and shirtings in abundance, with a piece of fine shirting for General Lee, one for General Cooper, and a third for the ladies of our hospital. Everywhere were the same generosity and hospitality. The dweller in the poorest cottage would give something "for the soldiers,"—a package of precious rags, a bunch of herbs for teas,—things which would be of little value in time of peace, but were now priceless. At Macon the priest and his sister came to the station and took me to their house; and from kind Mr. and Mrs. Gilmartin, of Savannah, it was difficult to get away. I came home laden with spoils.

Stopping in Charleston, I went to see my friends the Sisters of Mercy, who had now enough to do in their own city. One of these, full of courage, proposed to show me the beautiful houses on the Battery, which were fast being torn to pieces by the shells of the enemy. There had been an intermission in the firing that day, and the Sister was sure we would have time to see everything and get back before the guns recommenced. While we were mourning over these ruined homes, the seats of renowned hospitality, and whose roses were clinging to the falling walls, we heard a whizzing above our heads, and down we went to the bottom of the carriage, and down went the latter into a cellar, to shelter us from the danger to which our curiosity had exposed us. On my return to Richmond I joined Colonel Tabb's Virginia regiment, and was with them when they had a fight for the possession of a bridge over Nottoway Creek, near Petersburg. The charming young colonel recommended me to leave the train, and go into one of the houses near. Here was a scene of fear and dismay. Women were hurrying with their beds and furniture to a hiding place in the woods, weeping, and shouting to one another, sure the Yankees would be upon them immediately to burn and rifle their houses. Happily for them and for us all, our people drove the enemy away, and with one wounded man and one prisoner we reached Richmond without further delay.

Amongst the sad events of 1864 was the death of General J. E. B. Stuart, who was wounded mortally in one of the raids around Richmond. We hurried to town to see once more this *preux chevalier.* President Davis knelt at his beside, and life was flowing fast away. Of all the military funerals I have seen, this was the most solemn. As we walked behind the bier which carried this hero of the Song and Sword, who, like Körner,

> "Fought the fight all day,
> And sung its song all night,"

the stillness was broken only by the

> "distant and random gun,
> That the foe was sullenly firing."

Every one recalled the lines:—

> "Slowly and sadly we laid him down,
> From the field of his fame fresh and gory;
> We carved not a line, we raised not a stone,
> But we left him alone with his glory."

Eleven months later came "that day of woe, that awful day," which saw the evacuation of Richmond. All day and night streamed forth the people who could get away. Every carriage, wagon, cart, every horse, was in demand, and sad-faced people on foot, with little bundles, thronged the one outlet left open from the ill-fated city. By night it was deserted: only a few old men, with women and children, remained, and the swarm of negroes awaiting the triumphal entry of their Northern brethren, whom we knew to be the advance of the army of occupation. The next morning dawned on a scene truly demoniacal. Fire seemed to blaze in every quarter, and there was no one to combat it. Our people had set fire to the Tredegar Works before leaving, in order to deprive the enemy of them. My brother-in-law had gone with the President, and my sister, in her terror, prayed me to come into town to protect her when the enemy should enter. I set out from the hospital on foot, taking along a big South

Carolina soldier named Sandy, who was full of fight and strength, to pilot me through the perilous way. Between us and the city lay the penitentiary in flames, and from out of the building poured a hideous throng, laden with booty, and adding to the general uproar by their shouts. We hid behind a wall till they passed, when next was encountered a hearse drawn by two negroes, from out of which streamed ends of silk and calico and cotton stolen from some shop. Farther on came another hearse, from behind which oozed upon the ground tea and coffee and sugar, ill secured in the hasty flight of the thieves. On every side of us were falling walls and beams from the burning houses, and with every explosion from the factories of arms the earth would tremble, as it seemed, and the shock would sometimes throw us to the ground. We were long making our way to the pandemonium which awaited us in the town. Here tottered a church steeple; there a friend's house was on fire, and women and children were trying to save the household goods which the negroes were appropriating to themselves. We met some women who told us that the railway station was on fire, filled with wounded men from Petersburg. Happily, the men had been withdrawn by the ever helpful women. But here was a sight! The street ran flames of burning spirits, which had been emptied from the stock of the medical director in order to prevent their being used by the incoming soldiery. On the roof of my sister's house wet blankets were laid by her servants; and a few doors below was Mrs. Lee, infirm, unable to walk, yet in danger from the falling of a burning church and the houses across the way. My cousin Mrs. Rhett and I proposed to make our way to the commandant and ask for means to meet this danger. The fire raged furiously between us and the Capitol, the "headquarters," and we made a long detour through Broad Street to reach it. Here we encountered the regiment of negro cavalry which came in the advance. Along the sidewalk were ranged our negroes, shouting and bidding welcome, to which the others replied, waving their drawn sabres, "We have come to set you free!" My little nephew, who held my hand, trembled, but not with fear. He kept repeating, "I must kill them. I must strike them." "Be still, or you will be killed," was all I could say. It was not that we were afraid of our own people. The Southern negro never forgot the love and respect he had for his master. There is not one record against their true, warm hearts. Yet what might we not have encountered but for the prompt and kind care of the officers in command! In a few hours sentinels were at every corner; the thieves were compelled to yield up their ill gotten gains, and every instance of insult to ladies was summarily punished.

Coming into the presence of General Weitzel, we hastily explained our errand. "Mrs. Lee in danger!" he cried. "The mother of Fitz Lee,— she who nursed me so tenderly when I was ill at West Point? What can I do for her?" We explained that it was as well for her as for the other Mrs. Lee that we claimed his aid. In an instant he wrote upon his knee an order for the ambulances we needed; and at the head of five of these conveyances we led the way through the fire and smoke, our sleeves singed and our faces begrimed with soot and dirt. We posted an ambulance at every door where there were sick and infirm, and little children; and when I reached my sister's with the last one, the driver had unaccountably become so drunk that I could hardly hold him upon his seat. At the door were my sister's little girls, each with her bundle of most precious things to be saved. In vain would I "back up" to the pavement; my man would jerk the horse, and off we would go into the middle of the street, where he would hiccough: "Come along, Virginia aristocracy! I won't hurt you!" An officer galloping by, seeing my dilemma, stopped, seized the horse's head, backed him, and gave the driver a good whack with his sheathed sword, which sobered him for a moment. We loaded up, and moved off to the lovely house of Mrs. Rutherford, which, with its fine furniture, lay open and deserted. Here we took refuge, and leaving our driver without an encircling arm, I am persuaded he went under the horse's heels before long.

There came in with the first division Dr. Alexander Mott, of New York, as chief of the medical department. I had known him from his boyhood, and his wife was our friend and connection. He sought me out, and begged me to go instantly to our officers' hospital, left vacant by the Sisters of Charity, into which he must put his sick and wounded, and for whom he had no nurses. He could not provide nurses until the way was well opened with the North. I was glad to do this, especially as there were many of our officers yet remaining, who had been recommended to my care by the Sisters, and the few men who were still at Camp Winder could well be cared for by others.

I had naturally many *contretemps* in this my new hospital, though the surgeons in charge knew that I was nursing their people for sweet charity's sake, and not for their "filthy lucre." They first laid hands on the furniture of my room, which I had removed from Camp Winder, and which had been given me by friends to make me comfortable. I assured them it was private property, yet they contended it could be "confiscated" for their use. Fortunately, Dr. Simmons, a surgeon of the "old army," was now medical director, and, knowing him to have been a friend of General

Lee and General Chilton, I went to him with my report of the matter. He roundly declared there should be no "stealing" in his department: so next day my bed and wardrobe came back, with many apologies. We had been afraid that these surgeons would put their "colored brethren" in the same ward with our officers, but the latter were spared this humiliation. Apropos of the colored soldiers, one day the doctor in charge of these wards came to tell me he had great difficulty in managing some of them. They were homesick, would not eat or be washed and dressed.

"Perhaps they are Southern negroes," I said, "and accustomed to the gentle hand of a mistress. I will see."

And so it proved. As I went from bed to bed, I asked, "Where did you come from, uncle?" "I come out der family ob de great Baptis' preacher Mr. Broadus, in Kentucky," said one. "I ain't used to no nigger waitin' on me when I'se sick. My ole missis always 'tend me, an' gib me de bes' ob brandy toddy wid white sugar an' nutmeg in it." When I could say I knew his illustrious family, I was admitted to the privilege of washing his old black face, cleaning his fevered mouth, and putting on his clean shirt, and he drank eagerly the toddy made like that of "ole mis'." And so with them all. They did not "want to fight" and be killed; all they wanted was to be "carried back to Ole Kentuck."

These were the days which tried women's souls. Not one of our friends came to see us whose pocket was not examined by the sentinel at the gate, to see if I had given her a bit of bread or a few beans for the starving people outside. I had to make a compact with my surgeons to draw my ration of meat and give it away if I pleased: and it was thus I obtained for Mrs. Lee her first beefsteak. After General Lee came in from "the surrender," he might have had the rations of half the Northern soldiers, had he been willing to receive them. I have seen an Irishman who had served under him in Mexico stand at his door with a cheese and a can of preserves, praying him to accept them. General Lee thanked him, and sent the things to the sick in the hospital. As soon as provisions could be brought in, rations were distributed to the inhabitants. It was not infrequent to see a fine lady, in silk and lace, receiving timidly, at the hands of a dirty negro, the ration of fat pork and meal or flour which her necessity obliged her to seek. Fortunately, many people had hidden under the cellar floor rice and beans, upon which they lived till the better days came. These came on the first steamer, heralded by Mr. Corcoran from Washington, who, with his pockets filled with ten and five dollar notes, placed one in every empty hand, and soothed every proud heart with words of sympathy. There came also Mr. Garmandier, of Baltimore, with wine and brandy and whiskey for the old and feeble, distributing them from house to house.

I must not fail to relate my visit to the Libby Prison and its changed inmates. Upon what pretext these men were crowded into the Libby I cannot conceive, since they were paroled prisoners, who expected to be sent to their homes by the terms of the surrender. Hearing that this prison was filled with men to whom no rations were distributed, I went there, to find the house besieged by women seeking their missing friends, weeping and, crying out: "John, are you there?" "Oh, somebody tell me if my husband is in there!" and again, "Let down your tin cup, and I'll send you up something in it!" With difficulty I entered, and with greater difficulty moved about. The very staircases were crowded with men, packed like herrings in a box; they could neither lie down nor sit down. I was able to satisfy the women and send them away. The sentinel at the door was very civil. He said the men could not be fed without bread, none having come. He was sure they would soon be released, etc. Alas, the cruelties of war, and its abuses!

When I applied to the commandant, General Gibbon, for a pass to go to the North, I was asked if I had taken "the oath." "No," I replied, "and I never will! Suppose your wife should swear fealty to another man because you had lost everything? You would expect her to be more faithful because of your misfortunes." "She has you there, general," said a young aide-de-camp. "Let me give her the pass." And he did so.

My first visit was naturally to our old home, near Alexandria, and here I found several of the neighbors trying, like myself, to trace the once familiar road. Trees gone, fences burned, houses torn down, the face of the whole country was changed. From the débris of the ruined houses the freedmen had built themselves huts, in which they swarmed. In vain I tried to buy out those who sought refuge in our ruins. The offer to send them to Boston was received with scorn. They had no notion of leaving "Ole Virginny." My next visit was to see the man whom we all delighted to honor,—now more than ever, as he was suffering imprisonment and wrong for our sakes. I went to Old Point, made my way into his presence, and spent a day in talking with him and Mrs. Davis of the sad past, the sadder present, and that future which looked saddest of all.

I could not stay long in the North, though it contained the dearest object of my affections, the only child of my only brother. Lost without my accustomed employment, I asked myself what remained for me to do in the world. The work was at hand, as I found. Soon I was occupied in Baltimore, in taking food and clothing to the sufferers on the Rappahannock. Mr. John S. Gittings gave me transportation on his steamers to Fredericksburg and back, and every week I had boxes and barrels to distribute along the river, collected by the generous Baltimoreans; while Miss Harper, Major Mathias, and others made me welcome to their houses and to their stores. From the highest to the lowest, the hearts of the people were open to us. In a grocer's shop, one day, I was telling a lady I knew of an Episcopal clergyman and his wife who had been two years without flour. "I'll give you a barrel for them," said the kind grocer, and I had the pleasure of delivering it the next day. One Sunday, in Fredericksburg, I asked the lady with whom I was staying why she did not go to church. She glanced down at her feet, and I perceived she had no shoes,—only bits of black woolen made in the shape of shoes. Next time I brought a good load of shoes for distribution amongst the ladies and gentlemen living in the ruined cellars of their once fine houses.

In the intervals between these trips, and when I paused with my family, then living in Tappahannock, we commenced to collect the Confederate poems of the war, with which to make a volume. The poems which we had preserved from patriotic feeling must now be made to bring aid to the helpless orphans of the Confederacy. Many of the children I had promised to look after when the war should be over, and some of them had been confided to me by dying parents. Money must be had for this purpose. Murphy, of Baltimore, agreed to publish this book, providing it be made ready and sold while men's minds were busy with our fate. Done! The first edition went off in three months, and a new edition was called for. The first payment, one thousand dollars, enabled me to dispose of half of my "daughters." Schools were kind, friends helped me to clothe my girls. I had free travel on every Southern road, and Mr. Robert Garrett gave transportation for ten to go to St. Louis. These the Southern Relief Association took from me, educated and clothed them, and returned them to their homes,—those who had home! Miss Harper's house was the rendezvous in Baltimore. Friends far and near would adopt a girl for me. My old friend Miss Chew, of New London, Connecticut, and her niece Miss Lewis, each took a "daughter," and many boxes of clothing came from these and other charitable persons at the North. Here I must relate that the first money which I received for these girls came from that admirable and charming woman Mrs. Hamilton Fish, whom I had known in Washington when Governor Fish was in Congress. Hearing of my undertaking, she bade me Godspeed and sent me twenty dollars. During the war we had had a most interesting correspondence. I forget from which of us the proposal first came: that she should send to the Federal sick and wounded prisoners the medicines, clothing, and dainties which we did not have to give them, while I pledged myself to see these things distributed according to her instructions; and she, in turn, was to give to our prisoners what we could spare from our necessities. Unreasonably, as it seemed to us, the Northern government refused to sanction our interchange of charity, greatly to the distress of those in whose hearts I had raised hopes to be disappointed.

Several firms sent me half-worn books and music. I had even a sewing machine given me for the use of these children, and the Adams Express sent them free to the schools at which they were placed. Another thousand dollars from my kind publisher freed me from all embarrassment, paid all my debts for schooling and clothing, and my friend Miss Harper inviting me to travel with her in Europe, I gladly left my responsibilities and my memories behind me, and went to another world and another life.

After several years of interesting sojourn in France, Germany, Spain, and Italy, we came home to learn from the pilot who met our ship that General Lee was no more. Full of that love and veneration which we all bore him, I resolved to write his life in a popular form, with Mrs. Lee's approval. Manuscript in hand, I went to see this dear old friend, this heroic wife of our great hero, and with her went over my poor pages; modifying everything which she thought my love had exaggerated, and changing incidents and anecdotes which she thought of doubtful authenticity. When we came to a striking story in which General Lee rebukes the men who are jeering at a clergyman, she paused. "Does that sound like General Lee?" "To take this away will spoil my best chapter," I pleaded. "But you would not put into this book what is not true?" she asked. So I sacrificed my story. What trials of heart and sufferings of body this noble woman bore! Sustained by a faith I have never seen surpassed, and by accomplishments of mind which made her independent of discomforts which would have crushed others, she lived serenely on her own high level. The sale of The Popular Life of Lee canceled all the liabilities I had incurred for the education of my "daughters." Of the first comers, many had remained at school only two years, and had gone home to teach, while others took their places. And I am proud and happy to say that, of them all, I do not recall an instance of one who has not done honor to her people, and who has not profited by the opportunity afforded her to advance the interests of her family and make herself a useful member of society.

16 For Better or for Worse

Richard Addison Wood and Joan Faye Wood

*H*ENRIETTA STOCKTON ADDISON'S marriage to Benjamin Johnson Darneille, like most marriages, began with a honeymoon. Leaving from Baltimore, Maryland, where "Nettie" was temporarily living with her family (having left the commotion of Washington, D.C.), the couple set out for Darneille's home in Virginia. A year earlier, the trip may have been a relaxing journey enjoyed with friends and family, as was customary of the time. But the year was 1861, the Civil War was in its infancy, and Benjamin, a Southerner, and Henrietta and her family, Southern sympathizers, had no desire to be trapped inside Union territory. So following a wedding that was planned in just two days, the couple embarked on a bridal trip with Henrietta's father, hoping to safely make it to their destination of Richmond, Virginia. The escapade, as remembered by Henrietta in her postwar journal, was an event full of danger, intrigue and just a touch of fun.

* * *

I AM REQUESTED to give some items of interest for the benefit of my grandchildren, those present as well as in the future, of events which occurred a few months before the Civil War, as well as of my marriage, which took place on July 18, 1861, and of my wedding trip, which, owing to the war, was full of strange coincidences.

Great changes were taking place in Washington. Both Houses of Congress were debating upon the separation of the Union between the

245

North and South, all was excitement. My brother, William, from California, came on to bear arms for the South when called upon.

Benjamin Johnson Darneille, a lawyer of high repute from Albermarle County, Virginia (and my future husband), arrived in Washington the 2nd of March, 1861. On the 4th of March he hired a carriage for the day and we went from my family home on the Heights of Georgetown, now west of Washington, to see all the excitement due to Lincoln's being sworn in as President. Soldiers were stationed all around Washington, fearing an attack would be made by the South upon the Capital. It was a solemn time, and we all felt it, and too soon were our fears realized, war was declared immediately, and encampments of soldiers stationed all around us. Afraid to voice our sentiments, we commenced to live a life of dread, not knowing how soon my father and brother, Walkins (both hold fat offices under the government), would be offered the oath of allegiance to the United States to sign, which upon refusing to do so they would lose their positions.

When mother died in April 1861 we waited three days in hopes my sisters from Petersburg [Virginia], Wheeling [Virginia], and Baltimore [Maryland], could attend the funeral but the railroads were all seized to convey troops to the South, as fighting had begun in earnest, and only those right around in the district saw her remains laid to rest in Oak Hill Cemetery.

We all realized that God, in His mercy, has removed our mother from fearful troubles which were to come, and were even then upon us. The day upon which she was buried [April 15, 1861], in history is called the "Blue Monday." Marshal law was proclaimed, southern families were leaving all and fleeing to the south; every warehouse was taken for the government's use; you could see nothing but soldiers and the artillery flying everywhere, until we all felt it would be better far to rest in quiet Oak Hill Cemetery.

The next day Mr. Darneille arrived, having just heard of our affliction, and he was so tender in his sympathy we all loved him more. He urged my father and all of us to leave as soon as possible, as all communication with the south would be cut off. Brother William left in a few days for Richmond [Virginia], also the Hester's (my sister and brother-in-law), and their family. Emily Harry, my best friend, came and stayed with me, and helped me to break up housekeeping, Pa having decided to send a portion of our effects down to Petersburg to Mr. Sprigg, where we would stay for awhile; others we stored in Georgetown.

I suppose it must have been the last day of May when we sent down several large wagons of furniture to Alexandria [Virginia] to await our arrival on our way to Petersburg, the day after. Alexandria was put under marshal law, owing to the Union soldiers tearing down the Southern flag, which was hoisted over the Marshall Hotel. Captain Elverson [Colonel Elmer Ellsworth], on the Union side, was shot down, also the proprietor of the Hotel. That stopped our passage; our goods were all lost to us, and our plans all changed. My brother-in-law, cousin Thomas Addison, came down from Baltimore, and insisted that Pa and myself should come right up there and await a chance to get to Virginia. I do not remember the exact time Pa and I left for Baltimore.

William Meade Addison was District Attorney of Baltimore at this time, which gave us all the influence to act upon [Union Major] General [Nathaniel P.] Banks at Fort McHenry [Maryland], just beyond Baltimore, and he wrote personal letters of friendship to [Union Major] General [Benjamin F.] Butler, asking the favor of conveying us through their lines, or we never would have gotten those passes.

July 16, 1861—Mr. Darneille made his appearance (after the most hair breath escapes) on yesterday week, having been on the road for over a week from Buckingham County, Virginia, and his baggage all taken and left in Winchester [Virginia]. As both he and Pa were crazy to reach Richmond just as soon as possible, where business is urgently calling them, we decided that on Thursday the 18th in Christ Church, Baltimore, Benjamin Darneille and Nettie S. Addison would become "man and wife."

A beautiful day, and all seemed propitious for a joyful wedding trip— a number of friends at the church, the solemn services performed, and off we started, some five or six carriages full, to escort us to the landing of one of the large [Chesapeake] Bay steamers, with all necessary passes to convey us to Old Point Comfort [Virginia], where General Butler was to send our party under especial [*sic*] escort to New Port [Newport News, Virginia], where we would soon be within our own Southern lines and be safe. Four young men from Baltimore begged to join "the bridal party," so they could get south to take arms. We let them start on our pass, but whatever became of them after that eventful evening, no one knows. Our state rooms were all paid for; baggage deposited, some friends had left, among them Emily and brother, as they had to catch the train back to Washington, when all of a sudden some great excitement seemed to prevail on board the steamer. A look of alarm seized everyone. The Captain came up and handed back all the money, saying a telegram had just been received from Washington, demanding his steamer for Government use, as a large battle had been fought down South, and

"Billy Wilson's roughs, of N.Y." [Union Major William C. Wilson of the 104th New York Infantry] were to be carried down at once, and it would not be safe for any lady to be on board, as there might be a mutiny on the steamer.

In one minute all was confusion, as upon looking up the long street leading to the wharf we saw thousands of the most awful looking creatures, not even dressed in uniform as soldiers, but many hatless and in rags, coming for the steamer, while we were making for any carriage we could get to convey us back to my sister's. Mr. Richie, a lawyer of Baltimore, persuaded cousin Thomas to take our pass and go to Fortress Monroe [Fort Monroe, Virginia] and see what could be our chances of getting off in a few days, and if it would be safe for us to travel. Poor Mollie, my sister, tried to prevent their going, but Pa said he would go if they did not, so off they went with that vile crowd of humanity, while we all returned to Mollie's home, feeling cheaper than I can express. Conflicting news was reaching us of a great Southern victory, which we were afraid to believe, it being the day of the Battle of Bull Run [Virginia], followed by our great Manassas victory in the two next days. It looked as if we would not get away for weeks, and Pa and Mr. Darneille were most restless about going. Mollie got miserable about cousin Thomas, and feared they were arrested, for they did not return for a week, but then they came with the good news that General Butler said he would do all he could for us, but the flag of truce had been fired upon by our soldiers, and he feared it would not be safe to venture; but Mr. Darneille said he would risk it, and off we started the next day, on another steamer bound for Old Point, where we were received with the greatest courtesy by General Butler and staff. We were shown to handsome apartments, and my meals were all sent to my room, saying it might not be agreeable to be where there were so many officers and soldiers. After an early dinner, we were sent aboard a Union vessel, and sent to New Port News, where two large covered wagons were prepared for us at their own expense, with a file of twenty soldiers to walk by the side of us for five miles with a flag of truce, to prevent our being fired upon by pickets stationed all along the road, both Northern and Southern soldiers, making it very dangerous to travel.

Great embankments of brush would be placed across the road, which would take much time to remove, and very often a squad of soldiers would rush forward and present arms before they would realize our peaceful intentions. Finally, about sundown, we drew up to a deserted looking farm house, showing it to be the border lines of the two armies, fences, trees, everything gone that could be burned up. An old gentleman came out, looking scared to death at the sight of the Yankee soldiers, and plead[ed] that they would do his wife and himself no harm. Mr. Darneille soon assured him that we were on our way to Richmond, and it was only through the kindness of General Butler that we were brought that far, and we now placed ourselves upon his honor and mercy for protection, and would pay him well to give us shelter for the night, until we could procure conveyances to carry us to Yorktown [Virginia], where our troops would fully protect us, as the Yankee wagons could not go any further with us in safety. He seemed to breathe more freely, and invited us in the house, where his poor wife looked the picture of terror, but we soon comforted her by giving her tea, sugar, etc. from our effects, which she prepared us a supper from, and seemed truly happy to feel that she was among friends, for they were good Southern people. Our accommodations for sleeping were something awful. We insisted that Pa should have the only comfortable room, while we took a loft, the ceiling being so low that we could not stand up, even to try to slay the insects of various kinds which tried to devour us that night. Oh, it was a terrible experience for a bridal tour, and I never slept at all and longed for day break; and when I was summoned to breakfast, to eat fat meat and ash cake, I thought alas, if this is Southern hospitality? We tried to eat what was put before us, but tried to get away just as soon as possible, and the only conveyances to be gotten were two old country carts, without springs, and drawn by mules. The ridiculousness of the bridal party going in such style at first amused us greatly, but after riding several hours we were jolted nearly to death, and Pa protested that we must land at the first house we came to, and try to get some other conveyance, which we did towards evening, when we came upon the battlefield of "Bethel" [Battle of Bethel Church, Virginia], which was fought about a month before. We were directed to a Methodist minister and his wife, Simpson by name. They were most clever, and seemed delighted to see someone who was not in a fighting humor; said they would share the best they had, entertained us with the most heart rending accounts of the battle, and of the death and suffering of our noble officers, who had died right in their house, and pointed out to us large blood stains all over the floor, which they would never come out. We walked out through the battle field, had pointed out to us just where such and such a one fell, saw the bullet holes through all trees left standing, and got the horrors by nightfall, so that I did not care to remain, but there was no alternative. They gave us much better fare than we expected, and the bed rooms looked clean and nice, and we were all so tired that we soon proposed sleep. But alas, when I was shown into my room and Mrs. Simpson turned down the sheets and said to me: I hope, my dear, you won't mind the large blood stains, no water will get them out, and poor Captain "somebody" was so fearfully and mortally wounded and died in this very bed. It was too much for me. I just cried and said I would prefer sitting up all night, but Mr. Darneille had one of my trunks brought up in the room, and I got out several large skirts and put them over the sheets, and insisted, in talking to him, that I would much rather contend with the legion of live things, like I did the night before, than to be surrounded by ghosts all night. He calmed my fears, and indeed we were all so tired that nothing could keep us awake. In the morning, Pa insisted that he would stay there a week before he would travel in another cart. After breakfast, Mr. Simpson went off on horseback, and told Mr. Darneille he knew where he could get a "carryall" which could take us, and then a cart could take the baggage; so we waited patiently and, in fact, did not get off until early the next morning, as there was much of interest to see around there, and we did not have more than half a day's journey before we would reach York Town, [Yorktown, Virginia] where our troops had possession, and there we could take a steamer for Richmond. Mr. and Mrs. Simpson were very sorry to have us go, and would have liked us to remain and board with them for a month; but our desires were different. The trip to York Town [*sic*] was rather pleasant. Mr. Darneille knew as soon as we got there he would meet with numerous friends, which he did, and more than surprised them by presenting his wife. Some would not believe the truth, for they had looked upon him as a confirmed old bachelor, being twenty-two years older than myself; but he was remarkably young looking and well preserved for a man of forty-five, while I was very matured for my age, twenty-four.

We had a great time at Yorktown. The officers made us dine with them, and there was so much to tell on both sides that we enjoyed it greatly, and late that evening took the steamer for Richmond, and arrived the next day; and such surprises as we gave all our friends there were truly amusing. Not even brother William or sister Eliza's family knew of our marriage, and the innumerable friends we met while staying at the "Exchange Hotel" for a week were very agreeable. Our experience had to be gone over so often that it was funny. The newspapers had it that Mr. D. had attempted to "run the blockade," was arrested, and was now within the enemy's lines, etc., etc., and his friends were almost uneasy about him; and when they found that he had been treated so finely and brought back a wife, it was the joke of the community, and we were lionized during our stay. Pa left us and went on to Petersburg to see my sisters, Mrs. Sprigg and Mrs. Hester, and to tell them of our marriage and journey. We followed him in a week's time, and a real happy reunion we all had. Mr. D. stayed with us a week, and then he went back to Buckingham Court House [Virginia] to engage board for us both, until he decided to go to his own home over in Albermarle County [Virginia], his native place. He did not remain away more than ten days, when he returned and took me with him to dear old Buckingham, where I had visited three years before, and had many true friends. All was quiet and calm there, and for a time we forgot there was a war going on. Pa and Mr. Hester were given offices under the new Confederate Government, and they all went to Richmond to live.

Startling events were crowding rapidly upon the South; our losses were heavy, and there was such urgent demand for more troops that old and young were drafted into service, Mr. Darneille among the number, which nearly broke my heart, but I had to submit like all other wives and mothers. I cannot go over the details of those unhappy days—it makes my blood run cold to think of the horrors of that Civil War. Towards the close I felt that I could say with the poor woman whose husband was fighting with a bear: "That she didn't care which whipped, so they would only stop fighting." How we ever lived to tell the tale after the [Union Lieutenant General] Phil[ip Henry] Sheridan raid upon us in '65 is more than I can understand. Our house was on a very high eminence, and could be seen from afar. Generals Merrett and Costa [Union Major Generals Wesley Merritt and George Armstrong Custer] took it for headquarters, and ordered accommodations for their whole staff, killed all the chickens I had, ordered my servants to cook up everything they could find and give them a big supper, and they would pay back when the commissary wagons come up (but they never did). I tried to be polite and served them as best I could, which is the only thing that prevented them from burning the roof over our heads, for they were robbing and burning wherever they went. They stayed all night and the next day. Not a bridge or a mill or a fence was left behind them; you could look all over the country and see the houses on fire. One sad instance of [Confederate] Colonel Charles Scott's handsome home, right near us, where they found a Yankee gun behind the front door, which seemed to infuriate them, and they would take no reasons why it was there, but ordered Mrs. Scott out of the house, with six little children, in the cold—would not even get their clothes, then fired the house with all its contents. Poor colonel Scott had left the house to prevent being arrested, and hid somewhere near in a secluded sp-ot [*sic*], and seeing the house on fire, dropped dead, and it was not known for days where he was, even. When found, his watch and money were still on his person, which showed he had not been killed. Mr. Darneille was impoverished by the war. Richmond he knew would be taken, and he had ordered thousands of dollars of tobacco to be brought up on the canal, to try and save it; also a large portion was stowed in the mill at Scottsville [Virginia], all of which was burnt. Losses of every kind overtook him; but while our lives were spared we tried to thank God and be cheerful.

After the different Yankee raids had destroyed everything we had, then came our own poor soldiers, returning to their homes, asking shelter and food, and oh, for weeks before [Confederate General Robert E.] Lee surrendered to [Union General Ulysses S.] Grant we had to share what little was left us with our own men. Life had to be commenced over again; every one in the South was poverty stricken after April '65, when the war ended. By oh, what joy it was to feel that peace was once more to be enjoyed, even if poverty did come with it. I soon wrote to my friends at the North, and relief most unexpectedly came from my dear friends, Mr. and Mrs. Hebb, who, although strong Union people, sent me a large dry goods box full of everything for myself and children, and during that summer came down and spent a month with us, and made Mr. D. promise to let me visit them the next winter (all expenses to be paid), which was a glorious prospect for me to live upon, that of seeing all my dear friends at the North.

17 Letters from the Heart

Edited by Chris Fordney

CONFEDERATE CAPTAIN George Washington Nelson Jr. was captured near Winchester, Virginia, in October 1863 and spent the rest of the Civil War in prison camps. "Wash" endured extreme hardship in prison, at one point reduced to eating cats to stay alive.

Nelson's lifeline during his captivity was his correspondence with his second cousin and fiancée, Mary "Mollie" Scollay, a doctor's daughter in the tiny village of Middleway, in Virginia's Shenandoah Valley.

The letters between Wash and Mollie are held by Virginia Polytechnic Institute and State University. Edited for conciseness and capitalization, they are reproduced here in chronological order.

The correspondence opens with a letter Mollie wrote to Wash before his capture. A few days earlier she had seen him when the Army of Northern Virginia passed through her town on its way into Pennsylvania during the Gettysburg Campaign.

"Home" July 6, 1863

My Dear Wash

Your kind and interesting letter gave me much pleasure and although I do not know of any way to send an answer I will write, hoping that Providence will soon favor me with an opportunity. We had not been able to hear anything definite from our army until the receipt of your letter. Of course reports of all kinds both good and bad are current, the latter of which I generally try not to believe.

Yesterday evening we heard that a severe fight had taken place near Gettysburg in which we had been rather unsuccessful losing ten thousand men &c. &c. I sincerely hope this report may not be true. Though I do not doubt there has been a fight, still I hope it has pleased a kind Providence again "to bless our arms with victory. . . ."

I fear it will be sometime before we can hear any reliable news from the fight. Please write as soon as you can, and tell us all about it. O! how it would grieve me to know that any of my dear relations had to be buried upon Yankee soil. Remember Wash if you get wounded you are to come to [Middleway]. . . .

I think Genl Lee is the sweetest old fellow I ever saw. I had quite a nice little chat with him that morning at Uncle Mann's. He told me that no soldier was to see his wife or sweetheart now until the war was over, so I concluded that he intended to end it before he came back from Pennsylvania. . . .

After the Gettysburg Campaign, Nelson slipped into the Union-occupied valley to visit Mollie on furlough. He was captured at the home of a friend's parents in Clarke County, Virginia, as he made his way back to his unit.

Winchester Oct 28th 1863

I am caught at last, my darling Mollie, and that too when I thought I was all safe and sound. Tom Randolph and I were caught Monday while eating our dinner, and not dreaming that there was a Yankee in twenty miles of us. We are very fortunate however—have been treated as well as we could have been. We stay at night with the officers of the regiment & if it were not the fact of guards being all around us you would not know we were prisoners. It is through the kindness of the commanding officer, Col. Boyden, that I am now writing. Whither we will go from here I have no idea, nor in fact do I much care. If I am carried away from Dixie & you, my own love, one place is as good as another. Probably I will pass thro' [Middleway] to morrow. If so I will have this for you. Even if I should be allowed I think it better not to try to see you. It would be an excuse for the soldiers to poke about the house, which would be anything but agreeable to you all. . . .

And now, my beloved, good bye. We may not hear from each other for a long time. But the fire of our love needs no more fuel. *Our faith &*

trust cannot fail. God Almighty bless and keep you & restore us to each other soon.

Nelson was held briefly in Harpers Ferry, Virginia, before he and other prisoners were loaded on trains and transported to Johnson's Island, a prison on Lake Erie near Sandusky, Ohio.

"Home" Jan 16th 1864

My Dear Wash

I have set apart today for writing letters, and since *you* occupy the first place in my heart, my first letter shall be to you. After spending a week in the country I have returned to settle down quietly in [Middleway] for the rest of the Winter.

That little visit did me a heap of good. I enjoyed it so much. We had three dinner parties given us, and had more cake and other nice things than I have seen since the War commenced. You must not think that because I have been so gay, that I am less mindful of your unpleasant situation, for I assure you that there was not one hour in any day I did not think of you, and wish you could share my pleasure, and with what eagerness did I retire from the crowded room to devour the contents of your last two letters, which came to hand while I was there. . . .

Do you ever see the papers? I hear the prisoners [at Johnson's Island] have all been ordered to Point Lookout. I trust the exchange will soon be resumed. . . .

Johnson's Island Feb. 9th 1864

I wrote you yesterday, my darling Mollie, what I thought would be my last letter from this place. . . .

It is mighty sweet in you to tell me what a comfort my letters are to you; I can easily imagine so, if I may compare them with what yours are to me; They can't give you much satisfaction though, they are so short and cramped. There is no limit or measure to the feeling that goes from my heart to you, & how can it express itself in the narrow limits of a page? But I don't mean to complain. I am very thankful that this much is granted me. . . .

To day is Ash Wednesday, and we have had the services of the church in this room. The Rev. Mr. Helm, (a fellow prisoner) holds services two or three times a week. You would be surprised at the interest manifested in them. This imprisonment will, with God's blessing, prove eternal salvation to many of us. . . .

"Home" March 2nd 1864

My dear Wash

I had just been wishing for a letter when yours of the 23rd was handed me. I have been very fortunate lately, receiving on an average, one, and sometimes, two letters a week. . . .

A few nights ago, I stepped over to Mr Hanks to sit until bed-time, and staid rather later than usual. No one at home knew where I was, and among numerous conjectures, it was finally concluded, that your humble servant had started to walk to "Johnson's Island." I should love dearly to see a certain prisoner there, but don't think I could walk *quite that far*, were I sure of not *freezing* before reaching my journey's end. . . .

Johnson's Island March 27, 1864

[To Mollie]

It is Sunday evening, my own love, and such a lovely evening too—nearly every one around me is asleep and the room is perfectly quiet. I have been lying down for the last hour or so, but my thoughts have been so busy that I could not sleep. I have been thinking of you more intensely than ever . . . and they are mighty happy thoughts, for they are bright, sweet hopes—hopes that I feel are nearer their fruition. My belief that we will soon leave for "Dixie" has been growing every day. You, dear, can imagine how much happiness such a belief must bring me. . . .

I stopped writing a few moments to watch a "Baptizing" in Lake Erie. That ceremony has just been performed upon 12 prisoners. It made me feel very solemn, as I watched the poor fellows march out into the Lake, loose ice floating on it, singing their hymns, and the guard drawn up on the shore. . . .

"Home" April 5th 1864

My dear Wash

I heard through Cousin Bettie Randolph that you were expected by the "Flag of truce boat," which was due last Thursday week, so I suppose by this time, you are enjoying the sweets of freedom in our dearly loved Confederacy. Would that I could have been in Dixie, to welcome you home! but alas! that privilege was denied me, and I fear it will be a long *long* time before we meet, for I must forbid your coming to the valley again, until you can come with safety, and I believe it is the general impression that our army will not be here this Summer. O! I trust we are not destined to be shut up in Yankee lines all Summer. We are surrounded by them on all sides now. No one can get out of town—even to get a stick of wood, and what we are to do I don't know, but I trust the Lord will provide. We had an old house in the yard pulled down to burn, and I hope by the time that is gone, the Yankees will be removed. . . .

It was my painful task to communicate a few days ago to a friend of mine, the sad intelligence of her lover's death. Poor child! she is completely heart-broken, and I feel most tenderly for her. On her 18th birthday, they were to have been married, death alone preventing, and as it has pleased God to take him, she says, she cannot help praying that they may be united in Heaven on that day. This cruel war has crushed so many-many young hearts, and I fear the same trial is in store for me. O! may Heaven avert this blow from me. . . .

Nelson fell ill at Johnson's Island and in April 1864 was taken to Baltimore, Maryland, where he expected to be part of an exchange of sick and disabled prisoners. But he ended up at a prison hospital at Point Lookout, Maryland.

Hammond General Hospital.
Point Lookout May 30th 1864

I am glad to learn from your last letter, my darling Mollie, that some of the many letters I had written had reached you. You may relieve your mind altogether as regards my health; I am well, and expect to leave the Hospital for Camp to day or tomorrow. You are wrong though, in your prejudice against hospitals; this is certainly the best berth I have had since my capture. . . .

June 3rd 1864

Why is it my dear Wash that you have not been exchanged? Until last night, I had not heard for so long that I was sure you were with your friends in "Dixie," but alas! your letter of the 29th assures me of the *sad, sad* fact that you are still a prisoner. I am afraid you have been sick again. Tell me. Since I last wrote, I have been quite sick myself, but am entirely well now, and feel better than I have done for many months. Am still thin, but improving in flesh. Tell me about Lt. R[andolph] when you write again, so that I may let his friends know. They have not heard from him since early in March. I sent him a letter from his Mother, telling of his Brother Willie's death. He was killed in the last terrible battle. . . .

Do write again soon. Don't you expect to be exchanged? My letters go through so many hands, even to get to the office, and of course are

read by almost every one. You must not think them *cold*. I scarcely know
how to write them.

Officers Camp Point Lookout
June 7th 1864

As I foretold in my last letter to you, dearest Mollie, I have been
moved from the Hospital to the Camp, and indeed, I have so entirely
recovered that I am not even considered a fit subject for a hospital tent,
but allowed to rough it with the best of us. I like the change. It is pleasant to have no bottles around, no doctors whispering about you. I even
enjoy such a night as I have just spent. Rain driving through the tent—
wind blowing under it. Every now & then a rope or a peg giving way,
making it necessary for someone to go out & fix it, and thus get full benefit of wind & rain. I like it because it reminds me of other tents I have
been in, of other winds & rains I have gone through, or rather, which
have gone through me. I am this explicit, that I may convince you of my
entire recovery. There is one thing that troubles me very seriously, and it
is the only reason I regret leaving the Hospital—and that is, I had just
begun to get letters from you—and now, as has always been the case in
any change of place I have made heretofore, I may have to go a month or
six weeks without hearing from you. And this, my darling, is the hardest
trial that can be put upon me. . . .

Officers Camp Point Lookout
June 12th 1864

[To Mollie]
. . . I can well believe how gloriously beautiful your lovely country is right
now. It grieves me, my love, that you can't enjoy it. It is true that viewed
only in the light of contrast, Nature, with its beautiful garb, its sweet fra-
grance and its soft melodies, seems to mock the broken hearted and the
sorrowing of the land. But look upon it, dear, as the bow of promise, as
the type of peace, sent by the Almighty, for our comfort, to let us know
that *He* still ruleth, and that *all* will be well, and you will enjoy its beau-
ties & be comforted by them. You speak of the hardness of the times. I
trust you do not speak from experience. Tell me, my love, has any want
come to *you*? Tell me your sorrows, let me at least share with you the
knowledge of them. You know that I love you better than my own life.
Grant me then the privilege of comforting you with words of love. Alas,
that I can do no more. . . .

June 26th 1864

My dear Wash

Although I have written so recently, as I hear of an opportunity to the depot, I will send you a few lines of love, fearing I may not have another for some time. I fear you suffer much this warm weather; should think the confinement must be terrible. . . .

Don't you remember how happy we all were together this time last year? We spend our time thinking and talking over what happened on each day. But how many, who were then full of life and joy, are now under the sod. O! for an end to this shedding of blood. It is inhuman.

Fort Delaware June 28th 1864

If my last letter has reached you, my darling Mollie, you see by the above that I was a true prophet. I had hardly mailed my letter when we received orders to start and in due course of time arrived at this place and here we are safe enough. I told you I had heard from Cousin Posey through Dick Page, up to June 15th. I was very much grieved on coming here to learn that he was killed on the 17th and I fear there is little room to doubt the truth of this report. It comes from an officer of his brigade captured after the 17th. I am so sorry, my darling, that the little short letters I write you should ever contain bad news. But you know the love that prompts me to tell you the truth, and will, I trust, feel the less pain because you know that I sympathize with you in your loss & share with you your sorrow.

I found two old college friends here waiting to meet me. One was Rodes Massie, you have heard me speak of him. My respect & admiration for him are very much increased, since he has shown himself the sensible man, I thought him, by getting married. He tells me he has the best wife, and the sweetest wife that ever existed. I tell him I have no doubt of the truth of his statement as to the wives that *have been*. . . .

Fort Delaware July 11th 1864

[To Mollie]

You said in one of your late letters that you didn't hear from me as often as when I was farther off. Indeed, my love, the fault is not mine. I have written very often, even when I thought there was little chance of my letters going. I know you have not blamed me for this; you know too well the depths of my heart to believe that I could let pass any chance of sending the little notes, that are permitted. Why, my beloved, the dearest pleasure of my life, is interchanging with you, as often as I dare, some few words. . . .

I think the sun has been trying himself, just to see if there is any limit to the supply of heat. All we ask is that he will not overwhelm us with proofs of his power; we are ready to accord him credit for an infinite amount, and we are good judges, for we have no green trees, with cool breezes blowing beneath, to distract our attention from the *great* mass of heat about us. I have been finding pleasure and employment lately in a game of whist. Our object is to pass the time pleasantly and at the same time not allow the mind to become a dead letter. . . .

In August 1864, Nelson and 600 other prisoners were packed into the hold of a steamer and taken to Morris Island, in the harbor of Charleston, South Carolina. There they were confined in an open pen under the fire of their own batteries. In October, they were moved to Fort Pulaski, Georgia, where their rations were reduced to the starvation level to retaliate for the treatment of Union troops at Andersonville Prison, Georgia. Nelson withheld details of his suffering in the one letter that reached Mollie during this period.

Fort Pulaski Ga. October 31st 1864

[To Mollie]

O for a letter from you, my darling, is the burden of my song, and has been for some months. But I know it is not your fault that I don't hear from you. I doubt whether you have any idea where I am. . . .

I had very little idea, when leaving Johnson's Island for Dixie on the 22nd of April, that the 31st of October would find me in Fort Pulaski, Ga. It does seem impossible for me to be exchanged; no matter how fair a start I make, there is always some Jonah in the party to stop the whole business. Well, I am hopeful still, thank God, looking to what the next month or two may do for me. Who knows, I may *see you* by Christmas yet! How my heart beats at the very thought. . . .

In spite of all I have been through since this time a year ago, I can hardly regret my imprisonment, because it has shown me, perhaps more thoroughly than perhaps I could have learned under any other circumstances, how completely my heart is yours.

The constant stir in your part of the country keeps me mighty uneasy, and the absence of all news from you during it all is mighty hard to bear. May God shield you and yours. . . .

In early March 1865, Nelson and other prisoners, in rags and suffering from scurvy, were taken back to Fort Delaware. Friends gave him vegetables and clothes, and he immediately wrote to Mollie to explain his long silence.

Fort Delaware March 13th 65

My darling Mollie

I arrived here from Fort Pulaski yesterday; have just seen Dick Page; imagine my joy at learning that the mail route to you is open. I tried until there was no use in trying to communicate with you. . . .

We left Pulaski expecting to land at City Point, but, with such a Jonah as myself along, the party might have known we would stop at Delaware or some such safe place. Well I suppose I will be exchanged one of these days. Sometimes I think if I were one of those generous people we read about in books, I would write to you not to waste your youth & beauty on me, but, my own love, I can't find any where in my heart, so selfish is it, any such inclination. . . .

"Home" March 21, 1865

My dear Wash

. . . Really the fates seem to be against your being exchanged. How often have I pictured to myself your arrival at home, and the joy of the loved ones to have you with them again. Little did I think that when next I heard from you, you would be back in Fort Del: But I suppose we must be patient; one thing we know they cannot hold you forever. Until a few days ago, it had been five months since I had heard one word from you. O! how my heart ached for only one line, to tell me you were well. . . .

"Home" March 24, 1865

My dear Wash

I wrote you a short letter a day or two ago, but judging you by myself, I think you will not object to reading another so soon. I cannot express my joy at hearing from you again. . . .

What have you been doing with yourself all this *long long* time? How have you managed to pass away the dreary hours of eighteen months imprisonment? Little did we think when we parted that you would have to endure such a series of trials and hardships. Though I could not hear from you my thoughts were with you constantly and I have not thought of bestowing my *"youth and beauty"* upon any other soldier, so your generosity is not likely to be put to the test *yet a-while*. I don't know what *might* happen *if you don't get out of prison before the Summer is over*. . . .

I read a great deal last Winter, and in that way managed to keep my time so fully occupied that the long months slipped away very rapidly, and now spring has opened, bringing with it bright hopes to cheer our sad hearts. I don't think I ever enjoyed a spring as much as I have this one. We have had such sweet weather lately, and the country, tho terribly devastated is still beautiful. . . .

Has Lt. Randolph been exchanged? I suppose you know he has lost another brother. I am anxiously looking for another letter tomorrow. Hope I may not be disappointed. I wish there was no War in the land, and you were here this evening, would we not be *happy?*

"Home" April 4th 1865

I have written to you twice my dear Wash since the receipt of your note, telling me of your arrival at Fort Delaware, which was two weeks ago, and not another line have I received from you in all that time. . . . *Surely* you have written, I *cannot* think you would allow so long a time to elapse without sending me a word of love. . . .

[Middleway] is as dull as ever, and looks rather the worse for wear. The upper street is a wreck of its former self, four houses having been burned. Many of the houses on the street are perforated by bullets and shells, ours among the number, however *we* have added an improvement to the place by having a new porch built. Yesterday the dull monotony of our lives was broken in upon by the arrival of the news of the fall of Petersburg, which report we received "cum grana salis" as we do all such. . . . The campaign has opened, and battles are raging furiously. I wonder which of our friends have been killed. . . .

Three days after General Robert E. Lee's surrender at Appomattox, the despair of the Southern defeat was evident in Nelson's letter to Mollie.

Fort Delaware April 12th 1865

[To Mollie]

It is not a happy time with me at present, as you may well believe, my love, and Oh! with what delight I look at the one bright place in my heart, which even in this sad time consoles me beyond all description. You, my darling, have for the last few days been more in my thoughts than ever. And though made happier the more, I think, from the conviction of possessing your constant love, yet I must confess to some very anxious thoughts about you now. How could it be otherwise, believing as I do that your happiness & mine are identical, when I can form no idea what will be my future fate and how it will affect you. . . .

I suppose that after a little while letters will go directly through Richmond. Who would have thought it? If we could be disinterested spectators of our own lives, the ups & downs and unexpected turns would be very amusing. How knocked to pieces your little town must be. Carter Berkeley gave me an account of the fight there. Where were you, Mollie, when bullets were flying through your house and the porch blown up? You are quite a veteran. . . .

Sunday morning April 23rd 1865

My dear Wash

Your last [letter] I did not exactly understand. Surely you do not think that because of late events, my feelings towards you should change. I cannot think less of a brave soldier, because he has been overpowered by numbers. We have acted as we believed to be right; we were inspired by the noble principles of duty, then why should we feel humiliated? Though we have ceased to strike for success, and bright hopes for the future have ceased to animate us, still it is very comforting to have the approval of a quiet conscience, and to feel we have always followed in the path of duty. Cheer up then, and do not for one moment feel that you are disgraced by what has happened. Nearly all the soldiers from this place and vicinity have returned. It looks quite like old times to see them, and the young ladies have ceased to lament the want of beaux. . . .

Did I in my last letter lead you to infer that our porch was blown up by a shell? If so, I must undeceive you. A shell *did* burst at the steps, when we were all at the door, but no damage was done, except to the windows, which were shivered. . . .

Fort Delaware May 8th 1865

My darling Mollie

The events of the last few days have worked a great change among the officers confined here. The surrender of Johnston's Army, together with the voluntary surrender of one or two members of President Davis' Cabinet have combined to force upon us the conclusion that the Southern Confederacy is indeed a thing of the past. . . . The state of things was discussed from every point of view, opinions were fully & freely interchanged, and the conclusion arrived at that our government no longer existed in fact, that therefore our obligations to it were at an end, and our honor could in no way be compromised by any course we might pursue with regard to it. Then came up the question, "what is our duty under the circumstances?" And the opinion was almost unanimous that we ought to return to our loved ones, to support and comfort them. Under the state of things on the following day our names were called for the third time to know whether we were willing to take the oath of Allegiance to the United States. The result was that out of 2300 officers only 161 said "no." I myself am with the majority. I acted with the approval of both my reason and my conscience, as well as with the advice of my friends and brother officers. God alone knows the struggle I have had with my pride, but I have overcome it, and I feel that I have done what was right. And now, beloved, may I look to you, whom I love a thousand times better than all else in the world, for a little comfort—for the cheering word that you will sustain me in the path of duty and conscience? Ah! my darling, if you only knew the rack I have been upon from the fear that by a false step now I might loose you forever, you would have some idea of how I love you. God bless you always. If you love me write immediately. Love to all.

May 14th 1865

You are a sweet comforter, my own Mollie, and have made me very happy by your last letter, assuring me not only of your acquiescence in what I had done, but of your hearty approval. The one great question with me now is when will I be free to come to you . . . but whatever happens the Valley is the point on which my eye is fixed, and the *gem* of the Valley the object I am striving to reach. I have seen its beauty, I have proved its genuineness and know its value. It is the treasure in which my Whole heart is absorbed, and to win & to wear it is the aim of my existence. . . .

Nelson was released from Fort Delaware on June 13, 1865, a few days after his 25th birthday. He and Mollie Scollay were married on October 17, 1865. He became an Episcopal minister in Warrenton, Virginia, and they raised eight children. He died in 1903, at 63, of ill health that friends attributed to the hardships of his imprisonment. She lived another 20 years and died at the age of 79. They are buried side by side in a cemetery in Warrenton.

Reflections

18 The Siren of Bull Run

Michael Clune

$\mathcal{I}$N READING the story of the extra session of '61 in Blaine's *Twenty Years of Congress,* I was led to wonder what sinister influences had prevented Mr. Lincoln's fair and generous policy from exerting its due influence upon the generous and warm-hearted people of the South. I little anticipated that in after years, from the South itself, in the person of a great participant in the struggle, I should learn what precipitated it.

In February, 1902, I took passage on the good ship *Celtic* for a tour of the Orient. The voyage was remarkable in many respects. The *Celtic* was the largest ship that up to that time had sailed the Mediterranean. It was an object of curiosity to the inhabitants of the ports and was visited incognito by the King, the Queen, and the Prince Royal of Greece.

The tourists were largely people of affairs who had undertaken the voyage for the preservation or the recovery of health. Among the distinguished voyagers there was none more notable either in appearance, in character, or in experience than Burton Harrison, who had been private secretary to Jefferson Davis during the last three years of the rebellion. Physically, Mr. Harrison was the handsomest man I had ever seen of his years. He had reached what has been beautifully described as the high plateau lying just beyond middle life, where the passions lie vanquished. His character, as revealed by his tender devotion to his wife and his manly, cordial bearing toward all, was a revelation of that chivalry which seems to be passing away. It was, however from the deep well of his experience that the cool waters could be drawn which should quench the feverish thirst for war.

Among the entertainments usual on such it voyage, it was arranged to have an address upon Mr. Lincoln, and later another upon Mr. Davis. I was asked to speak on the martyred President and Mr. Harrison was asked to speak on the Confederate President. My treatment of Mr. Lincoln had made Mr. Harrison feel kindly toward me, and when he had finished his address on Mr. Davis I took a liberty which I would not otherwise have taken.

I said: "Mr. Harrison, you have told us, what any one could tell. What we wanted from you is what no one else could tell us." He replied: "I shall go to confession to you and tell you everything." I answered: "If you did go you would not tell everything." From this bantering came an agreement to meet with no one else present and exchange views. In a secluded nook on one of the great decks, and with the Mediterranean sparkling at our feet, and the scenes of Old World battles appearing and disappearing, we exchanged views. I asked what the South thought of Mr. Lincoln. He answered that up to the time of Lee's surrender the South's estimate of Mr. Lincoln was low. It wondered that he held the North together and gave him credit for shrewdness in doing it. There was, however, a brief period before the war when Mr. Lincoln both surprised and pleased an influential and intellectual minority of the Southern people. It was after his first inauguration. His kindly words and his hesitation to employ force made many of the ablest Southerners say: "Let us take him at his word. He promises a constitutional amendment making slavery a matter for the States only. What better could we get after a successful war?" Others said: "We have been preparing for this thirty years. We would be foolish to pause now." Mr. Lincoln was making converts every day. The war propagandists said to Davis, "You must sprinkle blood in the face of the Southern people or the Confederacy will collapse in a month." The assault on Fort Sumter was ordered, and fired the Southern heart so that Virginia was swept into the secession vortex. But the battle for peace did not end even then. The conservatives said: "It is true that the South is united more than it was, but the North is united from the sea even to the sea. The mad assault on Sumter has united twenty millions of whites against eight millions." Then the war party said to Davis, "It is necessary that the first battle shall end in a victory for the South or the Sumter card will have been played in vain."

Now comes the important part that only the secretary could tell. A lady endowed with wonderful beauty left Richmond for Washington with the tacit approval of Davis. She ingratiated herself into the confidence of McDowell's chief of staff. The officer, intoxicated by her beauty, ensnared by her wiles, undreaming of consequences, told her the time of McDowell's advance. She sent the information to Richmond by a trusty messenger, and along all the telegraph wires around Richmond there ran the summons for troops from all adjacent places. The battle of Bull Run was decided by troops from North Carolina who debouched from the cars while the battle was in progress. The Confederate victory was complete. It was made to appear as if gained by fifteen thousand Confederates against thirty-five thousand Federals. The peace party was silenced and grim war was on,

It was the opinion of Mr. Harrison that the cipher despatch of which he afterward had the custody for three and one-half years was the cause of the war. Had not distant troops been summoned on account of it, Bull Run would have been a Union victory and would have strengthened the Southern peace party in preventing the war. I told Mr. Harrison that I considered it his duty to give the matter to the world. He replied that the confidential revelations by secretaries in literature had instructed rather than edified him. I replied that there was no comparison between revelations made to satisfy a morbid curiosity and one that afforded a grave warning against war; that, although he was an Episcopalian and I a Catholic, he should receive my request as the voice of Christianity. Here the chivalry of a Southern gentleman shone at its best. He said that Mrs. Davis was yet living, but that if she should die he would think seriously of what I said and probably would comply with it.

Mrs. Davis outlived Mr. Harrison. He went to his honored grave and made no further sign. He had previously told his wife, however, and his son, Congressman Harrison, when approached upon the subject, knowing nothing of the matter, referred me to his revered mother. That lady recalled the matter at once and gave me permission to publish it.

What lessons flow from the incident! The Civil War was preventable. The issues had been debated for thirty years by able statesmen. On one side preparations had been made over a wide land and distant seas for the combat. And yet the act of a false siren was needed to precipitate the war. Wisdom and fairness were opening the way of peace. If that war was avoidable, what war is necessary? A continent was drenched in blood; millions of men incurred death and disease not because the conflict was, as Seward said, irrepressible, but because a foolish official betrayed a secret to a designing woman.

Did the emancipation of a race justify the war? For answer let us ask ourselves whether the cataclysm of the French Revolution left France as fortunate as the slow development of liberty left England?

All the happy emancipations of history have been peaceful and gradual. Emancipation was foreseen by the South and was only forestalled, as it thought, by the war. The effects of the war were unhappy for black and white. I need mention only carpet-bag rule, The Ku-Klux. That they have not yet ceased the horrors of lynching and its attendant cause bear witness. It is easier to invoke the demon of war than to lay him. Would that this story might help to keep him enchained forever.

19 The Rose of Mississippi

Joseph Hergesheimer

*V*ARINA HOWELL, for me she was the rose of Mississippi, was born in Natchez in the May of Eighteen-twenty-six. The Howells were Scots and Welsh and her grandmother had married an Irishman, James Kempe. The Kempes settled in Virginia before Sixteen-forty, but James removed with his young wife to the Mississippi Territory, and there he fought under Andrew Jackson. His third daughter, Margaret Louisa, married William Burr Howell—she was a great beauty and Howell was handsomely blond and tall in the tradition of his blood—and they settled in Natchez. Before his marriage, Joseph Davis, Jefferson Davis' elder brother, had tried to persuade Howell to buy land on the River forty miles below the town, in the rich alluvial bottom near The Hurricane, a Davis plantation, but William Howell preferred the lands near Natchez. His house was a large rambling dwelling, white on the high eroded Bluff, called The Briers—a tangle of Cherokee roses and bamboo bound together the magnolias and oak trees and pines that surrounded it. The Bluff was very high there; it fell away in almost perpendicular red walls to little valleys magnificent with uncut woods, bayous worn by floods sweeping far back into the low tablelands east of the Mississippi River.

William Howell was not a provident planter; but then neither was he above the help of houses, of families, intimate to him; and he lived in a region and times of extraordinary plenty. His first child was a son, Joseph; a trip into the North was undertaken in the interest of the infant's health;

and the Howells visited Jefferson Davis at West Point. Jefferson was then eighteen, a cadet at the Military Academy, and he was impressed by Mrs. Howell's charm. It was after that Varina, Varina Anne Banks Howell, was born, and a black slave held her—her long white embroidered robe reached to the floor—for christening in the Old Trinity Episcopal Church. She became a vivid and strong little girl and played freely with Joseph, and subsequent smaller brothers and sisters, in the dry bayous near the River. She slid and rolled down steep declines smooth-carpeted with pine needles and magnolia leaves, and in the bottoms was engaged by robust games and ventures.

Varina's childhood—the influences and surroundings of her earliest impressionable years—was set in a vast and solemn land; the sombre immensity of the Mississippi River swept between sheer irregular bluffs and dark forests, impenetrable swamps, draped with Spanish moss. Natchez on the Bluff, tranquil and deep in trees on a wide green esplanade, was constantly filled with the carriages and horses of planters, ladies in rose-colored muslins and gentlemen in white à cheval, bearing themselves with a careless elegance. They dressed carelessly and lounged in an insolence of pride on the high Spanish pommels of their saddles. There were six streets leading from the Bluff, seven streets parallel to the River intercepted them, and the Mansion House, the principal blocks, were built of brick.

Varina's freedom of extreme youth was soon interrupted by education—she attended two terms at Madame Greenland's school for young ladies, in Philadelphia, and then came under the private instruction of a tutor, Judge George Winchester. In addition to such formal instruction her grandmother, Mrs. Kempe, repeated for her the heroic episodes of her grandfather's life in an earlier day, stories of General Jackson, and Thomas Hinds, who led Jackson's cavalry at the Battle of New Orleans. Mrs. Kempe, as well, made Varina familiar with the traditions of her family in Virginia, in Prince William County. Her time then—she was perhaps sixteen—was filled with study and a companionship appropriate to the daughter of the dominating planter class. Judge Winchester, who had come to the deep South from Salem, Massachusetts, was a learned jurist; and in his charge, Varina wrote, she studied hard to finish a course in the classics before her seventeenth year. At that age, in that society, she was considered old enough to put on long dresses and do up her hair, to appear at balls and supper parties.

She went, when she was seventeen, to a long party at the Davis plantation, The Hurricane. Varina was, at that time, mature in appearance, a seductive girl with the dark coloring of the Kempes. Her skin was ivory, pale like a tea rose, her eyes were dark and her features softly curved, she had full vividly red lips and beautiful teeth. She was vigorously graceful: already she owned the bearing that later grew into what was currently described as a haughtiness of manner. However, she was highly animated, Varina laughed a great deal and delicate flushes of color rose easily into the paleness of her cheeks. She followed with intense interest the elaborate preparations for her visit to The Hurricane—a number of seamstresses, hired for the occasion, were active in the sewing-room, a multiplication of maids was kept busy.

She went, finally, under the care of Judge Winchester, on the steamboat Magnolia, one of the most palatial boats of the era. The steamboats of that time, she found, were literally floating palaces of ease and luxury. They were larger than now and she had never seen any hotel where food was so exquisitely prepared. Fresh fruits and most beautiful flowers were sent to the captain at almost every stopping place, by the planters, to whom the boat meant ice, new books, all the luxuries New Orleans could afford. This fell at Christmas time, Varina stopped first at Diamond Place, Mrs. David McCaleb's plantation, thirteen miles north of The Hurricane, and the house was green with great clusters of holly and mistletoe gathered from the trees along the River. Mrs. McCaleb was the eldest daughter of Joseph E. Davis; the day after their arrival Judge Winchester returned to Natchez. He left her reluctantly—Winchester was unmarried—and with the caution that she was not to fall in love.

There rose, for the moment, a question of Varina's remaining at Diamond Place for the holiday season; and, while this was being discussed, a handsome and distinguished-appearing gentleman arrived on horse. He was, Varina was informed, Jefferson Davis, Mr. Joseph Davis' younger brother, and he bore a message that nothing must be allowed to stop her journey to The Hurricane. In addition she learned that he was hurrying to a political meeting at Vicksburg. Jefferson, Mr. McCaleb assured Varina, was a man of highly elevated qualities. She wrote to her mother:

"Today Uncle Joe sent by his younger brother—did you know that he had one?—an urgent invitation for me to go at once to The Hurricane. I do not know whether this Mr. Jefferson Davis is old or young. He looks both at times; but I believe he is old for from what I hear he is only two years younger than you are. He impresses me as a remarkable kind of man but of uncertain temper and has a way of taking for granted everybody agrees with him when he expresses an opinion that offends me, yet he is most agreeable and has a peculiarly sweet voice and a winning manner of asserting himself. In fact he is the kind of person I should expect to rescue me from a mad dog at any risk but to insist upon a stoical indifference to fright afterward. I do not think I shall ever like him as I do his brother Joe. Would you believe it, he is refined and cultivated and yet he is a Democrat."

The day following a Miss Mary Bradford, with a man servant, rode up to Diamond Place to conduct Varina to The Hurricane plantation. The servant led a noble horse—one of the finest in the celebrated Davis stables—with a side saddle and complete riding habit; there was a family carriage drawn by a pair of bays to fetch Varina's bags; and "all in blue unclouded weather," she remembered, "we rode over the rustling leaves through the thick trees to The Hurricane." She rode gay and free through the whispering leaves, under the shade of massive trees, calling in a young clear voice to Miss Bradford, accompanied by the carriage bearing her virginal finery, her crinolines and bracelets and ribbons and colognes.

IT IS difficult to dwell on Varina Howell's girlhood, in reality it is impossible to consider any stage of her active being, aside from politics. Fortunately the politics that so closely surrounded and influenced her was far more vital and engaging, intensely more personal, than what later it became. When Varina wrote amazed to her mother that Jefferson Davis, who was refined and cultivated, was yet a Democrat she simply expressed the feeling of the whole Whig aristocracy of planters. There was, then, no actual intimation of the War for Secession, no general consciousness in the deep South of the approaching attempt at separation from the Union; the planters, quite differently, after long and practically unbroken control of the government, regarded themselves, their interests and lands, as preponderant, the major part of the United States. They would not have believed that the nation could continue without them. With practically no exception the planters of Mississippi were Whigs; their paper, the National Intelligencer, was edited by a Mr. Gale and Mr. Seton, both strong Federalists—the earlier Federal party had become Whig—and only the poor and the inconsiderable upheld Mr. Jefferson's principles. Varina had heard nothing but a violent denunciation of Martin Van Buren and his rabble; the general opinions of Andrew Jackson she was familiar with were hardly more complimentary.

The Democrats were wholly abhorrent to the ladies of Mississippi; even at the height of General Jackson's popularity in the district of Natchez, after his triumph at New Orleans, feminine opinion and the leadership of Judge Winchester and of the brilliant young Mr. Prentiss kept the Whigs firm in command. The further truth was that Virginia, the ideals of Thomas Jefferson, had lost their power over the South; the feeling that slavery would, at some future time, be ended, had changed to the realization that slaves were grown too valuable for surrender. The Whigs, the traditionally aristocratic party, still, in Varina's eyes, supported that self-evident fact. But Jefferson Davis, practically alone in his class, had foreseen that ultimately the Democrats must represent his necessities and beliefs and he had attached himself to the increasing political eminence of John C. Calhoun.

Mr. Davis had already, before Varina Howell knew him, been defeated for the State Legislature. The Whigs, recognizing his inherent ability, his resemblance to Calhoun, put forward against him their most effective speakers. He had, however, equalled even Sargeant Prentiss in the grace and manner of his bearing; Jefferson Davis, it was admitted, had surpassed him in the logic and depth of his argument. Mr. Davis' democratic logic had little connection with the beginnings, the fundamental spirit, of that doctrine. It was, now, local to the lower cotton states, Georgia and Alabama, Louisiana and Mississippi. It fashioned Davis' ideas precisely as it had bred Mr. Calhoun and William Lowndes Yancey. Back of it lay the dramatic change, the improved machinery, of cotton spinning—in one period of twelve years the export of cotton had risen from two hundred thousand pounds to forty million pounds. The deep South had grown immensely rich. The result of this was evident to Varina, but, blinded by prejudice and education, she was unable to see what was clear to Mr. Davis.

Varina thought of him, however, with the very great deference then offered to any superiority of years. She thought about him, in reality, very often indeed. He was a romantic personage—after the death of his first wife, Sara Knox Taylor, he had lived in almost complete seclusion for eight years on his plantation, Brierfield; he had confined himself to the company of his brother and to his books. Then Jefferson had emerged from his retirement to take his astonishing stand with the vile Democrats. Everyone bows down before the younger brother, she told herself after a few days at The Hurricane. She had, it was plain, a great confidence in her own opinions. Varina was, in reality, unusual—a combination of personal charm and beauty with an acute intelligence. Her education had gone further than was common for young ladies of birth. Judge Winchester had early discovered that she thought for herself. Jefferson Davis was astonished when, reading aloud to Joseph and himself, she adequately translated Latin phrases into English.

She would, Joseph Davis asserted, take high rank in the world of femininity when she blossomed out and came thoroughly to herself. Jefferson, to whom he was speaking, made no reply and the elder added, "By Jove, she is as beautiful as Venus!" After a long pause Jefferson Davis said quietly, "Yes, she is beautiful and has a fine mind." Joseph liked to walk with her through his beautifully planted grounds. They picked scarlet camellias—throughout her life Varina, whenever it was possible, wore a scarlet camellia low in her hair—and he teased her about her friends the Whigs. She was never slow, never at a loss, to reply. There were other things in the National Intelligencer besides attacks on Martin Van Buren. Varina gave him the benefit of her views of the Duke of Wellington, on Lord Brougham, on London, she had command of a score of wordly topics.

Joseph Davis, an old man, was delighted with her, walking lightly by his side, dressed in a "rose-colored marino made with a corded waist and a full skirt." It was a style that set off her strong, graceful body wonderfully well. They explored everything in the plantation—the general store room, filled with boxes and bridles, saddles and guns. The guns, Varina commented, made the room like the Arsenal at Natchez. There were blankets and osenburgs, shoes and calico and pocket knives for the negroes. He pointed out to her all the aspects of his place: the heavy roof of the great house glittered in the sun with dormers; it stood in deep lawns cool with the shadow of immense forest trees brought, many of them, from Europe; the dwelling had an air of isolated and sombre grandeur. Part of it had been swept away by storms, by "the hurricane," and numerous rambling additions gave it a strange air of appropriateness to the rank luxury of vegetation that enclosed it. There were long rose gardens and arbors, peach and apple orchards, and, beyond the heavily constructed stables and cribs, green streets of white-washed cabins.

He showed her the house from the heavy and turbulent, the yellow, waters of the River; from the River the plantation was as wide and various and inhabited as a little town. They walked in the drawing-room, the tea room, and through the high-arched music room where portraits filled the walls. He showed her a painting of a thin-faced handsome man of sixty. "My father," he said. "Samuel Davis. He was a good soldier—none better, a good citizen, a good master to his negroes and the best rider in the country—looked like one of Charles' Cavaliers on horseback, like one would imagine Peveril of the Peak looked—Jefferson reminds me of him at times so much that it startles me." From the music room, Varina continues, they walked through high-panelled glass doors into the garden. Her world was thick with the golden light of late afternoon, and into it Jefferson Davis suddenly, romantically, rode. When she saw him then, she admits, she instantly thought of Wallace and Glendower and Bruce and like heroes of history.

Jefferson Davis remained at Brierfield and Varina walked with him in place of his elder brother. They rode the winding country lanes and through groves of magnolias grey with moss, by live oaks and cotton-wood and gum trees. They saw the Mississippi River shining through clearings in the forest; sweeping down in an irresistible flood of great sullen waves; quiet in smoky crimson sunsets; immense and leaden and ineffably sad. Varina knew and related all the legends of the River; Jefferson Davis repeated miraculous passages from Virgil. She wore, on horseback, a long dark blue habit and a small hat with a curled plume. She managed her bay horse, selected for her with great particularity by Jefferson, with a perfection of ease. He rode Grey Medley, the horse that Federal soldiers were later to steal and present to General Grant.

* * *

The evenings were filled by a light elegance of conversation and dialogues and reading in a more classic form. There was a great deal of rhetorical Latin. Ladies, in the widest crinolines imaginable and with towers of ornamented hair, exhibited their adroitness with French turns of speech and showed a pleasant taste in poetry. That, usually, together with the domestic engagement, made up the whole polite feminine world. But men of superior accomplishments demanded more—they required a not inconsiderable political understanding, some apprehension of philosophical systems in addition to an indispensable charm.

Jefferson Davis was a highly-organized, a rigid and sensitive man; he was, even then, morbidly intense; and his requirements were peculiarly difficult. It was clear, however, at least to his brother Joseph, that Varina perfectly fulfilled them. Her good looks and mind, he asserted, fit her for any sphere that the man whom she married might well feel proud to reach. On the day before her departure from The Hurricane she sat through the late afternoon with Jefferson Davis in the music room. There was a fire of hickory logs on heavy brass andirons. Close beside her Davis saw that Varina had not put on what she called her sub-treasury brooch, an emblem of her Whig sympathies. That, commonly, had been the subject of humorous comment at The Hurricane, a Democratic house, but there was no politics in Jefferson Davis' sudden discovery of its absence. It was the sign of Varina's surrender to him. They became—if Jefferson secured the approval of her family—engaged. They stayed with their heads close together, lost in their planned happiness, until the sun had withdrawn from the room and dusk enveloped them.

The Howell family, Varina quickly found, not only approved of Jefferson Davis, it was delighted with him. Her mother remembered him, a handsome youth, from the long passed visit to West Point; her father, Whig and vestryman of Old Trinity Church, declared that the whole state was comparing Jefferson with Sargeant S. Prentiss. What, he rather surprisingly asked, did political parties amount to anyhow? It was the man after all. Yes, he reiterated—the complete parent—it was the man after all. Both the elder Howells now insisted that Jefferson Davis' politics was not a cause for concern. The truth was, William Howell intimated, that the Democratic party was growing daily stronger. The Whigs, he thought, but not too loudly, might not quite understand the new and rising power of the deep South. It is doubtful if Mrs. Howell ventured so far—the Whig spirit was last supported by the feminine world; it was attended with genealogical research, gilded with the identification of coats of arms; it served to distinguish the ladies of superior pretensions from what they universally called the common herd.

Varina herself went quickly through a political transformation: at first she had determined to ignore Jefferson's beliefs because she loved him; then she decided that, since his beliefs were his, she should meet them with affectionate regard; and then she adopted them, she adopted all of him, for her own. Varina, at first, was a little fearful of the opinion of her world; she was anxious to discover Judge Winchester's attitude toward Mr. Davis' convictions. But almost at once her vigorous mind and determined character, the power of love in her, killed all her questioning and doubt. From that moment until the end of her life she knew that Mr. Davis was right. The people who disagreed with him were wholly wrong. Her passionate loyalty, her absorption in the man she married, was characteristic both of Varina and of her times.

Women, then, thought themselves well lost in the men they loved and married; they made every effort to sink themselves in their husbands' personality; his necessity was theirs; his breath was their breath. In that way only, it appeared to Varina, could she be happy and justified, fulfilled. She didn't lose her spirit, her individuality, but found it. She became, in a very real sense, one with Jefferson Davis. There was no subserviency in this; she willingly and freely accepted Jefferson's ideas; the quality of her love made that not only possible but imperative. The quality of their love, of course, was at once passionate and ordered; it was love safety contained in the formal necessities of religion and a social system. Varina's society, her world, was primarily masculine; it was founded on the agreement that men, in the abstract, were superior in strength and in mentality to women; the superiority of women was totally different—it lay in purity and fidelity, beauty and all the domestic virtues. That—at least it seemed so then—was the ideal of happiness and marriage. There was no direct competition of duties, of responsibility, and so there was no implied or actual inferiority. A man and a woman were different; singly they were incomplete; together, married, they accomplished the perfection of human relationship.

It was, then, unthinkable that Varina should continue to be a Whig when Jefferson Davis was all active Democrat. He was, through the period of their engagement, more active than ever before. He came very often to The Briers in the spring and summer of Eighteen-forty-four, he was campaigning for the nomination of elector for Polk, and his struggle against Prentiss, who represented Henry Clay, lasted into the fall. A very short while ago, indeed, Varina had regarded Mr. Clay as the noblest figure in the country! Her interest now was all Mr. Calhoun's, all Jefferson's, and she addressed herself to the problems, the growing difficulties, of Democratic power and management. Her sheer youth, her lightness of talk and spirit, left her; she grew thin, worn, and intent; a grim determination—well recognized and dreaded in Southern women—settled upon her mouth.

Varina's love for Jefferson Davis, her anxiety in his political situation, finally overcame her, and she fell ill of a fever. When the month arrived for her wedding she was far too exhausted for that supernal ceremony. It was February, spring again; the gardens of Natchez were bright with the scarlet camellias Varina kept in her hair. Davis arrived and it was noticed in the family that at once she was better. She was almost gay. He returned soon upon that, she was almost recovered, and the date for their marriage was settled. The Reverend David Page, rector of Old Trinity Church, married them on the twenty-sixth day of February, in Eighteen-forty-five, with the simplest ceremony that could be devised. Varina was wedded at home, only a few people were present, and there was no breakfast. That caused a very wide comment and speculation in Whig society—could it have been because the Davis family were Baptists? Why, in addition, had practically no one seen Varina's trousseau?

Jefferson, on their wedding trip, took Varina to his sister's plantation in Louisiana, Locust Grove, on the Bayou Sara. His first wife had died there, and it was conceivable that Varina might have felt some private resentment; but it was clear that she didn't. She was deeply, romantically, interested in her husband's early tragic loss. Varina wrote, "We carried flowers to her grave in the family burying ground down by the garden before we left." They went from Locust Grove to Rosemont, to see Jefferson's mother. Rosemont was a wide cotton plantation; the dwelling had the columned portico, the tangle of roses and jasmine, usual in that region. Varina found the elder Mrs. Davis still beautiful at eighty-five and of a poetic temperament. Her eyes were bright, her hair was a soft brown, and her complexion as clear and white as a child's. They continued then—the main affair of their trip—on to New Orleans.

They stayed, inevitably, at the St. Charles Hotel, where there was the most elaborate bridal suite in the country. A great many fashionable people, Varina commented, but one she remembered most clearly was Mr. Wilde, the poet, whose sonnet, My Life is Like a Summer Rose, had made quite a local success. He was the uncle, she thought, of the poet and aesthete Oscar Wilde. General Gaines, at the request of some lady friends, was in full uniform. He had stern blue eyes and carried himself proudly. General Gaines indulged himself in a caustic comment at the expense of General Scott's System of Tactics. After six weeks she returned with Jefferson to Brierfield.

JEFFERSON DAVIS had planned and built the dwelling at Brierfield, in the great tract known as Davis Bend, a simply constructed house with cat-and-clayed walls set in a grove of live oaks with the elaborate strangeness of a fig tree at each gable end. The slave quarters were nearer the plantation house than was common; Davis and John Pemberton, his body servant, had put the land into a high state of cultivation. Varina was an extraordinarily pure example of her day and situation and education—a child, in reality, who had devoted almost all her time to formal and classic books. She now entered into the domestic obligations of her existence, and they were difficult and continuous—she was, in effect, the sole mistress, the controlling moral and spiritual force, of a complete village. The very number of servants, of slaves, at once made her duties light and her responsibility serious.

Brierfield, except for the plantations beside it, was isolated from the resources, the immediate supplies, of cities—its only doctor was Jefferson, assisted by Varina, its principal nurse was Varina herself. Negroes, under slavery, were absolutely dependent on their masters; they bore, for the most part, no trace of any responsibility. They were, outside the performance of their simple unvaried tasks, helpless. Varina, in all that had to do with the house, in everything that touched the personal life of the negroes, had to depend on her own wisdom and patience and tact. Jefferson's concern was with the fields and field hands, with justice and discipline. He rode in the morning over his land, conferring with Pemberton and overseeing the planting and harvest. Varina was busy supervising the affairs of her primitive kitchen, directing the maids who washed her delicate tea china and the boys polishing her silver and cleaning the brasses.

The rooms she described to be of fair size and opening out on a paved brick gallery surrounded by latticework. It was her husband's first experience as an architect. "As he carried me over the house," she continued, "he dwelt specially on the great doors as most desirable for admitting plenty of cool air. However, when they were opened the side of the house seemed taken down. The fireplaces were very deep and looked as though they might have been built in Queen Elizabeth's time to roast a whole sheep. It was a cool house, comfortably furnished, and we passed many happy days there, enlivened by daily rides in which we indulged in many races when the road was smooth. The game was more abundant than chickens now. There were wild geese in great flocks made fat by the waste corn in the fields; and white and blue cranes adorned almost every slough, standing on one leg among the immense lily pads that yet covered the low places with lemon-colored flowers as large as coffee cups."

Great flocks of wild geese and blue cranes, immense lily pads and lemon-colored flowers! Varina had a deep affection for flowers, for plants and trees; she constantly rode over the plantation with Jefferson; and she came to know almost every individual tree and lilac bush. That was a time of happy and pastoral tranquillity; it was serene with a perfection of companionship and passionate with love. The negroes surrounded her with affectionate pride; old slaves confused her with their earlier mistress, Jefferson's first wife. It did not last. Spring was lost in summer; the crops were laid by; myrtle and star jasmine were in flower; and a renewed insistent political pressure was brought upon Jefferson Davis.

A widening recognition of his powers forced him to stand for election to the Twenty-ninth Congress, and at once there was a sharp change in the contentment of Varina's life. I could easily take the sense of her own words and make it comprehensible, simplify quotation out of existence; but, aside from all exactness, there is an acute beauty in her formal phrases, a living breath of sweetness, that it would be a fault to lose. "Then," she admitted, "I began to know the bitterness of being a politician's wife, that it meant long absences, pecuniary depletion and ruinous absenteeism, illness from exposure, misconceptions, defamation of character, everything which darkens the sunlight and contracts the happy sphere of home."

She made, however, no effort to restrain Jefferson—his life, his success, were entirely hers. Varina was a very proud girl; she became a woman proud to the point of difficulty; when the serenity of her earliest married life was over she clothed her spirit in a determination as fine as the muslins that adorned her body. Mr. Davis went to Vicksburg to introduce John C. Calhoun to a political gathering, Varina accompanied him, and her first view of Mr. Calhoun completed her allegiance to the Democratic party. The speaker was late and the audience restless. Then she saw Jefferson, tall and thin, beside Mr. Calhoun. She had never heard her husband speak publicly before; they had written his speech together and she made a fair copy of it, and they both were profoundly moved. He had asked her not to look at him, so she listened tensely to his voice: Davis proceeded slowly, insecurely; it was evidently difficult for him to remember his words; and they never formally prepared another. Dates and some names were noted on a minute square of paper. After the meeting she talked for a long while to John C. Calhoun, and a deep mutual regard began that lasted throughout their lives. The statesman sent Varina tremendous communications on government in which it was evident he felt no necessity to mitigate the difficulty of the subject for her comprehension.

Jefferson Davis had been elected to Congress and, with Varina, he continued journeying north from Vicksburg: they proceeded toward Washington by the Mississippi and Ohio Rivers to Wheeling, from Wheeling they went in a stage coach sixty-six miles over the turnpike to Pittsburgh; they left Pittsburgh by steamboat for Brownsville; and, again by stage, accomplished the seventy-two miles that lay between them and Cumberland. They took up their journey at Cumberland on a steam railroad and finally reached Baltimore; the last forty miles required near three hours by rail. It was a very rough and various trip. On the Ohio the river was filled with ice, the boat was frozen into a solid expanse, and they were forced to wait for a thaw. This was Varina's first actual contact with democracy—the common herd—and, the change in her had been so absolute, she responded to it with a gay good humor. A pilot's wife, who had been indignant at Varina's superiority, ended by giving her a paper of apricot seeds. She planted them, at Brierfield, and an apricot tree grew that Varina called The Pilot's Wife.

In Washington she was very alert; her mind, her curiosity, was as active as her movements in society. Varina was a success at once: she carefully noted Mrs. Gaines, not then, she added, ankle deep in her great suit; the lovely Mrs. Ashleigh who afterward was Mrs. John J. Crittenden; Appollonia Jagello—a Polish heroine with a moustache and bass voice; Mrs. James Gordon Bennett; Mr. Calhoun and his family, newly moved into a house on Missouri Avenue. Mr. McDuffie, from South Carolina, Varina saw, closely resembled Mr. Calhoun but "bearing aloft a Cavalier's head, and who, like Launcelot, was not averse to dalliance for a while with pleasures of society." She doubtfully considered Judge Douglas, from the West, but Judge Woodbury of the Supreme Court impressed her immensely. He had brilliant eyes and gentle manners, and a beautiful daughter who became Mrs. Montgomery Blair. Mrs. Woodbury was well-preserved, a handsome and elegant woman, and a most amiable and charitable creature. A sentence and opinion of inexplicable feminine texture. Mr. Bedisco was the Russian Minister; he had married a school girl in Washington; and she, although scarcely more than a child, was equally admired by men and women.

MR. LINCOLN, Varina heard, was a member of that session of Congress. A Mr. Seddon was accompanied by his handsome bride. Colonel Dix, he became a general, was a senator from New York and one of the few members of government who possessed a house. Mr. Slidell passed through Washington on his way to Mexico; the Davises called, and the beauty of Mrs. Slidell—which was of the best Creole type—impressed them agreeably. The French empressement of her manner had an effect on Varina that was never effaced. Mr. Slidell, years older than his wife, owned features that were regularly handsome. Mr. Buchanan, then Secretary of State, came to see Varina Davis—he was tall and of fine presence and always wore a wide and immaculate white cravat, faultlessly tied. He was fair and delicate in color, his eyes, one had been seriously injured, were blue. A difficulty existed, however, in the nervous jerking of his head. His unwilling footsteps then were just upon the boundary of middle age, and a more charming man could hardly be imagined.

Varina's success swiftly increased; Washington society—except for a few individuals who resented the superiority of her bearing and the quickness of her wit—accepted her wholly. Her eyes, it was generally agreed, were her best feature, but her face had pride and beauty; it was charming with the freshness of youth. She talked for an evening with Robert Walker, the Secretary of the Treasury, Charles Ingersoll and George Dallas. No young men of this or any other day, Varina asserted, equalled them. Together they explored Byron and Wordsworth, Dante and Virgil. She knew Sam Houston and declared that he had a noble figure and handsome face. He had, in addition, a catamount skin waist-coat and ostentatiously left open his coat to show it. It was alternated with a waistcoat of scarlet. His manner was swelling and formal. When he was presented to a woman he took one step forward, bowed very low, and said, "Lady, I salute you." If she chanced to please him he took from his pocket a small snakeskin pouch and produced a wooden heart the size of a twenty-five cent piece. "Lady," he would continue, let me give you my heart." He spent days in the Senate whittling out these hearts and he had a jeweller put rings in them.

Congress was stirred by the agitation over Texas and Jefferson Davis—who had a solid knowledge of the West—took a brilliant part in the consequent discussions. The War with Mexico became a reality, Davis was notified by Colonel James Roach, who bore the message from Vicks-burg, that he had been elected to the command of the First Mississippi Regiment, and he immediately accepted that change of employment and responsibility. Jefferson and Varina Davis left Washington in June, they retraced their former passage, but the weather, the countryside, were now ideal. The rattle of the stage coach was lost in a heavy rumbling of artillery wagons. Jefferson was quick to inquire about it, and Varina had a sudden overwhelming premonition of loneliness. It was, he informed her, Duncan's Battery going down to Mexico. Jefferson was constantly preoccupied with a small book of military tactics, and, in a sudden irre-pressible unhappiness—she felt quite unnecessary to him—Varina rebelled. She recovered almost at once and became part of his enthusi-asm in the formations and maneuvering of soldiers. When he left Brier-field for the War, on an Arabian horse named Tartar, with a mounted body servant, Varina felt that it was like death.

She removed, while Jefferson was away, to The Hurricane, but on every day that it was possible she rode home, caring for her flowers and shrubs, watching every detail of the plantation. She began to worry about a fatality to her husband—she would never, then, have the children that were imperative to her. Varina grew thin with sharp shoulders, and eyes melancholy in large dark circles; her complexion lost its freshness; she was sallow, no longer beautiful. She imagined that she was the mother of a miraculously beautiful child, a boy. He would grow up to exactly resem-ble Jefferson. Varina wrote nothing of that to Mexico, fearful of distress-ing Mr. Davis, but her condition grew steadily worse and she was obliged to leave The Hurricane and return to Natchez and her parents. Jefferson Davis finally learned this, and, after the Battle of Monterey, where his services were distinguished, he obtained a sixty days' leave of absence—that, in the difficulties of travel, allowed him two weeks at home—and came back to Mississippi.

When he was forced to leave her again Varina was far steadier in spirit; she was fired by his stories of border warfare. His letters stayed for days warm in the bosom of her dress. Then he wrote that he had been wounded. She had a note from Thomas Crittenden praising Jefferson's valor at Buena Vista. Varina began to realize that he belonged to the nation as well as to herself. It might even be that the nation came first. She would, then, have to give him up. The world was a masculine world and her part, with all her spiritual and physical closeness to Jefferson Davis, was principally acquiescent. The last of her sheer youth, her untroubled gaiety, was gone.

When Mexico was defeated and Davis returned he was welcomed in New Orleans by Prentiss, his Whig opponent, with a speech of boundless eulogy; Jefferson Davis replied eloquently; the balconies of the city were crowded with women who threw down armfuls of yellow roses on the soldiers. Varina waited for him in Natchez, he arrived on a special boat, and a throng of people swept forward ahead of her. The crowd parted and he came forward, thin and pallid and on crutches. He was, actually, extremely ill; although, in the complete peace of Brierfield, his wound healed he was never well again. When he was once more comparatively active the governor of Mississippi, Brown, appointed Davis to fill the vacancy in the Senate created by the death of Jesse Speight. He continued to be weak; Varina was constantly troubled about him; she was far from well but she ignored that in her concern for Jefferson Davis.

He was, immediately, a conspicuous figure in the Senate; their position in Washington was now highly important. Varina brought her brother Beckett North and placed him in a school at Alexandria; her younger sister Maggie was constantly with her. National events were charged by a dangerous and explosive excitement, and Varina was intimately occupied by the public and social affairs that surrounded her. She began to assert her personality and opinions more decidedly; she dressed with an increased expensiveness. Men were drawn to her. She was, however, deeply religious; never tactful beyond the point of insincerity. Her supreme talent lay in the conduct of her marriage with Mr. Davis. They lived next to the United States Hotel; a bridge connected them with the dining room of that famous establishment. They had, appropriate to their time and position, a mess that always dined together. Governor McWillie and Mr. and Mrs. Burt of South Carolina belonged to it. The Toombses from Georgia were often present. Mr. Robert Toombs was very tall, he was very broad, he had very long black hair; and, when he was speaking, he contrived to toss it about in the manner of Danton. Varina was devoted to Alexander H. Stephens. A question rose of Jefferson's going to Cuba; General Lopez had come from Havana to beg his assistance; he conferred with Robert E. Lee, who asserted that such a venture would not be consistent with his obligations to the United States, and Lopez's representations came to nothing. That was the first meeting of Lee and Jefferson Davis and Varina. The controversies of the Thirty-first Congress increased in sectional bitterness, and when it adjourned Davis returned to the deep South for debate with the Whigs. He was, however, defeated in the next election, and he again occupied himself with the pastoral affairs of his plantation. Even in retirement the political and social fame of the Davises continued to grow; their prestige spread throughout the state. Varina, at last, was going to have a child.

SAMUEL EMORY DAVIS was born at Brierfield on the last day of June, Eighteen-fifty-three, the slaves brought him their customary gifts of hens and eggs and yams, and, in the interest of their baby, Varina tried to persuade Jefferson to stay quietly on his plantation. Instead he went to the inaugural ceremonies of Franklin Pierce at Washington and accepted an invitation from the new President to become a member of his cabinet. Jefferson Davis was made Secretary of War. His family left Davis Bend again in a great stir; Pemberton had died and the plantation was put under a white overseer. They took a furnished house on Thirteenth Street, and Varina brought Beckett and Maggie again North with her. Her life in Washington was even more impressive than before; her child grew finely; she spent many placid evenings in the company of Mrs. Franklin Pierce. Varina read French and Latin, she practiced new fugues, and dominated the formal and official activities of society.

The brilliant human pattern in the kaleidoscope of Washington had changed since Jefferson Davis was in the Senate. Captain McClellan, commissioned to study warfare in the Crimea, looked even younger than he was; he blushed deeply when unexpectedly addressed and appeared to be a modest and gentle and sensible young man. Mrs. Pierce—a brokenhearted woman—was continually sick and encountered strangers with difficulty. Franklin Pierce, in Varina's opinion, combined a flawless courtesy with a gravely sincere and plain habit of speech. Professor John Le Comte impressed her favorably. He had an exquisitely beautiful wife. Varina conversed with Professor Agassiz and Doctor Pearce. She saw a

little of General Scott—a grandiose man. "General Totten was an exceedingly elegant man in his deportment, and most kind-hearted and obser-
vant of all the courtesies of life, being a soldier in the scientific sense of
the word." Mr. Charles Sumner was handsome and displeasing; his bril-
liancy, Varina Davis felt, was studied; his deference obeyed nothing better
than a social policy.

The Davis house proved uncomfortable and they moved to another a
few blocks away. Samuel, their son, died after a brief painful illness. For
weeks Davis lost himself in work through the day and walked in bitterness
of grief at night. The cries of children in the street were unsupportable to
him. Varina was quiet. Soon her second child, Margaret, was born.
Buchanan was elected President and the sectional difficulties were revived
in Congress. Jefferson Davis was again elected to the Senate; he resigned
from the cabinet in the March of Eighteen-fifty-seven and took his seat
together with Douglas and Crittenden and Robert Toombs. The national
tension fast increased; in the winter of Eighteen-fifty-eight party differences were so acute that they were reflected in social relationships. Varina
managed to keep a cordial air in drawing-rooms of many different political colors, but it grew daily more difficult. Generally, the ordinary courtesies were wholly cast aside, public and private gatherings were rent with
controversy. Jefferson was ill and Varina was again worried about him.

She developed, for the necessities of her situation, an apparently light
attitude and humorous comment; she declined, it seemed, to take the
declarations of either party entirely seriously. Davis contracted laryngitis,
in addition, for the time, he was practically blind—he lay for two months
in a darkened room, unable to speak, writing almost illegible communications on a slate. He needed, his doctors insisted, a long rest and
change, and with Varina he went North for the summer; they proceeded
by steamer from Baltimore to Boston, and from there to Portland in a
packet boat. Varina had had a third child, Jefferson, and she was splen-
didly well. The faint blue circles around her eyes gave her beauty a deepened romantic interest. The Fourth of July fell when they were on
shipboard, and Davis made a speech supporting the Constitutional
Union; they found Portland charming; and, returning to Washington at
the end of summer, Varina remained there while Jefferson Davis went on
to his plantation. Varina, apparently occupied with the social calendars of
her younger sister and brothers, actually was wholly delivered to the gravity of her husband's political position.

The situation in Washington became steadily worse, the deep South
was torn in bitter disagreement, and Davis was caught in the local

struggle. His letters to Varina were the reverse of optimistic, and when she again saw the sombre pallor of his face she knew they were confronted by an imminent and perilous dilemma. She continued, however, to attend dinners and balls; Mr. Seward, who was opposing every Democratic movement, kept up a habit of calling upon her. Varina went with Mr. Davis to the Democratic Convention at Charleston; it was Eighteen-sixty, and no one there followed its strategy with a more detailed interest or greater understanding: she watched with a cold enmity—Varina was now passionately partisan—the persistence of the Douglas faction; she was concerned at the diffuse organization, the poets and scholars, the lawyers and country gentlemen, behind Rhett and the South Carolina extremists; she was openly scornful of the failure of the Northern delegates to understand the spirit of the South.

Varina was, as usual, engaged by the stir and excitement of the crowds and events. A Mississippi delegate assured her that she was all that made the funereal Convention endurable. It entertained her when a Southern Free-soiler told her that the Convention was pied, very much pied, and not very much of anything else. When it became evident that the Douglas squatter sovereignty was lost her delight was unconcealed. John C. Breckenridge, upon his nomination, realized her ideal of a high chivalry. He said to her, "I trust I have the courage to lead a forlorn hope." He led the forlorn hope to preliminary defeat in his person, and Varina was inconsolable; she sent Breckenridge letters of bitter regret stained with her tears. Something more of her serenity departed; for the first time in her memory she found herself disliking, even actively hating, people. Her pleasure in Mr. Seward evaporated. The President, Buchanan, was pointedly indifferent to Jefferson Davis, and this served to stiffen Varina's pride of bearing; she dressed with an increasing carefulness; her manner was absolute in correctness. Beneath a mere appearance, however, her nerves were strained. She expressed her love for Davis with small emotional restraint; Varina was never, if it could be avoided, away from him. Their marriage reached a new perfection.

The Congressional representatives of Mississippi and Alabama and Florida gathered in grave consultation, and Varina was in a state of unbearable suspense. There was an enormous crowd in the Senate Chamber for the last day of that session and Varina sent a servant to hold two places; Jefferson's condition was again precarious and it was doubtful if he'd be able to speak. He did speak and, although there were many tears at his eloquence, Varina left with a sense of accumulating heavy trouble. The long suspense was over, the South was free, but she was an utterly hopeless and miserable woman. "We left Washington," she wrote, "exceedingly sorrowful and took our little children with us."

Their journey to Mississippi was turbulent; the people everywhere demanded to see Jefferson Davis, to hear him speak; and Varina was fanatical in her efforts to prevent him from overexertion. In the Alabama hills there was a scent of violets. The city of Jackson received them with a universal enthusiasm, and they proceeded immediately to Brierfield. A sense of tragedy, of loneliness, settled over Varina. The negroes crowded about the door asking for little Samuel, forgetful that he was dead. The plantation was invested with all air of neglect; the Cherokee roses had spread in a wild and unattended tangle. Jefferson Davis and Varina were in the garden, pruning a rose bush, a Glory of France, when a messenger arrived on horse from Montgomery—Mr. Davis had been elected President of the Confederate States of America.

VARINA KNEW that Jefferson Davis belonged in the military and not the civil branch of government, but she was overwhelmed by the honor that had come to him: standing later on the gallery of the plantation house she cried, "Holy, Holy, Holy, Lord God of Hosts!" Jefferson left, it was arranged for her to meet him in Montgomery, and she was swept into another hurried activity of departure. She unpacked and packed again ball dresses; the sewing-room was filled with seamstresses. Varina's love for the South grew more intense; her heart, she thought, would break with it. On her way to Montgomery she stopped at New Orleans, to see her parents. Captain Dreux, at the head of his battalion, serenaded her, but she couldn't command her voice to speak to him when he came up on her balcony. He brought her immense bouquets from his men. Her journey up the Alabama River depressed her; the Exchange Hotel, the President's temporary residence in Montgomery, was no more encouraging—their rooms were crowded with men seeking preferment, with statesmen and lawyers, congressmen and planters and merchants. There was a confusion of contrary pressures and interests and individuals—the Honorable William C. Rives of Virginia, Pierce Butler, Butler King, William Lowndes Yancey, James M. Mason, John Preston, Steven Mallory and James Chestnut.

They moved to a house at the comer of Bibb and Lee Streets; it was filled; together with politicians, with hampers of roses. Davis went to his office at nine in the morning and returned at six completely exhausted. He slept but little. He ate practically nothing. His first Presidential message closed with the solemn protestation that the South desired peace at any sacrifice save that of honor. When the government was removed to Richmond, Davis, sick from labor and anxiety, was carried on a bed. Varina was forced to see him go without her; when, a week later, she followed, the country was filled with soldiers in butternut trousers and grey homespun coats with epaulets of yellow cotton fringe. Richmond was an armed camp; the Spottswood Hotel—they were again in temporary quarters—was no more relieving than the Exchange in Montgomery. After the battle of the First Manassas, Varina was distraught by the growing antagonism to the President. The question of cotton, the paramount question of finance, came up and found no solutions. Davis' physical condition had improved little if at all; he was unable to eat under any excitement; and Varina gave up all entertainment except formal receptions and the most informal breakfasts. In the evening Mr. Davis could bear to see no one. The Provisional government came to an end and in February, Eighteen-sixty-two, Davis was elected President of the Confederacy. It was a morose day with a pall of cloud, pouring rains; Mr. Davis stood under an insufficient awning in the public square but the gathered and cheering people were unprotected from the weather. The President, dedicating himself to the service of the South, was so pale and emaciated that he seemed to Varina a willing victim going to his funeral pyre; she was so affected by emotion that she was obliged to offer some excuse and leave the ceremony.

The mainly passive activities of women in a state of war began—they made clothing for the soldiers and sewed together the silks of battle flags, they fed families in poverty and supported orphans, they played guitars, sang, for the wounded in tobacco warehouses turned into hospitals. The cause of the South became worse; it rapidly grew desperate. Women, like Varina, bred in an aristocratic and luxurious pride covered their worn out shoes with pieces of satin from old boxes; old faded scraps of silk were cut in strips and picked to pieces, they were carded and spun into thread, and stockings knitted from them. The only dyes were barks and copperas. Guinea wings decorated palmetto hats; goose feathers were transformed into camellias for trimmings; antique velvet jackets made their unabashed appearance; black silks, more often than not, were the remainders of old umbrella coverings. The buttons from soldiers' uniforms decorated dresses everywhere. Raspberry leaves were used for tea; persimmons and black pepper, with hickory nuts and walnuts, were put in fruit cake. The coffee was ground-nuts and parched okra, often sweet potatoes. For figs there were persimmons in brown sugar. The sad little pretenses and courageous delicacies of privation.

The brief hopes raised by the Confederate successes in Eighteen-sixty-two collapsed in Eighteen-sixty-three. The victory at Fredericksburg was the only light that, for a little, stayed the advancing shadows of ruin. Shiloh was lost, Vicksburg and New Orleans fell, Gettysburg turned General Lee back from the richness, the promise, of Northern conquest. Disaster became universal; and when, in the spring of Eighteen-sixty-five, it was clear that Richmond would be invested, Jefferson Davis begged Varina to go into the deeper South. She protested bitterly against leaving him, but she obeyed his desire. Varina sold everything she could not take; Davis, who still had a little gold, reserved a five-dollar piece for himself and gave her the rest. Mr. Burton N. Harrison, President Davis' secretary, accompanied her to Charlotte, North Carolina. Rumors of fresh defeats reached Varina there: when the treasure train of the Confederacy and of the Richmond banks, escorted by Captain Parker and her brother, Jefferson Davis Howell, arrived at Charlotte, she decided to continue on with it.

At Chester, where the tracks were destroyed and further progress impossible, Varina was met by General Preston, General Hood and General Chestnut. Preston said, "We of this day have no future. Anything that a man can do I will do for you or the President." An ambulance was secured for Varina, it was overloaded, her maid was too weak for any effort, and Varina, with a cheerful baby in her arms, walked through the darkness and mud five miles into Abbeville. She reached the little church that was her destination for the night, past one o'clock; others were before her, but they were sleeping on the floor; the communion table had been kept for Varina. From there she proceeded to Washington in Georgia.

Jefferson overtook her beyond Washington; he travelled with his family for three days; then left it for the care of state papers. Near Macon he was surrounded by Union troops, secured, and taken to the Macon hotel where General Wilson had his headquarters. Davis, who thought his family would be permitted to accompany him, asked to be sent North by the greater safety of water. This was agreed to, but he was denied Varina's support. A tug boat came up to the ship in which they were confined and bore off Varina's brother; a second tug went away with Mr. Stephens, General Wheeler and Davis' private secretary; the following day a third appeared with a detachment of German soldiers. Jefferson Davis conferred with their officer and returned to Varina. "It is true," he told her, "I must go at once." He begged her not to gratify their enemies with any signs of grief, and she said goodby to him quietly. They parted in silence. Varina watched him as he was carried away from her, standing erect and bare-headed between files of foreign soldiers, and Jefferson seemed to her a man of another and higher race.

A provost guard, with female detectives, came on the ship and searched her baggage; Varina asked permission to debark at Charleston where her sister was ill; this was refused and they left for Savannah in a half gale. Soldiers broke open and robbed her trunks. Mr. Davis, again in a precarious condition, was confined to Fortress Monroe, and Varina, with great difficulty, got a permit to see him. He was so sick it didn't seem possible to her he would live through the month. She then labored ceaselessly for the release that was later granted him. Their money was gone, the plantations at Davis Bend wasted or seized; but Varina, at last, had Jefferson Davis for her own; for the remainder of his life he was wholly in her tender and immaculate hands. She wrote, "I watch over him ceaselessly . . . twenty years difference asserts itself . . . I am in terror whenever he leaves me."

20 Queen of the Confederacy

Cynthia Myers

$\mathcal{I}$T WAS an unusual scene, hundreds of Confederate soldiers dressed up, in formation, and standing at attention for review—by a woman. The troops in Adams Run, South Carolina, seemed less impressed by the rarity of the occasion than by the sight of the young belle who walked about their ranks in the spring of 1861. Blessed with large blue eyes, and red-gold hair that she wore tucked under an ostrich-plumed hat, she held the troops' undivided attention. They watched intently as she presented their commander with a blue silk banner of her own design that depicted a white palmetto tree—the symbol of South Carolina—and the words "Lucy Holcombe Legion."

Lucy Holcombe Pickens could boast of many distinctions besides having a Confederate army unit named after her. As the wife of Governor Francis Wilkinson Pickens, she was the first lady of South Carolina. She was a friend of the czar and czarina of Russia. She was the only woman who would ever get to see her picture on Confederate currency. She was so renowned throughout the South as a woman of charm, elegance, and strong character that she was known as the "Queen of the Confederacy." All of this, and she was not yet 30 years old.

Born Lucy Petway Holcombe in Fayette County, Tennessee, on June 11, 1832, Pickens was a Texan at heart, having moved to the Republic of Texas at a very young age with her parents, Mr. and Mrs. Beverly Lafayette Holcombe. The family settled near Marshall, a town in eastern

Texas, and her father established a plantation that would one day serve as headquarters of the Confederate Post Office Department's Trans-Mississippi agency. He named the home "Wyalucing," supposedly an American Indian term for "home of the friendless."

The name of their estate notwithstanding, Lucy and her folks never lacked friends at Wyalucing. They frequently hosted plantation owners from nearby Shreveport and Marshall and made social trips by steamboat to New Orleans. One family story credits Lucy with inventing iced tea for the refreshment of guests, using ice imported by steamboat from Jefferson, Texas, to cool glasses of mint and sugar-laced tea in imitation of the Southern gentleman's mint julep. Lucy attended a finishing school in Bethlehem, Pennsylvania, at age 13, and after two years returned to her parents' home and a routine of social events in Marshall, New Orleans, and Virginia.

Lucy was quite popular at these gatherings, drawing a host of eligible men into gentlemanly competition. One suitor from Charleston drank wine from her slipper, toasting her as "the belle of the South." While staying in the home of Mississippi Governor John A. Quitman, Lucy attended a session of the Mississippi legislature and succeeded in distracting the men from their political duties. When the time came for her to return to Texas, several of the lawmakers accompanied her as far as New Orleans.

Though Lucy had a generous assortment of young bachelors from which to choose a husband, none of these hopefuls won her hand. There were rumors that at age 19 she had fallen in love with a young man, but that he had been killed during a stint as a revolutionary in Cuba. The closest Lucy would ever come to confirming this alleged relationship was in a novel she wrote in her later years, remnants of which are preserved at the University of South Carolina. Titled *The Free Flag of Cuba,* this precursor to the modern romance novel told the tale of a heroic young soldier fighting in Cuba, and of his beautiful sweetheart back home.

In the end, the coveted prize of Lucy's betrothal went to twice-widowed Francis Wilkinson Pickens, a former South Carolina state legislator and U.S. Representative who, at age 48, was 22 years her senior. He was a friend of President James Buchanan, a slaveholding plantation owner, and an ardent supporter of states' rights. Lucy met Pickens while she was visiting relatives in Virginia. Upon her return to Texas, she found herself courted by mail and through a series of cross-country visits. The couple married on April 24, 1858, at Wyalucing and moved to South Carolina.

Shortly after the wedding, President Buchanan appointed Francis Pickens as U.S. ambassador to Russia. Apparently, Pickens was reluctant to accept the post but eventually succumbed to his wife's coaxing. Lucy arrived in St. Petersburg that summer and began to make her imprint on Russian society. She served her favorite Southern dishes at state dinners, introducing a curious Russian nobility to sweet potatoes and mayhaw jelly.

Lucy became a favorite of Czar Alexander II and Czarina Catherine II. The royal couple welcomed her into the palace, where Lucy's only child, a daughter, was born. The Russian rulers nicknamed the infant "Douschka," or "little darling," and served as her godparents. To celebrate the birth, they presented Lucy with a collection of diamonds and emeralds.

The Pickenses returned to South Carolina in 1860, and Francis entered the race for governor. He won the election and assumed office on December 16, 1860. Four days later a state convention voted unanimously to leave the Union. Three months before the Civil War would begin, Pickens would order the first overtly aggressive act of the secession period, commanding the Morris Island battery in Charleston Harbor to fire on the U.S.S. *Star of the West* as the ship attempted to deliver supplies and reinforcements to the U.S. Army garrison at Fort Sumter on January 9, 1861.

Soon, powerful South Carolinians became dissatisfied with Pickens's seeming unwillingness to take dramatic and decisive action against U.S. forces still in the state. Late in 1861, the committee that oversaw the seceded state appointed a five-man council to exercise the executive powers formerly held by the governor. The council consisted of Pickens, Lieutenant Governor W. W. Harllee, Attorney General Isaac Hayne, former governor William H. Gist, and former U.S. Senator James Chesnut, husband of famous diarist Mary Boykin Chesnut.

Despite Pickens's wavering popularity, Lucy continued to reign as "Queen of the Confederacy" from the governor's mansion in Columbia and from the Pickens plantation, "Edgewood," in nearby Edgefield County. As the war trudged on and common commodities became scarce, visitors looked forward to receptions at the mansion, where they could drink fine champagne and sip Russian tea, served in a silver samovar. William Wyndham Malet, a vicar from Hertfordshire, England, met Lucy while he was visiting his sister in South Carolina in the summer of 1862. "In the evening, at a veritable tea, I was introduced to Mrs. Pickens," he wrote, "one of the fairest of the fair daughters of Louisiana [*sic*]."

Lucy was not content, however, to limit her domain to the boundaries of domesticity. She is credited with playing a behind-the-scenes role in the Confederate government as an advisor and confidante to her husband. "The men say she is as clever as she is handsome," wrote Mary

Chesnut, who, along with her husband James, frequently socialized with the Pickenses. "Governor Pickens is angry because of the council appointed him, and it is evident there will be no concord among them. Someone said today he would outwit them all yet, with the aid of the lovely Lucy, who is a host in herself."

Chesnut, for one, does not appear to have been among Lucy Pickens's admirers. She calls her "Lucy Long-tongue" and remarks on her exaggerated low voice and slow manner of speaking. Her diary entries paint Lucy as a meddlesome, self-centered flirt. "Miss Lucy Holcombe, who was not accustomed to play second fiddle or to be overlooked, was on her high horse," she wrote on one occasion.

Owing either to vanity or to patriotism, Lucy made a generous contribution to the war effort in 1861. She sold her Russian jewels and used the money to finance the Holcombe Legion. Consisting of seven companies of infantry and one of cavalry, the soldiers of the legion were recruited from Newberry, Barnwell, Spartanburg, Anderson, Abbeville, and Atwell Counties. Colonel P. F. Stevens, superintendent of the Citadel military academy in Charleston, served as the legion's first commander. After the Second Battle of Manassas, Virginia, in August 1862, Colonel William L. Crowley succeeded Stevens. Crowley was shot a year later at Stony Creek, Virginia, and Major Andrew Woodruff assumed command through the end of the war.

Confederate Treasury Secretary Christopher Memminger, a South Carolinian and an admirer of Lucy Pickens, proposed that she be honored with her portrait on Confederate currency. One-hundred-dollar bills minted in 1862, 1863, and 1864 feature a profile of her with abundant hair and wearing a crown of laurel leaves. One-dollar bills from 1862 show her large eyes and, again, a laurel crown.

Francis Pickens died on January 29, 1869, and was buried at Edgewood Plantation. He left an estate deep in debt. Lucy continued to manage Edgewood and two properties in Mississippi. She looked after her daughter, wrote *The Free Flag of Cuba,* and worked to have George Washington's home at Mount Vernon declared a historical monument. She was a member of the Mount Vernon Association and the United Daughters of the Confederacy. Naturally, she continued to entertain, keeping Edgewood at the center of social activities in the Columbia area. Though only 36 when her husband died, Lucy never remarried. She died in July, 1899, and was buried at Edgewood.

As seems appropriate for the "Queen of the Confederacy," Lucy was memorialized in marble. A bust of her, originally displayed in the South

Carolina room at Mount Vernon, now sits in the South Carolinian Library at the University of South Carolina in Columbia. The statue's classic proportions and smooth lines recall her acclaimed physical beauty, and the marble suggests her strength of character and will. In retrospect, it is a monument not just to Lucy Holcombe Pickens, but to the ideal she exemplified: the Southern belle.

21 The Battling Belles

John Hunt and Bill McIlwain

*C*HILL AUTUMN winds rippled through the mountains of southwest Virginia, and in a clapboard farmhouse, two girls in their late teens engaged in earnest debate.

The year was 1862.

"But do you think we can get away with it?" the younger girl asked doubtfully. "All those men and . . ."

"Unk's gone over to the Yankees, damn him," the other declared, "and we should try to make up for him."

Thus began the fabulous, but little-known, Civil War saga of the fighting Bell girls, Mollie and Mary.

Cousins, they had grown up together on the mountainside farm. But, when the opportunist uncle who had reared them skipped to greener Yankee pastures, Mollie Bell was infuriated. Hot-blooded and Rebel to the bone, she persuaded Mary to join her in a fantastic scheme to enter the Confederate Army.

Definitely not lacking the pleasing but obvious characteristics of their sex, the girls planned carefully to effect a disguise. Thick woolen workshirts hid the curves of young womanhood, and they cropped their hair to conform to the male styles of the day. And when brought from way down *here,* their voices were not a whit higher than those of many fuzzy-faced lads who left their Dixie homes to fight for the Great Cause.

At last they were ready to face the recruiters. Mollie, a fierce, dark-haired little warrior—always the leader of the two—signed up as Bob Morgan; and Mary, younger and more reserved, as Tom Parker. Farm backgrounds stood them in good stead. Their riding ability quickly won them the saddles and sabres of cavalrymen.

Their baptism of fire came quickly. Less than a month later, a Federal force overran the troop and took every living member prisoner.

Brief indeed had been the fighting careers of Mollie and Mary Bell, it seemed at the moment. But they weren't meant to sit out the war in a Union prison. For within a few hours, Confederate General John Hunt Morgan thundered in to liberate them.

Perhaps because of this hairbreadth brush with failure, the Bells soon shifted to the infantry. Fighting now under General Jubal A. Early, they faced—and fired—minnie balls in some of the classic battles of the war. They were in the bitter, bloody fighting around Chancellorsville, where Stonewall Jackson was mortally wounded. They took part in the push into Pennsylvania and the smashing Southern defeat at Gettysburg; and they were at Spotsylvania Court House, where Early's men (and two women) licked General Burnside.

THEY PROVED their soldier careers were not girlish whims. Mollie was on picket duty one night when explosions rent the darkness and the cry arose, "They're charging!" Coolly she stood her ground and was credited with killing three men, a remarkable record in the day of the muzzle-loader. Singled out for heroism, she was promoted to the rank of sergeant, while Mary became a corporal. Their mates rated the girls "gallant, first-class fighting men."

Their sex posed nearly as great a problem as the enemy, however. Of necessity, they revealed the secret to one person, a young captain who could provide protection against physical checkups and other Army routine that would have exploded their soldier-boy lives.

But then in action one day, Mollie was struck in the arm by a shell fragment. Other soldiers gathered around. At last Mary reached the scene.

"We'll have to find a doctor," Mary said, bending over her cousin. They exchanged glances. Both were aware what medical examination and treatment would mean.

"No sawbones for me," Mollie retorted, rising to her feet. "Why, it's just a scratch." She won her point—and emerged, in the eyes of the others, as an even tougher, hell-for-leather soldier.

Now Early's forces were moving into the spectacular Shenandoah Valley campaign—a high point of the war for both sides, and for the Bells. Union General David Hunter was driving on Lynchburg when Early attacked and swept him out of Virginia. Flushed with success, the Confederate commander and his 8,000 soldiers pushed north and crossed the Potomac River to threaten Washington from the west.

Two corps were rushed in to reinforce the Capital, and Early dropped back into Virginia soon afterward. But alarm in the North brought pressure on General Grant to deal with Early in a hurry. For that task, he picked stocky, gruff General Sheridan, ex-Indian fighter who had already distinguished himself with a daring charge up Missionary Ridge in Tennessee.

Twice, at Winchester and at Fisher's Hill, Sheridan's speed and superior numbers struck staggering blows at Early. Still game, the Southern forces, with the Bells in their midst, wheeled and lashed back at Cedar Creek.

This battle, on Oct. 19, 1864, came almost two years after Mollie and Mary had entered the war.

Perhaps, in the strange fates of battle, it went sour because another woman faced them on the battlefield that day. One of the greatest camp-followers, Bridget Divers—known widely as Irish Biddy—rode with the First Michigan Cavalry, just as she had since early in the war.

Raging fiercely, the battle seemed at first a terrific Southern victory. At one point, Irish Biddy, nurse-messenger-handyman, herself was almost captured. But then Sheridan, the master-cavalryman, turned the tide and the Bells' captain-protector was taken prisoner. Hastily the girls conferred.

"Do you think we can *trust* him?" Mary asked, glancing at the lieutenant who had assumed command of the company.

"We'll have to have his help," Mollie replied. "We've got to take the chance."

It was a bad decision.

Itching for an official pat on the head, the lieutenant rushed the startling news straight to General Early.

THE WORD that women were in the Army swept consternation through the battle-toughened Confederate command. Questions arose. Could they be allowed to continue fighting? Had they committed an offense? Nothing in the rules of war quite seemed to cover the situation.

The Bells pleaded with Early for the chance to stay and fight, but he turned them down. While the top brass fussed and fumed, the girls were sent off to Richmond and Castle Thunder, the notorious Confederate military prison.

Mollie fired a parting barrage, however. In his Army, she vowed to Early, were six other women masquerading as men. She refused to name them, however, and Early was left to wonder and worry.

Was it true, or simply a disquieting try for vengeance by the Bells? This question was never answered.

The women warriors should have found consolation in the declaration of writer-statesman Edmund Ruffin, himself an old war dog. The girls had proved themselves fine soldiers, he said, and should be allowed to stay in service. But a controversy stormed. The other camp cried that even the best women warriors posed a threat to the morality of the men.

Shortly afterward, the Bells were released from Castle Thunder and told that their war was over.

Side by side, Sergeant Mollie Bell and Corporal Mary Bell, veteran infantrymen, rode silently back to their native mountains.

22 Sally Tompkins, Captain, Confederate Army

Robert S. Holzman

*J*EFFERSON DAVIS dedicated his autobiography "To The Women Of the Confederacy . . ." Many of them aided the military in invaluable ways, and some proudly bore honorary titles; only one woman was granted a regular army commission by the Secretary of War.

The opening of the Civil War in 1861 found Miss Sally Louise Tompkins living at the Arlington House in Richmond with her mother and sister. Sally was then 28 years of age. She was quite small, not over five feet in height, but there was dignity and force in her presence. She was not a beauty, but it was said of her that she had "a splendid face." A portrait of the period shows her long, determined mouth, narrow eyes, her hair parted straight down the center and tightly drawn back to expose her ears.

Sally was born on November 9, 1833, at Poplar Grove, Mathews County, Virginia. When her father died, the family left their rambling frame house with its tall portico and moved to Richmond. It would have been easy for her, by reason of the family wealth, to take a steamer from the Cape Fear River, and go to Europe to stay "for the duration" but she felt it her duty to remain in Virginia.

At the start of the war, Richmond had a population of about 37,000 persons, but there were few hospitals. The South had no effective national hospital or relief organization such as that in the North. Caring for the first of the war wounded was thrust upon untrained civilians. Warehouses

were overcrowded with disabled soldiers. Temporary structures were
hastily nailed together. But that was not enough. "Every house was
opened for the wounded," recorded one Southern woman. "They lay on
verandas, in halls, in drawing rooms of stately mansions. . . ."

After the first Battle of Manassas, the great vans of the Southern
Express Company brought in cargoes of suffering, gray-clad men. Judge
John Robertson sent Sally a message that, as his family had moved to the
country for an indefinite stay, she could make use of his spacious town
house. She equipped this building (at the northwest corner of Third and
Main Streets) at her own expense. On July 31, 1861, ten days after First
Manassas, she opened the doors of what she called the Robertson Hospital for the care of wounded and sick men from the battlefields. The government assigned six surgeons to the hospital.

Sally took her mother's old cook to the hospital to handle the
kitchen. Another cook was loaned by Dr. Spotswood Welford. Bandages
and linen were supplied by townspeople of high and low station; and
women who could not stand the sounds, sights, and odors of a hospital,
rolled bandages at home. Food was purchased by Miss Tompkins or was
donated by patriotic Southerners. Medicines were from captured Northern stocks. Later, when medicines and drugs were declared by the North
to be contraband of war, the necessary articles were furnished by blockade runners.

AT FIRST there was no shortage of assistance. An observer told how one
young girl approached a sick man with a pan of water in one hand and a
towel over her arm. "Mayn't I wash your face?" she asked him. "Well,
lady," he replied, "you may if you want to. It's been washed fourteen
times this morning. It can stand another time, I reckon." Because of the
Tompkins' family name and social prominence, the Robertson Hospital
became the focus of Richmond's wealth, beauty and fashion each day. But
after the first flush of patriotic enthusiasm, the hospitals were regarded as
the place for only the most stout-hearted women. Sally directed the work
and provided what was needed. So careful was the attention furnished
here that word of it spread widely, and many wounded men from distant
places begged to be taken to her establishment.

In the midst of everything was Sally Tompkins. She had a medicine
chest strapped to her side, a Bible always in her hand. The patients
quickly learned that they could not argue with her. She used her own
ample means generously but unlike certain private hospitals, she did not
charge her patients. Outrageous charging was only one of the abuses that

led the Confederate government to order that private hospitals be discontinued. Because of lack of over-all control, and for reasons of economy, the government thought it advisable to consolidate Richmond's numerous hospitals into a few large ones, such as Chimborazo, Camp Jackson, Camp Winder, and Howard Grove.

The order directed that all soldiers in private hospitals be transferred to institutions under direct governmental control. Soldiers could be treated at no hospital except one that was under a commissioned officer with a rank not lower than that of captain, which was the rank of an assistant surgeon.

While ambulances for the transfer of her patients waited at the door, Miss Tompkins went to see the president of the Confederacy to ask that her hospital be exempted from the order. She brought along her hospital register. Dr. William Berrien Burroughs later wrote in *Southern Practice:* "The number of men returned to the army was very large; in fact, her hospital record of deaths was lower than—and her record of soldiers returned to their commands was greater than—that of any other hospital in Richmond."

Sally was determined that "her boys" should not be taken from their beds. But, as the order had been the result of an act of the Confederate Congress to absorb the private institutions into the military organization, President Davis felt he could not ignore the law. His methodical mind worked out a solution: he would have her commissioned as an officer in the Confederate army; then she could continue to direct her hospital as an integral part of the military organization. On September 9, 1861, L. P. Walker, the Secretary of War, signed her commission as Captain of Cavalry, unassigned. As a captain, she could issue orders and draw army rations. She accepted the commission, but would not let her name be placed upon the payroll.

"I had the rank and title, everything except the pay," she explained.

WOMEN BANDAGED wounds, fanned flies, brought water, washed the disabled, hunted for ice and supplies. Some volunteer workers discharged their own obligations by bringing in their servants for the less glamorous tasks, but the work got done. Women of means visited the hospitals daily with gifts. Some women cultivated poppies for opium and laudanum. A generation after the war, a minister wrote that "more than to the surgeons, the credit of any comfort or sunshine in the hospital was due to our noble women. . . ."

Many southerners resented the presence of females in the hospitals. One worker declared that "There is scarcely a day passes that I do not hear some derogatory remarks about the ladies who are in the hospitals, until I think, if there is any credit due them at all, it is for the moral courage they have in braving public opinion."

But such carping made no impression upon Captain Tompkins. The only personal reaction that she noticed was the frequently-repeated offer of marriage. She would smile and say, "Poor fellows, they are not yet well of their fevers."

Her hospital functioned until June 13, 1865. During this period there were 1,333 admissions. Only 73 men died in the institution, a very low record for those days.

After the war, Captain Tompkins did not forget her interest in the soldiers of the Confederacy. She was a prominent figure at military reunions for many years. The family fortune was lost in the war, but at the 1896 reunion in Richmond, she rented a large house to provide shelter for the veterans.

As her meager funds failed, she went to live in the Home for Confederate Women in Richmond. She was not forgotten, and her eulogies did not wait for her death. The Sally Tompkins chapter of the United Daughters of the Confederacy was formed in her honor.

The only woman officer of the Confederate army died in Richmond on July 25, 1916, at the age of 83. She was buried with full military honors.

23 The Bread Riot in Richmond, 1863

William J. Kimball

*A*MPLE RECORD exists that long before April, 1863, many of the inhabitants of Richmond were in dire need of the necessities of existence, to say nothing of the luxuries which had been commonplace to some before the war. Slightly more than three months after the fall of Fort Sumter the *Richmond Daily Whig* (July 19, 1861) stated that the "stock of provisions is so nearly exhausted that it is unnecessary to give quotations." This statement, of course, did not speak for all of the citizens; some like the Chesnuts had sent from their country home wine, rice, potatoes, ham, eggs, butter and pickles about once a month,[1] and the Tabb-Rutherford wedding supper served during the waning months of the Confederacy was "doubt it as you may . . . a sumptuous repast."[2] Nevertheless in a city whose prewar population of 38,000 had more than doubled before 1865, one which depended for its supplies of all kinds upon long and exposed lines of railway, the grim specter of starvation was an unwelcome resident in many overcrowded homes.[3]

There are adequate reasons for believing that near-starvation prompted many people in the crowd to march on the stores, but it seems to be equally obvious that once the riot was underway, general looting prevailed. To President Jefferson Davis' mind, it was not bread they wanted; the mob was bent on nothing but plunder and wholesale robbery.[4] The causes of the "disturbance" which "darkened the annals of Richmond" on that day can never be fully known.[5]

Early on April 2, within the gates of Capitol Square, a crowd of several hundred women and boys stood quietly together. One of their number— a pale, emaciated girl, not more than eighteen—who could no longer stand, took a seat on a nearby bench. As she raised her hand to remove her sunbonnet, her loose calico sleeve slipped up, and revealed a mere skeleton of an arm. Perceiving that the sight of her emaciated limb had startled a woman who was sitting on the bench and who was not a member of the crowd, she hastily pulled down the sleeve with a short laugh and exclaimed, "This is all that's left of me; it seems funny don't it?"

In answer to a question of whether there was to be some celebration, she answered that there was. They were going to celebrate their right to live. They were starving; and as soon as enough of them got together, they were going to the bakeries and each of them would take a loaf of bread. It was little enough for the government to give them after it had taken all their men, she added.

Just then a fat old Mammy waddled up the walk to overtake a beautiful child who was running before her. "Come dis a way, honey," she called, "don't go nigh dem people," adding in a lower tone, "I's feared you'll ketch somethin' fum dem po' white folks. I wonder dey lets 'em into de Park."

The girl turned and with a wan smile rose to join the long line that was formed and was moving. She said simply, "Good-by! I'm going to get something to eat!"

The mob now rapidly increased, and numbered more than a thousand women and children. They impressed all the light carts they met, and marched along silently and in order.[6] They were led by Mrs. Mary Jackson, a painter's wife, who was a tall, daring Amazonian-looking woman with a white feather standing erect from her hat.[7] They marched through Cary Street to Main, where they encountered the Mayor and the Governor, who, even with the state forces under their command, were not able to repress them.[8] Mr. Mumford, the President of the Young Men's Christian Association, quieted them in another street by inviting them to come to the rooms of the Association, where their wants would be supplied. Those who were really in want followed him.[9]

Mr. Davis, having been informed of the serious disturbance, proceeded to the scene of trouble. He mounted a dray from which the horses had been taken and it was particularly noticeable to him that, though the mob claimed that they were starving and wanted bread, they had not confined their operations to food supplies, but had passed by, without any effort to attack, several provisions stores and bakeries, while they had completely emptied one jewelry store and had looted some millinery and clothing shops in the vicinity.[10] From the vantage point of the dray, he made a brief address to the formidable crowd, urging them to abstain from their lawless acts. He reminded them of how they had taken jewelry and finery instead of supplying themselves with bread, for the lack of which they claimed they were suffering. He concluded by saying, "You say you are hungry and have no money. Here is all I have; it is not much, but take it." Emptying his pockets, he threw all the money they contained among the mob.[11] He then took out his watch and said, "We do not desire to injure anyone, but this lawlessness must stop. I will give you five minutes to disperse, otherwise you will be fired upon."[12]

The order was given to a Captain Gay who commanded a military company comprised of a number of armorers and artisans who were enrolled by General Josiah Gorgas, Chief of the Ordnance at the Confederate arsenal in Richmond.[13] Captain Gay, who knew the women—some of whom were the wives, sisters, and daughters of the men in his command—became nervous. Instead of ordering the muskets loaded with a ball and two buckshot, in strict observance of military usage, he told the women that he would order "two balls and a buckshot" into them.[14]

Nevertheless, the mob realized that the men might be forced to shoot and at once began to disperse; before the five minutes had expired the trouble was over, and the famous misnamed bread riot was at an end.[15] However, although the rioting and looting were brought to a halt, the repercussions did not disperse with the crowd.

Later that same day the Assistant Adjutant-General in the name of the Secretary of War sent an appeal to the editors and reporters of the Richmond press in which he requested them "to avoid all reference directly or indirectly to the affair. . . . The reasons for this are so obvious that it is unnecessary to state them."[16] The reasons were not obvious apparently to the *Daily Richmond Examiner,* and its editor, John Muncure Daniel, the voice of the archenemy of the Confederate government. On Saturday, April 4, readers of the *Examiner* could find in the report of evidence in the Police Court, a "true account of a so-called riot in the streets of Richmond." It made fascinating reading. According to the paper, "A handful of prostitutes, professional thieves, Irish and Yankee hags, gallow birds from all lands but our own, congregated in Richmond, with a woman huckster at their head, who buys veal at the toll gate for a hundred and sells the same for two hundred and fifty in the morning market, [and] undertook the other day to put into private practice the principles of the Commissary Department. Swearing that they

would have goods 'at government prices' they broke open half a dozen
shoe stores, hat stores, and tobacco houses, and robbed them of everything but bread, which was just the thing they wanted least." It went on
to say that those who followed Mr. Mumford to the YMCA were miscre-
ants who "were seen to dash the rice and flour into the muddy street,
where the traces still remain, with the remark that 'if *that* was what they
were going to give, they might go to h—l.' It is greatly to be regretted
that this most villainous affair was not punished on the spot. Instead of
shooting every wretch engaged at once, the authorities contented themselves with the ordinary arrest, and hence the appearance of the matter in
the police report of the morning."

It was impossible to doubt, according to the paper, that the concealed instigators in the riot were emissaries of the Federal government.
"Plunder, theft, burglary and robbery, were the motives of these gangs;
foreigners and Yankees the organizers of them." The writer (if not
Daniel, certainly an ardent emulator) felt that a "most contemptible
notion, that such disturbance is a shame, which must be hidden—(as well
try to hide the sun!)—led them to coax and wheedle the audacious mis-
creants engaged in it." The editorial ended with this final broadside: "If
the officers of the law, with the ample force and power in their hands,
have not enough decision and energy to do more than arrest highway
robbers and disperse a mob of idlers at their heels, whose presence there
deserved immediate death quite as well, no words or arguments can furnish them with the pluck they lack."[17]

The decision (much to the complete disgust of the *Examiner*) was to
arrest those who were apparently leaders or ardent violators rather than
shoot them on the spot. By April 13, all the parties arrested had either been
discharged or sent on for trial before the higher courts. A reporter for the
Examiner was aware of a glaring incongruity which had existed from the
beginning of the examination: "the large amount of means at the command of the parties charged with being engaged in a 'bread-riot.' All with
a solitary exception [Mrs. Jackson, the leader] have been able to give bail,
all with a solitary exception have had counsel employed at enormous fees."

Mary Jackson was confined to jail awaiting a trial for felony. She
"petitioned for a *habeas corpus* that she, being innocent of the charges
against her was illegally detained in jail." The judge, "not thinking the
suspicion of her guilt light, and not believing that her health would be
endangered by confinement," refused to set bail.

Many of the people arrested were found guilty and sentenced in varying degrees; one woman, a Mary Johnson (whose name was often con-

fused with Mary Jackson's) was sentenced to five years in the penitentiary. Although there are no periodic accounts in the police court proceedings of Mary Jackson's fate, her case probably came up from time to time, for in the *Examiner* of October 12 it was stated that she was the "prime instigator and ringleader of the riot, but she was too smart to commit any overt act which might fix a penalty on her. . . . She was very circumspect in her own actions. It being found that no charge of felony could be sustained in her case, she was sent to Judge Meredith's court to be tried for a misdemeanor . . . and it is more than probable that if she is not acquitted altogether, she will get off with some merely nominal punishment." And thus, the *Examiner* was done with Mary Jackson.

The Bread Riot led to much use of the vitriolic pen and to many continuing court cases, but it apparently did not result in increased foodstuffs for the needy. Notwithstanding the fact that the staples may have been thrown in the mud, as the *Examiner* claimed, the number of needy persons was great. Former residents and helpless refugees who, driven from comfortable homes, were compelled to seek relief in the crowded city, insufficiently furnished with the means of living for the resident population and altogether inadequate to the increased number thrown daily into the progress of events, were forced to dispose of all their articles of taste and former luxury, and frequently necessary articles of clothing to meet the essential demands of life.

In spite of many facts to the contrary it would be ennobling to believe that "these miseries and inconveniences were submitted to in no fault-finding spirit; and although the poverty of the masses increased from day to day, there is no doubt that the sympathies of the people were unfalteringly with the revolution [the war] in all its phases." In any event, a bread riot notwithstanding, it would not be difficult to agree that "of all the *nil admirai,* the people of Richmond must be accounted the foremost."[18]

24 Coping in Confederate Appalachia: Portrait of a Mountain Woman and Her Community at War

John C. Inscoe

*L*ATE IN the summer of 1863, an anonymous "Voice from Cherokee County" wrote a letter to the *North Carolina Standard* in Raleigh, bemoaning the oppressive impact of Confederate policy on the state's mountain region. He paid tribute to those highlanders he maintained were most victimized by the hardships—its women, that "class of beings entitled to the deepest sympathy of the Confederate government. . . . the wives, children, mothers, sisters, and widows" left behind by those troops fighting for the southern cause. This voice from the state's westernmost county went on to extol "the thousand instances of women's patriotism, in resigning without a murmur the being in whom her affections centered, to all the horrors of war, and after her husband's departure, uncomplainingly assume all the duties of the sterner sex; accompanied by her little brood, labor from morn to night in the corn-field, or wield the axe to fell the sturdy oak."[1] The glorification of Confederate womanhood was obviously well under way by the war's midpoint and was pervasive enough to have reached what was among the remotest parts of the Confederacy and of the Carolina highlands.

Among those "thousand instances" so glorified by the chivalric Cherokee County resident was Mary Bell in adjacent Macon County. She did indeed spend much of the war laboring in the cornfield, chopping wood, and caring for a growing "little brood." But she did not do so "uncomplainingly" or "without a murmur," and most assuredly, she did not do so from any patriotic sentiments toward the Confederacy or sense of duty to the southern cause.

This article is an examination of Mary Bell's Civil War experience. Her husband left home in November, 1861, and, except for intermittent visits and an extended stay in 1863, was gone until February, 1865. Throughout that period, Mary wrote lengthy letters at frequent intervals that provide the basis for reconstructing in considerable detail the impact of the war on her, her family, and her community.[2] Her account of those years thus serves as a case study of the plight of Appalachian women on the Confederate home front. At the same time it provides perhaps another variable to the growing collection of individual experiences through which historians are coming to new understandings of how the Civil War shaped the status and role of southern women and how those women, in turn, affected the war effort.

In *Womenfolks,* her 1983 paean to her southern distaff ancestry, Shirley Abbott maintained, with tongue somewhat in cheek, that "the fortitude of upper-class southern women during the Civil War is one of the sacrosanct themes in the mythology of the region: great-granny defying those blue-coated sons-of-bitches under the portico, just after she had personally buried the silver and put down a small mutiny among the field hands. . . . The backwoods women (lacking any such melodramatic props) had little to be heroic about."[3] That view may well have reflected not only popular perceptions but also the focus of scholarly scrutiny at the time. The latter at least has changed substantially in the intervening years, thanks to significant work dealing with the ways in which southern women at all socioeconomic levels and in various parts of the Confederacy coped with the crisis.[4] Even for Appalachian women, who would certainly qualify under Abbott's categorization of those whose efforts were so unappreciated, such neglect is being remedied as historians of the region are providing new insights on the dynamics of highland home fronts from a variety of angles.[5]

Thus Mary Bell's version of the war years does not so much fill a void as it corroborates, amplifies, and personalizes the conclusions drawn by other studies of wartime women at community, regional, or national levels, while at the same time offering some unexpected variations on a number of those conclusions. Bell's vivid descriptions and often outspoken assessments of both her own problems at home and those of her neighbors provide a unique perspective of a mountain community caught in a war from which in some respects it was snugly insulated, yet that in other respects intruded daily into the lives of its residents. Bell's letters also portray a woman who grew over the course of those years without her husband. Though not always conscious of the direction or degree of that change, she left in her letters a rich chronicle of the adjustments in her life and in her attitudes from 1861 to 1865 that allows historians to trace the course of her personal development in the midst of crisis.

Mary Bell was twenty-six years old when she moved with her husband to his North Carolina hometown only a year before the Civil War broke out. Little is known of the early life of either husband or wife. A native of Rome, Georgia, Mary married Alfred Bell in 1856 and moved with him three years later to the mountain community of Clayton in Georgia's northeasternmost corner, where Alfred's older brother was a physician. Alfred himself was a dentist and went into practice with his brother for about a year, when he decided to return to Franklin, North Carolina, just thirty miles north of Clayton, where his father, Benjamin W. Bell, among the community's founding fathers and the county's first sheriff, lived and operated a jewelry and clock-making business.[6] The Alfred Bell family, which then included two young daughters, bought a house in the village and a nearby farm. Alfred quickly established a thriving dental practice and took an active role in his father's enterprise as well. The farm he turned over to a tenant and hired slaves, whose activities he closely supervised.[7]

Franklin was a small community of fewer than 150 residents in 1860, when the Bells made it their home. The seat of Macon County, Franklin was also the county's only village, serving the commercial and governmental needs of its more than 6,000 inhabitants. Situated in the Little Tennessee River valley on the edge of the Great Smoky Mountains about seventy miles southwest of Asheville, Franklin was built on the site of what had once been a sacred Cherokee village and was settled by whites only after the area was wrenched from that tribe in the 1820s. In some respects it remained a frontier community throughout the antebellum period. The few travelers who reached that remote southwest corner of North Carolina all commented on the physical beauty and fertile setting but noted too the only partial appearance of civilization. British geologist George Featherstonaugh, in moving through the area in the early 1840s, wrote of Franklin: "What a dreadful state of things! Here was a village, more beautifully situated . . . that might become an earthly Paradise, if education, religion, and manners prevailed. . . . But I could not learn that there was a man of education in the place disposed to set an example of the value of sobriety to the community."[8] Some progress may have been made by the time Charles Lanman journeyed through the area five years later, for his comment, after encountering a few leading citizens, was that they, "like all the intelligent people of this county, [were] very polite and well informed." He went on to describe the village: as "romantically situated on the Little Tennessee surrounded with mountains and as quiet and pretty a hamlet as I have yet seen among the Alleghanies."[9]

In 1860, Macon County was extremely rural, even by Appalachian standards, with Franklin the only semblance of a concentrated community. Like most mountain holdings, Macon's 632 farms were relatively small; almost 60 percent consisted of less than fifty acres and only 12 percent consisted of more than 100 acres. The diversity of the farms' output was also typical. Corn was the basic commodity produced, but it was supplemented by a variety of grains, as well as apples and peaches (the majority of which were distilled into their more potent liquid form). Sixty-two slaveholders (6.5 percent of the household heads) and 519 slaves (8.6 percent of the population) lived in Macon County in 1860, both totals higher than those of adjacent counties. Only two men owned more than twenty slaves; one of them, Dillard Love, a member of one of western North Carolina's oldest and most influential families, owned seventy-one.[10]

During the secession crisis, feeling in the county was strongly divided as to whether or when North Carolina should withdraw from the Union. But unionism never gained the firm foothold there that it did in other parts of the Carolina highlands, and Macon County residents rallied to the Confederate cause as soon as the opportunity presented itself. Soon after the war broke out, Franklin became a recruiting center for Confederate troops, and Macon County, like the rest of the southwestern counties, quickly fulfilled its initial enlistment quota as called by Governor John Ellis.[11] Alfred Bell delayed in joining that surge. Only in the fall of 1861 did he raise a company of Macon County volunteers and, as their captain, lead them to Asheville, where as part of North Carolina's Thirty-ninth Regiment they spent three cold and frustrating months awaiting assignment to active duty. "We are very willing," he assured his wife at the end of January, 1862, "to leave this Buncombe War & goe to Jeff Davises War."[12]

Two days after he left home in November, 1861, the correspondence between Alfred and Mary Bell was under way, and her new roles as wife, manager, and local citizen began to take shape. Among the most striking of those roles as reflected by her early letters was her very active interest in Captain Bell's military affairs. She was never shy about expressing her views or dispensing advice as to how he should conduct himself in his relationships with his officers and fellow soldiers or in commenting on the military affairs of other local residents. In her first letter, Mary reported to Alf that two Macon County men who she felt should have gone into his company were thinking of organizing their own instead. She expressed contempt for such unrealistic ambitions and for those of another acquaintance who had stayed home "to attend to his business," waiting to enlist until he could do so as captain of his own company. "I am in hopes he will not get into your regiment," she wrote, "unless he would volunteer & risk his chances" regarding officership.[13]

Mary continued to provide regular reports of the comings and goings of her husband's volunteers and of other Macon County men who had or had not enlisted, along with her speculation as to their motives for doing so. On several occasions she told him of efforts to retrieve his men and others who either temporarily or permanently abused furlough privileges. Because his company remained so close to home for so long, keeping the men in camp and committed to the cause proved difficult. By the end of January, Bell was referring to some in his company as "traitors and deserters" and inquiring of his wife as to their whereabouts.[14]

One of those, Tom McDowell, fled south into Georgia to avoid arrest. Mary reported that McDowell's wife at least blamed Bell for his fugitive status and that "she would rather see him die than see him go into your company." Mary feared that Mrs. McDowell and others "were making up rumors against" Bell, presumably for his role in the attempt to reclaim his troops. Those rumors were the first hint of military tensions growing out of the discontent of fellow residents. Mary was quick to dismiss the worth of those elusive charges, advising Alf that he should tell Tom McDowell what she had heard another wife tell her defecting husband: that he "was a disgrace to the Southern Confederacy and Jeff Davis would blush to own him." "If I were you," Mary mused, "I would blush to have such a man as Tom in my company. If you were to ever get in a close place he would be certain to stump his toe and fall down. The yankees would get him and great would be the loss."[15]

Mary was just as resentful of wives who were not yet having to make the same sacrifice she was making. In March, 1862, she admitted that for herself and a neighbor, "our daily prayer is that a draft will come and take every married man that can leave home as well as our husbands could. It makes us very mad to see other women enjoying themselves with their husbands and ours gone."[16] A month later she repeated in even stronger terms her discontent at the inequality of local sacrifice as she saw it: "whilst some are made to mourn all the days of their lives on account of some dear one who has died whilst fighting for their country, others will be glorying in the wealth they have made by staying at home and speculating while the war was going on and other poor wretches were fighting for them."[17]

It was quite apparent, however, that Mary's resentment of those not serving the cause militarily or otherwise had little to do with her own commitment to the Confederacy. As early as March 5, 1862, she urged Alf not to reenlist when given the option. Only the week before he and his company had been sent to East Tennessee, already the site of considerable activity as what amounted to a Confederate occupation force sought to control a large and unruly Unionist populace. That move, along with the arrival of the first of many corpses to be returned to Franklin, may have inspired sudden concern in the young Mrs. Bell for her husband's safety. "I do not care what inducements is held out," she insisted, "you must not enlist." Nor did she hide her very personal reasons for such a request: "I hope for my sake you not think of doing it for I am a poor miserable wretch without you—the world is dark and dreary and everything is a blank without the presence and cheering smiles and devoted love of my dear husband."[18]

She laid blame for this bleak situation squarely at the feet of one man and more than once cursed him for the misery he had inflicted upon her. "I believe we have a just God, and that sooner or later Abraham Lincoln will meet with his just rewards. I may be called heartless and wicked, and doubtless am, but it does one good to think that a retribution awaits such tyrants as old Abe."[19] But such hatred of Lincoln did not necessarily entail any patriotism for the new nation created in response to his election. Mary's apathy toward the Confederate cause was apparent from her earliest letters. Never did she profess any patriotic sense of duty as a motive or reason for pride in her activities and considerable achievements during the course of the war. Indeed, on more than one occasion she showed as much contempt for Confederate policies and efforts as she did for the Union cause and its most localized manifestation, the detested "Tories."

In her first letter to Alf, Mary wrote of some dresses she was having made and asked him if he could obtain needed materials more cheaply in Asheville than she could get them in Franklin. "I do not ask the Yankees any odds if I can get thread and dye stuffs . . . I see no sense in relying on things that are made entirely in the South."[20] The following May she was somewhat derisive in describing the efforts of local women who, at the request of Governor Ellis's wife, were "getting up a subscription here to make a gunboat for the defense of North Carolina." "Don't you think it is too late to think about making gunboats?" she asked Alf. She only contributed 50 cents to the cause, and her daughters gave 25 cents that "their grandpa gave them to throw in." She claimed she "told the girls I had sent all the gunboat I thought I ought to send, that I would be willing to subscribe a good deal more if I had you at home."[21]

By April, 1862, Mary could take some satisfaction in the fact that a Confederate conscription act had passed, but she was realistic—or cynical—enough to predict that it "will take some who ought to go as well as some who really are excusable, whilst some will be left behind still who ought to go." She was quick to agree with her husband that the proposed age span of eighteen to thirty-five should have been extended, for she observed, "there are men here at 45 just as able and who have just as much right to go as men at 35."[22] Ultimately, her interest in any conscription policy was how it would affect her beloved Alf, and she was not particularly optimistic, fearing that "it will also hold on some who are already gone that ought to have the privilege of coming home a while if they wish too."[23]

Like many wives, Mary Bell expressed grave concern about her husband's moral character. Perhaps the most typical aspects of her letters to him included admonitions on his sobriety: "Mashburn says that he got drunk while he was gone with you, I am afraid that you had it on the road and by so doing gave him encouragement to drink"; urged him to take up religion: "My earnest prayer is that you will prepare yourself for a better life"; and questioned various vices of which she had heard rumors, especially infidelity: "Reports are that you, Capt. Bell, a man in whom evry one had the utmost confidence as being a true devoted and virtuous husband, could play cards, drink whiskey, and ——— as many women as any man in camps and by so doing had won the love and respect of nearly every man in the regiment . . . I should think that if by such acts I had to gain the love of men, I should consider it dearly."[24]

Strikingly, the pervasiveness of alcoholism filled her letters and homilies. As even outside observers had noted of Franklin and other mountain villages, alcohol abuse was very much in evidence among the citizens well before the war, and the strains of the crisis merely aggravated the situation.[25] Mary commented frequently on the drunkenness of local soldiers on leave. When Bell had sent men back home to round up deserters, she reported, "in place of going sober as they ought to have done, they had to have whiskey and get drunk." She particularly resented the fact that they had drawn her younger brother Dee into their company. He got "drunk with the rest of them & has been drinking ever since." She hoped that Alf could persuade Dee to go to war "as the best thing that can be done for him." Nor was she alone in seeing the therapeutic value of military service for alcoholic menfolk. She told Alf of an acquaintance whose public and reckless displays of drunkenness had made his wife so "perfectly miserable" that "I think she would be glad for him to join the army hoping it will do him some good."[26]

But where Mary's advice and wifely wisdom proved most needed—though there is little indication that Alf listened—was in her counsel on a series of disciplinary actions that stemmed from the mutual dislike of Bell and his commanding officer, David Coleman. That situation, which took most of the war to play itself out, is revealing not only in regard to Alfred Bell's problems and his wife's insights into them, but also for its indication of the active if long-distant roles wives could play in company politics and military relationships.

Soon after Bell's regiment moved to East Tennessee, it reorganized and elected new officers. Much to Alf's chagrin, David Coleman, a well-connected Asheville businessman and legislator who had served as the regiment's colonel since its formation, was reelected to that position.[27] Captain Bell conveyed his bitter disappointment to Mary, who knew her husband's hot temper and independent streak better than anyone else, sensed problems arising from his resentment, and urged him "not to be too hasty" in any decision he made about leaving the regiment for another. "Remember," she cautioned, "you are all fighting for the same cause and there ought not to be any tumult or strife among you." Perhaps unconsciously, she even adopted Lincoln's biblical epigram to make her point. "A house divided against itself," she concluded, "cannot stand."[28]

Mary's fears were confirmed when in June, 1862, her husband initiated and circulated a petition among his fellow officers calling for Coleman's resignation as colonel on the grounds that he spent far too much time drunk and was reluctant to lead his men—or allow others to do so—into battle. Coleman responded by promptly arresting Bell and four other officers, suspending their commands, and threatening them with courts-martial.[29] Mary showed greater concern over Alf's fate than he did because much of her information on her husband's behavior came from other wives in Franklin. She urged moderation, writing Alf that "I do not want you to be satisfied with men who do not do their duty, but I do not want you to get prejudiced and think everything they do is wrong. Perhaps you are prejudiced against Coleman," she gently suggested. "It is rumored here that you have been, or are about to be, reduced in rank for some hand you took in the election. Has anything happened that could start such a rumor?"[30] Alf refused to take the situation seriously and remained cocky, claiming that he welcomed a court-martial because it would accomplish his ultimate goal, "an investigation of the facts as they are." He reported that "our prayers is peace or a battle that our rongs may be avenged . . . nobody scared thoe."[31]

Mary's letters during that period were far more consumed with Alf's predicament than his own were, and she mustered a variety of tones in responding to it. In the same letter she could boost his ego: "I do not want to make you vain, but the news got back home that you are the most popular captain in the regiment"; gently humor him: "you must not get too saucy and get into mischief . . . if you do and I find it out I will request Coleman to put you to digging up stumps"; offer serious advice: "please be calm and do nothing in your difficulties that you can be reproached with. I do not think you will do anything wrong if you will govern your temper"; and even rationalize the situation from her own perspective: "I feel almost in hopes that you will be cashiered and then your men cannot blame you . . . as I have a use for you at home."[32] Only rarely was she explicit in laying out her worst fears: "I am in dread continually for fear that you will in a mad fit do something you ought not to do. I hope for my sake and the sake of your little children that you will be willing to take more than you would otherwise do." That was not the first time nor the last child of which she reminded him: "You must not forget that you have a darling babe at home that you have never seen."[33]

Though the situation seems to have abated with no real resolution by the end of the summer, Alf's problems with his colonel continued. He had to write Mary in September, "I am againe under arest againe not by my self." Coleman had ordered the arrest of all officers for "not marching our companys in line." Bell dismissed the trumped-up charge as more indicative of the disturbed commander's state of mind than of Bell's own behavior. "He is drunk all the time," he claimed. "The boys pray for a fight."[34]

The ongoing divisiveness within this western Carolina regiment was apparently a major topic of discussion among the women of Franklin. Sooner or later many sided with either Coleman or Bell, most likely reflecting the biases of husbands who served with both. Yet even women whose husbands were not associated with the regiment had opinions on the matter. Mary Bell reported a visit from Lizzie Woodfin, the wife of the community's only physician, who thus was still at home. She assured Mary that she was "as bitter against Coleman as any of us." Mary had doubts about her sincerity, however. Earlier Mary had written of a public spat between Mrs. Woodfin and a Mrs. Copeland, and now she feared that the former would hear that "I had written to camp about her quarrel" and "will probably not like it if she hears it."[35]

The role of wives at home proved even more central to a later episode in the ongoing feud. In March, 1864, with his regiment still intact and stationed near Pollard, Alabama, Bell wrote Mary that once more Colonel Coleman had arrested him. The charges this time, said Alf, related to "my neglegince of my dutys assigned me in western N.C. and absents without leave all for spite." The charges originated from local reports that during an extended mission in Macon and surrounding counties the previous fall to roundup deserters and gather new recruits Bell had built a house, practiced dentistry, and (in connection with his father's business) made jewelry. His service record summed up the charges as "alleged speculation."[36]

The sources of these accusations, Bell informed his wife, "were my good lady friends at home who have been writing their husbands." He blamed their maliciousness on regimental politics: "all caused by my being the Sen. Capt. and the Office of Maj. to fill and others more desirous of promotion than I."[37] Salena Reid seems to have been the primary culprit, and Bell saw in her action, among other things, a lack of gratitude that serves as yet another indication of the interdependency the war forced upon the mountain community. She "ought to remember my father halled wood for her when her own father would not do it and my wife loned her money when she needed it. Such ungrateful women I have no use for."[38]

Mary too, of course, deplored the new trouble Mrs. Reid had apparently brought upon her husband and as much as anything else seemed bothered by the fact that as a result of correspondence home from Bell's fellow soldiers, the story "is going evry where here." "The first time I see that good lady friend of yours I shall tell her of it good," she ranted but then, deferring to Alf's judgment, added, "unless you say for me not to."[39] Though John Reid and his wife insisted to Mary that they were not the source of the reports of Bell's activities at home and earnestly sought to make amends, Mary's opinion of them softened only when the bright side of her husband's latest arrest and confinement became apparent: it kept him out of harm's way during the Atlanta campaign in which his regiment was by midsummer fully engaged. Both Bells took satisfaction too in the fact that Reid never was promoted to captain, "as that was his sole object to get me out of the way."[40]

The involvement of Mary Bell and other wives in their husbands' military affairs resulted in part from the small close-knit community from which they came and the fact that so many of that community's residents served together in the same unit during the course of the war. Tensions, disputes, or rivalries that may have had prewar roots carried over from home to camp and from camp back home. As the Bell situation demonstrates, the behavior of wives and other family members could and often did exacerbate such tensions, if only through the very effective and all-important conduit of correspondence to and from the field. That power of the pen in linking home and battlefront gave gossip or hearsay added force in shaping the relationships, ambitions, and rivalries among soldiers from the same area who served together.[41]

If the closeness of Mary Bell's mountain community proved a sore point in her husband's ongoing problems in his regiment, it also had much to do with her success in coping with the hardships of the war years. For, far more than many in her situation, she succeeded in making the best of the hard realities she faced. Equally significant, perhaps, was the fact that she was fully aware of her achievements and viewed them with great self-satisfaction.

Mary Bell was unlike the many southern women who began the war as determined and duty-bound partners in the Confederate war effort, only to be worn down by frustration, weariness, and self-pity that led to anger or indifference toward that very cause. As already demonstrated, she never professed a commitment to anything more than herself and her family, which perhaps explains why her bitterness and anger were vented so early during her husband's Confederate service. Yet as the war progressed, the tone of her letters suggests that her continued efforts to cope with home-front hardships without her husband made her an increasingly independent and self-confident woman who almost thrived on meeting the various challenges thrown her way.

In addition to the care of her growing family—she bore two children during the war (thus spending over a third of the war pregnant) and lost one—Mary's new responsibilities in Alfred's absence were as manager of their farm and as fiscal agent for her husband's dental practice and other business interests. His early letters to her included detailed instructions as to how she should deal with a variety of financial concerns, from negotiating with hired hands or, in the case of slaves, with their owners to collecting debts owed him, paying his own debts, and authorizing new loans, most often to men in his company or their wives. During the same period her letters to him were full of questions that reflected her unfamiliarity and uncertainty in fulfilling those new responsibilities.

Mary reported in April, 1862, that Alf's brother had proposed a swap of some property but that she declined what was most likely an advantageous bargain. She stated: "I was afraid to do it for fear I might get cheated" by her own brother-in-law and "for fear it might not prove good and you would not like it." Later that month, she informed Alf that a note he held on a debt owed him was not in their money box and reluctantly confessed that their young daughters had somehow removed it, used it for drawing paper, and since misplaced it.[42]

Otherwise Mary's reports indicated dutiful adherence to his instructions and demonstrated little initiative or judgment on her part in so doing. It was also obvious that she took little pleasure in those duties. Yet her success quickly boosted her self-confidence and earned the respect of other Franklin residents, male and female. By the summer of 1862, she had begun to exercise her own discretion in making loans to Captain Bell's men, all of which she reported to him so that he might collect from them when they returned to camp and were paid. She wrote in August that "as usual I had to loan some of your men some money." After laying out the particulars—in that case $5.00 loans to three different men and the mother of another—she wrote, "I hope I did nothing wrong." Her rationalization for such generosity—"I seem to have their good will as well as their Capt. and I thought perhaps I had better keep it by being good to them"—is yet another indication of how conscious she was of the impact wives at home could have on their husbands' interests in camp.[43]

Shortly thereafter, however, Mary began to express misgivings about Alf's generosity. She confided to him her fear "that in your dislike to do anything that appears stingy or niggardly, you would allow yourself to become a looser." After a gentle warning not to overextend himself with hand outs merely to assure his popularity among his troops, she concluded, "please don't think your little wife is medling with things that don't concern her dearest, or if you do, try to excuse her."[44]

Mary grew more and more self-assured in conducting other types of business as well. She was especially proud of her skill in bartering transactions, which as the war went on became an increasing—but never exclusive—means of doing business locally. She became more adept and confident in handling often complex transactions that sometimes involved a variety of currencies as well as produce. In one typical report she described a series of barters she negotiated in April, 1864. Those transactions also revealed the community's interdependency and the degree to which Mary Bell had made herself an integral part of an intricate local trade network:

John McConnel has paid me five bushels [of corn] and says that I will have to wait until he goes south after corn before he can pay me any more. Mr. Lores Ell owes me 4 bushels of Apples which he promised to bring this week but has not done it yet. Alfred and Simeon still owes the 4 bushels they have not brought any corn yet. Alfred sent me two hams which I credited on the old account which leaves him $1.64 in debt. Albert has only paid 1¼ bushels which leaves him in debt 3¾ bushels, Joe 2½ bushels, Arther 1 bushel, Adie McConnell 1½ bushels.

She continued in the same letter to explain her attempts to get payment for corn sold on credit to a neighboring woman, payment of which was to include dried fruit; her own unsuccessful attempts to obtain straw from some of those who still owed her for corn; and another neighbor's payment of a past debt in wheat freshly milled into what she reported was good flour.[45] By December she had swapped milk cows with Amanda Cunningham and in a deal in which she took particular pride traded a calf to Benny Dobson for his pregnant sow. "I want to raise my own meat," she wrote Alf, and two men told her "they would have give two such calves for such a hog" as that she acquired. One of them, Mary boasted, "says I can cheat."[46]

Her role in the Bells' jewelry business also provided Mary with experience that made her a shrewd businesswoman by 1864. In December she informed her husband with great satisfaction that she had charged a soldier $20.00, which he willingly paid, for the repair of his watch. She explained that she had arrived at the fee based on what she believed was the current equivalent of two bushels of corn, apparently a standard for such a service for much of the war. When she asked her father-in-law the next day whether that had been a reasonable charge, he replied that he would have asked for a mere dollar and "sorter opened his eyes wide" at her minor windfall in acquiring twenty times that amount. "So you see," she concluded to Alf, "I did not learn to cheat from either of my dadies, it must have been from my husband!"[47]

The grain, produce, and other goods accumulated through Mary's increasingly aggressive bargaining skills were supplemented by other goods Alf was able to supply from the various locales in which he served. Mary constantly sought such opportunities and asked him to obtain and send her a variety of goods, including thread and "dye stuffs" from Asheville and nails and tallow candles from Knoxville (which Mary had noted in a newspaper were cheaper than any available in Franklin).[48] By 1864 she was even being supplied with rice—"as cheap food as we can buy"—from acquaintances coming from South Carolina. Meanwhile, Alf sent shoes from Atlanta for her children and slaves.[49]

As for her responsibilities in agricultural production, Mary never lacked for male workers on her farm a mile or so from town or on her garden plot in town; nor for that matter did she ever lack for male advice. Hired day labor and tenants made up a substantial part of the southern highlands' agricultural work force, and in the early months of Alf's absence, a tenant and a hired slave continued to work different sections of the Bell farm under close supervision by Mary.[50] Though on occasion she referred to Bill Batey, the white tenant, as an overseer, there is no indication that he had any supervisory authority over Tom, the hired slave. Alf's father and brother, both Franklin residents, were also regular sources of support, advice, and on occasion, manpower. Mary's father-in-law even stayed with her and the children sometimes, and she spent a good bit of time at his house. In November, 1861, Mary wrote to Alf in the first of what would be for her a typical combination of reporting and inquiry: "Your father is shucking corn tonight. Tom is done sewing your wheat, he did not sew any rye for you, did you want him to sew some?"[51]

Other local men were available for short-term hire or volunteered their services or equipment. In April, 1862, for instance, Mary wrote: "I got Charles to work for me one day and have got everything that I wanted planted now. I paid him in irish potatoes." When she was "quite busy" helping to get her corn shelled, a neighbor "found out we were shelling and loaned us his sheller so we got it shelled out pretty quick." While she was firmly in control of her own garden plot, her early reports on farming operations indicated a detachment and uncertainty of what was happening there. In the same letter cited above, she admitted that "I have not found out whether Batey has sowed your cloverseed or not but I guess he has. Pa [Alf's father] is going to let me have some flax seed and some sugarcane seed." She went on to say that she planned to plant both "in this lot here," an indication that she did not entirely trust the more distant operation out of town or its overseers.[52]

Perhaps because of that lack of full confidence in Tom or Batey, Mary constantly plied her husband with questions regarding their activities. "Had I better get Bill Batey to haul your lumber?" she asked in June, 1862. "He seems to be a pretty good hand to wagon. I told Pa to inquire if it was ready. I can get Dan to cut my wood, how much did you give Jule's negro to cut by the month? Dan wanted to charge me 75 cts a month." She found these new responsibilities burdensome and after such reports to Alf usually concluded by stating, "I should like so much for you to come home."[53] At one point, she wrote out of utter exhaustion: "I wish I could be both man and woman until this war ends."[54]

Alf was always quick to respond to her letters with extensive and often specific instructions and advice, detailing the timetable and procedure for what and when to plant, much of which she was to pass on to her "overseers." When she complained of Batey's uselessness after their apple crops had been converted into liquid form—"I do not think he will do much while his brandy lasts"— Alf told Mary to tell his tenant that "if he turns his attention to drinking and is letting the place and things go to rack I shall not let him stay. . . . Tell him he must divide the brandy with me. You must lock it up in the stove for me."[55]

In January, 1862, Mary reported "a big scrape up in town." The slaves of a Mr. McCay had stolen around 600 pounds of meat and sold it to slaves on neighboring farms. McCay apparently whipped his slaves into a confession that revealed a wide variety of co-conspirators in the operation, including at least one of the Bells' hired slaves and their overseer Tom. Alf responded by instructing his wife to guard their smokehouse closely (which she had already informed him she was doing) and to "have a clasp and staples and lock it with the best padlocks that we have."[56]

By the end of that first summer on her own, Mary demonstrated considerably more knowledge of what was transpiring on both their own and other farms. On August 29, 1862, she began a letter practically gushing with farm statistics:

> Father has had his thrashing done this week and had only 54 bushels of wheat. Jesse Guffee had 31. You had 4½ of your own and 5 from Wm. Guffee. You have 16½ bushels of very good rye . . . I would like to know what land you want rented for that and who to. Pa says we should plant more rye. Grain is very high and can hardly be bought. There is a great cry for seed of both wheat and rye. Wheat is bringing $4.00 in Haywood [County]. Two bushels of your rye will have to go for thrashing and about ⅔ of a bushel of wheat. . . .

She continued in the same vein for another paragraph. Yet she still deferred to her husband's opinion on dispensation of their crop and reported that Mr. Batey too was "very anxious for you to come home."[57]

There is very little correspondence in existence between the Bells in 1863, in part because Alf spent much of the year at or near home. In 1864, as a more regular exchange of letters resumed, one can detect a subtle role reversal in the Bells' correspondence. Mary conveyed a new assurance in her reports of her activity and decision making in both financial and agricultural matters. More often than not, Alf, not Mary, asked the questions. At times he had to remind her merely to keep him abreast of the farm's progress. At other times he barraged her with questions that reveal the range of her agricultural responsibilities:

> how is your wheat and rye doing. what ground have you in corn, is the oats any account. is your clover doing good . . . is there any apples or peaches. is your horses poore. who does your blacksmithing. you can have those old Sythes fixed up so they will [be ready] for your harvest . . . is your potatoes any account. have you any lettice and onions. Have you old rye enough for coffee, do you get any milk. how does your cowes look. is the pasture good. has your foot got well. what hurt it. have you plenty to eate.[58]

Alf fully realized how much Mary had developed as a farmer and resigned himself to her newfound independence in that role. "As for your farming operations," he told her, "I have nothing to say nor advice to give. Besides if I had, Caty [his nickname for Mary] takes no advice but acts for herself and on her own judgement."[59] Her letters did indeed contain mere reports, often only casual references, on what she had done or decisions she had made regarding all aspects of the farm, from planting and harvesting to storage and marketing. Particularly revealing is the extent to which she described the operation in first person singular: "I think I will have a clover patch by next year"; "my horses are fatter than any of my neighbors work horses"; "I like my darkies better I believe than I did at first."[60]

While Mary still complained about the burden she bore, she seemed to do so with far less rancor than had been the case two years earlier. "I have almost overdone myself this week," she informed Alf in April, 1864, "spinning, coloring blue, and making soap. I have been gardening some today too." She later mused that "you have three broke down women on your place [his sister and a slave were the other two]. I believe I am the stoutest one and I am almost give out. We can all eat hearty and that is all you can brag on." She took pride in how hard she worked, and on occasion she openly acknowledged her achievement: "I do not want to boast any but I think you can say now that you have a wife that does not eat any idle bread although she can eat a good deal when she can get it."[61] But her spirits remained high because of her sense of accomplishment. In July she was exuberant over how well the farm was going: "I felt so good that evrything went right with me I do not think any person could have made me mad for two or three days if they had of spit in my face."[62]

Mary's references to her father-in-law and other men on whom she had depended at home were less and less frequent, as were her pleas, so desperate throughout 1862, for her husband's return. She continued to express her love for Alf and was at times eloquent in how much she missed him; yet her pleas for his return often seemed perfunctory. She ended a letter in February, 1864, with the rather matter-of-fact question: "Are you going to reenlist or what are you going to do? Get out if you can honorably."[63] Perhaps most revealingly, she began a letter in June by exclaiming, "O! Would that you were here today." But the reason behind her urgent desire for her husband's presence at that point was not, as it had been in the past, to pass onto him the work and responsibilities that were then hers alone, but rather, as her next sentence indicated: "I would take you over the farm and show you our prospect for a crop."[64]

Even the threat of that scenario most feared by those on the home front—attack by enemy forces—hardly shook Mary's newly gained confidence. In early February, 1864, 250 men of the First Wisconsin Cavalry moved across the Tennessee border into southwestern North Carolina and got as far as Macon County before turning back.[65] Though the party was never closer than twenty miles from Franklin, the residents panicked at this first real threat of enemy incursion into their area. By the time Mary reported the incident to Alf, the excitement had waned and fears subsided. But she was smug in mocking her fellow townspeople for the panic to which she apparently never succumbed. "I guess you have heard," she said, "of the great yankee and tory raid we had or at least expected to have. . . . It was the most ridiculous thing I ever heard of. I think evry man in Macon Co., except those that were too old to get away, skidadled—home guards, preachers, doctors and all, except Cousin William Roane and he ventured far enough to find out that they were not coming." She was no more sympathetic toward the frightened women left behind by Franklin's male population as she described the two or three days in which they had had to endure the prospect of "fine times during yankee holadays." In a somewhat scornful tone, she detailed a variety of mishaps other women encountered in their efforts to hide their valuables and livestock and safeguard their homes, much of which comes across as little more than slapstick in her irreverent retelling of various incidents.[66]

Alf's response was just as lighthearted. He had heard newspaper accounts of the raid before he received Mary's letter but waited until he had read her version before commenting that "we are glad to hear that the people at home had all excaped the yankees so well by flying to the mountains and staying there untill the women and children, ran the yankees back." He later commented that "the home guards of Macon should have a flag presented to them by the ladies for their galantry."[67]

It was only a month after that scare that Mary Bell's confidence in her business and farm management skills culminated in the achievement in which she took most pride and satisfaction: her purchase of a slave family. With no trepidation of either long- or short-term risks in such an investment and no sense at all that she and Alf might well have become among the last Americans ever to achieve slaveholding status, Mary, with the help of Alf's brother, negotiated the purchase of three slaves. In so doing, she achieved what had been a major goal since the war began.

The Bells had discussed the purchase of one or more slaves on several occasions, and as the value of Confederate currency became increasingly questionable, Alf urged Mary to convert their accumulating cash into property of some sort. In December, 1862, he declared: "I don't think it good policy to keep money on hand. I want you to invest what you have in something, either for a negro or land."[68] Unfortunately, she chose the former. The fact that Alf entrusted his wife to undertake so momentous a transaction indicates how much he respected her growing business acumen. In effect he gave her a free rein in terms of whom or what she purchased and how much she paid. "I want you not to ask me anything about it," he told her. "Its enough for you to know that I want you to buy it . . . I have a wife, and I thank god for it, who is not extravagant and [is] always trying to lay something up for the future."[69]

Mary backed off from making such a purchase at that time, but late in the summer of 1863, while Alf was at home, they accepted a teenage slave girl, Eve, as payment for a long-held note owed Alf. From the beginning, Eve proved a source of irritation to Mary, and by early 1864 Alf was encouraging her to trade Eve for a tract of land he badly wanted, again leaving the negotiations to her discretion. The extent of his advice to her was simply that, in addition to Eve's value, she "give any price for it that you think we can pay and live afterward."[70]

It was advice that came too late. A week earlier, Mary wrote to Alf with great excitement: "Well I believe I told you that you need not be surprised if Katy Holcomb [her own nickname] made a nigger trade. Well she has done it. I have swaped Eve for a man, woman an[d] child." She explained the complex transaction, which had actually been carried out by Alf's brother Benjamin. It involved payment of $1,800 in addition to Eve to a local resident who had only recently purchased the family from Charleston and transported it to his farm in Macon County. By then he feared that he had overextended himself financially and, according to Mary, was eager to settle for a low price for the family of three. Mary was proud of her bargain but told Alf, "I recon you will have to petition for you[r] wages to be raised until you can pay up the debts that you extravagant wife contracts."[71]

Alf, who had earlier thanked God that he did not have an extravagant wife, was probably taken aback by her news. Yet assured by his brother that the deal had indeed been an advantageous one, he stifled any criticism of his wife and informed her that he was glad she at last had such able help at home and in the field. He added: "I hope we can git along without having to do with Love's negroes. I do crave to be independent and unbeholding to any body."[72] Mary's own enthusiasm for Trim, Patsey, and their daughter, Rosa, remained unabated through the rest of the year. Descriptions of them and her utilization of them came to dominate her subsequent correspondence to Alf as long as that correspondence lasted.

In many respects, Mary Bell's acquisition and management of her labor force—hired and purchased, white and black—provide the most dramatic reflection of how the war allowed her to mature and to assert a sense of independence she probably would never have known otherwise. Just as the war imposed new challenges and responsibilities on her, it also provided her with new opportunities of which she took full advantage. Neither hunger, poverty, nor material deprivation was ever among the hardships she faced. Her husband's comfortable financial situation and his position in the community helped to shield her, but Mary's skillful management of their resources in his absence also contributed substantially to her well-being. The relative lack of deprivation made Mary Bell's wartime experience quite different from that of many other women in the same region, on whom the war's impact was far more destructive, physically, emotionally, and materially, as Gordon McKinney has recently demonstrated in this journal.[73]

Yet her achievement was hardly unique or even unusual among Confederate women. In her general description of the plight of southern womanhood at war, Anne Firor Scott laid out the essence of the Bells' experience with almost uncanny precision. "Husbands hurrying off to the army," Scott stated, "sent back all kinds of instructions about the planting, harvesting, and marketing of crops, the management of slaves, the education of children, the budgeting of money, the collecting of old debts, and every other aspect of their business, apparently in perfect confidence that their wives would somehow cope. The women, in their turn, were polite about asking advice and begged for guidance, while carrying on as if they had always been planters, business managers, overseers of slaves, and decision makers."[74]

Yet Mary Elizabeth Massey noted in the opening sentence of her book *Bonnet Brigades* that "had every woman and girl of the 1860s described the ways in which she was affected by the Civil War, no two accounts would have been alike."[75] It is the particularities of Mary Bell's experience and the context in which it took place that make her letters worth such close scrutiny. While there was much that was typical about her response to the war, her individuality also bears examination. She was never subjected to the brutal and destructive forces that victimized so many Appalachian women as a result of the peculiar nature of the war waged in that region.[76] And unlike thousands of her counterparts, Mary Bell never offered her services to a military hospital or went to work in a factory; she was never part of any women's voluntary association or patriotic activity to support the men and boys in gray or the cause for which they fought; she never participated in a bread riot; and she never signed a petition or wrote letters on her own behalf or Alf's to President Jefferson Davis or Governor Zebulon B. Vance.[77] For the most part, she coped with the war in very private terms and reacted to it through purely personal means.

Mary's almost total self-absorption is among the most striking aspects of the self-portrait her letters provide; from beginning to end, her own and her family's well-being were her only priorities. She did not fit the pattern of the many women throughout the South and in western North Carolina who were initially caught up in the spirit of the war and the meaning of the Confederate cause, only later to be disillusioned and embittered by the increasing hardships that cause imposed on them, whose deteriorating willpower became a major impetus to massive desertions and much-weakened morale among Confederate fighting men. Mary was bitter and cynical about the war from the beginning and thumbed her nose at the patriotism of other Franklin women. If she ever consciously encouraged her husband's abandoning the military to return home, it was during his first few months away. Though she genuinely missed him throughout the war's duration, she was far more self-secure and her need for him far less acute during its final year.

Drew Gilpin Faust has noted the number of southern women who yearned to be men so that they might make themselves useful to the Confederacy. Mary Bell was among those expressing her desire for what Faust calls "a magical personal deliverance from gender restraints."[78] But when Mary proclaimed, "I wish I could be both man and woman," she had in mind nothing as magnanimous as contributing to the war effort; she simply yearned for the strength to keep her farm, family, and finances afloat for the duration. She was certainly not alone in her firm adherence to those limited and localized goals; if anything distinguished Mary Bell's efforts, it would probably be the degree to which she succeeded in managing all three and the tremendous satisfaction she took in doing so.

Yet she could not have done it on her own. Her success was very much the result of community interdependency, as reflected by the reciprocal nature of her relationship with fellow Franklin residents that emerges as a dominant theme in her letters. Despite her self-absorption, Mary relied heavily on her neighbors, just as they often called upon her for aid of various sorts. The war's demands forced new levels of cooperation and interaction on that mountain community as it did many others. Despite Mary's cynicism toward the "cause" and her disdain for many of those in whose midst she lived, she used them and was used by them.

Perhaps what most distinguishes Mary Bell's experience as Appalachian in nature is the sense of community that it so vividly conveys. Gordon McKinney maintains that it was the disintegration of community structure and economy that so victimized many western North Carolina women and placed them at the forefront of the bitter and often destructive divisiveness that plagued much of the southern highland populace.[79] But the conditions that rendered other communities dysfunctional do not seem to have been as acute in Franklin. While Mary Bell's descriptions suggest that the potential for internal disorder was present, the Macon County seat also enjoyed a variety of circumstances that insulated it from the worst ravages of the war and enabled it to weather the crisis far better than other mountain communities.

The flexibility of local trade patterns and labor arrangements that characterized the antebellum economy of much of the southern highlands proved a tremendous asset to the Bells and other Macon Country residents in adapting to the new demands imposed by the war. Faced with manpower shortages as acute as those elsewhere in the South, families, like the Bells, with the financial resources to take advantage of them filled the void with long-established practices of long- and short-term slave hirings and tenant employment. The great diversity of highland agricultural production allowed for a degree of local self-sufficiency that sheltered the community from the deprivation such a crisis might—and elsewhere often did—impose.

Franklin's physical remoteness shielded it from much of the military movement that disrupted so many southern lives and households. Even the brutal and destructive bushwhacking activity that plagued so many sections of the southern highlands was never a serious threat to that particular corner of Appalachian North Carolina.[80] Yet Franklin was never so inaccessible that constant contact with its men in the field or access to goods and services well beyond the local supplies was ever denied those of its residents with the means to utilize it.

Perhaps the most significant factor in Franklin's avoidance of internal collapse or upheaval was that political sentiments there were never as divided as they were in East Tennessee or other sections of the Carolina highlands. Though in neighboring Cherokee County, Unionists and deserters threatened Confederate wives and Confederate raiders harassed the wife of a prominent Unionist, unionism never achieved a stronghold in the state's southwestern corner; nor did Franklin residents (perhaps buffered by Cherokee County from spillover of Tennessee's Unionist influence) ever seem to have engaged in such confrontations.[81] The tensions and disagreements that arose between the Bells and fellow residents were limited to petty jealousies or personality conflicts that never split the community to the extent that more basic disagreements over commitment to the Union or to the Confederacy would have. Thus local animosities were never a threat nor a barrier to the mutual dependency on which Franklin residents came to rely so heavily, animosities that could well have negated the advantages their insulation and self-sufficiency provided.[82]

Unfortunately, Alf's return home in February, 1865, brought the Bells' vivid record of their wartime lives to a sudden halt. One can only guess what long-term effects Mary's "emancipation" had on her marriage, her household, or her place in the community. Nor can one know how either spouse reacted to the loss of their newly acquired slave property; how much of a role Mary continued to play in Alf's business affairs or farm management; or to what extent Confederate defeat and its subsequent burdens demoralized her or punctured her steadily growing self-esteem. From an 1890s perspective, John Andrew Rice wrote that "in 1860 the South became a matriarchy." If Mary's wartime role does not fully support such hyperbole, Rice's subsequent analysis seems a remarkably apt description of the Bells' situation: "The men went away from home to other battlefields, leaving the women free to manage farm and plantation directly, without their bungling hindrance; when they returned, those who had escaped heroic death . . . found their surrogates in complete and competent charge and liking it."[83] That being very much what Alfred Bell returned home to in February, 1865, it is hard to imagine that his household ever reverted to the full patriarchy it had been before he marched off to war.

25 Emily Lyles Harris: A Piedmont Farmer During the Civil War

Philip N. Racine

*E*MILY HARRIS, a South Carolina farmer's wife of the last century, might well have been missed as far as history is concerned except for the fact that she married a man who kept a journal. Her husband, David Harris, started his journal in 1855 to keep an accurate record of his farm work so he could eventually learn the very best time and method for undertaking his various tasks. With his wife, Emily Jane Lyles, his many children, and his ten slaves, he worked one hundred acres of a five-hundred-acre farm located eight miles southeast of the village of Spartanburg, South Carolina. In addition to recording his daily work, David often used his journal to comment on current affairs, family life, and his own state of mind. His records tell us much about farm life in the county, for he was a diligent and perceptive witness.

Yet, any investigation of the state of mind of people in Spartanburg District during the Civil War must also pay particular attention to Emily Harris. When David eventually went off to war, he asked his wife to carry on with his journal. He did us a great favor, for Emily made the journal her confidante. To it she confided her feelings, her opinions, and her fears. Through the entries in her journal we catch a glimpse of what it was like in the middle of the nineteenth century to be the wife of a farmer and of a soldier. There is no better contemporary record of life in Spartanburg District and not many its equal for the region. Throughout the literature on women in the Confederacy, including the recent work of

Bell Wiley, Mary Elizabeth Massey, and the diary kept by another South Carolinian, Mary Boykin Chesnut, there is no more introspective and brutally honest commentator than Emily Harris. Some women who left us records were closer to battle, some were closer to the government, most were richer, but none looked at themselves and their world as unsparingly as did this farm wife in Spartanburg.

In 1860 Spartanburg County was an overwhelmingly agricultural area with few industries outside of small grist and saw mills and cotton gins. The county population was 18,500 whites and 8,100 slaves. The village had about one thousand inhabitants, eighteen stores, a couple of hotels, four churches, and five schools. There were no troops in the county during the war outside of the wounded and men on furlough, and no battles were fought there. The first Union soldiers who officially came to Spartanburg were chasing Jefferson Davis after the war's end. They stayed only a few days. So, for the most part, Spartanburg was a backwater of the war, but, nonetheless, its residents felt the war's effects. This was the setting in which David and Emily Harris recorded their perspectives on the county in wartime.

Born in 1827, Emily Jane Lyles Harris grew up in Spartanburg village until 1840 when her parents moved to the country. Her father, Amos Lyles, was intent on educating his only daughter, and Emily soon found herself boarding in the village so she might attend Phoebe Paine's school. Phoebe Paine was a Yankee schoolmarm who believed that women should be educated to use their intellectual gifts. In later years Emily recalled Phoebe Paine admonishing her to remember her "buried talent."[1] Historians of Spartanburg owe Phoebe Paine much, if for no other reason than for preparing Emily Lyles to write well, with feeling and understanding about herself and her times.

Emily Harris had nine children. When war broke out a set of twins had died and her seven remaining children were ages one year and nine months, four, six, eight, ten, twelve, and fourteen. She was thirty-three years old. Since her marriage in 1846, Emily's life had been filled with giving birth to and raising children, sometimes teaching them, making their clothes, and tending a garden from which much of the food for the family was taken; she had at least one house servant to help her. Although she enjoyed church, attended some social functions, and at times received relatives at home, she did not often go to the village or much of anywhere else. Her elderly mother lived with her for a few years in the late 1850's. With all these responsibilities she stayed at home, and there is evidence that she was not altogether content. Her husband, David, often complained of her temper, which irritated him; they seem to have quarreled often. Emily's temper was appreciated by all on the farm, for she was sometimes angry enough to whip her female slaves, and at least once, she whipped a male slave.

Such frequent outbursts of temper may have been partly a response to the physical isolation of the farm which denied David and Emily adequate diversion to relieve the monotony of their rural existence. It was ironic that this isolation, of which both Harrises complained, did not afford them any personal privacy. In 1862 David Harris wrote:

> Solitude sometimes is my most pleasant companion. How nice it is to sit in a quiet room by a glowing fire of shining embers, and to live over the past and to mark out pleasant plans for the future. This is a pleasure almost entirely denied me. So many children, and many cares. Oftentimes I would sit by the fire, and read and wright and dream. But children will be children, and children will make a noise. Then my resort is the bed. To find rest for my wearied limbs, and my diseased boddy. Wife often asks me to remain up with her, but I am compelled to take refuge in the bed, until I have become so accostomed to retiring early, that I cannot well do otherwise.

David wrote this entry at a time when Emily was also feeling overburdened and depressed, but he made no mention of her need for the same privacy and solitude that he craved. Nor did he seem to understand her need for his adult company. He was shutting her out, isolating her even more, and finding his peace, such as it was, partly at her expense. In the war's later years Emily confided to the journal that she "craved a few quiet days and for several weeks they have been denied me. I may as well give it up and resign myself to live in hub-bub all my life." A few days later Emily spoke a general human complaint when she lamented that her seven "children have all been at home. I have been much troubled by their noise and confusion which has caused me to ask myself what I should do with them when the school was out, and then what I should do with myself if I had no children." Farm life was a paradox. These two adults did not seem to be able to find sufficient companionship in each other to fill their individual needs for adult society, and the press of humanity which resulted from nine people living in a small house only added to their frustration and anxiety. The farm was isolated, but the people were never alone.[2]

When David Harris learned that his departure for service with the state volunteers was imminent he worried about leaving his family. He

was sure Emily would care for the children, that she would work consci-
entiously and hard, but he also knew she would "be much at a loss with
the management of the farm and the negroes." She had never had to
assume the responsibility for the operation of everything and now, all of
a sudden, it was dropped in her lap. He knew she would try, and he was
ready to accept the consequences, whatever they might be. Emily was
not quite so reconciled.

> The trial has come at last, my husband has gone to the war, he left me
> yesterday afternoon. I thought I would rather not go with him to the
> depot but after he had gone I felt an almost irresistable impulse to
> follow him and keep his beloved countenance in my sight as long as pos-
> sible. It was a hard parting, a bitter farewell. Ninety days, how long to
> be without him, how long for him to bear the privations and hardships
> of the camp and . . . how I shudder to think I may never see him again.
> A load of responsibilities are resting upon me in his absence but I shall
> be found trying to bear them as well as I can.[3]

Among her difficulties was that faced by all mothers whose husbands
are away for long periods of time—how to deal with the children. These
were farm children used to having both their parents with them, or
nearby, almost all the time. The younger children did not understand
David Harris's long absence; one child, his father's namesake, in anger
about something ran from the house to the gate "expecting to be taken
up by his father. The tears would come a little in spite of one but I
choked them down because the children seem sad enough. . . ." Emily
controlled her emotions to help her children adjust, but the sensitivity,
good nature, and deep feelings for people she showed in doing so
rewarded her unkindly. Troubled and unsettled as she was, others among
her relatives and friends turned to her for support; to them she was a
strong woman, a realistic woman, a woman who could cope. Such had
always been her role, and she was sought out, ironically, for the very comfort and advice, the very intimate sharing she herself so desperately
needed. During a visit by a relative grieving a husband off to war, Emily
had to "laugh and be gay on her account. . . ." She was the one to whom
many turned, and thus "it has always been my lot to be obliged to shut
up my griefs in my own breast." As it turned out she could manage the
farm better than she could manage her griefs.[4]
    Even when Emily felt she had things under control her journal entries
are marked with sadness and a depressing sense of foreboding and loss:

> All going well as far as I can judge but tonight it is raining and cold and a soldier's wife cannot be happy in bad weather or during a battle. All the afternoon as it clouded up I felt gloomy and sad and could not help watching the gate for a gray horse and its rider but he came not, though all his family are sheltered and comfortable the one who prepared the comfort is lying far away with scanty covering and poor shelter.

Most of the time she did not feel under control but rather overwhelmed. Her days were full ones; she felt almost crushed by the myriad things she had to do:

> It has rained all day, the children have been cross and ungovernable. Old Judah and Edom [slaves] were both sick. Ann is trying to weave, and a poor weave it is, the sewing must be done, everything must be attended to, Laura is coughing a rough ominous cough, has scarcely any shoes on her feet, and no hope of getting any this week, West has the croup. I am trying to wean the baby and the cows laid out last night, and last and worst of all I know my husband is somewhere miserably cold, wet, and comfortless.[5]

No matter how badly things went for her, Emily always thought of David, and she took some comfort in the fact that he wrote her every day.

Emily did settle into the routine of running the farm, and some of her journal entries sound much like those of her husband. She planted, complained of the weather, meticulously recorded all the data of farm life her husband so cherished, constantly berated her slaves and, unlike her husband, always recorded the health of the children. "Family not well, negroes doing nothing but eating, making fires and wearing out clothes," was a typical entry. But she did grow crops, and grow them well. She had to hire extra field hands to help her bring in the harvest, although hiring was difficult; no one wanted money, everyone wanted food. Her record crop of oats—the best in her area of the district—almost went to ruin in the field because she had to pay her hired hands in wheat and she almost ran out. She exhausted everyone including herself in getting the oats in.

Yet, even her successes took their toll. Her persistence was in spite of herself: "I shall never get used to being left as the head of affairs at home. The burden is very heavy, and there is no one to smile on me as I trudge wearily along in the dark with it. I am constituted so as to crave a guide and protector. I am not an independent woman nor ever shall be." Emily felt insecure and incompetent, but to everyone around her she appeared just the opposite. She did get everything done but despaired of the life it meant she had to lead and the strength it meant she had to conjure up: "I am busy cutting our winter clothing, every thing is behind time and I'm tired to death with urging children and negroes to work."[6]

The pressures of farm, slaves, and family were almost too much. By late 1863 Emily was beginning to hate the farm, despair of her life, and fear herself: "If I am always to live as I have lived the last few months I shall soon tire of life and be willing to die. It seems that I have to think for every one on the place. . . . Every little thing has to pass through my hands in some way." Assailed as she was by self-doubt, lack of privacy, and burdens of responsibility, it is not surprising that the war itself began to take on an evil aspect for her. She blamed her husband's absence on the government, a government which she came to hate. In the spring of 1864 David Harris tried to get out of the army by securing an exemption as a farmer, but he was turned down. "Now of course there is no hope but for him to remain and fight our foes," she wrote, but as for herself she felt as much "like fighting our men who, standing at the head of affairs, are the cause of keeping such as him in the field, as I do the Yankees." This is self-pity; there were thousands like him and thousands like her. Her skepticism about the war grew until in 1865 she was openly hoping for a quick defeat. When she heard of a battle that was won by the Confederates she commented that it "will only prolong the struggle and do us no good I fear." She once remarked that she wished "the government would take all we've got and then call out the women and children and see if that would not rouse this people to a sense of their condition."[7]

These were lucid comments which reflected realities. But at times, she did tend to be a bit melodramatic: "There is no pleasure in life and yet we are not willing to die. I do not know how it might be but I feel like I should welcome the *Messenger* if it were not for those who need my services. . . ." And at another time she complained that "the great trouble is, there is no one on this place that has the welfare and prosperity of the family at heart but me. No one helps me to care and to think. . . . Losses, crosses, disappointments assail me on every hand. Is it because I am so wicked?"[8]

Yet, she was not self-centered. In addition to worrying about her own state of mind, she often thought and wrote of all the people who suffered around her. She might have been speaking for the whole of the county in 1864 when she wrote:

How we pity the brave men who are engaged in these battles. How we sympathize with the anxious hearts which almost stand still with suspense as they turn and listen in every direction for the last scrap of news from the battle. These hearts are more to be pitied than those that lie cold and still on the bloody field.

Every body is anxious and gloomy. Constantly we are hearing of some brave man who has fallen and whether an acquaintance or not he is somebody's son, somebody's friend. Some face will grow pale at news of his death, perchance some heart break, some soul pray, in its anguish, for death.[9]

As the year 1864 closed, Emily did become increasingly theatrical, yet there was a note of genuine desperation in her comments and a growing sense of self-doubt, a sense that there was something wrong with her. In late 1864 she confronted her depression:

It is seldom I stop to think of how I feel, much less write about it, but tonight I feel so unnaturally depressed that I cannot help casting about in my mind to see what is the matter. I left home . . . with Mary and Quin . . . to celebrate the anniversary of their marriage. I forgot all I wanted to carry with me. I lost some money. I felt unwell. I came home and found my sick ones not so well. I heard that the troops [with David] . . . were ordered *to sleep with their shoes and cartridge boxes on.* After supper the topic of conversation was Death. Our faithful dog, Boney, has howled ever since dark. What ails me, I do wonder?

Then late one night her husband returned on furlough. "After we all had hugged and kissed our best friend, we raised a light to gaze upon and scrutinize the beloved features which had begun to be something belonging to the past." David looked well and "his arrival has dispelled all gloom for the present."[10] David was well pleased with what Emily had done; by all measures she had managed the farm and the slaves with skill, making enough money and trading wisely enough for all to have lived fairly well. From the journal entries during his furlough it is difficult to know if Harris sensed his wife's state of mind. If he did sense the need and the fear, he did not record it, and in two weeks he was once again gone.

David's departure brought on all the old anxieties and fits of depression. Before he would come home again Emily would have to face two new problems, both of which might frighten even the most steadfast personality. By war's end slaves would grow impudent and rebellious, and desperate men—some soldiers and some deserters—would blanket the countryside; and Emily would have to face them both alone.

The war posed special problems for the Harris family and their Negroes. The very prospect of war had raised the remote possibility of

Negro rebellion in David's mind, and there had been one case of alleged planned insurrection in the district in 1860. The fear that war would trigger a Negro uprising was general throughout the South, but the fears were unfounded. David Harris remained skeptical of the possibility of a general slave uprising in Spartanburg District for much of the war as we see in this late 1863 description of a sortie prompted by an alleged black conspiracy. A friend came to the house "and warned me to take guns and equipment to repair at dusk to Cedar Spring to watch a big negro-frolick that was to take place. . . . I went according to request (but without my gun) and bravely charged upon the house. But it was dark, silent and quiet, so we charged home again."[11] Otherwise, until the summer of 1864, Harris's relations with his slaves did not change. Every once in a while a Negro ran off for a short period, usually because of a flogging, but that was not so unusual.

When David went off to war he was concerned about his wife's ability to manage his slaves. Running the farm was one thing, managing its labor was another. Emily was nervous about the prospect seemingly without much cause. Then the war turned decidedly sour, and an ominous series of strange events began to plague her. Her field hands began to find hogs butchered on her place. By the summer of 1864 a good many had been killed, by white renegades she at first believed, but then she was given cause to suspect blacks. Slaves from the neighborhood had been selling pork for some time, and whites were in such need as not to raise many questions about the source. Also, rumor among her own blacks had it that runaways hiding in the neighborhood were killing her stock. With the help of two neighbors she interrogated her slaves, but all they could agree upon was that one certain Negro, whose name was Pink, was selling pork. Pink said he had bought the pork from her own slave named Eliphus. She did not believe him and let the matter drop. Emily came to believe that her hogs were being killed "for revenge as well as gain. We have insulted a negro who is too smart to be detected in his villainy."[12] If true, it was the first sign that she could be the object of rebellion.

If the first, this was not the last sign, for by 1864, the relationship between masters and slaves was changing in ominous ways. Either because of the news that the war was going badly for the South (Negroes kept informed) or because they considered Emily less a master than David, or both, the Harris slaves began to take liberties. At Christmas in 1864 several of her blacks left the farm without her permission and stayed away at length, and others to whom she had given permission overstayed their time. The same was going on elsewhere in the district. Even more worrisome, for it showed where the sympathy of these "faithful blacks" lay, was the news she accidentally learned from slaves not her own: "I have learned through negroes that three Yankee prisoners have been living for several days in our gin house and have been fed by our negroes. The neighbors are seen watching for them with their guns." After putting together a surprise raid on her own slave quarters, Emily was disappointed that "the search for Yankee prisoners on our premises ended without success or information except the unmistakable evidence that some one or more had been lodged and fed in and about our gin for some days. We tried to get the negroes to tell something about it but in vain. We could hear of their telling each other about it, but they wouldn't tell us nothing."[13] The slaves were not rising up, but they were harboring the enemy, and they were keeping things to themselves.

As Emily began to lose control over her slaves, she started to fear them. Negroes were aware that the Yankees were coming and some began to act on that knowledge, or at least, on that hope. In early 1865 "old Will came to me and asked me to give him 'a paper' and let him go and hunt him a home. York [the Harris's Negro overseer] has given him a whipping and he wishes to leave the place." This was the first request for freedom ever made by a Harris slave. Emily denied it, but the altercation between the two Negroes created a crisis, for Emily was put in a position where she realized the actual limits of her authority, limits which were an outcome of the times. "I'm in trouble," she wrote; "York must be corrected for fighting the old negro and there is no one willing to do it for me. It seems people are getting afraid of negroes."[14]

But the loss of authority hurt two ways. The white leadership, which before 1861 had sought some justice for slaves in special Negro courts, was off to war, and wives found that there were severe limits on what they could do to protect their chattels from the irresponsible exercise of power. As whites grew more fearful of blacks late in the war, arbitrary punishments became more frequent and severe. In crises the niceties tend to get trampled. Emily Harris again:

NEGRO TRIAL, great trouble
    Today some runaway negroes were caught. One of them, Sam, who once belonged to Dr. Dean confessed a good deal and implicated others who were accordingly severely whipped without giving them a chance to prove their innocence. Eliphus [a Harris slave] and Guinn Harris' Pink were both whipped without proof of their guilt. I never will allow another negro of mine punished on suspicion. I understand that on next Monday the const[ables] are to go in search of evidence against Eli-

phus. Things are reversed. People used to be punished when found guilty, now they are punished and have their trial afterward.

Eliphus has cause to deplore the absence of his master as well as I. If he had been here it would not have been managed in this way.[15]

Whether Emily gave Eliphus cause to know her feelings on the matter we do not know, but her indignation was a little late to help him. It is worth noting, however, that she did expect her slave to receive justice.

In 1865, as the weeks of winter and spring passed, Emily lost more and more control over her slaves. She found it "a painful necessity that I am reduced to the use of a stick but the negroes are becoming so impudent and disrespectful that I cannot bear it." In March she set down the plain fact that "the negroes are all expecting to be set free very soon and it causes them to be very troublesome." David Harris reflected white reaction to the emerging Negro attitude when he said, on hearing of a Negro who had been shot, that the dead man was "a bad boy & I am glad that he is killed. There is some others in this community that I want to meet the same fate."[16]

The last few months of the war were among the most traumatic for Spartanburg district. When General William T. Sherman captured Savannah in December 1864, South Carolinians realized that he would soon invade their state. They also knew that, as the first southerners to secede, they were blamed by Union soldiers for the war and that their state stood as a symbol of rebellion. They expected the worst Sherman's army could dish out, and by reputation that could be pretty bad. Knowing that the end was near, some people in the village openly rejoiced at the prospect of peace and even flew a peace flag. There was little adverse reaction even to such a blatant act, for, as Emily put it, "every one seems to think we are to have peace soon and no one seems to care upon what terms." But peace was some months off. Word came to Spartanburg that Sherman was burning Columbia with thousands of women and children fleeing that part of the state. After hearing about Columbia, Emily Harris described her neighbors and herself as "in a dreadful state of excitement, almost wild. The Yankee army are advancing upon Spartanburg we fear. They are now destroying Alston and Columbia. . . . It has been impossible for me to sit or be still or do any quiet thing today. I am nearly crazy."[17] Emily had no need to fear, for Sherman turned toward Camden and never came near Spartanburg.

The Union army proved a chimeric threat but not so the deserters and renegades who plagued the northern part of the district. These desperadoes became bolder as the Confederate and state forces grew increasingly weak and ineffective. In the middle of 1863, that bad time for the Confederacy in general, the deserters became a serious problem. Their numbers, estimated at anywhere from six hundred to one thousand, were growing and many of them were "armed; are bold, defiant and threatening. Nothing but extreme measures can accomplish anything," wrote the officer in charge of the Greenville district requesting advice on how to control these marauders. The South Carolina troops were detailed to hunt down the deserters, but they were almost bribed into doing so. "By arresting a notorious deserter. . . ," David Harris recorded in his journal, "I was granted a twenty days furlough." Most deserters eluded capture largely because they were aided by local citizens who had never been in favor of the war or who were disgusted with it."[18]

By 1864 the deserters and others were getting bolder and stealing food and goods all over Spartanburg District. Food was disappearing from front yards of farms very close to the village. When Emily Harris heard that a barrel of molasses was stolen from under the bedroom window of her very close neighbor, Dr. Dean, she exclaimed of the thieves that "showing them is the only remedy." Her husband, frustrated by the imminent defeat of the Confederacy, railed at "the thieves about me [who] are troubling me as much as the war. It seems that they will steal all we have got, and leave us but little for my family." By March of 1865 state soldiers who were assigned for local defense despaired of providing adequate protection; one of them wrote to his comrade that "from what I can hear, in the Districts of Union, Spartanburg & Greenville the citizens have been almost overrun by Deserters and absentees from the Army."[19]

The absentees presented a special problem of their own. Throughout the war, the spring had been a time when men simply walked away from their units. Worried about crops and about their families running out of food, they suffered a special homesickness. In the spring of 1865 all was made worse by the obvious futility of continuing the war, and soldiers set off for home on foot by the thousands. Such movement by strangers through the district posed problems for Emily Harris: "Late this afternoon a cavalry soldier came and begged to stay all night. I allowed him to stay but shall do so no more. . . . There are hundreds of soldiers passing to and fro. This is a little dangerous for women and children and fine horses to trust themselves on the road." The fear was well founded, but it created pangs of conscience for women who were also loyal citizens and distressed wives. Emily Harris worried that "there are thousands of soldiers now passing through the District on their way to join Gen. Lee near

Richmond. Two have just asked to spend the night but I sent them away. In the same way my poor *husband* will be turned away to sleep in the rain and mud. . . ." These soldiers were dirty, raggedly dressed, and had not been paid in months. They found themselves thrown onto the mercy of farm and village people who, in turn, felt threatened by these strangers.[20]

Throughout all of her trials—the burden of raising children by herself, of managing a farm, of handling quarrelsome slaves, and the fear of the dislocation of defeat and the imminence of privation—Emily Harris constantly fought her personal war against depression. More than anything else she feared herself; she believed that her emotions and her mind threatened her world most immediately. In February of 1865, in the midst of rebellious slaves and national defeat, she got the answer to a desperate question she had put to herself months before. "What ails me, I do wonder?" One evening in February she recorded her answer:

> A Presentiment
>   When Mrs. Harris, my esteemed mother in law, among her various objections to her son's alliance with me mentioned that of insanity being an hereditary affliction of my family I laughed at the idea of ever being in any danger of it. But the years which have intervened since then have left upon me the imprint of the trials and sufferings they in passing listerred [carved] on me. I sometimes have days of misery for which I cannot give, even to myself, a cause. These spells are periodical and today for the first time I have thought perhaps they were the transitory symptoms of insanity. It is a dark dream to dread. I wonder if the hopelessly insane do suffer much. If it is to be so who can arrest the fate. . . .[21]

Emily Jane Lyles Harris faced the ordeal of increasing slave arrogance and the fear of wandering soldiers with the realization that she might be losing her mind. Luckily, her husband came home unhurt within a month. He took over the journal once again, and Emily faded from view, for David hardly mentioned her. However, we do know she did not go insane. Her ordeal stemmed not from insanity, but rather from overwhelming burdens, loneliness, and sensitivity. What is especially striking about her entries in the journal is not that she was depressed, but that her depression made her feel so guilty and incompetent. Indeed, her life gave her ample reason to be fearful and anxious, yet her society expected her to react to her burdens otherwise; being unable to meet society's expectations, she felt compelled to seek some unnatural explanation, such as her mother-in-law's comment on insanity, for her self-doubts. Emily's anguish stemmed from the unrealistic self-perception fostered in women during the nineteenth century, a self-perception which even an education by Phoebe Paine could not significantly alter. Emily's reaction to her condition was probably more typical of most women, and especially farm women, caught up in this Civil War than the bombast of men would have us believe. And in her remarks about the tedious work, the isolation, and the trouble of daily life, she spoke truly of what much of an ante-bellum farm existence was like.

David Harris died at age fifty-four in 1875. Emily lived with her children until her death in 1899 from a stroke suffered, according to family tradition, in a dentist's chair. The dentist reportedly was badly unsettled by the possibility that he might have brought on the attack; poor fellow, had he read the journal he would have known that Emily had always had a flair for the dramatic.

26 A Civil War Experience of Some Arkansas Women in Indian Territory

Edited by LeRoy H. Fischer[*]

*N*OT THE least of the sufferers during the Civil War years were the women who faced hardship at home while their husbands faced danger on the battlefield. Moreover, Southern women often suffered the direct effects of battle as campaigns raged about them. The following account is the story of five women and three children who sought to escape such perils by flight southward during the autumn of 1864. They began their trek in Fayetteville, Arkansas, with Washington, Arkansas, as their intended destination. Losing their way, they wandered into the war-desolated Choctaw Nation of Indian Territory. Only after a series of harrowing experiences did they eventually reach safety along the Red River.

The author of this account, Francena Lavinia (Martin) Sutton, was a resident of Fayetteville. Her husband James was a merchant there but apparently was away from home, probably in Confederate service. In 1864 Mrs. Sutton was twenty-four years old. Her son William Seneca, the author of the foreword of this reminiscence, was four years old. After the Civil War Mrs. Sutton returned to her home in Fayetteville and became an instructor at the University of Arkansas. Her son, who received degrees from the University of Arkansas in 1878, 1880, and 1905, became a professor at the University of Texas at Austin in 1897. In the course of his career he served that institution as dean of education and as president.[1]

Foreword

The story accompanying this note was written by my mother, Mrs. Francena Martin Sutton, of Fayetteville, Arkansas. From time to time, for
years prior to her death, which occurred in 1914, I asked her to write a
series of articles to set forth her experiences during the Civil War. Again
and again she promised to comply with my request; but she was always a
busy woman, and she repeatedly postponed the task which I hoped she
would perform. I thought that she had passed away without writing even
a portion of her war reminiscences. My sister, Mrs. Mary Sutton
Kinsworthy, who lives in Little Rock, Arkansas, some time after mother's
death found the paper which gives an account of a trip some Southern
women made in 1864 from Fayetteville, to Paris, Texas. This paper was
evidently written a short time before my mother's final illness. I greatly
regret that she did not live to describe other scenes which she witnessed,
and in some of which she was a participant, during the war between the
states, which tried not only the souls of men, but of women also.

University of Texas   W. S. Sutton
May 22, 1922

* * *

Nestled in the heart of the Ozarks, whose sides glowed with a wealth of
green in summer and sparkled with ice jewels in winter was the delightful
town of Fayetteville, Arkansas. It seemed securely sheltered from all possible foes. Though cut off from the busy marts of the world, undisturbed
by screech of railroad whistle or hum of factory wheel, she still was far
from idle. Picturesque scenery, fine climate, gushing springs, clear flowing streams, balmy breezes and a soil that yielded abundantly—these
were the inducements held out to the people of the older States. And
many responded by placing their families and their all into the ships of
the American plain—the prairie schooner—to find new homes under
fairer skies. The place grew steadily from a simple village in the forties to
a thriving town in the sixties.[2] Its people enjoyed a feeling of freedom
and contentment denied the strained life of the city. A few years sufficed
to make it quite a business and educational center. The number of
churches, colleges and nice homes indicated the refined, enterprising
classes of people attracted hither.

But time brought civil strife to the nation, and this unsuspecting
town with the adjacent country, became a common battle ground. Men

and lads were forced to take sides, and not infrequently families were divided. There was hot blood and bitter hate.

When the war cry resounded every yard stick was dropped on the counter; the plow left in the furrow, books piled on students' desks, and without regard to station in life, every man was expected to report for army service. The fortunes of war played fickle with this part of the territory—this special town being an object of dispute—sometimes held by one army; again, the other. But the close of the second year found it in the close grasp of the Federal forces. Yard-fences and garden-walls melted away as it were. The space they formerly enclosed was now occupied by soldiers' tents. In 1864, the fall campaign was over and the troops generally were going into winter quarters.[3]

The command at Fayetteville was already settling down to a long season of costly comfort and luxurious ease. The soldiers feasted and frolicked and sang their camp-fire songs. About this time, General Price of the Confederate Army, lovingly known among his men as "Old Pap Price," was on the march from Missouri to Texas.[4] With slight detour he could strike the town of Fayetteville. Colonel F's regiment was made up of soldier boys who were intensely fond of the girls they had left behind them, which girls were now forted up, and paying unwilling allegiance to the Stars and Stripes. An earnest appeal to General Price that this portion of the command be permitted to tap the Fort, and worry the garrison for a while, gained his consent. The Gray Coats were granted a few howitzers, some Enfields and a quantity of shot and shell. Off the bolted on double quick to surprise the napping Fort. They had no ambition to capture the place, as conditions made it impossible to hold it; but they so longed to catch glimpses of the sweet girl faces, get a few morsels of palatable food, snatch some articles of sorely needed clothing—then retire as surprisingly as they had dropped down.[5]

The early morning twilight was deepened by a dense fog, which concealed their approach until they were well upon the sentinels. As the bugle had not yet sounded, the Blue Coats were still wrapped in slumber. The Boys in Blue hastily threw on their uniforms, thrust sockless feet into their boots and with empty stomachs hastened to answer the call "to arms." By this time the hills were fairly teeming with Gray Coats, and they rained shot and shell into the inner lines of the enemies breastworks. Private dwellings were sometimes in range, and the inmates driven to cellar and basement. The bombardment was continued during the entire day, hence many citizens were pent up in these close, stuffy quarters during the entire time. When the conflict ceased, the women found their pantries and larders empty—even the churns and side-boards betraying proof that strange, hungry visitors had ventured in.[6]

The day, of course, was crowded with thrilling incidents, shading all the way from the most pathetic to the most ludicrous. Very early in the day it was discovered that the garrison was minus the commanding officer. Whereupon a subordinate, who bore his chief no love at any time, and whose love of drink was much stronger than his love of country, especially at the cannon's mouth, leaped upon a conspicuous part of the breast-works and screeched out: "Where is Colonel H?"[7] Echo answers, "Where?" These terse speeches found local fame and are still fresh in the minds of some who heard them on that long gone-by day.

A most amusing quarrel, (yet regrettable, as showing the debasing influences of war on woman), was heard by the teller of this story, between a Federal officer and a rebel woman of gentle birth and careful rearing, but who was now under the iron heel of fate, boarding Yankee officers for a livelihood. A few minutes after the cannonading opened she informed the first official of her household that there was no wood to get dinner with. (He always provided all things to run a first-class house.) He gruffly replied, and that in army terms; "In the name of G-d, Mrs. S., you must be crazy! Don't you hear those d-d rebel guns? I've no time to think of wood or dinner either!" In like voice and equally strong terms she retorted: "Yes, Major G., I hear them and thank the Lord for the music; and Major, maybe you'll not need any d-d dinner and, to be honest, I don't care a d-n whether you do or don't, so there!"

He got his dinner and supper at one and the same time—nine o'clock that night. And to his amazement, his landlady was in much sweeter temper towards him, for the Gray Jackets had sent a bomb crashing through her house that day, doing considerable damage; this she held against them as an unpardonable outrage.

One of the most touching incidents of the day was that of an old Black Mammy, a member of your story-teller's family. Mammy had again and again refused to listen to the appeals of Northern friends to leave her Southern Folks to go with them to the happy land of freedom. Early in the day she had gone with the family to the basement for safety, as the Enfields from the fort were being levelled towards the house, the balls now and then entering the windows and dropping upon the floor. She turned a large barrel sideways and crept into it, and remained there all day. Mammy not long afterwards, showed signs of mind failure, which grew worse and worse until she finally suicided by jumping into the well.

She insisted that schools for colored children would not be allowed by white folks, and if attempted the children would be waylaid and killed.

But Black Mammy still lives in the minds and hearts of those who knew her, and their mouths still water for her waffles, cake, pies, and turkey done to a brown.

The bombardment closed with the day, and strange to say there were few fatalities on either side.[8] The Gray Jackets had seen a happy realization of their dream—a sort of strategic feint worthy of veterans. They drew off as slyly as they had entered, leaving the Blue Coats greatly disconcerted, and filled with surmises as to how these Gray Foxes got into the Fort, and what would be their next audacious move.[9]

The smoke from the cannonading had scarcely lifted before the officers at the post began to cast up their losses and gains. They found they had held their own, though at the expense of considerable nerve tension and the agonizing dread of being bottled up, as at that time they had no knowledge of the near approach of General C. with a fresh force.[10]

Personal losses among the officers counted for much. These arch rebels had ventured over the dead line to get a feast for eye and appetite. On entering houses (usually of friends) after a hurried greeting, they put the question: "Have you Yankee officers stopping with you, if so where are their apartments?" A beck or nod would suffice to point the way, and they were usually rewarded by a rich find of good clothes, cigars, pistols, etc., for Federal officers revelled in citizens' dress when off duty, and enjoyed life to the full. To soothe their consciences these Boys in Gray sometimes left the most grotesque articles in lieu of those taken, arguing than an "even exchange was no robbery."

The attack on the Fort served to stir up fresh strife and suspicion grew stronger against the Southern sympathizers. There were blood signs on the moon—dark whisperings in the air—women convinced against their will were made responsible for the late mischief. Underground messages were received by these women that filled them with grave misgivings. They, too, began to hold what they called "councils of war." A few families would meet, bound by ties even stronger than blood, to recount the past, weigh the present and forecast the future. Some woman from the country would perhaps be the oracle of the occasion, coming, ostensibly to shop—in reality, to distribute the latest budget from the South-land.

Soon after the late surprise party, a council of this kind was held at the home of a representative family, a member of which had recently suffered because of a breach of loyalty. The meeting was on a night so dark,

the darkness could almost be felt—a night for witches to brew their broth
and ghosts to stalk abroad. To add to the gruesomeness of the night, rain
fell in weird chant upon roof and pane.

The little group comprised a mother, four children, a darling of a
little grandson and two visiting friends. All gathered close about the
smoldering fire, which struggled at times to a thin, blue flame, licking up
reluctantly between a few ill-shapen logs. It was the same generous fire-
place, however, whose blazing fires had sputtered and crackled and
sparkled and cheered so many hearts in days gone by when huge darky
Joe put on the regulation back-log at nightfall. But Joe's herculean arm
and the back-log, too, was missing; for Joe was rejoicing in his newly-
found freedom in stormy Kansas, and the back-logs had gone to feed the
fires of the Federal troops.

But the little party drew into a close knot and spoke in mysterious
whispers. The from out of town woman had things both tearful and amusing to tell. She related a thrilling episode of a maiden, who had recently
distinguished herself in a contest over a bag of coffee. A scouting party
from the Post had gone into the country, plundering and harassing the
people most unmercifully. At the home of Mrs. B. they emptied her
smoke-house and larder of their contents—a stalwart soldier seizing a last
and partly filled bag of coffee, when the daughter objected, saying: "I
have made no complaint at your taking the other things, but the coffee
my aged mother needs above all else, and I bid you leave that alone." The
soldier gave no heed to her demand, and had neared the door, sack in
hand, when the young lady seized a heavy iron poker and dealt him such a
blow upon the head that he instantly dropped to the floor. At length
regaining his feet he hurriedly left the house, leaving the coffee behind.

Soon the story of the heroic deed reached the ears of lovers and friends
of hers in far-away Dixie. The boys in Gray at once decided that such
incomparable bravery should not go unrewarded, and sent her a magnificent saddle-horse, with a glowing tribute to her matchless heroism.

The young lady still lives, under another name however, to tell her
story of the Blue Coat, the coffee, the poker and the saddle horse.

Another story related by the visitor was of a dear old lady whose piety
and precision had never been questioned, either by saint or sinner. Her
house was plundered, and when the looters had gone, leaving behind
them confusion worse confounded, her daughter began to pick up the
few remaining things, all the while choking with fury! Finally she burst
forth: "Confound the Yankees anyhow!" In drawling speech, and wholly

unconscious of its weight of meaning, the old mother chimed in: "Well I say so too, Sally!"

A pen portrait of the second visitor of the group, above mentioned, may be interesting, at least to the young reader, if not to the grown-up who has a weakness for consulting the Black Art. Not that the Fortune teller, Mrs. W., was a toothless old crone of the nomadic tribe, distilling from a pot of frogs, serpents, an bitter herbs a concoction whereby to drag up the hidden secrets of the past and reveal those of the future. She did not so much as consult kings and knaves, and attempt to divine the unknown through the medium of greasy paste-board. Her art lay in a simple "turning of the coffee cup." She was extremely fond of coffee any way and through this innocent method she afforded hours and hours of inexpressible pleasure to others, besides the individual solace she got from the coffee. The old lady, though connected with some of the most distinguished of American history, had enjoyed few educational advantages in youth; hence her English was extremely faulty, but this fact only lent novelty to the sport.

On one occasion a young lady in the country decided that she must consult Mrs. W. about her lover Zeke, who was then in the Trans-Mississippi department of the army. Mrs. W. was found and no time was lost to brew a fresh pot of coffee—coffee without pistols, for two, mind you! The coffee made, it must pass through that essential process of shaking to its very depths; after this a quick pouring into the cups, when a settling of the grounds to the bottom must follow. The coffee is then drunk. Next a second violent shaking of the grounds takes place, and the cup inverted in the saucer. Whereupon the old lady settles her spectacles upon her nose (the bows tied with a white cotton string). After a long and careful study of the figures on sides and bottom of the up, then—the fortune! All excitement the old lady exclaims: "Oh Miss Jinny, the Wah is a goin to end reel soon, an yore Zeky wil get thew without a scratch! You jest lookee heah! Don't ye see, thar's a big road and lots of men a foot and lots mo' ridin, an all of 'em a comin right this a-way. Heah's Zeeky sorty off to hisself. Oh, he's a comin home, an that mity soon, as shore as yore borned, and he will be ridin of a mule!"

"Zeeke" truly survived the war, and came home with heart and limbs all whole to Jenny, but minus the mule! He and Jenny were really wedded and a happier couple was never mated. The anecdote is still told by those familiar with it, though nearly forty-nine years have elapsed since the amusing incident occurred.

The old lady turned the cup again on the dreary night previously mentioned, and doleful sights were as plainly to be seen as A, B, C. The two visitors were of one mind—that trouble was ripening for Southern families and that they would sooner or later be "sent over the lines" if they did not go of their own accord—that a messenger should be dispatched at once to ascertain the prospects for new homes in the far South, and arrange for an early exodus.

But who could, or who would, or who should, go became the hard question. Some were too old to attempt so hazardous a journey, others too young. At last one who had become painfully inured to the hardships of the war and its bitter experiences, one who was possessed of more courage than caution, finally said she would willingly go if it were not for the darling little four-year old.[11] That his baby years had already seen quite enough of cruel adventure and hair-breadth escape, the little fellow having been in the midst of another battle, when some soldiers were shot dead from his mother's porch, while others sought safety in the attic from the volleys of musketry turned toward the house. But the Grandmother interrupted her, declaring that she and his Aunties would be his willing slaves until her return. The little mother swallowed the awful lump in her throat and said: "Well, then, I will go and spy out the land." But none will ever know what heartache it cost that mother to imprint the parting kiss on his little mouth, and press him to her heart for the last time; for of all the children round about he was the sweetest, the most beautiful—the idol of the household, the joy of the neighborhood, the admiration of strangers, with his dark curls reaching almost to his shoulders, his dark expressive eyes, his merry chatter and ringing laugh, filling the house with life and cheer while his manners were so charming, his little speeches so bright as to provoke suspicion of his having been coached by his elders. Sometimes in the presence of officers stopping at the home the little fellow would relate dreams he had had about war happenings, and perhaps something would occur soon to create suspicion concerning the little boy's dreams. His dress suits were of Confederate gray cloth of which he was intensely proud. For general wear he had butter-nut jeans— the uniform of the famous skirmisher Buck Brown and his men. When Buck Brown was killed, little Willie sat at the table as silent as the grave, while the matter was discussed by the officers and family. When the officers had retired, he cleverly spoke up: "Gan-mudder, I mustn't wear my butter-nuts now—Buck Brown is dead!"[12]

About this time three stranger ladies arrived at the Fort, enroute South in search of Confederate friends, and glad to join any parties thither-bound. The eldest of these was [a] woman perhaps sixty years of age. The first syllable of her name being in perfect harmony with her fiery nature, while the second was close kin to "ball," so it was decided no violence to her or our conscience to corrupt it to "Fireball." The second of the three was a woman with two small children, one three years old, the other eighteen months. The third of these women was a young lady that had already achieved fame by her deeds of valor and wonderful skill in the conduct and management of the affairs of her home and the community. Her Christian name being India, she was soon dubbed the gem of the whole party. At the last hour came another woman with an eight-year old son, pleading to be joined to the little caravan. So there were eight souls, including the teller of this story, starting upon a mission almost as novel and as faithtesting as was that of Noah, when he launched the Ark freighted with its eight human souls and all that was to be preserved of earth.

Friends looked on amazed, even awe-stricken, at the idea of such a perilous undertaking. But those stout hearted women went ahead perfecting their plans as best they could under frowning circumstances. It was a most difficult matter to get anything like valuable vehicles and teams through the military lines at that time; so there was but one conveyance, with an ill matched team of two horses, to accommodate this party of eight. Vehicle did I call it? Well, if its kind should be reproduced today on the principal street of any modern city, very soon the civic authorities would object. For each revolution of the wheels was followed by such dolorous screeches as would affect the nerves of the stoutest. It was hard for the most considerate to suppress a "ha, ha," at the grotesqueness of this turn-out. Three of the party were horse back, Mrs. Yett had the royal honor of being mounted upon the prize steed awarded Miss B. for rescuing the bag of coffee from the Yankee soldier previously described. The other two rode condemned cavalry horses.

The day of starting at last came. On the 18th of November 1864, the sun rose bright and promising, but by ten o'clock, (the hour appointed for leaving), the wind was blowing a perfect gale. The little band had arranged to cross the country to the next Fort, a distance of fifty or more miles, with the mail-party of the Post.[13] This they did for protection, as the mail-party always went heavily guarded; for at this time the mountains were full of bush-whackers and "mountain-boomers," names well-nigh obsolete to-day, much to the credit of present day civilization.

At this point, the party of women confidently expected to join a flag of truce that had been sent in from Doaksville, Ind. Ter. to escort families

out of Federal lines. This hope bouyed them for a most trying and hazardous trip over the mountains, which meant an all night ride, the darkness disturbed now and then by a few straggling moonbeams, with
strangers for escorts, and men mounted on white horses for way marks!
The distance, however, was covered without serious casualty, this to be
said in special praise of the mail-party. The Fort safely reached, those
women for a brief time were ecstatic. They breakfasted with loving friends,
and hurried away to headquarters to get the necessary information,
regarding the flag of truce, when lo! to their utter dismay and undoing
they found that the truce party had passed out several hours before.

The authorities assured them that by a little extra exertion they could
overtake the company. Passes were granted, and that, too, without the
rigid process of individual search for contraband—a custom that had
afforded no little amusement, as well as spoil, to the searchers in the past.

So much for the false estimates placed upon exteriors at times. One
of this party had a thousand dollars in gold—the remaining members had
from one hundred to five hundred dollars on their persons. By ten
o'clock they were ready to move. The post commander granted them a
guard beyond the danger line.[14] They were put upon the highway, taken
by the truce party and assured that it would be but a short time before
they could join it, if they traveled briskly.[15]

Luncheon had been provided for one day only. This the little people,
having nothing else to occupy them, helped themselves to every hour in
the day. All day long the company kept up the steady march, vainly
hoping and expecting that each turn in the road would bring the flag to
view. The barefoot prints of the children, and even of the dogs, were so
fresh and distinct it seemed truly absurd that they could not come up
with it. Another great astonishment and hardship to the travelers was the
utterly deserted condition of the country. Not a single roadside house
had an occupant; consequently these women did not see another human
face during the entire day. At night fall weary and somewhat discour-
aged, they took up quarters in a wayside cabin.[16] A division of chores was
soon agreed upon. Some were to gather fuel and keep fires, not to cook
with, for alas! they had nothing to cook, nor anything to cook in if they
had. Others were to care for the horses. The writer had some excellent
"Lincoln coffee" in her carpet bag, but sans a vessel to make it in, it was
useless.[17] Evidently the people that had lived in the houses on this thor-
oughfare did not subsist out of paper-sacks and tin-cans as do the civilized of the present day. Not one vestige of the kind could be found. The
company suppered on the scraps that the little folks had munched on

during the day, parched some corn that had been put into the go-cart for the horses, converted saddle-blankets, shawls and other wraps into pallets on the puncheon floor, with saddles and sachels for pillows, and all cuddled down to lose their senses of weariness and worry, if possible, in a few winks of sleep. And right here we would echo the sentiment of Sancho Panza who invoked blessings on the man that first invented sleep—that treasure which covers one all over so like a blanket!

The fire committee had provided an abundance of fuel in order to keep a blazing fire all night. Hardly were we settled to our new and strange conditions, before equally strange noises were heard in the distance. At first there was great rejoicing, the noises being mistaken for domestic sounds from some farmhouse not far away, but alas! it was the howling of wolves, seemingly making a bee-line for the company's quarters. So two of the party, urged by the traditional theory that wolves were easily terrified by fire, arose and went out to explore the premises, hoping to find some out-building that they might set on fire. Much to their delight they soon found one, and in a few minutes the flames were crackling and leaping sky ward. But a high wind was blowing and the wonder continues to this day that the lodgings as well were not burned. But fortune favored—the wolves changed their minds, and the wind its course,—these women were still safe and more impressed than ever that God was yet in His heavens and that they were creatures of His overruling providence. With the earliest dawn of the morning the party were all up and with a few simple preparations, again upon the road, feeling very sanguine they should overtake the flag that day, perhaps by ten o'clock, at least by noon. How they tried to hasten, but the horses were much jaded and like ourselves beginning to feel keenly the want of food.

Noon-time drew on and our hope was still deferred. We were forced to stop and graze the horses upon the dry grass. Besides we had lost our bearings and were in much perplexity as to whither we were traveling. Of one thing only were we sure—that we were still in the United States, as we hadn't crossed the oceans either side, nor yet the Rio Grande River on the South, or the Great Lakes on the North. All else was speculation of the crudest kind. Some suggested we turn back, but Mrs. Fireball said, "Nay," that we could not possibly make the return trip without risking our lives—the wiser part would be to push on—relief would certainly come soon. On we went and the day dragged drearily away bringing no better or brighter prospects than the one before. The fagged condition of the horses necessitated our stopping before night, but there was no food to be had for woman or beast, nothing but pure refreshing water of which the women freely drank, and dry grass for the horses.[18] The most heart-touching thing of all was to hear the little children's cry for bread when there wasn't anything except a few grains of parched corn to give them. The younger one was a very delicate child and the anxious mother was fearful it would die before help could be reached. She remarked that in the event it did die, there was no alternative but to carry its little body on, as we had nothing with which to make a coffin or dig a grave. These leaden words fell heavily into the hearts of all while tears flowed freely.

The second night was a barren repetition of the first, except the threatened invasion of the wolves and the house burning. Literally overcome by weariness and hunger we took more sleep. The first streaks of daylight, however, found us again upon the highway. The horse back riders walked much of the time fearing their horses might fail entirely. Cattle now began to appear on the prairies, some of them quite gentle. This afforded some little encouragement that their owners could not be far away. Still there were no signs of life in the roadside houses. The cattle, especially the calves were real fat and one of the company remarked that it was a burning shame that we should starve to death with choice food at hand. Finally the brave India spoke up: "Well, I know how to kill a beef and dress it too; for I have had some very practical training along that line right recently. I have had to kill the beeves for the neighborhood at home, but then I had a gun to shoot with and a sharp knife to dress with. There isn't a thing of the kind in all this crowd that would serve the purpose, unless I could kill it with this pocket knife, given me as a memento by a Federal officer as we came over the Boston Mountains on the first night out." Your story-teller replied that she too had a knife almost as good, and possibly between them they might do some execution. Of course, these things were first talked of in jest, without thinking of undertaking a task so unreasonable. But as the day wore on with no promise of help the suggestion became more and more serious. At last the horseback riders formulated a plan and summoned all their courage to submit it to "Mrs. Fireball," whom they had constituted commander-in-chief, referee, etc. The plan proposed was to camp earlier than usual, selecting a place near a slaughter-pen. There were many of these prepared, as we afterward learned, by Gen. Price's command which had passed that way only a few weeks before.[19] It was submitted only to meet with the keenest ridicule. However, she finally wound up by stating that she had already decided to stop early and give the horses a longer time to rest and graze before being tied up for the night. She still insisted that the projectors of the slaughter-scheme should "mother" it, as she would wash her hands of anything so perfectly absurd. Whereupon they cheerfully, yea, gladly, excused her from lending so much as her presence.

Shortly after this conference, the old lady who always led the van, pulled the rein before a rather comfortable-looking cabin.[20] This cabin was situated on a beautiful hill which easily sloped down to a large spring, gurgling from its foot, its waters meandering away in a silvery, purling brook. Just beyond this brook was an excellent slaughter-pen with a smaller one inclosed [sic] within it. The first, and an important, step was to select from the herd of cattle feeding close by, an old family cow with a calf or two—cut them out from the main herd and by some device tole [enticed] them into the pen. Your story-teller had a small quantity of salt which she had provided for her horse. It was brought forth and served the purpose. In a little while they had a mother cow and twin bossies in the toils. But it proved a more strategic matter to get one in the smaller pen. Success finally crowned their efforts, after which they turned the mother and the other calf outside, driving them out of sight and sound. We then tied bossy's head close up to the fence that it might not have room to jump about. India volunteered to cut its throat with her pocket knife, but some one must hold its rear leg on the side she stabbed from. The leg was soon secured with a rope, and the writer appointed to the mission of holding it. When all was in readiness, India gave the signal,—"one, two, three,"—and plunged the cruel knife into the little innocent's throat. No sooner done than the creature began to rear and struggle like mad. The woman at the rope put all her reserve force into the effort, when lo! the little one slipped the leash with as much ease as Sampson broke the cords. And the woman, oh where was she! Such a fall! She tumbled all in a heap among some sharp-edged rails, but there was no time to think of bruises, whether slight or serious. Another device was brought out, and a more successful [one]—this time both rear legs were to be fastened to the fence and two knives brought into play. It was not the work of two or three minutes by any means. The little victim made a bold defense for its life. At last the poor thing lay quivering on the ground.

By this time the evening shadows had deepened until every stump and bush was a spectre, and each rustle of leaf or noise from insect was freighted with dread. Graveyards are always lonely places and gruesome. We are filled with awe and solemnity, even in the broad light of day when walking through these silent cities.

Only a short distance from the spring mentioned, was a number of newly-made graves. Price's poor soldiers (some of them) had succumbed to hunger and exposure and fallen out by the way.[21] There they lay, their fresh mounds their only monument. No language is sufficient to describe the weirdness and awful depression of that sad scene!

Soldier-like, these women could not wait until life was entirely extinct, before entering upon the next disagreeable task, viz., the dressing of the beef. They had neither candle nor lamp to aid them, but just as they began their revolting work, the great round full-orbed moon (it never seemed so large before) rose, and as there was neither cloud nor tree to obstruct, she shone down upon them in regal splendor. Soon the disagreeable task was ended and with supreme satisfaction they hurried to the house to convince "Captain Fireball" that they could kill a beef, possibly a bear, without her assistance or advice. The old grumbler drew down the corners of her mouth into a smile of doubtful approval and looked a volume of astonishment. At once she recovered herself and was ready with advice as to what and how, to do with the meat. But India was regarded as authority in such matters, as she was well posted upon beef either on foot or on gridiron, so she was requested to give instructions as to how it should be prepared. She suggested that the steaks be cured over a hot fire by placing the meat on poles and holding it over the blaze. This was called jerking, she said. The liver she suggested would be very palatable if covered up without embers and coals, and thoroughly roasted like potatoes. Salt was called for, but lack-a-day! the little supply of salt had been exhausted in deluding the mother cow into the pen! So we had unsalted meat, without bread or coffee; for still no tin cans had been found in which to make that "Lincoln coffee."

Still they made the most of the blessings they had, and with spirits revived and hope rekindled they set out the next morning for a most eventful day. Just before starting, some one spied horsemen in the distance. The writer was requested to mount the prize horse and run them down. Obedient to the request she started at a lively gait, but the riders went like the wind, and were soon out of sight. Later it developed that they were Indians and few there be that can outstrip an Indian rider. When she returned to camp with the report of a failure, it was then proposed that India and she start out again leaving the main road, to see if they could not find a house or settlement that had not been deserted. Sure enough after a reconnoiter of several miles smoke was seen curling upward. Braced with fresh belief that help was at hand, they hastened on and soon came to a small hut; but to their dismay a full-blood Indian sat on the outside making moccasins! He looked a very wild Indian with tomahawk, bow and arrows, head-rig made of feathers, etc. The women were greatly frightened, still their urgent purpose made stout their hearts and they boldly attempted a conversation; but he only glanced up with a look of savage contempt for pale faces, remained doggedly silent, and resumed his work. In despair they hurried back to camp. The luckless story related, the whole party began to have grave suspicions that they had straggled into the Indian Territory, among an unfriendly tribe at that.[22] A few moments sufficed to put the caravan on the road again. They pushed up as fast as their ill conditions would permit, filled with an awful dread as to what might be their next experience. At noon they found they must stop on account of the horses.

In a short time a man was discovered coming towards the company. "Captain Fireball" issued the order that they all stay together—that there be no straggling. Perhaps she preferred a wholesale massacre if there were to be one at all. Maybe she thought to intimidate the stranger by presenting a bold front. As he approached he gradually slackened his pace. He rode a very fine mule, was equipped with tomahawk and flint lock, which of course betrayed his race. Nearer and nearer he drew to the wagon until our very hair stood on end—all were white as ghosts! Still he did not speak a word. "Captain Fireball" and the mother of the wee bairns [children] tried in vain to draw him out. They showed him the little hungry children—counted on their fingers the number of days they had been without food—told him the children must surely die if food was not gotten very soon.

Just as the man came up, India's horse died. She removed the saddle and told the Indian he might have it. However, she first offered to buy his mule, but he shook his head to indicate "No" for his answer. "Captain Fireball" added still more to the sum offered and made him a second proposition, but "No" was his sign. Mrs. Yeater then offered him two hundred dollars in gold, he still shook his head and coupled with it a grunt that signified an emphatic "No." India, on second thought, decided it would be unwise to give away her saddle as she might meet with an opportunity to buy another horse, so she put the saddle and other equipment into the wagon. After staying some time, the Indian started off across the prairie. At once we began a council as to what was the next best thing to do, when to our horror we saw the Indian rein his mule suddenly about and come flying at full speed to the wagon. All were sure their time had now come, and were silently offering up what we supposed was our last prayer to God! The Indian ventured close up and began to talk in extremely broken English—a word sometimes standing for an entire sentence. He pointed across the prairie and said: "Live six miles," pointing to us, "you Bush Creek, camp." Then pointing to himself and then across the prairie, "Go, corn bread." Pointing to the babies: "Pappooses starve." Pointing to himself: "Come, Bush Creek."[23] With this broken speech he galloped off at full speed. Having no faith in his promises, we lost no time in getting away, determined if possible to put many a mile between him and us. We construed his plan to mean he would bring a band of Indians and we hardly dared surmise the rest. We had traveled about two hours, as nearly in the opposite direction for that indicated by the Indian as we could, when we met another man, who to our overwhelming delight was a white man and could speak excellent English. Oh! it was a joy inexpressible to find some one once more who could speak the Mother Tongue! "Captain Fireball" questioned him as to our whereabouts on this lower world, and he replied by asking us where we started from and where bound, and we answered by stating that we had started from Fayetteville, Arkansas to Washington, Arkansas, when he wittily said: "Well, my friends, I must say you have taken a devil of a circuitous route for it." (He was a soldier.)[24] He said that Doaksville was the nearest point for us, which was not a great distance from Red River, in the Choctaw Nation—that at Doaksville we could find friends and get help—that it was headquarters for the Confederate commissaries in that part of the country and a part of the army was in winter-quarters not far away.[25] We confided our various experiences to him while he laughed and sighed by turns. We told him of our episode with the Indian that day and how we were living in mortal dread of his return with a band of tomahawkers, at least to take our horses and leave us helpless to perish. The man was much amused at our story more especially when we told him that we had revealed the fact to the Indian that we were Southern women in search of soldier friends and relatives of the Southern army. He said we need borrow no fear of being molested by that man, that the Indian was a Choctaw and that his tribe to the last man were Southern. [A page of typescript is missing at this point. When the next page begins, the party has traveled an undefined distance and has stopped at the cabin of a Negro woman.] race, never having felt the pangs of real hunger, or been pressed with extreme want of any kind. But the writer will say right here that a whiter soul never existed than was found under this black skin. The haste with which we dismounted, unsaddled, ungeared, and made our way into Mammy's quarters would have reflected credit on the double-quick movements of any body of soldiers!

Her little hut contained only one little room about twelve feet square with puncheon floor and cracks large enough to drop the babies shoes through. In this room were an old-time loom, a reel fastened to the wall, a rude bedstead also fastened to the wall, a broken chair and two or three stools, a few cooking utensils and some large flat gourds full of—good-ness only knows what! Picture, if you can, the putting in of eight other persons, with all their belongings, and making provision for them to sleep within the crowded space of that one room. The dear old Mammy began to busy herself about some supper. The storyteller brought out that "Lin-coln coffee" which had so long lain useless in the bottom of her sachel, and had Mammy make some. She fried some delicious venison and made some genuine Indian cornbread, the meal having been beaten in a mortar. Never, never, in all our days had food meant so much to us! Still we suffered much uneasiness, fearing we should over-eat and fall sick in that desolate land. However, the supply was not abundant, which was doubtless in our favor. The supper over we began vigorous preparations to get some sound sleep—a thing we had had little of since leaving home. We were compelled to use our saddle-blankets, shawls, etc., as Mammy's supply of bedding was very scant. But the crucial moment came for the cuddling down—it was a sure case of "first come first served," as it was soon discovered that there was not room for all on the pallets; so Mammy, (noble soul), offered her bed, saying she must go in Massa's house and patch and darn until mighty late. When she came back, sure enough she found Mrs. Yell on her bed, she having lain down on top of the cover with her riding skirt drawn over her. Mammy said: "Law, honey, why didn't ye git unda the kiver? I knows ye haint ben comfable!" Before going to bed we had attempted to bar the door securely, (there was no such thing as a lock). We stood in dread of intruders during the night. Sure enough near two o'clock horses hoofs were heard and mum-bling voices. A few moments later a pounding on the door and an effort to push it open. Instantly we rose to our feet and some of us rushed to the fireplace to make a light. Black Mammy had just fallen asleep when this tumult came up, but she bounced up and answered the call. She went out closing the door behind her and held a long confab with the visitors. Finally returning, she reported that there was an Indian man outside who had met a party of women and children on the prairies that afternoon and that the little ones were about to die of starvation, having nothing whatever to eat—that he lived some six miles away from where he met them—that he told them where to camp and that he would go home and get bread and corn and come to them. He said he had no meal ready for cooking when he got home; so he had to pound the meal, and his daugh-ter to bake the bread. He had come back to the place he had directed them to with some bread, and corn for the horses. Failing to find them there he had started in search of them when he met a man that had seen them after he had, that the man had told him about where he might find them. He expressed great sympathy for the poor hungry children. However, he wished as a reward for his trouble, the saddle offered him the day before by the young lady. India brought it forth and cheerfully gave it to him.

Next morning Black Mammy made another delicious cup of coffee and gave us some more venison, gravy and corn-bread. Just as we were on the eve of starting, Mammy was standing around talking and eating her breakfast from a tin plate, when your storyteller stepped up and said to her: "I don't know, Mammy, when I shall ever have another opportunity to eat, so I take the liberty of taking a few more mouthfuls with you." She replied: "Yes, honey, gist hep yosef to all ye want," and the dear old soul (heaven rest her in peace if she has passed over) would have had me take it all, her heart was so big with sympathy.

Again we started upon a long hard day's travel, mostly on foot, or in the rumbling old wagon, which brought us to another Indian cabin where we found somewhat better fare, as we had plenty of room and a blazing fire. The Indians could furnish us nothing to eat, so we had to supper and breakfast on the jerked beef we had saved and the corn cakes the Indian had ridden eighteen miles to bring. We awoke next morning to find it very cloudy and the wind blowing furiously; a gentle shower of rain had fallen and we feared worse conditions were in store.

About ten o'clock the wagon, which had held together astonishingly, broke down. This meant a dreadful predicament as there was no possible means of repairing it. There we were, stranded on the roadside, not knowing how far it was to a repair-shop. Again the mounted members were sent on ahead to get help if possible. After a ride of perhaps five miles, we came to the very delightful home of the Choctaw Chief.[26] The Chief himself spoke very little and very broken English, but to our surprise and joy we found his wife to be a most cultured New England lady, who had some years before come out to the Nation as a missionary. After she had taught a few years, the Chief's wife died and in time he married the missionary.[27]

Quite a village had sprung up around him as he owned vast estates and numbers of slaves. We first saw and talked with some of the men in one of the shops, and told them our errand. One of the men went at once to the Chief and spoke to him of the matter. The Chief was not long in getting up an interest in the unfortunate people and sent a man to bring them, with the request that the entire party come to his house. We messengers went up at once and when we had related our forlorn story, he had a hack sent immediately for those who were staying by the stuff. His charming wife was much moved when we told of our narrow escape from starvation, and burst into tears when she heard that there were three children in the party, two of them very small. She expressed the tenderest sympathy and begged we should all make ourselves comfortable and have dinner with her that day. It took little persuasion for we had been so long without table-comforts so long since we had tasted really palatable food, that we were almost wild at the prospects.

After admiring the house and its unique appointments, we strolled out into the spacious yard and garden. The yard was a large old-fashioned one, full of forest trees, flowering shrubs, and old-time flowers. Here and there were still to be found autumnal flowers meekly blooming among the grass. The rear position of the yard had been converted into a cemetery. The Chief's first wife and several children by her, together with six babes by the last wife, slept here side by side. Beautiful white marble slabs and shafts told their short sad story, while the myrtle and ivy rambled in rank profusion over the graves and gracefully twined about the shafts. The weird impressiveness of the scene may be better imagined than described in words.[28] Soon dinner was announced. The rich Chief had felt nothing of the ravages of the war, hence his table fairly groaned with good things. His slaves knew nothing whatever of the prospects of early freedom, [and] there were servants to attend our slightest want. How we regretted to part from our lovely new-found friends! But the hospitable hostess and the overseer who also spoke fluent English, had given most careful directions as to the remainder of the journey to Doaksville—our first objective point.

Just as night came on we reached the village—some riding, others walking, a few in the wagon. Imagine our joy on arriving to find some old-time friends who were in a position to render us needed assistance! We were comfortably quartered at the village tavern, [and] except for the crowd, we had to sleep three and four in a bed. Here we stopped for two days enjoying solid comfort and rest, and eating three square meals per day.

Having rallied from our awful strain, the party divided—a portion making for that division of the army in winter-quarters at Washington, Arkansas. The rest including the writer for Northern Texas, where we had many friends and relatives.

Captain Rector of the Confederate army most kindly escorted us to Paris, Texas, in a splendid turn-out.[29] Arriving in the beautiful town, we were not long in locating some relatives, who judging from the luxurious manner of their living, were totally oblivious of the war, knew nothing indeed of what war meant. The women, and the men, too, for that matter, lived lives of perfect ease and indolence, with little concern about anything, except eating and drinking and making merry. Nor was it a difficult matter for us to fall in with this happy-go-lucky sort of life. How to kill time was the all absorbing question. There was plenty of slaves, as the Thirteenth Amendment was not yet effective in those parts.[30] So the white women had absolutely nothing to do but "chop time," and your storyteller did her part of it most effectively.

27 The Impact of the Civil War on a Southern Marriage: Clement and Virginia Tunstall Clay of Alabama

Carol K. Bleser and Frederick M. Heath

*A*LTHOUGH THE Southern belle is frequently depicted in popular novels of the Old South, she is harder to find in the actual historical records. Nevertheless, authentic belles did exist in the nineteenth-century South, and they were sought after by men, both young and old, who expected them to be pretty, unmarried, affluent, charming, fashionable, and flirtatious. In addition, the classic Southern belle was expected to have rudimentary skills at a musical instrument, the French language, and the art of flattering conversation. Playing this dependent and ornamental role not only trained women to manipulate men, important in a patriarchal society, but also had immediate practical compensations because an accomplished player could hope to marry a man of wealth and social position. While the goal for a belle was to marry for love, marry they did in any case, for, rightly or wrongly, they believed that marriage would provide them with social rank, material benefits, freedom, and companionship, and thus was far more desirable than remaining single.

Once married, the belle usually disappeared from the social scene. The burdens of bearing children in rapid succession, of caring for a husband, and of managing a household left them little time to amuse either themselves or others. As Scarlet O'Hara put it, "Married women never have any fun." A few married women, however, never stopped behaving as if they were still belles. They continued to flirt, to pose at the center of groups of competing males, and to spark the devotion of prestigious men. These wives, including the famous diarist Mary Boykin Chesnut, were often free from the responsibilities that occupied most married women. Having no children and usually no home of her own to manage, Chesnut collected admirers in order to escape from boredom and to wield influence over the men around her, many of whom she considered inferior to herself.[1]

Similar on the surface in many ways to Mary Boykin Chesnut was Virginia Tunstall Clay. Both women dazzled men. Virginia's 1843 marriage to Clement Claiborne Clay united her with a husband whose political prominence gave her opportunities to seek attention from men of importance. Their childlessness and his failure to provide her with a home of her own freed Virginia from the responsibilities borne by most wives. Virginia Clay, ambitious, self-centered, energetic, attractive, and sociable, attempted for over twenty years to be a married belle, a role through which she enjoyed some of the delights of her single days and achieved both recognition and influence. The Civil War, however, which altered so many lives in so many ways, brought changes which enabled Virginia to apply her talents to purposes other than merely pleasing men.

Virginia Tunstall was born on January 16, 1825, in Nash County, North Carolina. Her mother, Ann Arrington Tunstall, died before Virginia was one year old, and her father left his daughter to be raised by relatives, of which there were more than enough. Her mother had twenty half-brothers and half-sisters.[2] Sometime before she turned eight, Virginia went to live with her aunt and uncle, Mary Ann and Henry Collier, in Tuscaloosa, Alabama. There she grew up, living at times with the Colliers and at other times with her mother's half-brother, Alfred Battle, and his wife, Millicent, both families being members of Tuscaloosa's elite. Collier became a state judge in 1828, a member of the state supreme court in 1836, and its chief justice the following year. Alfred Battle, a merchant, was one of the town's wealthiest citizens. Both uncles owned sizable homes in town, plantations, and large numbers of slaves.[3] Her aunts and uncles took good care of Virginia, but she was always somewhat of a guest in their homes and, of necessity, learned the importance of being adaptable and congenial—traits that later served her well. Her father, Dr. Payton Randolph Tunstall, seldom visited her. Little is known of him except that he apparently mismanaged his personal finances.[4] Nevertheless, her other relatives had money and social position so that Virginia could aspire to be a belle. She attended the Female Academy in Nashville, Tennessee where young women of her class studied arithmetic, composition, and geography and learned to play musical instruments, to draw, and to do needlework in the school's "Ornamental Department." Virginia, although only fourteen when she graduated from the academy in 1840, was already receiving a great deal of attention from male admirers.[5]

Her father, on one of his rare appearances, took her to Mobile, where he escorted her to a play and a ball, bought her a peach silk dress, and introduced her to Octavia Le Vert, whom Virginia and others would remember as one of America's most sophisticated women and famous belles. Virginia wrote in her memoir that in "those few charmed days, I saw, if not clearly at least prophetically, what . . . beauty and joy life might hold for me."[6]

In December 1842, Virginia, staying with the Colliers in Tuscaloosa, then the state capital, attended a round of parties marking the opening of the legislative session. At these gatherings she often saw Clement Claiborne Clay, a new member of the Alabama legislature and an old family friend. Clay, then twenty-six years old, was the son of Clement Comer Clay, one of the most prominent men in the state. Clement Comer had moved in 1811 from Tennessee to Huntsville, Alabama, which was the center of a fertile region in the bend of the Tennessee River, ideal for growing cotton, and which would be home to Clay and his sons for the rest of their lives. Within a month of Alabama's statehood in December 1819, Clement Comer, only thirty years old and a planter-lawyer, became the first chief justice of the state supreme court. He also served three terms in the national House of Representatives from 1829 to 1835, was governor from 1835 to 1837, and was a United States senator from 1837 to 1841. In that year, he resigned from the Senate to return to Alabama to look after his personal fortune. Clay owned two plantations which included over 2,700 acres and at least seventy-one slaves, and he had a law practice and a fine home in Huntsville. Part of his financial success came through his marriage in 1815 at the age of twenty-five to sixteen-year-old Susanna Claiborne Withers, the daughter of John Withers, a prosperous planter. Clement Comer and Susanna had three children, Clement Claiborne, John Withers, and Hugh Lawson. Both parents expected a great deal of their sons, especially of their eldest son, Clement, born December 13, 1816.[7]

In January 1833, when Clement Claiborne Clay was sixteen years old, he entered the University of Alabama, graduating a year and a half later. While still an undergraduate, young Clay decided that he wanted to study mathematics at Harvard. His father insisted that he study law at the University of Virginia. After father and son visited Charlottesville, the son described the dormitories as "uncomfortable & unhealthy" and the students as "wild" and "harum-scarum." Clement became ill, law school was postponed, and he served as secretary to his father when the latter was the governor of Alabama. After two years as his father's aide, Clay acceded to his parent's wishes and entered the University of Virginia, earning a law degree in 1839, while his father was in the United States Senate. Returning to Huntsville, he worked as a junior partner in his father's law firm, helped manage the family's plantations, and wrote editorials for a newspaper controlled by his father. After the elder Clay's return from Washington in 1841, apparently dissatisfied with his son's management of the family properties, the younger Clay was elected to the Alabama legislature in the fall of 1842, but this did not result in his escaping from paternal domination. Soon after he arrived at the state capital, his father followed him to Tuscaloosa and moved into an adjoining room.[8]

By the time of his father's arrival, Clement and Virginia were already in love. He sent her candy, books, and romantic verses. Clay admitted to being "a *small* poet," but he claimed to be a "great lover." By the end of December, Clement had convinced Virginia to marry him.[9] She had found his appearance "striking and pleasing," and his features "classic in their beauty." Their courtship lasted less than two months, a briefer time than most couples took to arrive at such a binding decision. Virginia was eighteen years old when she wed Clement.[10] Although she had many beaus and was not likely to become a spinster, she was eager to marry Clement for she loved him, had no permanent home, and was tired of being passed from relative to relative. Moreover, he was an excellent prospect for any ambitious belle.

At twenty-six, Clement had reached the average age of marriage for men of his class.[11] He wrote his father that he had fallen in love with "a lady of as tender a heart, as sensible a head, and as noble a spirit, as any one I ever knew." Nor did he overlook that Virginia owned "enough property to support her[self] comfortably," and numbered among her relatives "some of the most wealthy & respectable persons of this place." Moreover, Clement thought he "ought to get married," for a wife would make him "a better man and a more useful citizen." "I want," he wrote, "some anchor to give me greater stability of character. I want some incentive to an exercise of economy in my time & money. . . . I want, in brief, something more to live for—some constant & abiding sense of responsibility in the world." Even though by the 1840s it was no longer necessary for a son to request formal permission of his parents before becoming engaged, Clement Clay, still dependent on his family financially and emotionally, asked for their approval. There was no family opposition.[12]

The wedding took place in Tuscaloosa on February 1, 1843, at the spacious, columned home of Judge Collier. The realities of timing, social acceptability, and material prospects—as well as romantic love—lay behind the courtship and the marriage which had followed it so quickly. Clement and Virginia had known each other for some time. Governor Clay had appointed Virginia's uncle, Henry Collier, to the state supreme court when Clement had been his father's secretary. Moreover, a marriage between Clay's son and Collier's niece might advance the political fortunes of both families. Virginia and Clement anticipated a bright future.[13]

Clay, as noted, had been confident that marriage would make him a happier and more responsible person. During the early years of their union, he filled his letters to Virginia with lengthy declarations of what she and their relationship had done for him. Clement, like most nineteenth-century men, believed that the presence of a woman in his life would soften the harsher aspects of his male behavior. When he thought of his wife, Clement claimed, "I forgive my enemies, I am sensitive as a child to acts of kindness, & compassionate as a woman toward the unfortunate, & grateful as such a sinner can be for the protection & care of Providence." He even admitted his dependence on his wife who "has almost supreme power over me & leads me about, whither she will, by the silken cord of love."[14]

Nevertheless, before their marriage Clement had revealed to his mother that he knew "one objection to herself—it is that she is a belle!" Also, in a letter to Virginia written two weeks before their marriage, Clay told her, "You love admiration quite to a sin & sometimes pay much too dearly for it." Marriage and maturity, Clement hoped, would cure her of her need to play the belle. That was not to be the case. Afterwards, Clement began to worry that Virginia's refusal to abandon the role of a belle might hurt his reputation. "You are so pretty & fascinating," he told her, "that I fear some fine looking fellow will forget you are a married woman & make love to you. Beware of the follies of yr. sex. I know you love me too much to say or do willingly anything improper or unbecoming my wife; but yr. haste and vivacity may betray you into seeming errors." She must not forget that "yr. future is made—you are not beau-catching."[15]

Two weeks after their marriage Clement took Virginia to Huntsville to live with his parents. Few of Virginia's letters of the early years of their marriage are extant, but it is clear that life under the eyes of the elder Clays could not have been very pleasant or satisfying for Virginia. Her mother-in-law, Susanna Clay, was demanding, overly sensitive, and critical of others, especially of her daughter-in-law whom she considered a social butterfly. Virginia had little to occupy her time except paying and receiving calls, doing needlework, gardening, practicing the piano, and seeking out whatever entertainment Huntsville could offer a wife with time on her hands. She did accompany Clement to Tuscaloosa in 1844 while he attended the legislative session. "The winter promises to be very gay," Virginia wrote enthusiastically to her mother-in-law. "[T]o be in the parlour you might imagine me Miss T. again!!"[16]

The Clays remained childless. Most of their contemporaries thought that wives without children were incomplete. Mary Boykin Chesnut referred to herself as "a childless wretch" and noted that "South Carolina as a rule does not think it necessary for women to have any existence outside of their pantries or nurseries. If they have not children, let them nurse the walls." Clement may have feared that in the eyes of the world their lack of children might seem to reflect a conspicuous flaw in his manhood. Nevertheless, he tried to cheer his wife when comments about their not having children undermined her normally good humor. On one occasion when she was off visiting relatives, he imagined "that they are rigging you about yr. *imputed wants* & our *connubial poverty* & bragging of some people's 'thumping luck & fat babies.'" There is no indication, however, that the childlessness of their marriage caused any major strain between them.[17]

More stressful to the Clays was their perception that Clement's political career was languishing; also, the reality that they were still financially dependent upon his parents was of great concern. Huntsville's voters did send Clement back to the state legislature in 1844 and again in 1845, and in 1846 the legislature chose him to be the judge of the newly established Madison County Court at Huntsville, but the salaries from these offices were inadequate to support the life-style envisaged by the Clays. They also received small sums from the rental of ten slaves that Virginia had owned since before her marriage, from the rental of an office building Clement owned on the Huntsville public square, and from the fees of his law practice. In 1846, Clay estimated his annual income to be $2,500. Then thirty years old, Clement, who had suffered since his teens with feelings of low self-esteem, wrote to his father and apologized for having "achieved so little to the credit of myself or family or to the substantial welfare of my spiritual or temporal interests."[18] Self-reliance and self-confidence had eluded him despite his marriage and what appeared to be a promising career.

As his letter revealed, Clement needed to do something to seek his independence and to escape from what he called the "squalls & storms" in his parents' home. In early 1847, Clement bought a house on three and one-half acres one block from his father's residence. In December 1851, they sold the place for $7,000, more than twice what they had paid for it and moved back home.[19] Following the sale of their house (probably against his wife's wishes), Virginia persuaded Clement that she needed to take a holiday in the North to escape the tensions of living once again under her in-laws' roof and to seek a medical opinion for why she could not become pregnant. Clement, not able to leave his law practice, sent Lawson, his youngest brother, who had yet to establish himself in a profession, as Virginia's escort, an arrangement which caused some local gossip. Lawson and Virginia spent most of their time at the Orange New Jersey Mountain Water Cure, one of the many hydropathic spas which flourished at the time. There, a German physician diagnosed her condition as a displaced womb and prescribed hydrotherapeutic baths and douches. Virginia wrote her husband, "I never can leave Dr. W. till a new woman. If he fails, I shall die, or at *least try to, for my life shall no longer burden you or me.*"[20]

When Clement received this letter, he was distraught. It is apparent from their correspondence that throughout the first decade of their marriage, he was frequently depressed with most aspects of his life except his relationship with Virginia and had relied upon her to pull him out of recurring dark moods. Now, he rose to the occasion: "The whole secret of yr. unhappiness is the want of children. . . . It is the greatest grief to me, because you know that I take my full share of the cause of this want." He, too, yearned for children, he confessed, but insisted that he was determined not to give way to "paralyzing grief" and to "be thankful for what I have rather than thankless because I have not all I want." If he could live without children, so must she.[21]

Clement's optimism proved temporary. Soon he wrote Virginia: "I am making scarcely anything by the law [and] your property is too small to support us. . . . I own nothing of value compared with yr. happiness and contentment. I wd. give everything up & commence life with nothing but my poor talents & faithfulness, if I could ensure yr. happiness and contentment." She answered: "I have been away from you too long, & I know it, & shall come home as quickly as possible. If there is any real cause for despondency, I do not give way as you do, & you miss the usual counterbalance. . . . I wish we had more money, but we might have less."[22]

In the fall of 1853, Virginia and Clement's prospects brightened. Clement was nominated for Congress, and although he lost to the Whig candidate, W. R. W. Cobb, his political sacrifice for the Democratic party helped turn around his own fortunes. Three months after his defeat by Cobb, he won the endorsement from the Democratic caucus to the United States Senate. The Alabama legislature followed suit and elected him to the Senate by a vote of eighty-five to forty-three.[23] Two weeks after his victory, the Clays set out for Washington. In the nation's capital, Clement anticipated following in his father's footsteps, while at the same time he hoped to become independent of his parents. Virginia, as a United States senator's wife, looked forward to entering into a society much more sophisticated than that of Huntsville. Moreover, after ten years of marriage, Virginia was seven months pregnant. Motherhood might give her sense of place in Southern society, and fatherhood could signal Clement's long sought after release from self-doubt.

In mid-January, however, Virginia gave birth to a daughter, stillborn. One wonders shy she made the difficult journey from Alabama to Washington in her advanced state of pregnancy. She seldom thereafter mentioned the death of their daughter although she wrote a favorite cousin, "I, poor mortal, would give all else on earth to be a mother."[24] Clearly, that must not have been the case, since Virginia undertook a trip which was recognized as potentially hazardous for one so far advanced in pregnancy. Virginia never became pregnant again.

Washington, however, offered Virginia many distractions. During the congressional sessions, since they lived in boardinghouses or small hotels, Virginia was free to spend her days paying and returning calls, gossiping with friends, and planning for the receptions, balls, and trips to the theater which filled many of their evenings. Although nearly twenty-nine years old and married for over ten years when she arrived in the nation's capital, Virginia, in her memoir of these Washington years, referred to herself as "a belle of the fifties." While away from Washington on shopping sprees in Philadelphia and New York, or on trips to visit relatives or to stop at health resorts, Virginia continued her search for admirers. At one spa, she thought she was "such a belle I was almost ashamed of it," she confessed to Clement.[25]

Frank Carpenter, a well-known news reporter, described Virginia as one of the most brilliant women, "and the finest conversation[al]ist he had ever met of either sex." Virginia seems not only to have been skilled at making conversation, but also to have taken a natural interest in what others said. One Alabaman considered her "an eloquent listener." Noted also for her wit, Virginia played the part of Aunt Ruthy Partington at a lavish costume ball given in April 1858 by Senator and Mrs. Gwin of California. Aunt Ruthy, a fictional character created by the humorist Benjamin Shillaber, was famous for her rustic quips and malapropisms. Virginia, dressed against type in a plain black dress and black apron, displayed a cleverness that made her the hit of the evening. Her barbs tweaked not only President James Buchanan and Senator William Henry Seward but even the wife of the British Ambassador whom she addressed as "honey" and asked if Queen Victoria had recovered from her latest "encroachment." She was the star of the evening.[26]

Virginia Clay's sparkling personality also led men to fall a little in love with her. The man she most cared for, however, other than her husband, was her cousin Tom Tunstall. When teen-agers, Tom had given Virginia her "first kiss of love." After Clement had become a senator, he helped Tunstall obtain a position as United States consul to Cadiz. After Tom had left for Spain, Virginia wrote him: "Would to Heaven I cd. clasp my arms around your neck & burying my head in yr. fragrant hair, whisper in yr. ear how much I love you, how much pride & solicitude I feel for you, and how much dearer than almost all the rest of the world you are to my heart." It was a very intimate sounding letter, even by the effusively romantic standards of the day. But Clement demonstrated no jealousy toward Tunstall or his wife's other admirers. He no longer warned her, as he had in the early years of their marriage, of the supposed dangers to his reputation that male admiration of her might bring him.[27] The confidence Senator Clay had gained by his recent political successes enabled him to accept his wife's flirtations. He became proud of her continuing ability to attract attention.

Clay no longer worried about rivals, but he still fretted about money. Virginia's extravagance had long been a problem. Once, before she married, she had within ten months bought fifty-two pairs of shoes. While shopping in New York in 1854, Virginia wrote to Clement that she and her cousin, Evelyn Collier, were short of cash after purchasing twenty new dresses. She added that if they did not reduce their spending and if his salary were not increased, they would go bankrupt, but she did not suggest that she had any responsibility for curbing their expenditures. Nevertheless, despite her overspending and his fretting over finances, the Clays were far happier and much better off financially than they had been in Huntsville.[28]

Clement, like Virginia, won some fame in Washington though he never ranked among the leading politicians of his day. Senator Clay, having considerable ability as an orator, used this talent to defend the South and its institutions by supporting the Kansas-Nebraska Act and the Lecompton Constitution and by attacking "Black Republicanism," particularly two of its leading representatives, John P. Hale of New Hampshire and Charles Sumner of Massachusetts. In 1857, the Clays returned to Alabama in time to campaign for his reelection to the Senate. Clement won easily following the withdrawal of his chief opponent, Governor John A. Winston.[29]

The sectional antagonisms which were clearly visible at the time of their arrival in Washington increased with the passing of the decade. Virginia, not very interested in political issues unless they were entwined with social relationships, reacted to the crisis by refusing to socialize with Northerners, except with those who sympathized with the South. She bragged to her father-in-law that she and Clement would have nothing to do with "free-soilers, black Republicans & Bloomers." On the other hand, she recalled in her memoir that Southerners expressed shock when she danced with Anson Burlingame, a Republican from Massachusetts who once challenged the South Carolinian Preston Brooks to a duel. Virginia could not pass up the opportunity to glide across the floor with a handsome man, even if he were a Yankee.[30]

At the same time that tensions between the North and South accelerated, Clement's health, never robust, began to deteriorate. In the spring of 1860, asthmatic seizures forced him to leave the Senate even before the session ended. For many years, respiratory infections and a persistent cough had bothered Clay, but, seemingly, the stress generated by the impending Civil War had triggered these new attacks. The best medical experts of the day recommended a change of scene, and for almost a year, Clement and Virginia moved from place to place seeking relief from his asthma until he improved sufficiently to return to Washington in early January 1861. They arrived just in time for Clay to resign his Senate seat following the secession of Alabama. A relapse of asthma followed; the Clays returned to Huntsville where Clement gradually regained his health. By October, he was well enough to travel to Montgomery to campaign for his election to the Confederate Senate. Clay won and the way now seemed open for their return to prominence, this time in Richmond.[31]

Virginia and Clement reached the Confederate capital in February 1862. In April they received word that federal troops occupied

Huntsville. Officials arrested and briefly detained Clay's seventy-three-year-old father and confiscated livestock and provisions. Some slaves ran away. On August 31, 1862, the Union army withdrew from the town, and Virginia and Clement, concerned about his family's condition, came home in early October and stayed for several months before returning to Richmond at the end of the year. Federal troops reappeared in Huntsville in July 1863; and this second federal occupation prevented the Clays from visiting Huntsville until after the war. For almost all of 1863, Virginia stayed with relatives in North Carolina and Georgia, chiefly in Macon at the family home of her sister-in-law, Celeste Clay. Virginia wrote frequently to Clement urging him to let her and Celeste join him and Lawson, Celeste's husband, at the capital.[32]

Clement was eager to have his wife with him and knew that she would enjoy the social whirl in Richmond, but crowded quarters, expensive living conditions, and rumors of a possible Northern raid made him wonder if it were not better for her to remain in Georgia. Although Clay did not tell Virginia directly that she could not come, his letters continued to stress the adverse wartime conditions in Richmond. Virginia quickly tired of what she viewed as a manipulative game. "If you . . . *prefer* we shd. remain here," she insisted, "just *say so* as you shd. to grown up sensible people, & not be any more attempting to beguile or deceive us, like silly children into yr. wishes." Finally, he wrote her, "You can come on when you please," but she found this answer unsatisfactory. "At last you say we can come on & we, woman like, having gained our point, respectfully decline! . . . Women of our caliber must be wooed in more enthusiastic words I assure [you]." Clay must eventually have extended a satisfactory invitation, because Virginia and Celeste arrived in Richmond for a brief visit in late April 1863.[33]

Before Virginia left Macon, Clement mailed her one hundred dollars, "all the money I have. Do economize," he pleaded, "as we have nothing that we can rely on now, but my salary, & that is only for 11 months more." Her reply was vintage Virginia: "I am much obliged for the money, also the advice, but fear the *latter* will not do me nearly so much good as the former. However, I will *try*, but you know my blood."[34] Both now and at other times during their marriage, she revealed few, if any, feelings of guilt over spending more money than Clement thought they could afford.

In 1862 and 1863, Virginia Clay spent only a few weeks in Richmond, but she was with Clement from early January to mid-February 1864, during the winter session of the legislature. During this visit, she refused to let the high costs and other problems of living in the wartime Confederate capital prevent her from enjoying one final fling. The organizers of a production of Sheridan's *The Rivals* asked Virginia to play the part of Mrs. Malaprop, the character who was the model for Aunt Ruthy Partington's unwitting and hilarious misstatements. Despite the multitude of troubles now facing the South, many of the beleagured Confederacy's elite came to see the comedy. Mary Boykin Chesnut, a member of the audience, wrote that Virginia's performance "was beyond our wildest hopes." "The back, even," Mrs. Chesnut gushed, "of Mrs. Clay's head was eloquent."[35]

Virginia's appearance as Mrs. Malaprop was her last hurrah as the wife of a powerful officeholder. Clement had already begun a political decline that would eventually end their hopes of prominence and wealth and permanently rearrange the balance of strength within their marriage. Clay was a lame duck senator during the early 1864 session; in November 1863, the members of the Alabama legislature had elected Richard Wilde Walker to take his place. When Clay's term in Congress ended in mid-February, he and Virginia lost their only source of income, and they could expect no funds from his financially pressed father in occupied Huntsville. President Davis soon offered the former senator several positions, the most attractive of which was as a member of a commission to forward the Confederate cause of Canada. After a sentimental parting with Virginia, Clay ran the federal blockade and reached Halifax in the middle of May by way of Bermuda. He and the other members of the delegation talked of peace with numerous Northerners including Horace Greeley and former Attorney General Jeremiah Black on the one hand, while on the other hand they concocted a grandiose and impracticable scheme to separate the Midwest from the East which foundered as did other plots. None of these efforts had any discernable impact on the outcome of the war, nor were these months a happy time for Clement. He quarreled with other members of the delegation, and one of his associates described him as a "peevish invalid." The eight-month Canadian adventure was the sad final chapter of his political career.[36]

Life within the shrinking Confederate lines was equally disturbing for Virginia. She first took refuge in Petersburg; then when the enemy army came close, she fled again to Georgia and to Celeste's family. Most of Virginia's letters to Canada never reached Clement. In one that did, she asked him to bring home for herself and their female relatives a long list of items including four French corsets, two dozen pairs of gloves, some books on the latest fashions, and an assortment of dresses, bonnets, handkerchiefs, and furs.[37] Her continuing extravagances were totally unrealistic at a time when so many others were making major sacrifices.

During the war, Virginia Clay not only failed to feel guilty over her improvidence, but she usually avoided caring for wounded soldiers, rolling bandages, or knitting socks for the troops, activities that occupied the time of many women of her class. As Celeste Clay conceded to Clement, "Sister, & myself, deserve *no* credit for *any thing*. We have done *as little* for our country as any other two worthless women I know." Virginia made no such confession.[38]

In late December 1864, Clay began the slow journey home from Canada. Husband and wife were reunited at Macon in February 1865. Caught up in the turmoil of the last days of the Confederacy, the Clays were almost constantly on the move for the next three months. In May, they were near Lagrange, Georgia when someone at the railroad station handed Virginia a newspaper which contained a copy of a proclamation offering sizable rewards for the capture of Jefferson Davis along with Clay and other members of the Canadian delegation and accusing them of conspiring with the assassins of Abraham Lincoln. Clement, confident that he was innocent of the charge, decided to surrender and turned himself over to a federal general in Macon. Guards took Clay, accompanied by Virginia and by fellow prisoner President Davis and his family to Fortress Monroe, Virginia. There, troops imprisoned Clay and Davis. Virginia, as she parted from Clement, gave him a Bible with a message inscribed on the flyleaf: "With tearful eyes & aching heart, I commend you, *my own precious* noble, idolized husband to the care & keeping of Almighty God."[39]

Clay remained a prisoner for almost eleven months. The government charged him with general treason, authorizing raids from Canada, conspiring with Lincoln's assassins, and with carrying out germ warfare by sending infected clothing across the border. Evidence for the last two accusations, of which Clement was almost certainly innocent, came primarily from the testimony of several individuals who eventually admitted that they had lied. At first, however, government officials believed him guilty of all the charges.[40]

While Clay was in Fortress Monroe, his wife worried about his health. Beginning in January 1866, Clement's asthma recurred, and prison doctors gave him "heavy doses of opium," a drug nineteenth-century physicians prescribed for numerous diseases and chronic conditions including asthma. Clay also suffered in prison from nervous dyspepsia and depression. He confessed to Virginia, "I am quite worn out & of very little

value to you or anybody. You would probably be better off without me."
Only his awareness of the love of his wife and parents for him kept
Clement from the final depths of despair. He told Virginia, "I'll try to
live to see you," but "if you & they cared less for me & were less dependent on me for happiness, it would be better for us all."[41]

Virginia slowly made her way back from Fortress Monroe to
Huntsville, harassed along the way by federal agents who searched her
baggage in an attempt to discover incriminating papers. Life in
Huntsville was even more unpleasant for Virginia than before the war.
The people of the town were deeply divided between those who had
supported the Confederacy and those who had worked with the federal
army during its occupation. Slaves were free, but new labor agreements
had not yet emerged. Clement Comer and Susanna were old, sick, dis-
couraged, and in debt. Withers, the second son, was back from the war
but could not earn a living for his wife, Mary, and their six children.
Lawson had gone to Georgia to Celeste's family to try to become a
planter. When Virginia urged Lawson to return to Huntsville to help
care for his ailing father, he refused.[42]

With her husband incarcerated and immersed in melancholia, and
his father and brothers paralyzed by their own problems, Virginia undertook a letter-writing campaign to free Clement. When her initial efforts
brought no results, she resolved to go to Washington. A contact there
had written Virginia, "'Tis said that the President likes the opportunity
of granting personal favors direct to the parties on their own application
. . . and that the ladies never fail with him." A president who reportedly
could be swayed by feminine charms was a challenge too tempting for
her to pass up. In November 1865, she borrowed one hundred dollars
and enough silk from a local merchant for a new dress and took the train
to Washington.[43]

Virginia wrote several letters to Andrew Johnson in which she sought
to obtain the release of her husband by flattering the president and by
pointing out to him that both her husband and her father-in-law were in
ill health. She also called on Johnson at the White House where, she
recalled, she and her female friends begged for Clement's release. On
one occasion, she encountered Benjamin F. Perry who wrote to his wife:
"I met Ms. Senator Clay of Alabama at the White House and spent an
hour with her whilst waiting to see the President. . . . She is one of the
most intellectual women I ever met, a noble lady, a devoted wife. She
seemed pleased when I introduced myself to her and told me all her history and troubles and trials. We took seats in one corner of the room and

had quite a tete a tete for one hour. She is with all very fine looking. The President gave her a package and she smiled as if her whole soul was radiant with joy. I hope it was the release of her noble husband."[44] Clay, however, was not released until two months later. Virginia claimed in her reminiscences that during one late evening visit to the White House she had become so angry at the president's excuses and delays that she had threatened to remain until he complied with her demand. Her display of temper supposedly brought about the president's capitulation, and the next morning, April 18, 1866, the authorities freed Clement. The details of Virginia's account of her final confrontation with President Johnson must be viewed with some suspicion. Nevertheless, Johnson's practice of humbling proud Southerners but ultimately granting their individual requests for pardons and Virginia's ability to get what she wanted from men probably worked in tandem to bring about Clement's liberation. Virginia and her husband both believed that *she* had rescued him.[45]

Following Clement's release, the Clays returned to Huntsville. Susanna Clay had already died on January 2, 1866. Clement Comer Clay did not long survive his wife, dying September 6, 1866, four months after a reunion with his eldest son. Clement Claiborne, acting as his father's executor, sold several of the estate's most valuable assets, including his parents' Huntsville home. Cash from the sale of the house, which brought $10,600 and from other transactions went to pay Clement Comer's debts which totaled over $30,000. It would be six years before Virginia and Clement gained clear title from his father's estate to 1,420 acres of land located about twenty miles east of Huntsville near the village of Gurley.[46]

Like other members of the Southern elite, the Clays, especially Clement, found it extremely difficult to cope in the postwar years. Following the sale of the old family home, Clement and Virginia moved in 1868 to a small house on the farm called "Clay Lodge," and then later on to a nearby cottage which Virginia named "Wildwood." Clement took up farming. They raised cotton, corn, oats, peas, other grains and vegetables, chickens, cattle, and hogs. The sale of cotton and grain brought in some cash. Clay tried at different times several systems of farm management including renting parts of his land, sharecropping, and using hired laborers. None of these arrangements proved profitable. His attempts to establish a shingle business and a saw mill on the farm and to mine soapstone also came to nothing. Although the income from the farm and from the rental of a Huntsville office building they owned kept the Clays minimally supported, they were forced to sell other assets to pay off some long-standing debts. Among their creditors was William W. Corcoran, a Washington banker and friend from the 1850s, who had lent Virginia $1,000. Corcoran finally gave up hope of repayment and returned Virginia's note.[47] The Clays' troubled and complicated finances dominated their final years together.

Clay, seeking to improve their economic situation, accepted a position in 1871 as the chief Alabama agent for the Life Insurance Association of America and spent much of the next two years traveling throughout the state attempting to sell policies and to recruit and supervise other agents. Clement discovered that old friends whom he considered prospective buyers welcomed him cordially into their homes and offices but were not interested in purchasing life insurance. He disliked traveling and being away from Virginia, and after two years he resigned.[48]

Before their financial burdens and the responsibility of running the farm overtook them, they had taken several trips together. Virginia also went to New York in July 1868 to attend the Democratic convention and to Washington in November 1868 to apply to friends for a loan. There, a letter from Clement arrived stressing their lack of funds. Virginia responded that he had saddened her soul, and she threatened to come home without even trying to borrow money. "Reserve yr. gloomy views of mankind & life for my ears not my eyes," she insisted. "When I see . . . luxurious homes . . . & trousseaus from Paris, & think of my lot, my home & my one black silk dress, I do not need in addition one word from you or any other one to realize my situation."[49] Although Virginia was quite aware that their fortunes had dropped, she had not accepted fully his pessimistic view of their future.

Clement was fifty-seven years old in 1873 when he left the insurance business and returned to the farm. Unable to escape from debt and often ill, Clay became more and more depressed and dependent on Virginia. "I can't understand or conceive," he woefully confided to his wife, "how some persons endure debt—it is worse than asthma, even to me. It robs life of all its enjoyments, makes death appear as a friend in need." He confessed on another occasion that "the cares & responsibilities of my present life, my short comings & long sinnings," had caused him to lose "all self confidence & courage, as well as hope & faith." These and other doleful laments naturally troubled Virginia, as did her husband's frequent illnesses. Also, she had cause to worry about his drinking, which apparently had become a major problem following the war. Her letters to him are filled with pleas and admonitions to avoid all intoxicating beverages. He admitted in his letters to her that his slips had caused them both much pain, and he assured her that he was, as he once put it, "dry as a powder horn." His incessant claims that he was avoiding strong drink show that he had great difficulty staying on the wagon and suggest that he occasionally fell off it. Three years before his death, he wrote to his wife that he was "as sober as I ever was, & as sad."[50]

Virginia, only forty-three years old when they went to live on the farm in 1868, missed the social activities to which she had been addicted in the prewar years. Activities such as supervising the farm chores, making jelly, mending clothes, and raising flowers and vegetables kept her busy but not happy. Virginia complained to Clement that she was bored, restless, and discontented and blamed him for their financial problems which forced her "to do without what I wd. dearly love to have." Clement, aware of her need to get away from the farm and its isolation, furnished a small apartment for her in his Huntsville office building where she often stayed for several days at a time. She also managed most years a two-week trip to Memphis, Louisville, or St. Louis to visit friends and relatives.[51]

Men continued to seek out Virginia Clay. Jefferson Davis, her husband's old colleague and fellow prisoner, wrote her forty-three letters between 1870 and 1878. Davis, like Clement, was disenchanted with the postwar world, and he found in Virginia a sympathetic woman. "When woman's rights become the law of the land," Davis wrote her, "you will become an available southern candidate for the Presidency." Davis could imagine no higher compliment, but another famous Southerner, L. Q. C. Lamar, who like Davis had been a friend for years, did as much, if not more, for her morale. The Mississippi congressman sent Virginia a poem as overflowing with sentiment as those composed for her during her days as a young belle. Lamar offered to return from the dead if Virginia called. She did not ask him to resurrect himself, but requested instead that he endorse a note extending a loan.[52]

Nevertheless, Virginia had changed. No longer the flighty belle, she became the stronger partner during the final years of her marriage. Even in political matters Virginia was preeminent. Jefferson Davis, as noted, recognized her political abilities, and friends and relatives wrote asking her to endorse their applications for office.[53] As the antebellum correspondence between husband and wife reveals, Virginia always had the potentiality for becoming the dominant personality in their relationship. Clement, in the early years of their marriage, expressed in his letters to his wife a dependence upon her, especially when ill health and self-doubts overcame him. He became more confident following his election to the Senate and his political successes in Washington, and his dependency upon her might have remained only a minor and privately acknowledged component of their relationship had not the Civil War destroyed his health, his political career, and his hopes of prosperity. After the war he wrote to Virginia that "nothing is worth living for me, but you, and it is only my love for you that saves me from despair and total darkness—I confess this to you, and only with some shame." Her postwar letters are full of compassion for him, but she refused to allow his pessimism to undermine her self-confidence. "You wrong me," she wrote him, "when you think I am not troubled at yr. debts, but it is not my style to die in advance of death's summons."[54]

Although Virginia was able to keep some emotional distance between herself and her self-tormented husband, their letters suggest that their physical desire and affection for one another remained strong despite other changes in their marital relationship. When separated from each other, Clement and Virginia typically wrote how much each missed the other. Off on an insurance trip. Clement wrote that he wished his wife were there to fill his bed. Virginia declared that she missed him especially at night. Trapped by a snowstorm in an overheated Huntsville room, Virginia once wrote, "If I am obliged to be cooked let it be with my old rooster."[55] Given the Victorian unwillingness to discuss sex, these and other statements are indications that intimacy remained an important part of their relationship, even as the marriage drew to a close.

On January 3, 1882, nine years after he gave up the insurance business and settled back on the farm, Clement Clay died at the age of sixty-five. His health had been poor for many years, and the end could not have come as a surprise to Virginia. She was, at first, melancholic, but she soon recovered enough to make a trip to Europe. Nonetheless, she found life as a widow unsatisfactory. In 1887, Virginia married David Clopton, an old friend and a political colleague of her husband in both the United States and Confederate Congresses. The bride was sixty-two years old; the groom, five years older, was twice widowed and had six grown children. At the time of their marriage, Clopton served as a justice of the Alabama Supreme Court; they lived in Montgomery for five years until Clopton died suddenly in 1892. Virginia inherited one-seventh of his property, much less than she had expected.[56]

Following the death of Judge Clopton, Virginia adopted the name Virginia Clay-Clopton, returned to Wildwood, and supported herself for the remaining twenty-three years of her life apparently from the proceeds of the farm. Virginia, convinced by her own personal observations that woman's talent for politics was equal to that of man's, joined in the crusade to win the vote for women and served from 1896 to 1900 as president of the Alabama Equal Suffrage Association. She remarked that the opponents of equal suffrage thought that woman had her own sphere and should not go beyond it, but Virginia noted that "if woman does not now suffer from the absence of political power, it is the only instance in History where a class so deprived has not been the worse because of the disability." Since women are, she declared, "almost as often found in positions of responsibility as men, the same is required of them, and they should be given the same means of attainment and defense," in this case the franchise, to determine their destiny. Although Virginia was more of an adornment to than an active leader in the women's suffrage movement, her name carried weight. Interestingly enough her activities in the suffrage movement do not appear to have damaged her social standing.[57] She also joined and held office in several organizations devoted to keeping alive the memory of the Confederacy, and she particularly enjoyed attending their reunions. At a Confederate gathering in New York City in 1902, she was, she bragged, "the belle of the ball."[58] Her need to feel that she was the center of attention had not at all diminished.

Virginia began working in 1900 on her memoirs, which were published in 1905 under the title *A Belle of the Fifties*. Of the book's thirty chapters, only one discussed her life before her marriage to Clement, nine described Washington society in the 1850s, and an equal number recited her movements and impressions during the Civil War. The final eleven chapters detailed Clement's imprisonment and especially Virginia's role in freeing him. The first ten years of her marriage were omitted entirely, and the period after 1866 received one sentence. She simply blotted out those years which she did not care to recall.

Virginia lived for ten years following the publication of her reminiscences. On January 16, 1915, she celebrated her ninetieth birthday at a party in Huntsville. Hundreds of friends and relatives attended and almost as many others sent telegrams. Six months later she died on June 23.[59]

At the time of Clement and Virginia's marriage, their expectations for continued political, economic, and social success rested in part on the assumption that Clement, the able and eldest son of a prominent father, would achieve much in the antebellum world of which they were a part. Their anticipations ignored the fact that Clay, like many other sons in patriarchal families, had remained in a state of prolonged dependency. Although he became a United States senator and an advisor in the Confederacy to Jefferson Davis, Clement's economic and psychological dependence upon his authoritarian father kept him from gaining the self-

confidence and maturity necessary to make the most of these opportunities and prevented him from sustaining himself after prominence and
prosperity disappeared. Clay, forty-nine years old when he was released
from prison in 1866, retreated to the farm, to the bottle, to ill health,
and to gloomy thoughts.

After 1865, Virginia emerged as the stronger spouse, demonstrating
confidence, buoyancy, and optimism in good times and in bad. Eight
years younger than her husband and light years away from him in temperament, Virginia more easily readjusted her sights at war's end, surren-
dering the lavish, the fashionable, and the expensive to make the best of a
simpler style of living. Clement had written Virginia in 1868 that "if it
were possible for you to love me & to enjoy my company as I love you
and enjoy yrs., we might be happy in our seclusion."[60] He recognized,
however, that her preference for city life left her discontented on the
farm, and so they worked out an arrangement that enabled her to stay in
town often and to take trips out-of-state to visit friends and relatives.
Clay's willingness to reach such an accommodation was a rare occurrence
among nineteenth-century Southern husbands.

This case study of the marriage of Virginia and Clement Clay seems
to support the hypothesis that the South's defeat in 1865 and the resulting political, economic, and social changes produced a profound change
in the internal dynamics of marriage. In the Clays' case, moreover, we
know that Virginia, who had seemingly been destined to be a Southern
belle in perpetuity, stepped forward after the war to become the stronger
spouse. Their reversal of roles did not, however, result in their alienation
from one another. Virginia and Clement's ability to accommodate themselves to each others' needs and their romantic love for one another,
which was a constant force in their relationship from their engagement in
1842 until Clement's death almost forty years later, made it possible for
their affection to survive in the midst of vast historical change.

28 The Trial of Mrs. Surratt and the Lincoln Assassination Plot

Benjamin B. Williams

*N*INETY-EIGHT YEARS ago on the evening of Good Friday, April 14, 1865, a pistol shot, and a figure in black dropping to the stage of Ford's Theater in Washington brought to a climax a series of plots and intrigues and marked the beginning of legal controversies which extend into the present. The event, of course, was the assassination of Abraham Lincoln by John Wilkes Booth. For Booth it was a successful conclusion to his elaborate schemes. Twelve days later Booth was dead on the Garrett farm near Port Royal, Virginia. With his death, Booth escaped the misery that befell the people whom he had implicated in the assassination, both the culpable and the innocent.

On May 10, 1865, eight persons were charged before a military court with conspiracy in the assassination of Lincoln.[1] On July 5, 1865, four were sentenced to death by hanging, three received life imprisonment, and one was sentenced to six years at hard labor.[2] The sentences were carried out two days later. One of the four persons to receive the death penalty was Mrs. Mary Eugenia Jenkins Surratt,[3] convicted on a few scraps of circumstantial evidence. What is perhaps worse, she was the victim of suppressed evidence and a suppressed clemency plea signed by a majority of the military court.[4] The suppressed evidence might have acquitted her, and the suppressed clemency plea, no doubt, would have assured her release within four years.[5]

Almost all who have reviewed the trial and execution of Mrs. Surratt hold it to have been a miscarriage of justice. In an attempt to find the reasons for Mrs. Surratt's execution it is necessary to examine much more than the legal aspects of the case. Three elements, it seems to me, conspired to bring about her execution—the temper of the times, the political ramifications of the trial, and the state of the law when the events happened.

It is dangerous to make a judgment on a single historical event without some knowledge of the background circumstances which inevitably exert an influence on that event. Let us look briefly at this background.

First, I think it is instructive to know that the air was rife with plots to assassinate Lincoln throughout his administration. In fact, the most celebrated early plot, the so-called "Baltimore Plot," was planned in 1861, before Lincoln's first inauguration.[6] The plot was uncovered by the Pinkerton detective agency whose agents infiltrated the groups in Baltimore and learned of their designs. At that time Lincoln was making appearances in various cities on his way to Washington. He was scheduled to stop in Baltimore, and the assassination was planned to take place as he progressed from the train to a carriage which was to take him to a Baltimore hotel. On the advice of Allan Pinkerton, Lincoln took a night train from Philadelphia to Washington the night before his scheduled appearance in Baltimore, thus foiling this earliest assassination plot.

During the war, the secret service and the War Department were constantly checking on plots to assassinate Lincoln. These agencies had files on various plots, including the names of suspects. Lincoln himself kept a folder in his desk, passed on to him by the secret service, of many of the plots and threats against him.[7] For the most part, the War Department and the secret service suspected a connection between the plots and the Confederate Government. It was a suspicion that these agencies never relinquished, and when the assassination did take place, every effort was made to trace it to the Confederacy.[8] It was perhaps the absence of suspicion of a small private plot, or of an individual public figure such as Booth that made the assassination possible.

Booth's shooting of Lincoln has almost obscured the fact that the actor had, some times earlier, planned an elaborate kidnap scheme.[9] Soon after Lincoln's reelection in 1864, Booth plotted to kidnap the President and spirit him away to Richmond where he hoped to use his hostage to end the war or at least as an instrument to effect the release of large numbers of Confederate prisoners. Exactly when Booth changed his plan from kidnapping to assassination is not certain, but we can surmise that the fall of Richmond and Lee's surrender at Appomattox would have rendered the kidnap plan unfeasible.[10]

It can be seen that the actual assassination was confirmation of four years of threats to the powers in Washington, and certainly must be considered an influence on the speed and severity of the trial and punishments. Although this does not mitigate injustice, it may help to an understanding of one of the most important nonlegal circumstances surrounding the trial—the temper of the times. Adding to this consideration, we must note that at the time Lincoln was shot, Washington and the North were celebrating their successes in the South. The assassination of Lincoln and the attack on Secretary of State Seward led many to think that these were only parts of a general conspiracy in terrorism, an all-out effort by the Confederate government to stave off defeat. Unfounded as these suspicions proved to be, they were none the less real to the powers in Washington at the time.

One other aspect that certainly played a part in the trial was the character of the men in charge of the trial—Secretary of War Stanton and Judge Advocate General Joseph Holt. There were few men in power in Washington who boded more ill for those on trial than these men who would have control of the evidence and would be in charge of the prosecution. Both men were extreme Unionists, and both were willing to believe the most disreputable witnesses who supported their own predilections and bias in the case.[11]

One of the most frequent questions raised with regard to the trial is the legality of the military court. This and other matters in connection with the trial can only be understood in terms of the state of the law at that time. This was but one of many trials by military commission between the years 1862 and 1866. The genesis of the military trial at the North came about as a result of difficulties arising from draft riots and actions of some Southern sympathizers in the Union states. On September 24, 1862, Lincoln issued a proclamation establishing martial law throughout the Union states, under which the writ of *habeas corpus* was suspended. This proclamation was given legislative sanction by an Act of Congress on March 3, 1863.[12] The challenge to the constitutionality of this act was being litigated at the time of the Lincoln assassination trial, but unfortunately for Mrs. Surratt and the others, the famous *Ex parte Milligan* decision was not rendered by the Supreme Court until 1866. The essence of the Milligan decision is that civilians can not be tried by military court where the civil courts "are open and in proper and unobstructed exercise of their jurisdiction."[13]

The results of the trial, especially the convictions of Mrs. Surratt and Dr. Samuel Mudd, may be attributed in large part to the political ramifications of the trial. As was suggested earlier, the Union government suspected complicity of Confederate leaders in the assassination. In the original charge, the Confederate leaders were named along with the eight prisoners at the bar. Since the court was insisting on a general conspiracy plot instigated by President Davis, Clement C. Clay, and other Southern leaders, it can be seen that the slightest connection with the plot by any of the eight people on trial would, in the eyes of such a court, involve them more deeply than would have been the case had they been tried merely for their part in the assassination alone.[14] It has also been suggested that Secretary of War Stanton and Judge Advocate General Holt were inclined to believe any dubious evidence that would tend to support their general conspiracy theory. In this regard, most of the damaging testimony was that of one Sanford Conover who came from Canada to produce an elaborate web of evidence linking Booth's act to a meeting with Clement C. Clay and other Confederate ministers in Canada. Conover also produced two witnesses to testify to the accuracy of his charges. Even though men in Canada and General Dix in New York warned the court of Conover's unsavory character, the court remained convinced that the testimony was to be believed.[15] Again, too late to be of help to those on trial, it was proved that Conover was a perjurer and had suborned his two witnesses to perjury.[16] These disclosures did, however, aid in attaining the release of Jefferson Davis.

With this background on the events, the times, and the men in charge, I will turn to the Booth plots and the involvement of those brought to trial.

JOHN WILKES BOOTH was born at Bel Air, Maryland, May 10, 1838, the youngest child of the famous actor Junius Brutus Booth. His older brother, Edwin, became perhaps the greatest Shakespearean actor produced in America. John Wilkes Booth had followed his father and brother in a stage career, and was quite successful. He is said to have earned as much as $20,000 a year in the early 1860's. His original plan to kidnap Lincoln has already been mentioned. This plan had some appeal among the young men who fell under Booth's influence, and it was during the plotting of it that Booth attracted most of his adherents. It was this kidnap plot in which John H. Surratt, son of Mrs. Surratt, was involved. Booth also interested two paroled ex-Confederate soldiers in the idea, Samuel Arnold and Michael O'Laughlin. The others taking part in this plot were George Atzerodt, David Herold, and Lewis Paine. These last three were to some degree mentally retarded, and were the only ones who were active with Booth in the actual assassination.[17]

Booth's first "capture" plot was to take place on January 18, 1865, when it was believed that Lincoln would attend the Ford Theater. This plan would have followed the sequence of the assassination, except that Lincoln was to have been bound in his box and lowered to the stage to be spirited away by the route Booth and Herold used after the assassination. The plan fell through as Lincoln did not appear at the theater that evening.[18]

The second kidnap plan was to intercept Lincoln's carriage on the road to the Soldier's Home on the outskirts of Washington. On March 20, 1865, Booth and his cohorts were lying in wait on the road. A carriage appeared and as Booth and Surratt rode up to it, they discovered that the one passenger was not Lincoln. Several members of the group were now convinced that the government secret service was aware of their plot. Arnold, O'Laughlin, and Surratt decided to break away from any further involvement with Booth, the first two returned to Baltimore, while Surratt returned to his Confederate courier activities. Surratt left for Richmond, and on April 3, 1865, passed through Washington on his way to Canada.[19] As a result of these defections, Booth was left with only the three mental defectives, Herold, Paine, and Atzerodt to carry out his designs. In the assassination, according to the best evidence available, these four were the only ones involved directly.

Everyone knows the part Booth played in this last desperate game, but the actions of the others are not so well known. Booth arranged for Paine to enter Seward's home and stab the Secretary of State at the same time that he was entering Lincoln's box at Ford's. Herold was detailed to accompany Paine, hold the horses outside, and lead Paine, who was unable to find his way around in Washington, to a rendezvous with Booth on the escape route into Maryland. Atzerodt was probably assigned the task of killing Vice-President Johnson. Booth's part in the plot was the only one successfully completed. Seward was spared by the fact that he was wearing a metal jaw brace when Paine struck with his knife. Herold panicked and left Paine to wander aimlessly around the capital for three days before he was arrested. Atzerodt, a drunkard and coward, never went near the room of Vice-President Johnson. Herold joined Booth on the road to Maryland and was with him until captured in the barn where Booth was killed.

These three men who were involved in Booth's final plot were tried, convicted, and hanged. Arnold and O'Laughlin, involved in the earlier kidnap plot, were sentenced to life in prison, and Dr. Samuel Mudd, who set Booth's leg and whose complicity in the plot was as tenuous as Mrs. Surratt's, was also given a life sentence. Edward Spangler, a scene mover at Ford's Theater, was sentenced to six years for allegedly aiding Booth's escape from the theater.[20] The question then is: Why was Mrs. Surratt hanged and what was her part in the conspiracy?

Mrs. Surratt was born near Waterloo, Prince George County, Maryland, about the year 1820. She married John H. Surratt in 1835. Her husband operated a farm and a tavern some fifteen miles south of Washington. He became postmaster at that place which was designated Surrattsville. After her husband's death in 1862, Mrs. Surratt decided to move to a house at 541 H Street in Washington. On October 1, 1864, she went to live in Washington, renting her tavern and farm to John Lloyd for $500.00 a year. She took in boarders to support herself and her daughter Anna.

The connection of the Surratts with Booth began on January 1, 1865, when Booth came to see John Surratt, probably to enlist his aid in the kidnap plot. Between January and April, Booth, Atzerodt, Herold, and Paine all were at the Surratt house on various occasions. Paine, whose real name was Lewis Powell, boarded in the house for four days under the assumed identity of Rev. Wood, Baptist minister. None of the others did more than visit the house.

Part of the evidence against Mrs. Surratt was the assumption that her house was the headquarters for the conspirators, and the presumption was that she could not have been unaware of the plotting taking place under her roof.[21] Other evidence introduced at her trial was the fact that she delivered a package for Booth to her tenant Lloyd on the day of the assassination. On the testimony of Lloyd she was reported to have told him to "have the guns" ready. The last damaging evidence against her was the fact that on the night of April 17, as the government officers were arresting the entire Surratt household, Paine who had been wandering about the city since the night of April 14 showed up at Mrs. Surratt's boardinghouse. When asked by the police if she knew him, Mrs. Surratt claimed that she did not. This fact was used at the trial to further the government case that she was shielding the assassins.[22]

The two principal witnesses against Mrs. Surratt were a boarder at her house, Louis Weichmann, and her Surrattsville tenant, John Lloyd. Mrs. Surratt's attorneys, Frederick Aiken and John Clampitt, tried to impeach both by showing that Weichmann knew more of Booth's plans than she did, and that John Lloyd, by his own admission, was very drunk on the day in question. There is strong evidence that both witnesses were testifying out of fear for their own lives. These two and several others who aided Booth in one way or another were never brought to trial. President Lincoln's bodyguard who had left his post at the theater box door, making Booth's task easier, was never tried for negligence or fired from the police force.[23]

In answer to the charges against Mrs. Surratt, her attorneys produced letters to show that Mrs. Surratt had had legitimate business in Surrattsville on April 14, and submitted that her delivery of a wrapped package for Booth was no more than a favor. Her failure to recognize Paine on the night of the arrest was explained by the fact that he was quite altered in appearance from his pose as the Rev. Wood. Several witnesses also testified to Mrs. Surratt's poor and failing eyesight. Many witnesses, including ex-slaves, told of her good character and kindness. Several priests confirmed that she was a devout Christian woman. Not a single witness was brought forth to testify against her character.

One point that further influenced the court and those in charge against Mrs. Surratt was their belief that her son John had taken an active part in the assassination on April 14, 1865. John Surratt had eluded police and military dragnets and during his mother's trial was in hiding in Canada. Both Stanton and Holt were probably annoyed at not being able to bring young Surratt to trial with the others and may have let their disappointment weight against his mother.

Even though in conspiracy the aiders and abettors to the crime are equally guilty with the one who commits it, it seems strange that Mrs. Surratt should have been sentenced to hang when the court was able to spare the lives of Mudd, Spangler, Arnold, and O'Laughlin. The information that would surely have spared her life, the suppressed evidence and the clemency plea, was not brought to light until the trial of John Surratt two years later.

John Surratt was apprehended in Egypt and was brought to trial in Washington on June 10, 1867. Fortunately for him the Milligan decision had been rendered in 1866 so that he had the benefit of a civil court trial. It was never proved that he was in Washington at the time of the assassination and the jury could not agree on a verdict. He was finally released from custody on June 22, 1868. The charge was *nol prossed*. Out of this trial, however, emerged the facts of the suppressed information in the earlier trial. It was learned, for instance, that the diary taken from Booth's body contained information that might have cleared Mrs. Surratt, and that someone had cut several pages from the book.

For the first time also it became known publicly that five of the officers on the nine-man military court had signed a clemency plea in behalf of Mrs. Surratt. When President Johnson heard of the clemency plea, he asked for the records of the court, claiming that he never saw the plea.[24] Judge Holt insisted that he had taken the plea with other papers to the President in order that the latter could sign the death warrants. Recent investigation of the records indicates that either Holt withheld the plea or that it was so placed among the papers that were brought to the President that he never saw it. In either event, Holt or his superior, Secretary of War Stanton, must bear the blame. It is reasoned that had the clemency plea accompanied the other papers to the President it logically would have been the last page of the record on which the President would have had to sign the death warrant. However, Johnson's signature appears following the sentences pronounced by the court, and not on the sheet bearing the clemency plea.[25]

A word should be said with regard to the frequently maligned members of the military commission. Nine Union officers served on the court, three major generals, four brigadier generals, a colonel, and a lieutenant-colonel. The best known of the officers on the court was Major General Lew Wallace, author of *Ben Hur*, Major General David Hunter was the ranking officer on the court, and was one of the five who signed the clemency plea. The other four officers joining General Hunter in the plea were: Major General August Kautz, Brigadier Generals Robert Foster and James Ekin, and Colonel C. H. Tomkins. (Generals Wallace, Howe, and Harris and Lieutenant-Colonel Clendenin did not sign the plea).[26]

On July 5, 1865, the sentences were announced. Mrs. Surratt's attorneys, Aiken and Clampitt, as well as the prison commander, General Hartranft, and the military commander of the Washington District, General Hancock, were shocked that she had received the death penalty. Clampitt and Aiken sought the advice of Reverdy Johnson, the famous constitutional lawyer who had worked with them on Mrs. Surratt's defense. Johnson suggested that they secure a writ of *habeas corpus*. The two attorneys persuaded Judge Andrew Wylie of the Supreme Court of the District of

Columbia to issue a writ directing General Hancock to produce Mrs. Surratt in his court. The writ was delivered to Hancock who sent it to the White House. Operating under the March 3, 1863, Act of Congress which suspended *habeas corpus,* President Johnson, in an executive order, directed Hancock to return the writ to the court of Judge Wylie.[27]

Some hope of a last minute stay was held. Paine made a deposition to the prison director, General Hartranft, that he believed Mrs. Surratt innocent, and the General endorsed the statement stating that he thought Paine was telling the truth.[28] However, time was running out, and it is unlikely that this statement ever reached the President who alone, at this time, could have halted the execution. Other attempts were made to reach the President on July 7, the day set for the hangings. Mrs. Surratt's daughter, Anna, waited in vain for a meeting with the President. The widow of Stephen Douglas was the only one who got to see Johnson, but he rejected her petition. President Johnson, on the evidence he had seen, felt that all efforts to save Mrs. Surratt were based solely on her being a woman, and not on the possibility of her being innocent.

The executions were set to take place between 10 A.M. and 2 P.M. General Hancock delayed as long as he thought he could before ordering the executions. He took up a position so that he could learn of any last minute stay, but none came. The traps fell and the four were pronounced dead at sixteen minutes to two.[29]

Dr. Mudd, Edward Spangler, Samuel Arnold, and Michael O'Laughlin were sent to prison at Dry Tortugas Island off the Florida Keys. They arrived there on July 24, 1865. In a yellow fever epidemic which swept the prison in August 1867, Michael O'Laughlin died. Dr. Mudd was commended for his services during the epidemic, and in one of his last acts before leaving office, President Johnson pardoned Mudd, Arnold, and Spangler in February 1869.[30]

Judge Holt, who must bear a large part of the responsibility for the injustice to Mrs. Surratt, received a great amount of criticism during the last twenty-nine years of his life as uncovered evidence weighed in favor of Mrs. Surratt's innocence. The judge tried vainly to clear his name in many articles to the press, but was never able to vindicate himself before his death in 1894.[31]

Holt's assistant judge advocate, John Bingham, was also taken to task for his part in the proceedings. While serving in Congress in 1867, Benjamin Butler, of all people, charged Bingham with helping to hang an innocent woman—Mrs. Surratt.[32]

It is fairly certain that had the trial been conducted under civil court procedures or in times of less vindictive emotionalism or under the control of men of different temperament than that of Stanton and Holt, Mrs. Surratt's life would have been spared. History indicates that her guilt was never more than a guess.

Notes

Chapter 3: A Contemporary Account of the Inauguration of Jefferson Davis

1. Mary H. Noyes, age 57, and Emma Noyes, age 17, both natives of Massachusetts, were listed as members of the Jackson household, in Montgomery, Alabama, on the Census of 1860.
2. William Noyes Jackson, third son of the J. F. Jacksons, was about four years old when the letter was written.
3. John B. Garrett (of Garrett & Pollard Hardware Dealers) lived on Catoma Street, between Tallapoosa and Bibb Streets.
4. Thomas Hill Watts (Governor of Alabama 1863–1865) was a law partner of J. F. Jackson, in the firm of Watts, Judge and Jackson.
5. On Jan. 21, 1861, Benjamin Fitzpatrick and Clement C. Clay, Jr., Senators from Alabama, with the Senators from Florida and Jefferson Davis, then Senator from Mississippi, announced in the Senate their intention to withdraw from that body, and they did withdraw.
6. Sampson Willis Harris was a Representative from Alabama in Washington, 1847–1857. He died in Washington on April 1, 1857. Jefferson Davis was Secretary of War, 1853–1857. In April 1856 J. F. Jackson was admitted as counselor to the U.S. Court of Claims, at Washington.
7. William Wallace Screws read law under Thomas H. Watts and was admitted to the bar in June, 1859. He was about 22 years of age, had a room in the Jackson's house, and was one of the first young men to volunteer for military service and left with the "True Blues" for Fort Barancas.

Chapter 6: Personal Recollections of the Battle of Chancellorsville

1. A 'Chancellor' of Chancellorsville—a child of fourteen years." Mrs. Chancellor's story is furnished by her great, great niece, Lynda Williams of Stanford, Kentucky. Members of the Chancellor family now residing in Kentucky are: George Chancellor, Lexington; James C. Pruitt, Millersburg; Mrs. Sherman Anderson, and William Chancellor, Stanford; Beverly Chancellor, Harrodsburg; Lee and Ves Chancellor, Mt. Washington; J. W. Williams, James Wesley, III, and Cynthia Reed Williams, Stanford.
2. Five roads converged at Chancellorsville House. The house was a large brick mansion with ample wings and was formerly used as a tavern for entertainment of travelers journeying to and fro from Fredericksburg to the mountains. Standing in front of the Chancellorsville house and looking southward were extensive fields bounded by forests. Lenoir Chambers, *Stonewall Jackson*, (New York, 1959), II, 403.

3. General Stonewall Jackson was removed from the battlefield to Reverend Melze Chancellor's house, 2 miles west of Chancellorsville where his surgeon Dr. McGuire administered to his wounds. Later the wounded General was removed to "Wilderness Tavern." John Esten Cooke, *Stonewall Jackson: A Military Biography* . . . (New York, 1866).

4. The North and the South: "The Foundation of an Enduring Friendship Laid at the Battle of Chancellorsville." The death of Mrs. Fannie L. Chancellor, of this county, recalls an incident of the war that in after years caused a strong and abiding friendship to spring up between a gallant Northern officer and a Southern woman.

   General Joseph Dickinson, of Washington, is the hero of the story. In that time of carnage and destruction he took Mrs. Chancellor and her family and others that had refuged there, Miss Kate Forbes, now Mrs. Bastable, of this city, being among the number, from the dangers to which they were exposed in the Chancellorsville house, to a place of safety.

   Since the war the ties of friendship between General Dickinson and Mrs. Chancellor have been very strong, and whenever he visited the battlefields in this section he always called to see her and received the most cordial hospitality.

   He attended her funeral, manifesting in the hour of death the indissoluble ties that bound him to his friend while she was living. (Unidentified newspaper clipping—July, 1892.)

Chapter 9: A Confederate Girl Visits Pennsylvania, July–September 1863

Dr. Lander is Professor of History and Government at Clemson University, Clemson, South Carolina, author of *A History of South Carolina, 1865–1960*, co-editor of *A Rebel Came Home: The Diary of Floride Clemson,* and frequent contributor to historical journals.—Ed.

1. Charles M. McGee, Jr., and Ernest M. Lander, Jr., eds., *A Rebel Came Home: The Diary of Floride Clemson* . . . (Columbia, S.C.: University of South Carolina Press, 1961). The manuscript diary and all Clemson correspondence hereinafter cited are located in the Clemson Papers, Clemson University Library, Clemson, S.C.

2. The head of the Baker family was Elias Baker, younger brother of Thomas G. Clemson's mother, Elizabeth Baker Clemson. Elias Baker's family included wife Hettie, daughter Anna (Annie), son Sylvester, daughter-in-law Sarah (wife of deceased son Woods), and Sarah's daughter Luly. Floride usually referred to Uncle Elias and Aunt Hettie as "uncle" and "auntie." Elias Baker died on December 5, 1864. The Baker residence at Altoona today houses the Blair County Historical Society.

3. Carrie McClelland, Floride's cousin, had been a classmate when Floride attended Aunt Elizabeth Clemson Barton's boarding school (Sept. 1856–June 1858) in Philadelphia. McGee and Lander, *A Rebel Came Home,* pp. 12–15.

4. Catharine Clemson, sister of Thomas G. Clemson, married George W. North. Walter, Willy, and Clem were their sons.

5. Kate Barton, daughter of Elizabeth Clemson Barton, sister of Thomas G. Clemson. Elizabeth Clemson married George W. Barton (1807–1851).

6. Henry Onderdonk, president of Maryland Agricultural College. He was ousted in 1864 because of his Confederate sympathies. Letter from Mrs. Virginia R. Onderdonk, Baltimore, Md., Aug. 25, 1959.

7. D. Williamson Lee, son of Gideon Lee, onetime mayor of New York City and U.S. Congressman. Letter from Horace E. Hillary, Paterson, N.Y., Dec. 22, 1959. Thomas G. Clemson had business dealing with the Lees, and in 1869 Floride married D. W. Lee's brother, Gideon. In 1863 she obviously had a "cursh" on D. W. Lee.

8. William Clemson, brother of Thomas G. Clemson

9. Mattie Clemson, daughter of Episcopal minister John Baker Clemson, brother of Thomas G. Clemson.

10. Mrs. Lizette Daub, Mrs. Clemson's housekeeper, and her daugher, Freda; Mrs. Charlotte Augusta Norris Calvert (1815–1876), wife of Charles Benedict Calvert (1808–1864), neighbors of the Clemsons. See John Bailey Calvert Nicklin, "The Clavert Family," *Maryland Historical Magazine*, XVI (Sept. 1921), 316.

11. Henry McCeney (age 16), son of George and Harriet McCeney, who farmed nearby. MS. Census 1860, Washington, D.C. (National Archives).

12. Ella Calvert (1840–1902), daughter of the Charles B. Calverts, was married to Duncan G. Campbell. Nicklin, "The Calvert Family," *Maryland Historical Magazine*, XVI (Sept. 1921), 316.

13. General John Hunt Morgan, ill-fated Confederate raider, most of whose force had been recently killed or captured in Ohio.

14. The Clemsons had sold some of their furniture to the Elias Bakers.

15. Elizabeth Robinson (age 21), daughter of Conway and Mary S. Robinson, was one of Floride's best friends. Conway Robinson was a Virginia-born lawyer and Confederate sympathizer. The two oldest Robinson sons, Cary and William, were killed in action in Confederate service. MS. Census 1860, Washington, D.C. For the Robinson deaths see McGee and Lander, *A Rebel Came Home*, pp. 44, 66.

16. Mary Clemson, daughter of John Baker Clemson.

17. "Govvy" Morris, a frequent visitor at The Home and apparently a friend of D. W. Lee.

18. Sallie, a third daughter of John Baker Clemson.

19. Floride's dog.

20. Margaret Ritchie Stone, wife of Dr. Robert K. Stone (1822–1872), personal physician to President Lincoln and the Clemsons. Mrs. Stone was the daughter of Thomas Ritchie, founder of the *Richmond Enquirer*. MS. Census 1860, Washington, D.C.; *History of the Medical Society of the District of Columbia, 1817–1909* (Washington: The Medical Society of D.C., 1909), pp. 238–39.

21. Two nearby places of entertainment.

22. Benjamin H. Latrobe, Jr. (1806–1878), and daughter Mary Elizabeth Latrobe (1836–1916). John E. Semmes, *John H. B. Latrobe and His Times, 1803–1891* (Baltimore: The Norman, Remington Co., 1917), pp. 578–79.

23. Emily Wood (age 21), daughter of Elizabeth D. Wood, a Bladensburg neighbor. MS. Census 1860, Washington, D.C.

24. William M. Merrick (1818–1889), associate justice for U.S. Circuit Court for Maryland. *Biographical Directory of the American Congress, 1774–1949*, p. 1557. The Merricks were close friends of the Clemsons.

25. Laura Leupp, a frequent visitor to The Home and daughter of Charles M. Leupp, a New York businessman and friend of Thomas G. Clemson. Leupp committed suicide on Oct. 5, 1859. Laura Leupp to Mrs. Anna C. Clemson, Oct. 6, 1859, Clemson Papers.

26. Mary Latrobe and Henry Onderdonk were married on Dec. 17, 1868. McGee and Lander, *A Rebel Came Home,* p. 124.
27. Floride was named "Elizabeth Floride" but had customarily been called "Floride" since childhood. See ibid., p. 1.
28. Virginia King (age 18), daughter of U.S. Army surgeon Benjamin King, a Bladensburg neighbor. MS. Census 1860, Washington, D.C.
29. Jennie Cameron was probably Virginia Cameron, youngest daughter of Simon Cameron, President Lincoln's first secretary of war. Letter from Mrs. Clarkson T. Hunt, Lancaster, Pa., July 7, 1965.
30. Louisa Clemson, sister of Thomas G. Clemson, married Samuel Washington, a great nephew of George Washington, and lived at Harewood, now West Virginia. During the Civil War the family suffered great privation. "Lizzie W" and "Cousin Annie" were probably Elizabeth Washington and Anna Clemson Washington, daughter and daughter-in-law, respectively, of Louisa and Samuel Washington. See McGee and Lander, *A Rebel Came Home,* pp. 17, 55, 65.
31. Probably Mrs. Mary E. Dodge of the Bladensburg area. MS. Census 1860, Washington, D.C.
32. Confederate ranger John Singleton Mosby.
33. The British government intervened and did not permit the "Laird Rams" to leave England.
34. Tom Clemson, another cousin, apparently lived with Aunt Barton and Kate at that time.
35. Woods Baker, deceased son of Elias Baker and husband of Sarah.
36. Harriet Lane, ex-President Buchanan's niece.

Chapter 15: Memories of a Hospital Matron

1. The Daughters of the Confederacy, in West Virginia, as throughout the whole South, have this sacred duty now in charge,—the care of Confederate graves.

Chapter 23: The Bread Riot in Richmond, 1863

A member of the faculty at Mary Baldwin College, Staunton, Virginia, William J. Kimball is the author of *Richmond in Time of War.* He also has done extensive research on Civil War novels.

1. Mary Boykin Chesnut, *A Diary from Dixie* (Boston, 1949), p. 283.
2. John H. Wise, *The End of an Era* (Boston, 1902), p. 410.
3. When there was no tariff on domestic produce (as there was for a short period in the winter of 1861–62), foodstuffs were brought into Richmond by wagon from neighboring farms. Yet even after the tariffs were lifted, the inhabitants were at the mercy of the hucksters who charged what they pleased for their merchandise. On the very day of the bread riot, meal was selling for $16 per bushel. See Sally Brock Putnam, *Richmond during the War* (New York, 1867), pp. 113–14.
4. Varina Howell Davis, *Jefferson Davis . . . A Memoir by His Wife* (New York, 1890), II, 374. Hereafter cited as Davis, *Jefferson Davis.*
5. Judith W. McGuire, *Diary of a Southern Refugee* (New York, 1867), p. 203.
6. Mrs. Roger A. Pryor, *Reminiscences of Peace and War* (New York, 1905), p. 238. Although Mrs. Pryor specifically mentions women and children as comprising the mob, some male participants were also involved.

7. Ernest Taylor Walthall, *Hidden Things Brought to Life* (Richmond, 1933), p. 24.
8. Davis, *Jefferson Davis,* II, 374.
9. McGuire, *Diary of a Southern Refugee,* p. 203.
10. Davis, *Jefferson Davis,* II, 374.
11. Ibid., p. 375.
12. Ibid.
13. Ibid., p. 374.
14. Walthall, *Hidden Things Brought to Life,* p. 24.
15. Davis, *Jefferson Davis,* II, 376.
16. A similar appeal was sent to the president of the local telegraph company, U.S. War Dept., comp., War *of the Rebellion: A Compilation of the Official Records of the Union and Confederate Armies* (Washington, 1880–1901), Ser. 1, XVIII, 958.
17. The *Examiner*'s editorial writer feared that "the next arrival of Northern newspapers will be filled with lies about these thief-saturnalia which will shame Munchausen." A subsequent issue of the New York *Herald* contained "the statement of a refugee from Richmond," but the account of the riot was both inaccurate and grossly exaggerated.
18. Putnam, *Richmond during the War,* p. 210.

Chapter 24: Coping in Confederate Appalachia: Portrait of a Mountain Woman and Her Community at War

John C. Inscoe is associate professor of history at the University of Georgia and editor of *The Georgia Historical Quarterly.* A brief version of this article was presented at the annual meeting of the Organization of American Historians in Chicago in April, 1992. The author wishes to thank Mary Anglin, Jane Turner Censer, Catherine Clinton, Drew Gilpin Faust, Jean Friedman, Gordon McKinney, Richard Melvin, and LeeAnn Whites far their very helpful comments and suggestions.

1. *North Carolina Standard* (Raleigh), August 19, 1863.
2. The Bell correspondence is found in the Alfred W. Bell Papers, Special Collections Department, Duke University Library, Durham.
3. Shirley Abbott, *Womenfolks: Growing Up Down South* (New Haven: Ticknor and Fields, 1983), 62.
4. George C. Rable, *Civil Wars: Women and the Crisis of Southern Nationalism* (Urbana: University of Illinois Press, 1989); Marilyn Mayer Culpepper, *Trials and Triumphs: The Women of the American Civil War* (East Lansing: Michigan State University Press, 1991); Jean Friedman, *The Enclosed Garden: Women and Community in the Evangelical South, 1830–1900* (Chapel Hill: University of North Carolina Press, 1985), chapter 5; Michael Fellman, *Inside War: The Guerrilla Conflict in Missouri during the American Civil War* (New York: Oxford University Press, 1989), chapter 5; Drew Gilpin Faust, "Altars of Sacrifice: Confederate Women and the Narratives of War," *Journal of American History,* 76 (March, 1990), 1200–1228; and Camille Kunkle, "'It Is What It Does to the Souls': Women's Views on the Civil War," *Atlanta History,* 33 (Summer, 1989), 56–70.

Some of the best works on those issues focus on North Carolina women, including Paul D. Escort, *Many Excellent People: Power and Privilege in North Carolina, 1850–1900* (Chapel Hill: University of North Carolina Press, 1985), chapter 3, particularly pp. 63–67; Victoria Bynum, *Unruly Women: The Politics of Social and Sexual*

Control in the Old South (Chapel Hill: University of North Carolina Press, 1992), chapters 5 and 6; and Jane Turner Censer, "'A New Age A-Dawning': Genteel Women in North Carolina during and after the Civil War," paper presented at the annual meeting of the Organization of American Historians in Chicago, April, 1992.

5. Gordon B. McKinney, "Women's Role in Civil War Western North Carolina," *North Carolina Historical Review,* LXIX (January, 1992), 37–56; Phillip Shaw Paludan, *Victims: A True Story of the Civil War* (Knoxville: University of Tennessee Press, 1981); Barbara Howe, "The Impact of the Civil War on Women's Employment in Wheeling, West Virginia, in the 1860s," paper presented at the Second Southern Conference on Women's History in Chapel Hill, North Carolina, June, 1991; Ralph Mann, "Guerrilla Warfare and Gender Roles: Sandy Basin, Virginia, as Case Study," paper presented at the Fifteenth Annual Appalachian Studies Conference in Asheville, North Carolina, March, 1992; and Mann, "Family Group, Family Migration, and the Civil War in the Sandy Basin of Virginia," *Appalachian Journal,* 19 (Summer, 1992), 374–393.

   For more general recent work on Appalachian women during the nineteenth century, see Milton Ready, "Forgotten Sisters: Mountain Women in the South," in John C. Inscoe (ed.), *Southern Appalachia and the South: A Region within a Region,* Volume 3 of *Journal of the Appalachian Studies Association* (1991), 61–67; Sally W. Maggard, "Class and Gender," in Jim Lloyd and Anne G. Campbell (eds.), *The Impact of Institutions in Appalachia* (Boone, N.C.: Appalachian Consortium Press, 1986); Mary K. Anglin, "Reinventing: Working Class Women of Western North Carolina," paper presented at the Twelfth Annual Appalachian Studies Conference in Unicoi, Georgia, March, 1989; and Antlin, "Errors at the Margins: Rediscovering the Women of Antebellum Western North Carolina," paper presented at the annual meeting of the Southern Historical Association in Fort Worth, Texas, November, 1991.

6. Lawrence E. Wood, *Mountain Memories* (Franklin, N.C.: privately published, n.d.), 75.

7. Antebellum information on the Bells was gleaned from the inventory description, Bell Papers.

8. George W. Featherstonaugh, *A Canoe Voyage up the Minnay Sotor . . .* (London: R. Bentley, 2 volumes, 1847), II, 281.

9. Charles Lanman, *Letters from the Alleghany Mountains* (New York: G. P. Putnam, 1849), 81. For other nineteenth-century observations of Franklin and Macon County, see A. R. Newsome (ed.), "The A. S. Merrimon Journal, 1853–1854," *North Carolina Historical Review,* VIII (July, 1931), 313–314; Myron H. Avery and Kenneth S. Boardman (eds.), "Arnold Guyot's Notes on the Geography of the Mountain District of Western North Carolina," *North Carolina Historical Review,* XV (July, 1938), 282–283; and Wilbur G. Zeigler and Ben S. Grosscup, *The Heart of the Alleghanies; or, Western North Carolina* (Raleigh: Alfred Williams and Company, 1883), 82–83. For recent but impressionistic histories of the county, see Wood, *Mountain Memories;* and Jessie Sutton (ed.), *The Heritage of Macon County* (Winston-Salem: Hunter Publishing Company, 1987).

10. For Macon County statistics on population, landholdings, agricultural output, and slaveholdings in 1850 and 1860 in relation to other western North Carolina counties, see John C. Inscoe, *Mountain Masters, Slavery, and the Sectional Crisis in Western North Carolina* (Knoxville: University of Tennessee Press, 1989), tables 1.1,

1.2, 1.3, 3.2, and appendix. For general accounts of Macon County before and
during the Civil War, see special issue of the *Franklin Press,* June 26, 1925; and
Sutton, *Heritage of Macon County,* 43–51.

11. On early recruiting efforts in southwestern North Carolina, see Vernon H. Crow,
*Storm in the Mountains: Thomas's Confederate Legion of Cherokee Indians and Moun-
taineers* (Cherokee, N.C.: Press of the Museum of the Cherokee Indian, 1982),
10–15.

12. Alfred to Mary Bell, January 30, 1862, Bell Papers. All subsequent references to cor-
respondence refer to this collection. On January 30, 1862, the *Asheville News* noted
that "Coleman's Battalion is here and eager to meet the enemies of their country.
. . . They are tired of listless inaction and would hail with joy the order to march."
For a history of the Thirty-ninth Regiment and Bell's service record, see Louis H.
Manarin and Weymouth T. Jordan, Jr. (eds.), *North Carolina Troops, 1861–1865: A
Roster* (Raleigh: Division of Archives and History, Department of Cultural
Resources, projected multivolume series, 1966–), X, 104–109, 120.

13. Mary to Alfred Bell, November 13, 1861.

14. Alfred to Mary Bell, January 30, 1862. See her letters of Novemher 13, 1861, and
January 30, 1862.

15. Mary to Alfred Bell, February 10, 1862.

16. Mary to Alfred Bell, March 5, 1862.

17. Mary to Alfred Bell, April 28, 1862.

18. Mary to Alfred Bell, March 5, 1862. She expressed similar sentiments in letters of
April 4 and June 13, 1862. In Mary's letter of March 5, 1862, she noted that one
victim had died of measles, while another had been one of the men who wanted to
lead his own company.

19. Mary to Alfred Bell, June 20, 1862.

20. Mary to Alfred Bell, November 13, 1861.

21. Mary to Alfred Bell, May 22, 1862.

22. Mary to Alfred Bell, April 28, May 22, 1862. The act, the first draft in American history, was passed on April 16, 1862; in September the age of eligible draftees was
raised to forty-five and in February, 1864, extended again to cover men from ages
seventeen to fifty. See Emory M. Thomas, *The Confederate Nation: 1861–1865* (New
York: Harper and Row, 1979), 152–155, 260–261, for a thorough treatment of
Confederate conscription.

23. Mary to Alfred Bell, April 28, 1862.

24. Mary to Alfred Bell, January 20, March 5, August 26, 1862. Mary's reference to
Alf's encounters with prostitution was a legitimate concern as long as he was in East
Tennessee. A Confederate major stationed near Knoxville wrote of that region in
1863: "Female virtue if it ever existed in this Country seems now almost a perfect
wreck. Prostitutes are thickly crowded through mountain & valley in hamlet & city."
Quoted in Bell I. Wiley, *Confederate Women* (Westport, Conn.: Greenwood Press,
1975), 162.

25. See George Featherstonaugh's comment on Franklin on pages 305–6 above.
Franklin was not alone in its reputation for the insobriety of its citizenry. Augustus S.
Merrimon wrote in 1854 of Jewel Hill in nearby Madison County: "I do not know
of any rival for this place in regard to drunkenness, ignorance, superstition, and the
most brutal debauchery." Newsome, "A. S. Menrimon Journal," 319.

26. Mary to Alfred Bell, January 30, 1862. See also her letters of June 28 and August 26, 1862, and his letter of September 18, 1862.
27. Coleman, a nephew of David L. Swain, was an ambitious and accomplished young man, who seems to have been well liked and respected by most others who knew him. There seems to be no other evidence of the problems in his leadership or deportment as laid out by Alfred Bell. For sketches on Coleman, see F. A. Sondley, *A History of Buncombe County, North Carolina* (Asheville: Advocate Printing Company, 2 volumes, 1930), II, 768–769; John Preston Arthur, *Western North Carolina: A History from 1730 to 1913* (Raleigh: Edwards and Broughton, 1914), 403–404; and Frontis W. Johnston (ed.), *The Papers of Zebulon Baird Vance* (Raleigh: Division of Archives and History, Department of Cultural Resources, projected multivolume series, 1963–), I, 19n. For a vivid contemporary description of Coleman, see Newsome, "A. S. Merrimon Journal," 310. The most thorough treatment of Coleman's Civil War career is found in David C. Bailey, *Farewell to Valor: A Salute to the Brothers Coleman . . . of Asheville Days Remembered* (Asheville: Hexagon Company, 1977). Despite a detailed treatment of Coleman's leadership of the Thirty-ninth North Carolina Regiment, Bailey makes no mention of Alfred Bell or the dissension in his company.
28. Mary to Alfred Bell, May 29, 1862.
29. Alfred to Mary Bell, June 18, July 6, 1862.
30. Mary to Alfred Bell, June 28, 1862.
31. Alfred to Mary Bell, July 6, 1862.
32. Mary to Alfred Bell, July 20, 1862.
33. Mary to Alfred Bell, July 27, 1862.
34. Alfred to Mary Bell, September 1, 1862.
35. Mary to Alfred Bell, July 27, 1862.
36. Alfred to Mary Bell, March 31, 1864; Manarin and Jordan, *North Carolina Troops,* X, 120.
37. Alfred to Mary Bell, March 31, 1864.
38. Alfred to Mary Bell, April 8, 1864. Salena Reid was the wife of Lieutenant John Reid, who headed the other Macon County company of Coleman's regiment. The author is grateful to Richard Melvin for information on these and other individuals in Franklin with whom the Bells interacted.
39. Mary to Alfred Bell, April 22, 1864.
40. Mary to Alfred Bell, June 5, 17, 1864.
41. On the localistic nature of Union military companies and their linkage to communities, see Reid Mitchell, "The Northern Soldier and His Community," in Mans Vinovskis (ed.), *Toward a Social History of the American Civil War: Exploratory Essays* (Cambridge, England: Cambridge University Press, 1990), 78–92. On the impact of such community-composed units on desertion rates among North Carolinians, see Peter S. Bearman, "Desertion as Localism: Army Unit Solidarity and Group Norms in the U.S. Civil War," *Social Forces,* 70 (December, 1991), 321–342.
42. Mary to Alfred Bell, April 4, 28, 1862.
43. Mary to Alfred Bell, August 26, 1862.
44. Mary to Alfred Bell, August 29, 1862.
45. Mary to Alfred Bell, April 15, 1864.
46. Mary to Alfred Bell, December 16, 1864.

47. Mary to Alfred Bell, December 16, 1864.
48. Mary to Alfred Bell, November 13, 1861, June 28, 1862.
49. Mary to Alfred Bell, June 18, 1864; Alfred to Mary Bell, June 28, 1864.
50. Recent studies have made it increasingly apparent that tenantry made up a significant part of the antebellum agricultural work force in the southern highlands. See Frederick A. Bode and Donald F. Ginter, *Farm Tenancy and the Census in Antebellum Georgia* (Athens: University of Georgia Press, 1986), 116–117, table 6.1, p. 131 [for north Georgia mountains]; Joseph D. Reid, Jr., "Antebellum Southern Rental Contracts," *Explorations in Economic History,* XIII (January, 1976), 69–83 [for Haywood County, North Carolina]; Durwood Dunn, *Cades Cove: The Life and Death of a Southern Appalachian Community, 1818–1937* (Knoxville: University of Tennessee Press, 1988), 72; Tyler Blethen and Curtis Wood, "The Pioneer Experience to 1851," in Max R. Williams (ed.), *The History of Jackson County, North Carolina* (Sylva: Jackson County Historical Association, 1987), 83–95; and Wilma Dunaway, "Southern Appalachia's People without History: The Role of Unfree Laborers in the Region's Antebellum Economy," paper presented at the meeting of the Social Science History Association in Washington, D.C., November, 1989.
51. Mary to Alfred Bell, November 13, 1861.
52. Mary to Alfred Bell, April 5, 1862.
53. Mary to Alfred Bell, June 13, 1862. Mary referred to Julius T. Siler, who lived across the street from the Bells, and whose family was among Macon County's largest slaveholders. Siler's wife, Mary, was David Coleman's sister.
54. Mary to Alfred Bell, May 22, 1862.
55. Mary to Alfred Bell, August 26, 1862; Alfred to Mary Bell, September 18, 1862.
56. Mary to Alfred Bell, January 30, 1862; Alfred to Mary Bell, February 8, 1862.
57. Mary to Alfred Bell, August 26, 29, 1862.
58. Alfred to Mary Bell, June [n.d.], 1864.
59. Alfred to Mary Bell, April 10, 1864.
60. Mary to Alfred Bell, July 8, 1864.
61. Mary to Alfred Bell, April 22, 1864.
62. Mary to Alfred Bell, July 8, 1864. For context on the traditional roles of women as farmers, see Elizabeth Fox-Genovese, "Women in Agriculnire during the Nineteenth Century," in Lou Ferleger (ed.), *Agriculture and National Development: Views on the Nineteenth Century* (Ames: Iowa State University Press, 1990), 267–301.
63. Mary to Alfred Bell, February 19, 1864.
64. Mary to Alfred Bell, June 5, 1864.
65. Crow, *Storm in the Mountains,* 59. The most detailed account of this and earlier raids into adjacent Cherokee County appears in Margaret Walker Freel, *Our Heritage: The People of Cherokee County, North Carolina, 1540–1955* (Asheville: Miller Printing Company, 1956), 225–231. The only such incident reported in Macon County is an "unconfirmed story" of a Union man traveling through the county on his way to East Tennessee who was killed, beheaded, and buried between Franklin and Highlands. Sutton, *Heritage of Macon County,* 46.
66. Mary to Alfred Bell, February 19, 1864.
67. Alfred to Mary Bell, March 17, 1864.
68. Alfred to Mary Bell, December 9, 1862.
69. Alfred to Mary Bell, December 9, 1862.

70. Alfred to Mary Bell, March 17, 1864.
71. Mary to Alfred Bell, March 11, 1864.
72. Alfred to Mary Bell, March 31, April 8, 1864. Alfred referred to Dillard Love, who with seventy slaves in 1860 was Macon County's largest slaveholder. For a more detailed analysis of the Bells' slave purchases and Mary Bell's relationship with her new property, see John C. Inscoe, "Mary Bell and Her 1864 Slave Purchase: Opportunity and Optimism in Confederate Appalachia," unpublished paper.
73. McKinney, "Women's Role in Civil War Western North Carolina."
74. Anne Firor Scott, *The Southern Lady: From Pedestal to Politics, 1830–1930* (Chicago: University of Chicago Press, 1970), 82.
75. Mary Elizabeth Massey, *Bonnet Brigades* (New York: Alfred A. Knopf, 1966), ix.
76. Both Gordon McKinney and Ralph Mann provide richly documented accounts of the brutalization of women by the guerrilla warfare, military raids, bushwhackers, and deserters that plagued southern highlanders. McKinney, "Women's Role in Civil War Western North Carolina," 43–46; Mann, "Guerrilla Warfare and Gender Roles." For accounts of women in similar circumstances in Missouri, see Fellman, *Inside War,* chapter 5.
77. Perhaps because he was a western Carolinian himself, scores of mountain women wrote Governor Vance during the war. Much of McKinney's analysis of highland women is based on their letters to him. There is little evidence that women's aid societies or charitable associations were ever formed in the state west of Buncombe County. McKinney, "Women's Role in Civil War Western North Carolina," 54.
78. Faust, "Altars of Sacrifice," 1206–1207.
79. McKinney, "Women's Role in Civil War Western North Carolina."
80. Although Confederate colonel William W. Stringfield of Thomas' Legion had used Franklin as the base for his defensive patrols during the latter part of the war, the closest military action to Franklin was the war's final skirmish in North Carolina, which took place forty miles away in Waynesville on May 6, 1865. See Arthur, *Western North Carolina,* 602–621; and Crow, *Storm in the Mountains,* 136–137. For accounts of bushwhacker activity and its effects elsewhere in western North Carolina, including adjacent Cherokee County, see both of the above and Daniel Ellis, *The Thrilling Adventures of Daniel Ellis* (New York: Harper, 1867); Ina W. Van Noppen, "The Significance of Stoneman's Last Raid," *North Carolina Historical Review,* XXXVIII (January, April, July, October, 1961), 19–44, 149–172, 341–361, 500–526; William R. Trotter, *The Civil War in North Carolina,* Volume II: *Bushwhackers: The Mountains* (Greensboro: Piedmont Impressions, 3 volumes, 1988–1989); and McKinney, "Women's Roles in Civil War Western North Carolina," 43–45. For broader context on the impact of such activity elsewhere in the state, see Paul D. Escott and Jeffrey J. Crow, "The Social Order and Violent Disorder: An Analysis of North Carolina in the Revolution and Civil War," *Journal of Southern History,* LII (August, 1986), 373–402; and Wayne K. Durrill, *War of Another Kind: A Southern Community in the Great Rebellion* (New York: Oxford University Press, 1990), chapter 7 [on Washington County].
81. McKinney, "Women's Roles in Civil War Western North Carolina," 44, 49, 55; Freel, *Our Heritage,* 225–231.
82. Examples of mountain communities torn apart by ideological differences include Shelton Laurel in Madison County, North Carolina, and Cades Cove, Tennessee.

For analysis of how destructive an impact such divisions had on community life, see Paludan, *Victims;* and Dunn, *Cades Cove,* chapter 5. See also Kenneth W. Noe, "Red String Scare: Civil War Southwest Virginia and the Heroes of America," *North Carolina Historical Review,* LXIX (July, 1992), 301–322; and Mann, "Family Group, Family Migration, and the Civil War in the Sandy Basin of Virginia," 374–393.

83. John Andrew Rice, *I Came Out of the Eighteenth Century* (New York: Harper and Brothers, 1942), 116–117, quoted in Scott, *Southern Lady,* 100.

Chapter 25: Emily Lyles Harris: A Piedmont Farmer During the Civil War

Philip Racine teaches history at Wofford College in South Carolina. He is at present writing a history of Spartanburg County.

1. Reminiscence of Mrs. Laura L. Harris, typescript in private hands. Unless otherwise noted all quotations are from the David Golightly Harris Farm Journals, 1855–1870, a microfilm copy of which is in the Southern Historical Collection at the University of North Carolina, Chapel Hill.

2. July 1862, David suffered from severe headaches; 16 and 18 Oct. 1864.

3. 13 and 20 Nov. 1862.

4. 23 Nov. 1862.

5. 2 and 4 Dec. 1862.

6. 28 Jan., 7 Nov. 1863, 8 July 1864.

7. 24 Nov. 1863, 31 May 1864, 5 and 27 Jan. 1865.

8. 27 Aug. and 1 Oct. 1864.

9. 18 May 1864.

10. 20 and 29 Oct. 1864.

11. 26 Dec. 1863.

12. 13 June, 25 Nov., and 7 Dec. 1864.

13. 16 and 18 Dec. 1864.

14. 3 Jan. 1865.

15. 20 Jan. 1865.

16. 22 Feb., 6 and 27 March 1865.

17. 8 and 20 Feb. 1865.

18. John Durant Ashmore to (unknown), Greenville, S.C., 30 Aug. 1863, John Durant Ashmore Papers, South Caroliniana Library, University of South Carolina; The South Caroliniana Library will hereafter be cited as SCL; 6 Dec. 1863.

19. 25 Oct. and 8 Nov. 1864; J. A. Keller to Col. John M. Obey [place unknown], 16 March 1865, J. A. Keller Papers, SCL.

20. 6 and 3 March 1865.

21. 17 Feb. 1865. Emily's maternal grandparents were first cousins, which may have been what her mother-in-law objected to.

Chapter 26: A Civil War Experience of Some Arkansas Women in Indian Territory

* The editor is Oppenheim Regents Professor of History at Oklahoma State University, Stillwater, Oklahoma.

1. Biographical data supplied by Chester V. Kielman, Archivist, Barker Texas History Center, University of Texas at Austin; William S. Campbell, *One Hundred Years of Fayetteville* (1928), p. 100; manuscript returns of the 1860 federal census, Arkansas History Commission, Little Rock, Arkansas; *Who Was Who in America* (5 vols.,

Chicago: Marquis-Who's Who, 1943–1973), Vol. IV, p. 919. The original manuscript of the Mrs. Francena Lavinia (Martin) Sutton Civil War account is not known to be extant. A typescript is in the Barker Texas History Center of the University of Texas at Austin.

2. In 1860 Fayetteville had a population of 967,673 white and 294 slave. *Population of the United States in 1860; Compiled from the Original Returns of the Eighth Census* (Washington: Government Printing Office, 1864), p. 19.

3. Federal forces under Brigadier General Samuel Curtis scattered a few Confederate pickets and raised the Union flag over Fayetteville on February 23, 1862. The Federal hold on the city thereafter was threatened several times. In July, 1862, 550 mounted riflemen and detachments of cavalry under Major William H. Miller routed a Confederate force a few miles southwest of Fayetteville. The Battle of Prairie Grove was fought near the city on December 7, 1862. After this Fayetteville was garrisoned by the First Arkansas (Union) Cavalry Regiment under Colonel M. La Rue Harrison. On April 18, 1863, they repelled an attack by 900 Confederates under Brigadier General William L. Cabell. However, Southern partisan Captain William Brown seized the city for a few hours on August 23, 1863, while Harrison's regiment was absent from the city. In October Colonel William H. Brooks and the Thirty-fourth Arkansas (Confederate) Infantry Regiment besieged the city's garrison of 500 men of Harrison's regiment under Major Thomas J. Hunt. Hunt refused to surrender, and Brooks withdrew. In the fall of 1864, the entire First Arkansas (Union) Cavalry Regiment was in Fayetteville. United States Department of War, *The War of the Rebellion: A Compilation of the Official Records of the Union and Confederate Armies* (70 vols., 128 books, Washington: Government Printing Office, 1880–1901), Ser. I, Vol. VIII, pp. 68–70, Vol. XIII, p. 163, Vol. XXII, Pt. 1, pp. 67–158, 305–313, 594–595, 701–704. Hereafter cited as *Official Records.*

4. Major General Sterling Price's defeated army was retreating southward after his futile raid along the Missouri border and crucial defeat at the Battle of Westport, Missouri. Price had taken 12,000 men north in a desperate attempt to regain control of Missouri. Union forces under Major General Samuel Curtis pursued Price as far as northern Arkansas. Albert Castel, *General Sterling Price and the Civil War in the West* (Baton Rouge: Louisiana State University Press, 1968), pp. 238–255; *Official Records,* Ser. I, Vol. XLI, Pt. 1, pp. 303–729.

5 . "Colonel F" refers to Major General James F. Fagan, commanding one of Price's three cavalry divisions. Actually he did not bring his own regiment to attack Fayetteville. On November 1, 1864, Price was in Cane Hill, where Fagan learned that Brooks' regiment and Brown's partisans again were besieging Fayetteville. Price gave Fagan 500 men from Brigadier General Joseph O. Shelby's brigade and two pieces of artillery to join the attack. The "soldier boys" who had left their girls in Fayetteville were the men of Brooks' regiment, all or most of whom came from Fayetteville or Washington County. Harrison's men had erected a fort of extensive earthworks within the city. Fagan probably attacked the city to procure provisions for his men, who suffered from want of food and clothing. *Official Records,* Ser. I, Vol. XLI, Pt. 1, pp. 638, 397–400, Pt. 400, Pt. 4, p. 1004; Robert E. Waterman and Thomas Rothrock, eds., "The Earle-Buchanan Letters of 1861–1876," *Arkansas Historical Quarterly.* Vol. XXXII, No. 2 (Summer, 1974), p. 103.

6. Fagan led his detachment, Brooks' regiment and Brown's partisans in an attack on Fayetteville on November 3, 1864. The two Confederate guns bombarded the fort,

many shots striking nearby residences. The Confederates invested the city except for the fort. Three times the Confederate officers attempted assaults on the Federal works, but each time their weary men refused to attack. *Official Records,* Ser. I, Vol. XLI, Pt. 1, pp. 400, 515; Castel, *General Sterling Price and the Civil War in the West,* p. 247.

7. Colonel Harrison.

8. Harrison reported his losses as 1 killed and 8 wounded, and Confederate losses as 100 killed, wounded and taken prisoner, no doubt an inflated figure. *Official Records,* Ser. I, Vol. XLI, Pt. 1, p. 400.

9. The attack on Fayetteville was no "strategic feint," but it was the last engagement of Price's long retreat. The Confederates abandoned the city on November 4, 1864, and escaped just ahead of the advancing Federal troops of Major General James G. Blunt. *Official Records,* Ser. I, Vol. XLI, Pt. 1, pp. 400, 515, 638; Castel, *General Sterling Price and the Civil War in the West,* p. 247.

10. This was Blunt's army. A message from Harrison had reached Curtis the night before at Cross Hollows, eighteen miles away. *Official Records,* Ser. I, Vol. XLI, Pt. 1, p. 515.

11. Mrs. Sutton here refers to herself. The child was William Seneca Sutton, writer of the Foreword to this article.

12. Captain William "Buck" Brown, a former miller, was a guerrilla captain of northwest Arkansas, operating near Fayetteville. He led a band of 60 to 150 men that constantly harassed Harrison. Brown seized Fayetteville briefly on August 23, 1863, while Harrison's men were absent. In April of the next year he and his men dressed in Federal uniforms to surprise and kill nine Union troops. In March of 1865 a Federal patrol caught Brown near his mill in Benton County and killed him and three of his men. Leo E. Huff, "Guerillas, Jayhawkers and Bushwackers in Northern Arkansas During the Civil War," *Arkansas Historical Quarterly,* Vol. XXIV, No. 2 (Summer, 1965), pp. 136–137; *Official Records,* Ser. I, Vol. XXII, Pt. 1, pp. 594–595, Vol. XLIII, Pt. 1, p. 1185.

13. Their destination was Fort Smith, fifty miles southwest of Fayetteville, just east of the border of Indian Territory.

14. The commander of Fort Smith was Colonel William R. Judson, and the ladies' escorts were men of the Thirteenth Kansas Infantry Regiment. *Official Records,* Ser. I, Vol. XLI, Pt. 4, pp. 374, 986.

15. At least four roads led south from Fort Smith. The ladies intended to take the road south to Washington, Arkansas. Their escort failed to set them on the right road, and they followed a road leading southwest into Indian Territory. For maps of the country traveled by the ladies on this trip, see *Atlas to Accompany the Official Records of the Union and Confederate Armies* (Washington: Government Printing Office, 1891–1895), Plates CLIX, CLX.

16. The ladies' route that day carried them up the valley of the Poteau River. They camped on the prairie just north of the Winding Stair Mountains. The country was deserted because most of the Confederate residents of the northern part of the Choctaw Nation had fled south to avoid Union troops.

17. "Lincoln Coffee" was a name frequently used in the Confederate States as a substitute for coffee, which virtually became unobtainable within six months after the opening of the Civil War. Coffee substitutes used most frequently were parched corn,

rye, wheat, okra seeds, sweet potatoes, or chickory. Other coffee substitutes were acorns, dandelion roots, sugar cane, parched rice, cotton seeds, sorghum molasses, English peas, peanuts, and beans. Mary Elizabeth Massey, *Ersatz in the Confederacy* (Columbia: University of South Carolina Press, 1952), pp. 72–73.

18. The day's travel had skirted the north edge of the Winding Stair Mountains. The camp evidently was on a creek tributary to the Kiamichi River.

19. After leaving Cane Hill on November 4, 1864, Price had led his men on a wearying retreat across Indian Territory. His route lay north and west of that of the ladies. However, detachments left his main column to find and slaughter cattle for his starving troops. *Official Records,* Ser. I, Vol. XLI, Pt. 1, pp. 639, 647–648, 661, 692, 697, 705.

20. By this time the ladies were turning southward along the western border of the Winding Stair Mountains.

21. One of Price's officers reported that for twenty-three days his men had nothing to eat except beef without salt, and for three days they had nothing at all. *Official Records,* Ser. I, Vol. XLI, Pt. 1, p. 692.

22. The ladies were in the Choctaw Nation.

23. The Indian was directing the women to camp Bushy Creek, and he would bring them food.

24. A Confederate soldier.

25. Doaksville was close to Fort Towson. Both were located near where the Kiamichi River enters the Red River in the Choctaw Nation. Major General Samuel Bell Maxey, commander of Confederate troops in Indian Territory and also Superintendent of Indian Affairs, made Fort Townson his headquarters. Kenneth E. Lewis, "Archeological Investigations at Fort Towson, Choctaw County, Oklahoma, 1971," *The Chronicles of Oklahoma,* Vol. L, No. 3 (Autumn, 1972), p. 276; Allan C. Ashcraft, ed., "Confederate Indian Department Conditions in August, 1864," *The Chronicles of Oklahoma,* Vol. XLI, No. 3 (Autumn, 1963), pp. 270–271.

26. This "chief" was Robert M. Jones, the Choctaw planter. Jones had returned earlier in the year from Richmond, Virginia, where he had served as the Choctaw Chickasaw delegate to the Confederate Congress. His Rose Hill plantation was west of Doaksville on the Red River. Jones owned more than 200 slaves. T. Paul Wilson, "Confederate Delegates of the Five Civilized Tribes," *The Chronicles of Oklahoma,* Vol. LIII, No. 3 (Fall, 1975), pp. 362–364.

27. Jones' second wife, Susan Colbert, died in 1860. He married Elizabeth Earle on January 18, 1861. She had been a Presbyterian mission teacher at Armstrong Academy. Sketch of Robert M. Jones and sketch by W. B. Morrison titled "Rose Hill Mansion," Vertical Files, Library, Oklahoma Historical Society, Oklahoma City, Oklahoma.

28. Jones' three children by his first wife, Judith Walker, all died in infancy. There is record of only two children by Susan Colbert, one of whom died in infancy. The Rose Hill cemetery now is owned by the Oklahoma State Historical Society. Sketch of Robert M. Jones, sketch by Morrison, titled "Rose Hill Mansion" and family records in *Bible* of Robert M. Jones, Vertical Files, Library, Oklahoma Historical Society.

29. The name Rector was common in the Confederate Army in Indian Territory. Thus this person cannot be identified with any degree of accuracy.

30. The author's chronology is confused at this point. The Emancipation Proclamation issued by President Abraham Lincoln on January 1, 1863, technically, but not actually, freed the slaves in the Confederate States then in rebellion against the United States. The Thirteenth Amendment constitutionally freed slaves when it became effective on December 18, 1865.

Chapter 27: *The Impact of the Civil War on a Southern Marriage: Clement and Virginia Tunstall Clay of Alabama*

This article is a revised version of a paper read before a session of the Southern Historical Association's meeting at Charleston, South Carolina, in November 1983. The authors wish to thank Barbara Welter and Jane Turner Censer for their comments on that paper and also to express their appreciation to the National Endowment for the Humanities for awarding Professor Heath a summer stipend, 1980, and Professor Bleser a fellowship, 1983–84.

The marriage of the Clays is one of ten unions to be explored by the authors in a book-length study on marriage in the mid-nineteenth-century South. There they will explore, among other things, the hypothesis that the loss of the Civil War and its aftermath produced profound alterations in the internal dynamics of many Southern marriages.

1. Margaret Mitchell, *Gone with the Wind* (1936; reprint, Garden City, N.Y.: Garden City Books, 1954), p. 67. C. Vann Woodward, ed., *Mary Chesnut's Civil War* (New Haven and London: Yale Univ. Press, 1981), and Elisabeth Muhlenfeld, *Mary Boykin Chesnut: A Biography* (Baton Rouge and London: Louisiana State Univ. Press, 1981), describe and analyze the most quoted woman of the nineteenth-century South.

2. For information on Virginia's early years and biographical information on all the Clays, see Ruth Nuermberger, *The Clays of Alabama: A Planter-Lawyer-Politician Family* (Lexington: Univ. of Kentucky Press, 1958), p. 82, hereafter cited as Nuermberger. Bell Irvin Wiley, *Confederate Women,* Contributions in American History, No. 38 (Westport, Conn.: Greenwood Press, 1975), includes a chapter on Virginia Clay. Wiley stresses Virginia's eagerness to play the belle, but his conclusions differ substantially from ours. Ada Sterling, *A Belle of the Fifties: Memoirs of Mrs. Clay of Alabama, covering Social and Political Life in Washington and the South, 1853–66; Put into narrative form by Ada Sterling* (New York: Doubleday, Page & Company, 1905), hereafter cited as *Belle,* must be used with caution as it contains many exaggerations and numerous errors.

3. For information on Henry Collier and Alfred Battle see Matthew W. Clinton, *Tuscaloosa, Alabama: Its Early Days, 1816–1865* (Tuscaloosa: Zonta Club, 1958), pp. 18, 23, 64, 104–5, 109; William Garrett, *Reminiscences of Public Men in Alabama for Thirty Years* (Atlanta: Plantation Publishing Company's Press, 1872), pp. 718–19; Thomas M. Owen, *History of Alabama and Dictionary of Alabama Biography,* 4 vols. (Chicago: S. J. Clarke Publishing Company, 1921), 3:112, 115, 380; and U.S. Census Records, Alabama, 1840, Population Schedules, Tuscaloosa County, pp. 194, 201, 252, 254. Virginia had other prominent Alabamans among her relatives including her uncle, Thomas B. Tunstall, who served as secretary of state while Clement Comer Clay was Governor of Alabama.

4. An acquaintance of Dr. Tunstall recalled he was "too careless of money matters." Thomas J. Green to Clement Claiborne Clay, Sept. 9, 1854. Unless otherwise indicated, all manuscripts and other unpublished sources cited in this paper are from the

Clement Claiborne Clay Papers at Duke University. This collection contains over 8,500 items. On Tunstall, see also his obituary in the *Florida Democrat,* reprinted in *Huntsville Democrat,* Oct. 13, 1847; and Whitemore Morris, *The First Tunstalls of Virginia and Some of Their Descendants* (San Antonio: privately published, 1950), p. 52. The voluminous Clay Papers at Duke contain no letters from Virginia's father, and there are only a few references to him. As late as 1873, Virginia was able, however, to provide the home address of her father's widow. Virginia to Clement, July 5, 1873.

5. Diploma, Virginia Caroline Tunstall, Nashville Female Academy, Dec. 9, 1840; Volume of poems to Virginia Tunstall, Clay Papers, Duke, Box 2; "Little Mag" to Virginia, Jan. 12, 1848; Martha Fort to Virginia, July 13, 1845; and F. Garvin Davenport, *Cultural Life in Nashville on the Eve of the Civil War* (Chapel Hill: Univ. of North Carolina Press, 1941), pp. 42–43.

6. *Belle,* pp. 10–13.

7. Nuermberger, pp. 1–68, 85–87. Frances Cabaniss Roberts, "Background and Formative Period in the Great Bend and Madison County" (Ph.D. diss., University of Alabama, 1956), is an excellent study of the early history of the Huntsville area. Clement Comer Clay's early land transactions are recorded in Deed Books B, pp. 3, 177–78, F, p. 27, G, pp. 246–47, H, pp. 44–45, 621–22, K, pp. 23–24, L, pp. 54–55, M, pp. 319–20, 472–73, N, p. 387, P, pp. 498, 532, Madison County Courthouse. The number of his slaves can be found in U.S. Census Records, Alabama, 1830, Population Schedules, Madison County, p. 101; and 1840, Madison County, pp. 169–70, Jackson County, p. 70.

8. Clement Claiborne to Ann E. Withers, Dec. 25, 1834, Levert Family Papers, University of North Carolina at Chapel Hill; Clement Claiborne to Susanna, Dec. 26, 1834. See also other letters in the Clay Papers and Nuermberger, pp. 75, 77, 88, 89–90.

9. Clement to Virginia, Jan. 5, 1843. The poem which followed Clement's confession contained the less than immortal lines:

> Oh! Ginnie dear, I do declare
> You ought to have a lickin!
> Unless in mercy you forbear
> Your arrows in me stickin!

10. Virginia Clay-Clopton, "Clement Claiborne Clay," *Transactions of the Alabama Historical Society* 2 (1898):82. See also Maria to "Dear Cousin" [Virginia], Jan. 1, 1843; *Belle,* pp. 15–16. Ann Williams Boucher, "Wealthy Planter Families in Nineteenth Century Alabama," (Ph.D. diss., University of Connecticut, 1978), p. 42, arrives at 18.5 as the average age of first marriage of 39 women born between 1820 and 1839 and married to wealthy Alabama planters in 1860. Two other statistical studies of upper-class southern women in the early nineteenth century agree that the average age of first marriage was twenty. Jane Turner Censer, "Parents and Children: North Carolina Planter Families, 1800–1860," (Ph.D. diss., Johns Hopkins University, 1980), p. 175; Catherine Clinton, *The Plantation Mistress: Woman's World in the Old South* (New York: Pantheon Books, 1982), pp. 60, 233. The difference between Boucher's figure of 18.5 for Alabama and Censer's statistic of 20.5 for North Carolina may reveal significant differences between older and more recently settled southern areas.

11. Boucher, "Wealthy Planter Families," p. 42, and Censder, "Parents and Children," pp. 177–79, agree that the average age of marriage for upper-class men was 26.

12. Clement Claiborne to Clement Comer, Jan. 18, 1843; and Clement Claiborne to Susanna, Dec. 23, 1842. Censer, "Parents and Children," pp. 137–64, in the best discussion of the topic, maintains that children often informed their parents of an engagement only after a proposal had been accepted and that parental consent, when sought, was seldom refused. Carl Degler, in his book *At Odds: Women and the Family in America from the Revolution to the Present* (New York: Oxford Univ. Press, 1980), pp. 9–14, is in agreement with Censer's findings. Bertram Wyatt-Brown, *Souhern Honor: Ethics and Behavior in the Old South* (New York and Oxford: Oxford Univ. Press, 1982), pp. 206–12, disagrees and claims that the opposition of fathers, other family members, and community opinion often served to block an unacceptable union. Russell Blake, "Ties of Intimacy: Social Values and Personal Relationships of Antebellum Slaveholders" (Ph.D. diss., University of Michigan, 1978), pp. 63–70, asserts that couples were uncertain over whether or not they were obligated to request parental consent prior to becoming engaged.

13. Virginia Clay, "Biographical Sketch of Clement Clay," n.d., p. 2, Clement Claiborne Clay Papers, University of Alabama; Clement Claiborne to Clement Comer, Feb. 3, 1843. The home in which the marriage of Virginia and Clement took place is still standing. Frank L. Owsley, "The Clays in Early Alabama History," *The Alabama Review* 2 (Oct. 1949): 243–68, stresses the political dimensions of this marriage.

14. Clement to Virginia, Feb. 15, 1846.

15. Clement to Susanna, Dec. 23, 1842; and Clement to Virginia, Jan. 20, 1843, Mar. 20, 1846.

16. Susanna Clay lacked Virginia's interest in society. Susanna to Ann E. Withers, Dec. 16, 1830, Dec. 3, 1831, Feb. 10, 21, 1832, Levert Family Papers. See also Nuermberger, pp. 81, 84–85, 87; Susanna to Clement Comer, Jan. 4, 1847; and Virginia to Susanna, Jan. 1, 1850. Virginia to Susanna, Dec. n.d., 1844. See also Wiley, *Confederate Women*, p. 44; Nuermberger, p. 96.

17. Woodward, ed., *Mary Chesnut's Civil War*, p. 32; Mary Boykin Chesnut, *A Diary from Dixie*, ed. Ben Ames Williams (Cambridge and London: Harvard Univ. Press, 1980, first published 1949), p. 382; and Clement Claiborne to Virginia, Feb. 22, 1846. Wyatt-Brown, *Southern Honor*, p. 236, claims that "barrenness in women . . . had always been a point of shame, and sufferers were contemptible or at best pitiable in the eyes of others."

18. Clement Claiborne to Clement Comer, Dec. 18, 1846. See also Lawson Clay to Susanna, Dec. 15, 1845; Clement Claiborne to Virginia, Mar. 8, Apr. 26, 1846; and Nuermberger, pp. 15–17, 85–86, 103–5. For Clay's salary as a legislator see J. Mills Thornton, *Politics and Power in a Slave Society: Alabama, 1800–1860* (Baton Rouge and London: Louisiana State Univ. Press, 1978), p. 80.

19. Clement to Virginia, Apr. 2, 1846. See also Clement to Virginia, Mar. 8, Apr. 9, 26, 1846; Clement Claiborne to Clement Comer, Dec. 18, 1846; and Lawson to Clement Comer, Dec. 19, 1846. The deeds recorded at the time Clay purchased the house and lot state that he paid only $555. He wrote his father, however, shortly before closing the transaction, that he would offer $2,700 for the property. Clement, whatever the original price had been, more than doubled his money when he sold it. Deed Books W, pp. 313–14, 616, Y, pp. 392–93, Madison County Courthouse.

20. Clement to Virginia, June 27–28, 1852, quoting a letter from Virginia which is no longer extant. See also Virginia to Clement Claiborne, June 10, July 20, 1852; Susanna Battle to Susanna Clay, Oct. 22, 1852; and Wiley, p. 45.

21. Clement to Virginia, June 27–28, 1852.

22. Clement to Virginia, Sept. 30, 1852; and Virginia to Clement, Oct. 4, 1852.

23. Nuermberger, pp. 115–18; *Belle,* pp. 21–25; and Garrett, *Reminiscences of Public Men in Alabama for Thirty Years,* p. 582.

24. Virginia to Tom Tait Tunstall, Oct. 10, 1856. See also draft of entry for *Woman's Who's Who of America,* Oct. 1912; and Nuermberger, p. 120.

25. Virginia to Clement Claiborne, Sept. 16, 1856.

26. Undated clippings, Clay Papers, Duke, Box 56; James E. Saunders, *Early Settlers of Alabama by Col. James Edmund Saunders, Lawrence County, Ala., with Notes and Genealogies by his Granddaughter, Elizabeth Saunders Blake Stubbs* (New Orleans: L. Graham & Son, Ltd., 1899), p. 288; and undated newspaper clipping, Clay Scrapbook V, p. 5. Virginia long remembered success that night and devoted a whole chapter to the event in *Belle,* pp. 126–37. See also Mrs. D. Giraud Wright, *A Southern Girl in '61* (New York: Doubleday, Page & Company, 1905), p. 21; Mrs. Roger A. Pryor, *Reminiscences of Peace and War* (New York: Macmillan Company, 1905), p. 81; and Marian Gouverneur, *As I Remember: Recollections of American Society During the Nineteenth Century* (New York and London: D. Appleton & Co., 1911), pp. 276–77.

27. Virginia to Tom Tunstall, Jan. 25, 1857. See also Virginia to Tom, Oct. 10, 1856; Tom to Virginia, May 23, 1859, Sept. 13, 1894, July 6, 1897, and Nov. 14, 1905. For biographical information on Tunstall see Morris, *The First Tunstalls of Virginia,* p. 86; and Owen, *History of Alabama,* 4: 1689–90. For Clement's lack of jealousy of Virginia's male friends see his letters, 1853–61, passim.

28. M. A. Collier to Virginia, May 16, 1852; Virginia to Clement Claiborne, [Nov.] 19, 1854; Clement Claiborne to Clement Comer, Jan. 18, 1854; Clement Claiborne to Susanna, Dec. 15, 1854; "List of Notes & bonds due C. C. Clay, Jr., placed in the hands of J. Withers Clay by H. L. Clay—Jan'y 1858"; and Nuermberger, p. 296.

29. Virginia to Clement Comer, July 10, 1855, Nov. 17, 1857. For Clay's political views and stands see Clement Claiborne to Clement Comer, Jan. 18, 1854, June 7, 1856; Nuermberger, pp. 123–74; and Levi S. Vanderford, "The Political Career of Clement Claiborne Clay" (M.A. thesis, University of Alabama, 1935), pp. 23–56. The Alabama legislature reelected Clay to the Senate over fifteen months before his term would expire in March 1859 because no session was scheduled for 1858.

30. Virginia to Clement Comer, Dec. 25, [1855]. See also *Belle,* pp. 139–42, Wiley, pp. 51–53.

31. Letters in the Clay Papers discuss his asthma and other details. See also Nuermberger, pp. 164, 176–84, 189–90. For the suggested causes of chronic asthma in adults see Samuel I. Cohen, "Psychological Factors," in T. J. H. Clark and S. Godfrey, eds., *Asthma* (London: Chapman and Hall, 1979), pp. 67–78, 84–87; Peter H. Knapp et al., "Psychosomatic Aspects of Bronchial Asthma," in Earle B. Weiss and Maurice S. Segal, eds., *Bronchial Asthma: Mechanisms and Therapeutics* (Boston: Little, Brown & Co., 1976), pp. 1055–80. David McCullough, *Mornings on Horseback* (New York: Simon and Schuster, 1981), pp. 90–108, contains an absorbing account of the asthmatic attacks which Theodore Roosevelt suffered as a

child and young adult. McCullough maintains that unresolved conflicts between Roosevelt and his parents caused the illness. Infections, as opposed to emotional causes, seem to play a greater role in adult than in childhood asthma. Milton B. Rosenblatt, "History of Bronchial Asthma," Weiss and Segal, eds., *Bronchial Asthma,* pp. 10–12, provides a good summary of mid-nineteenth-century medical recommendations for the treatment of asthma. See also W. W. Gerhard, *The Diagnosis, Pathology and Treatment of the Diseases of the Chest,* 2d ed. (Philadelphia: Edward Barrington and George D. Haswell, 1846), pp. 130–34.

32. The Clay collections at Duke and at the Huntsville Public Library contain many letters describing conditions in wartime Huntsville. See also "Civil War Days in Huntsville; As Taken from the Diary of Mrs. W. D. Chadwick which Appeared in Regular Episodes of the *Huntsville Times,*" 3d ed. (Huntsville: *Huntsville Times,* n.d.), pp. 3–14, University of Alabama Library; and Nuermberger, pp. 191, 211–18.

33. Virginia to Clement, Feb. 14, 24, Mar. 2, 14, 19, 1863. See also Clement to Virginia, Feb. 13, Mar. 12, 19, 22, 25, 1863, and Wiley, pp. 58–59.

34. Clement to Virginia, Mar. 12, 1863; and Virginia to Clement, Mar. 19, 1863. See also Wiley, p. 59.

35. Woodward, ed., *Mary Chesnut's Civil War,* p. 553. See also Celeste to Virginia, December 24, 1863; Wiley, *Confederate Women,* pp. 54–56; and Constance C. Harrison, *Recollections, Grave and Gay* (New York: Charles Scribner's Sons, 1911), p. 176.

36. Clement to Virginia, Dec. 20, 1863; Withers to Clement, Aug. 17, Oct. 29, Nov. 29, 1863; Clement to Susanna, Nov. 11, 1863; Nuermberger, pp. 221–30, 233. Nuermberger's account, pp. 234–66, of the activities of Clement and the other commissioners in Canada is excellent. See also John W. Headley, *Confederate Operations in Canada and New York* (New York and Washington: Neale Publishing Company, 1906), pp. 256–73. The quotation on Clay's behavior in Canada is from the papers of Thomas H. Hines, quoted in James D. Horan, *Confederate Agent: A Discovery in History* (New York: Crown P:ublishers, 1954), pp. 84–85.

37. Virginia to Clement, Nov. 18, 1864. Virginia Clay Diary, 1859–66, provides the data to reconstruct Virginia's movements and her sentiments during Clement's absence in Canada.

38. Celeste to Clement Claiborne, Feb. 16, 1865; also quoted in Nuermberger, p. 220. Celeste exaggerated. For Virginia's occasional nursing of wounded soldiers see Virginia Clay Diary, 1859–66, entries for May 27 and Aug. 20 to Sept. 30, 1864.

39. Bible, Clement Clay Papers, Huntsville Public Library. See also "C. C. Clay memoranda *re.* return from Canada, 1865"; Typescript of copy from Virginia Clay Diary, 1865–66; Lawson to Virginia, Jan. 7, 1865; Clement to Virginia, Mar. 30, 1865; Philip Philips, "A Summary of the Principal Events of My Life Written between the 10th and 20th of June, 1870," pp. 54–58, Philip Phillips Family Papers, Library of Congress; and Nuermberger, pp. 262–69. The proclamation ordering Clay's arrest is in U.S. War Department, *War of the Rebellion: A Compilation of the Official Records of the Union and Confederate Armies,* 130 vols. (Washington: Government Printing Office, 1880–1901), ser. 1, vol. 49, p. 2:558–59, hereafter cited as *OR.* President Johnson's proclamation offered $25,000 for Clay's capture, but the newspaper which Virginia read gave the amount as $100,000.

40. The charges against Clay are summarized in Joseph Holt to Edwin M. Stanton, Dec. 6, 1865, *OR,* ser. 2, 8:859–61. See also in the same volume, Stanton to Andrew

Johnson, Jan. 4, 1866, pp. 843–44; Joseph Holt to Stanton, Jan. 18, 1866, pp. 847–55. The dispositions accusing Clay are in ibid., 867–69, 876–77, 878–80. See also *Report of the House Committee on the Judiciary,* 39th Cong., 1st sess., No. 104. The perjury of most of those who accused him is admitted in Holt to Stanton, July 3, 1866, *OR,* ser. 2, 8:931–45.

41. Clement to Virginia, Aug. 11 and Sept. 18 to Oct. 1, 1865. See also Thomas Withers to Virginia, Sept. 16, 1865; Clement to Thomas Withers, Oct. 11, 1865; Nelson Miles to Virginia, June 20, July 29, Sept. 8, 1865; handwritten copy of "Comments in *Jay's Family Prayers* made by C. C. Clay Jr. in prison." Reports of Clay's health by prison officials are published in *OR,* ser. 2, 8:570–892, passim. On the unpredictable impact of stress on asthma, see Donald J. Lane, *Asthma: The Facts* (New York: Oxford Univ. Press, 1979), p. 69.

42. Lawson to Virginia, Sept. 20, 1865. See also Typescript of copy from Virginia Clay Diary, 1865–66; Virginia to Clement, Sept. 3, Nov. 3, 1865; and Nuermberger, pp. 269–71, 295.

43. Ben Green to Virginia, Oct. 21, 1865. See also Virginia to Clement, July 27, Nov. 3, 1865; Virginia to Ben Wood, Aug. 4, 1865; Virginia to Joseph Holt, May 23, 1865; J. Carlisle to Virginia, June 11, 1865; Ben Wood to Virginia, June 15, 1865; J. S. Black to Virginia, July 3, 1865; *Belle,* pp. 301–2; and Nuermberger, pp. 278–79.

44. Benjamin F. Perry to Elizabeth Perry, Feb. 18, 1866, Benjamin F. Perry Correspondence, South Caroliniana Library, Columbia, S.C.

45. Virginia may have moved the president by threatening to obtain a writ of habeas corpus, an idea suggested by Jeremiah Black. Virginia to Mary Clay, Apr. 14, 1866.

46. Will Book 1, pp. 357–58; Probate Record Books 28, pp. 258–60; 32, pp. 564–65; Deed Books JJ, pp. 104–5, BBB, p. 123; Minute Book 10, pp. 533–34; Madison County Courthouse; Clement C. Clay, "Executor's Book, 1866–1869;" and Clement to Jefferson Davis, Oct. 25, 1870, Jefferson Davis Papers, Confederate Museum, Richmond, Virginia.

47. The date of the Clays' move from Clay Lodge to Wildwood is not certain, but it probably took place in late 1878. See Clement to Virginia, Dec. 15, 1878; Jefferson Davis to Virginia, Mar. 13, 1883. Although many of the numerous postwar manuscripts in the Clay Papers at Duke in one way or another deal with finances, many of the exact details remain unclear, such as how large their income was and how great their expenses were. Details concerning what crops and livestock they raised, how they sold them, and Clay's general dissatisfaction with his labor arrangements can be found in many of his letters. For the sale of their land, see Deed Book LL, pp. 368–70, CCC, pp. 108–9, Madison County Courthouse. Nuermberger provides, pp. 298–99, 301–11, 315–16, a useful general summary of their dismal financial situation. For Corcoran's loan, see William W. Corcoran to Virginia, Jan. 3, Oct. 12, 1880. Clay Papers, Duke; and Virginia to Corcoran, Oct. 16, 1880, William W. Corcoran Papers, Library of Congress.

48. Clay's disillusionment with selling life insurance can be followed in his letters to Virginia from July 1871 to Nov. 1872.

49. Virginia to Clement, Nov. 11, 1868.

50. Clement to Virginia, Aug. 27, 1871, July 5, Aug. 23, 1876, Dec. 15, 1878; and Thomas Withers to Virginia, Sept. 16, 1870. Clay's cousin, Dr. Thomas Withers, recommended that he abstain from using alcohol.

51. Virginia to Clement, Oct. 13, 1874. See also her other letters to Clement from 1870 to 1880 and Nuermberger, pp. 307–8.
52. Davis to Virginia, Aug. 8, 1870. Lamar's poem is in Lamar to Virginia, Dec. 20, 1874:

> My dearest, if beneath the sea,
> With all its waves above my head,
> I lay, and thou shoulds't call for me;
> Methinks that I would quit the dead
> And come to thee.

53. E. F. Brooks to Virginia, Nov. 17, 1876; Paul Hammond to Virginia, Jan. 13, 1877, A. C. Haskell to Virginia, Jan. 28, 1877; W. H. Forney to Virginia, May 9, 1877; Lionel W. Day to Virginia, Aug. 30, 1877; and Virginia to L. Q. C. Lamar, Aug. 30, 1877.
54. Clement to Virginia, July 5, 1876; Virginia to Clement, Dec. 19, 1874. See also many other letters exchanged between Clement and Virginia from 1871 to 1880.
55. Virginia to Clement, Jan. 6, 1877. See also Clement to Virginia, Sept. 27, 1872, July 5, 1873, Jan. 23, 1874; and Virginia to Clement July 31, Oct. 1, Nov. 5, 1872, Oct. 15, 20, 1874.
56. *Huntsville Democrat,* Jan. 5, 1882. For information concerning Virginia's reaction to Clement's death see Fannie Copon to Corrine Goodman, Jan. 27, 1882; Virginia to Jefferson Davis, Feb. 16, 1882; Virginia to Jeremiah Black, Feb. 28, 1882. Nuermberger, pp. 316–17, details Virginia's trips between her two marriages. Owen, *History of Alabama,* 3:352–53, summarizes Judge Clopton's career. On his estate, see "Settlement of Estate of David Clopton," Mar. 8, 1892, and the many letters exchanged between Clifford A. Lanier and Virginia regarding the settlement.
57. In speeches advocating suffreage, Virginia defended woman's right to be "strong-minded," emphasized what she believed was women's increasing responsibility to provide financially for themselves and others, and described the achievements of famous women including Deborah, Dido, and Queen Elizabeth I. See draft speeches in Box 48, Clay Papers, Duke. For Virginia's participation in the suffrage movement see Virginia to Mrs. Neblett, Apr. 28, 1895; Virginia Clay Diary, 1893–96, entry for Jan. 21, 1895; Ruth Ketring Nuermberger. "Virginia Caroline Tunstall Clay-Clopton," in Edward T. James et al., eds., *Notable American Women, 1607–1950,* 3 vols. (Cambridge: Belknap Press of Harvard University, 1971), 1:348–49; Elizabeth Humes Chapman, *Changing Huntsville, 1890–1899* (Huntsville: privately published, 1972), pp. 27–34; John Irvin Lumpkin, "The Equal Suffrage Movement in Alabama, 1912–1919" (M.A. thesis, University of Alabama, 1949), pp. 3–5; and Lee N. Allen, "The Woman Suffrage Movement in Alabama, 1910–1920," *The Alabama Review* 11 (April 1958):83–84. Virginia had literally made the transition described by Anne Scott in *The Southern Lady: From Pedestal to Politics, 1830–1930* (Chicago: Univ. of Chicago Press, 1970).
58. Virginia to Celeste, Jan. 25, 1902, Clay Papers, Huntsville Public Library.
59. Clipping from the *Houston Chronicle,* Jan. 31, 1915, Box 56, Clay Papers, Duke; and Octavia Zollicoffer Bond, "South of the Line: A Belle of the Fifties," *Southern Woman's Magazine* 5 (Sept. 1915):16–17, 33.
60. Clement to Virginia, Nov. 22, 1868.

Chapter 28: The Trial of Mrs. Surratt and the Lincoln Assassination Plot

1. Benn Pitman, *The Assassination of President Lincoln and the Trial of the Conspirators* (Facsimilie Edition; New York, 1954), p. 18.
2. Ibid., pp. 247–249.
3. Guy W. Moore, *The Case of Mrs. Surratt* (Norman, Okla.; 1954), p. 4.
4. Ibid., pp. 105–18. See also, Robert W. Winston, *Andrew Johnson: Plebeian and Patriot* (New York, 1928), pp. 286–290, passim.
5. Those sentenced to prison terms—Mudd, Spangler, and Arnold—were pardoned in 1869 by President Johnson, and it seems likely that she would have been too. O'Laughlin died in prison.
6. For an account of this plot see Norma B. Cuthbert, *Lincoln and the Baltimore Plot, 1861* (San Marino, Calif., 1949).
7. James A. Bishop, *The Day Lincoln Was Shot* (New York, 1955), p. 105.
8. See Pitman, op. cit., pp. 18, 64, passim.
9. See Moore, op. cit., pp. 11–12, and Bishop, op. cit., pp. 86, 88.
10. Evidence indicates that Booth did not inform his active accomplices of the murder plot until two hours before the deed. See Moore, op. cit., p. 101.
11. Moore, op. cit., pp. 113–14.
12. William Winthrop, *Military Law and Precedents* (2nd ed.; Washington, D.C., 1920), pp. 823, 829.
13. Ibid., p. 817.
14. Moore, op. cit., p. 33.
15. See Lloyd P. Stryker, *Andrew Johnson* (New York, 1929), p. 335; see also, Moore, op. cit., p. 33 n., and Pitman, op. cit., p. 33.
16. Moore, op. cit., pp. 32–33.
17. Bishop, op. cit., pp. 72–73.
18. Ibid., pp. 75–76.
19. Ibid., pp. 86–94, passim.
20. See Pitman, op. cit., pp. 247–49.
21. Moore, op. cit., p. 5.
22. See for example Judge Advocate John Bingham's summation in Pitman, op. cit., pp. 351–402.
23. Bishop, op. cit., p. 291.
24. Winston, op. cit., p. 286.
25. See Moore, op. cit., p. 112,
26. Ibid., pp. 106–07.
27. These proceedings are in Pitman, op. cit., p. 250.
28. Moore, op. cit., p. 60.
29. Ibid., p. 61.
30. Winston, op. cit., p. 285. n. 13.
31. See Moore, op. cit., pp. 11 Off.
32. Ibid., pp. 70–71.

For Further Reading

Abernathy, Martha. *The Civil War Diary of Martha Abernatthy: Wife of Dr. Charles C. Abernathy of Pulaski, Tennessee*. Edited by Elizabeth Paisley Dargan. Beltsville, Md.: Professional Printing, 1994.

Andrews, Eliza Frances. *The War-Time Journal of a Georgia Girl, 1864–65*. New York: D. Appleton & Co., 1908.

Andrews, Matthew Page, comp. *The Women of the South in War Times*. Baltimore, Norman Remington Co., 1924.

Bacot, Ada W. *A Confederate Nurse: The Diary of Ada W. Bacot, 1860–1863*. Edited by Jean V. Berlin. Women's Diaries and Letters of the Nineteenth-Century South. Columbia: University of South Carolina Press, 1994.

Beale, Jane Howison. *The Journal of Jane Howison Beale, Fredericksburg, Virginia, 1850–1862*. Fredericksburg, Va.: Historic Fredericksburg Foundation, 1995.

Beers, Fannie A. *Memories: A Record of Personal Experience and Adventure During Four Years of War*. Philadelphia: Lippincott, 1888. Reprint, Collector's Library of the Civil War. Alexandria, Va.: Time-Life Books, 1985.

Beller, Susan Provost. *Confederate Ladies of Richmond*. Brookfield, Conn.: Twenty-First Century Books, 1999.

Blashfield, Jean F. *Women at the Front: Their Changing Roles in the Civil War*. New York: Franklin Watts, 1997.

Breckinridge, Lucy. *Lucy Breckinridge of Grove Hill: The Journal of a Virginia Girl, 1861–1864*. Edited by Mary D. Robertson. Women's Diaries and Letters of the Nineteenth-Century South. Columbia: University of South Carolina Press, 1994.

Brevard, Keziah Goodwyn Hopkins. *A Plantation Mistress on the Eve of the Civil War: The Diary of Keziah Goodwyn Hopkins Brevard, 1860–1861*. Edited by John Hammond Moore. Women's Diaries and Letters of the Nineteenth-Century South. Columbia: University of South Carolina Press, 1993.

Brock, Sallie. *Richmond During the War.* Alexandria, Va.: Time-Life Books, 1983.

Brockett, L. P., and Mary C. Vaughan. *Women at War: A Record of Their Patriotic Contributions, Heroism, Toils, and Sacrifice During the Civil War.* Boston: R. H. Curran, 1867. Reprint, Woodbury, N.Y.: Longmeadow, 1993.

Buck, Lucy Rebecca. *Sad Earth, Sweet Heaven: The Diary of Lucy Rebecca Buck During the War Between the States, from Front Royal, Virginia, December 25, 1861–April 15, 1865.* Edited by William P. Buck. 1940. Reprint, Birmingham, Ala.: Cornerstone, 1973.

———. *Shadows on My Heart: The Civil War Diary of Lucy Rebecca Buck of Virginia.* Edited by Elizabeth R. Baer. Southern Voices from the Past. Athens: University of Georgia Press, 1997.

Burge, Dolly Lunt. *The Diary of Dolly Lunt Burge.* Edited by Christine Jacobson Carter. Southern Voices from the Past. Athens: University of Georgia Press, 1997.

Burger, Nash K. *Confederate Spy: Rose O'Neale Greenhow.* New York: F. Watts, 1967.

Campbell, Edward D. C., and Kym S. Rice, eds. *A Woman's War: Southern Women, Civil War, and the Confederate Legacy.* Richmond: Museum of the Confederacy; Charlottesville: University Press of Virginia, 1996.

Chesnut, Mary Boykin Miller. *A Diary from Dixie.* Edited by Ben Ames Williams. Boston: Houghton, Mifflin, 1949. Reprint, Cambridge, Mass.: Harvard University Press, 1980.

Clemson, Floride. *A Rebel Came Home: The Diary and Letters of Floride Clemson, 1863–1866.* Edited by Charles M. McGee Jr. and Ernest M. Lander Jr. Women's Diaries and Letters of the Nineteenth-Century South. Columbia: University of South Carolina Press, 1989.

Clinton, Catherine. *Civil War Stories.* Jack N. and Addie D. Averitt Lecture Series, no. 7. Athens: University of Georgia Press, 1998.

———. *The Other Civil War: American Women in the Nineteenth Century.* New York: Hill and Wang, 1984.

———. *Plantation Mistress: Woman's World in the Old South.* New York: Pantheon, 1982.

———. *Tara Revisited: Women, War and the Plantation Legend.* New York: Abbeville Press, 1995.

———, and Nina Silber. *Divided Houses: Gender and the Civil War.* New York: Oxford University Press, 1992.

Collis, Septima M. *A Woman's War Record, 1861–1865.* New York: G. P. Putnam's Sons, 1889.

Culpepper, Marilyn Mayer. *Trials and Triumphs: Women of the American Civil War.* East Lansing: Michigan State University Press, 1991.

Cumming, Kate. *Kate: The Journal of a Confederate Nurse.* Edited by Richard B. Harwell. Baton Rouge: Louisiana State University Press, 1958.

Dawson, Francis W. *Our Women in the War.* Charleston, S.C.: Walker, Evans & Cogswell Co., 1887.

Dawson, Sarah Morgan. *Sarah Morgan: The Civil War Diary of a Southern Woman.* Edited by Charles East. Athens: University of Georgia Press, 1991; New York: Simon & Schuster, 1992.

DeWitt, David Miller. *The Judicial Murder of Mary E. Surratt.* Baltimore: John Murphy & Co., 1895.

Edmondston, Catherine Ann Devereux. *Journal of a Secesh Lady: The Diary of Catherine Ann Devereux Edmonston, 1860–1866.* Edited by Beth Gilbert Crabtree and James W. Patton. Raleigh, N.C.: Division of Archives and History, Department of Cultural Resources, 1979.

Edmonston, Belle. *A Lost Heroine of the Confederacy: The Diaries and Letters of Belle Edmonston.* Edited by William Galbraith and Loretta Galbraith. Center for the Study of Southern Culture Series. Jackson: University of Mississippi Press, 1990.

Elmore, Grace Brown. *A Heritage of Woe: The Civil War Diary of Grace Brown Elmore, 1861–1868.* Edited by Marli F. Weiner. Southern Voices from the Past. Athens: University of Georgia Press, 1997.

Emert, Phyllis Raybin, ed. *Women in the Civil War: Warriors, Patriots, Nurses, and Spies.* Perspectives on History. Lowell, Mass.: Discovery Enterprises, 1995.

Faust, Drew Gilpin. *Mothers of Invention: Women of the Slaveholding South in the American Civil War.* Chapel Hill: University of North Carolina Press, 1996.

Felton, Rebecca Latimer. *County Life in Georgia in the Days of My Youth.* Atlanta, Ga.: Index Printing Co., 1919. Reprint, New York: Arno Press, 1980.

Forten, Charlotte. *Journals of Charlotte Forten.* Edited by Brenda Stevenson. New York: Oxford University Press, 1988.

Fox, Tryphena Blanche Holder. *A Northern Woman in the Plantation South: Letters of Tryphena Blanche Holder Fox, 1856–1876.* Edited by Wilma King. Women's Diaries and Letters of the Nineteenth-Century South. Columbia: University of South Carolina Press, 1993.

Greenburg, Martin H., Charles G. Waugh, and Frank D. McSherry Jr., eds. *Civil War Women: American Women Shaped by Conflict in Stories by Alcott, Chopin, Welty, and Others.* Little Rock, Ark.: August House, 1988.

———, eds. *Civil War Women II: Stories by Women about Women.* Little Rock, Ark.: August House Publishers, 1997.

Hagerman, Keppel. *Dearest of Captains: A Biography of Sally Louisa Tompkins.* White Stone, Va.: Brandylane Publishers, 1996.

Hague, Parthenia Antoinette. *A Blockaded Family: Life in Southern Alabama During the Civil War.* Boston: Houghton, Mifflin, 1888. Reprint, Lincoln: University of Nebraska Press, 1991.

Hall, Richard. *Patriots in Disguise: Women Warriors of the Civil War.* New York: Paragon House, 1993.

Hawks, Esther Hill. *A Woman Doctor's Civil War: Esther Hill Hawks' Diary.* Edited by Gerald Schwartz. Columbia: University of South Carolina Press, 1984.

Heyward, Pauline DeCaradeuc. *A Confederate Lady Comes of Age: The Journal of Pauline DeCaradeuc Heyward, 1863–1888.* Edited by Mary D. Robertson. Women's Diaries and Letters of the Nineteenth-Century South. Columbia: University of South Carolina Press, 1992.

Holland, Mary Gardner, ed. *Our Army Nurses: Stories from Women in the Civil War.* Boston: B. Wilkins and Co., 1895. Reprint, Roseville, Minn.: Edinborough Press, 1998.

Holmes, Emma. *The Diary of Miss Emma Holmes, 1861–1866.* Edited by John F. Marszalek. Library of Southern Civilization. Baton Rouge: Louisiana State University Press, 1979.

House, Ellen Renshaw. *A Very Violent Rebel: The Civil War Diary of Ellen Renshaw House.* Edited by Daniel E. Sutherland. Voices of the Civil War. Knoxville: University of Tennessee Press, 1996.

Hunter, Alexander. *The Women of the Debatable Land.* Washington, D.C.: Cobden Publishing Co., 1912. Reprint, Port Washington, N.Y.: Kennikat Press, 1972.

Johnson, Patricia Givens. *Confederate Woman of New River Border County.* Blacksburg, Va.: Walpa Publishing Co., 1993.

Jones, Katharine M., comp. *Heroines of Dixie: Spring of High Hopes.* 1955. Reprint, St. Simons Island, Ga.: Mockingbird Books, 1974.

———, comp. *Heroines of Dixie: Winter of Desperation.* 1955. Reprint, St. Simons Island, Ga.: Mockingbird Books, 1975.

Joslyn, Mauriel Phillips, ed. *Valor and Lace: The Roles of Confederate Women, 1861–1865.* Journal of Confederate History Series, vol. 15. Murfreesboro, Tenn.: Southern Heritage Press, 1996.

Leonard, Elizabeth D. *All the Daring of the Soldier: Women of the Civil War Armies.* New York: W. W. Norton & Co., 1999.

Loughborough, Mary Ann. *My Cave Life in Vicksburg.* New York: D. Appleton, 1864.

McDonald, Cornelia Peake. *A Woman's Civil War: A Diary with Reminiscences of the War, from March 1862.* Edited by Minrose C. Gwin. Wisconsin Studies in American Autobiography. Madison: University of Wisconsin Press, 1992.

McGuire, Judith W. *Diary of a Southern Refugee during the War.* New York: E. J. Hale & Son, 1867. Reprint, Lincoln: University of Nebraska Press, 1995.

Massey, Mary Elizabeth. *Women in the Civil War.* Lincoln: University of Nebraska Press, 1994.

Middleton, Lee. *Hearts of Fire: Soldier Women of the Civil War.* Torch, Ohio: L. Middleton, 1993.

Moore, Frank. *Women of the War: Their Heroism and Self-sacrifice—True Stories of Brave Women in the Civil War.* Hartford, Conn.: S. S. Scranton, 1866. Reprint, Alexander, N.C.: Blue Gray Books, 1997.

Preston, Margaret Junkin. *Life and Letters of Margaret Junkin Preston.* Edited by Elizabeth Allen. Boston: Houghton, Mifflin, 1903.

Rable, George C. *Civil Wars: Women and the Crisis of Southern Nationalism.* Urbana: University of Illinois Press, 1989.

Ropes, Hannah. *Civil War Nurse: The Diary and Letters of Hannah Ropes.* Edited by John R. Brumgardt. Knoxville: University of Tennessee Press, 1980.

Simkins, Francis Butler, and James Welch Patton. *The Women of the Confederacy.* Richmond, Va.: Garrett and Massie, 1936. Reprint, St. Clair Shores, Mich.: Scholarly Press, 1976.

Sterkx, H. E. *Partners in Rebellion: Alabama Women in the Civil War.* Rutherford, N.J.: Fairleigh Dickinson University Press, 1970.

Stone, Kate. *Brokenburn: The Journal of Kate Stone, 1861–1868.* Edited by John Q. Anderson. Library of Southern Civilization. Baton Rouge: Louisiana State University Press, 1972.

Sullivan, Walter, ed. *The War the Women Lived: Female Voices from the Confederate South.* Nashville: J. S. Sanders, 1995.

Thomas, Ella Gertrude Clanton. *The Secret Eye: The Journal of Ella Gertrude Clanton Thomas, 1848–1889.* Edited by Virginia Ingraham Burr. Gender and American Culture. Chapel Hill: University of North Carolina Press, 1990.

Trindal, Elizabeth Steger. *Mary Surratt: An American Tragedy.* Gretna, La.: Pelican Publishing Co., 1996.

Velazquez, Loreta Janeta. *The Woman in Battle: A Narrative of the Exploits, Adventures, and Travels of Madame Loreta Janeta Velazquez.* Edited by C. J. Worthington. 1876. Reprint, New York: Arno Press, 1972.

Wallace, Elizabeth Curtis. *Glencoe Diary: The War-Time Journal of Elizabeth Curtis Wallace*. Edited by Eleanor P. Cross and Charles B. Cross Jr. Chesapeake, Va.: Norfolk County Historical Society, 1968.

Whites, LeeAnn. *The Civil War as a Crisis in Gender*. Athens: University of Georgia Press, 1995.

Wolosky, Shira. *Emily Dickinson: A Voice of War*. New Haven, Conn.: Yale University Press, 1984.

Index